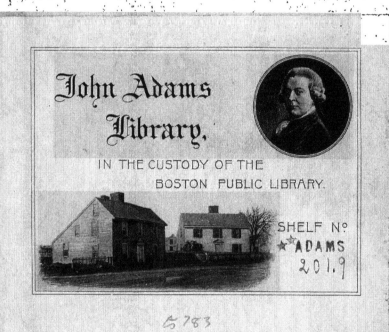

John Adams 1770

ALL THE

WORKS

OF

EPICTETUS,

WHICH ARE NOW EXTANT;

CONSISTING OF

His DISCOURSES, preserved by ARRIAN,

IN FOUR BOOKS,

The ENCHIRIDION, and FRAGMENTS.

Translated from the Original GREEK,

By *ELIZABETH CARTER.*

WITH

An INTRODUCTION, and NOTES, by the Translator.

DUBLIN:

Printed for HULTON BRADLEY, Bookseller, at the *King's Arms* and *Two Bibles* in *Dame-street.*

MDCCLIX.

The TRANSLATOR of EPICTETUS owes the Permission of inserting the following ODE intirely to the Friendship of the Writer of it; who, when she favoured her with it, had no Thought of its ever appearing in Print.

An IRREGULAR ODE.

To E. C. *who had recommended to me the* Stoic Philosophy, *as productive of* Fortitude, *and who is going to publish a Translation of* EPICTETUS.

I.

COME, EPICTETUS! Arm my Breast
With thy impenetrable Steel,
No more the Wounds of Grief to feel,
Nor mourn by others' Woes deprest.
Oh teach my trembling Heart
To scorn Affliction's Dart;
Teach me to mock the Tyrant Pain!
For see around me stand
A dreadful murd'rous Band,
I fly their cruel Power in vain!
Here lurks *Distemper's* horrid Train,
And *There* the *Passions* lift their flaming Brands;
These with fell Rage my helpless Body tear,
While *Those* with daring Hands
Against the immortal Soul their impious Weapons rear.

II.

Where-e'er I turn, fresh Evils meet my Eyes;
Sin, Sorrow, and Disgrace,
Pursue the Human Race!
There on the Bed of Sickness *Virtue* lies!
See *Friendship* bleeding by the Sword
Of base *Ingratitude!*
See baleful *Jealousy* intrude,
And poison all the Bliss that *Love* had stor'd!
Oh! seal my Ears against the piteous Cry
Of Innocence distrest!
Nor let me shrink, when Fancy's Eye
Beholds the guilty Wretch's Breast
Beneath the torturing Pincers heave:
Nor for the num'rous Wants of Mis'ry grieve,
Which all-disposing Heav'n denies me to relieve!

III.

No longer let my fleeting Joys depend
On social, or domestic Ties!
Superior let my Spirit rise,
Nor in the gentle Counsels of a Friend,
Nor in the Smiles of Love, expect Delight:
But teach me in *myself* to find
Whate'er can please or fill my Mind.
Let inward Beauty charm the mental Sight;
Let Godlike Reason, beaming bright,
Chace far away each gloomy Shade,
Till Virtue's heav'nly Form display'd
Alone shall captivate my Soul,
And her divinest Love possess me whole!

IV.

But, ah! what means this impious Pride,
Which heav'nly Hosts deride!
Within *myself* does Virtue dwell?
Is all serene, and beauteous there?
What mean these chilling Damps of Fear?
Tell me, *Philosophy!* Thou Boaster! Tell:
This God-like all-sufficient Mind,
Which, in its own Perfection blest,
Defies the Woes, or Malice of Mankind
To shake its self-possessing Rest,

Is it not foul, weak, ignorant, and blind?
Oh Man! from conscious Virtue's Praise
Fall'n, fall'n!——what Refuge can'st thou find!
What pitying Hand again will raise
From native Earth thy groveling Frame!
Ah, who will cleanse thy Heart from Spot of sinful Blame?

V.

But, See! what sudden Glories from the Sky
To my benighted Soul appear,
And all the gloomy Prospect cheer?
What awful Form approaches nigh?
Awful: Yet mild as is the southern Wind
That gently bids the Forest nod.
Hark! Thunder breaks the Air, and Angels speak!
"Behold the Saviour of the World! Behold the Lamb of [God!"
Ye Sons of Pride, behold his Aspect meek!
The Tear of Pity on his Cheek!
See in his Train appear
Humility and *Patience* sweet,
Repentance, prostrate at His sacred Feet,
Bedews with Tears, and wipes them with her flowing Hair!

VI.

What Scenes now meet my wond'ring Eyes!
What hallow'd Grave,
By mourning Maids attended round,
Attracts the Saviour's Steps? What heart-felt Wound
His spotless Bosom heaves with tender Sighs?
Why weeps the Son belov'd, Omnipotent to save?
But, lo! He waves his awful Hand!
The sleeping Clay obeys His dread Command.
Oh Lazarus! come forth!——"Come forth and see
"The dear Effects of wond'rous Love!
"He, at whose Word the Seas and Rocks remove,
"Thy Friend, thy Lord, thy Maker, weeps for Thee!"

VII.

Thy Walls, *Jerusalem*, have seen thy King,
In Meekness clad, lament thy hapless Fate!
Unquench'd His Love, though paid with ruthless Hate!
O lost, relentless *Sion!* Didst Thou know
Who thus vouchsafes thy Courts to tread,
What loud *Hosannas* wouldst thou sing!
How eager crown his honour'd Head!

Nor see unmov'd His kind paternal Woe!
Nor force His Tears, His precious Blood, for thee to flow!

VIII.

No more repine, my coward Soul!
The Sorrows of Mankind to share,
Which He, who could the World controul,
Did not disdain to bear!
Check not the Flow of sweet fraternal Love,
By Heav'n's high King in Bounty given,
Thy stubborn Heart to soften and improve,
Thy earth-clad Spirit to refine,
And gradual raise to Love divine
And wing its soaring Flight to Heaven!

IX.

Nor Thou, Eliza, who from early Youth
By Genius led, by Virtue train'd,
Hast sought the Fountain of eternal Truth,
And each fair Spring of Knowlege drain'd;
Nor Thou, with fond Chimeras vain,
With Stoic Pride, and fancied Scorn
Of human Feelings, human Pain,
My feeble Soul sustain!
Far nobler Precepts should thy Page adorn.
O rather guide me to the sacred Source
Of real Wisdom, real Force,
Thy Life's unerring Rule!
To Thee, fair Truth her radiant Form unshrouds,
Though, wrapp'd in thick impenetrable Clouds,
She mock'd the Labours of the *Grecian* School.

M. H.

INTRODUCTION.

§. 1. THE Stoic Sect was founded by *Zeno*, about three hundred Years before the Christian Æra: and flourished in great Reputation, till the Declension of the *Roman* Empire. A complete History of this Philosophy would be the Work of a large Volume: and nothing further is intended here, than such a summary View of it, as may be of Use to give a clearer Notion of those Passages in *Epictetus*, a strict Professor of it, which allude to some of its peculiar Doctrines.

§. 2. That the End of Man is to live conformably to Nature, was universally agreed on amongst all the Philosophers: but, in what that Conformity to Nature consists, was the Point in Dispute. The *Epicureans* maintained, that it consisted in Pleasure; of which they constituted Sense the Judge (*a*). The Stoics, on the contrary, placed it in an absolute

(*a*) *Sensibus ipsis judicari voluptates.* Cic. de Fin. L II. By Pleasure the *Epicureans* sometimes explained themselves to mean, only Freedom from Uneasiness: but the Philosophers of other Sects in general, as well as *Cicero*, insist, producing their own Expressions for it, that they meant sensual Delights. This, indeed, was more explicitly the Doctrine of *Aristippus*, the Father of the *Cyrenaics*: a Sect, however, which sunk into the *Epicureans*: whose Notions plainly led to the Dissoluteness so remarkable in the Lives of most of them.

Perfection of the Soul. Neither of them seem to have understood Man in his mixed Capacity; but while the first debased him to a mere Animal, the last exalted him to a pure Intelligence; and both considered him as independent, uncorrupted and sufficient, either by Heighth of Virtue or by well-regulated Indulgence, to his own Happiness. The Stoical Excess was more useful to the Public, as it often produced great and noble Efforts towards that Perfection, to which it was supposed possible for human Nature to arrive. Yet, at the same time, by flattering Man with false and presumptuous Ideas of his own Power and Excellence, it tempted even the best to Pride: a Vice not only dreadfully mischievous in human Society, but, perhaps of all others, the most insuperable Bar to real inward Improvement.

§. 3. *Epictetus* often mentions Three Topics, or Classes, under which the whole of Moral Philosophy is comprehended. These are, the *Desires* and *Aversions*, the *Pursuits* and *Avoidances*, or the Exercise of the active Powers, and the *Assents* of the Understanding.

Ορεξεις Εκκλισεις. §. 4. The *Desires* and *Aversions* were considered as simple Affections of the Mind, arising from the Apprehension, that any thing was conducive to Happiness, or the contrary. The first Care of a Proficient in Philosophy was, to regulate these in such a manner, as never to be disappointed of the one, or incur the other: a Point no otherwise attainable, than by regarding all Externals as absolutely indifferent. *Good* must always be the Object of Desire, and *Evil* of Aversion. The Person then, who considers Life, Health, Ease, Friends, Reputation, &c. as *Good*; and their Contraries as *Evil*, must necessarily *desire* the one, and be *averse* to the other: and, consequently, must often find his *Desire* disappointed, and his *Aversion* incurred. The Stoics, therefore, restrained *Good*

and

and *Evil* to *Virtue* and *Vice* alone: and excluded all Externals from any Share in human Happiness, which they made entirely dependent on a right Choice. From this Regulation of the *Desires* and *Aversions* follows that Freedom from Perturbation, Grief, Anger, Pity, &c. and in short, that universal Apathy, which they every-where strongly inculcate.

§. 5. The next Step to Stoical Perfection was, the Class of *Pursuits* and *Avoidances* (*b*). As the *Desires* and *Aversions* are simple Affections, the *Pursuits* and *Avoidances* are Exertions of the active Powers towards the procuring or declining any thing. Under this Head was comprehended the whole System of moral Duties, according to their incomplete Ideas of them: and a due Regard to it was supposed to ensure a proper Behaviour in all the social Relations. The constant Performance of what these point out, naturally followed from a Regulation of the *Desires* and *Aversions* in the first Topic: for where the Inclinations are exerted and restrained as they ought, there will be nothing to mislead us in Action. Ορμαι Αφορμαι.

§. 6. The last Topic, and the Completion of the Stoic Character, was that of the *Assents* (*c*). As the

(*b*) The Stoics define these Terms: the one, a Motion, by which we are carried toward some Object; the other, a Motion, by which we strive to shun it. The original Words, by a Happiness in the *Greek* Language, are properly opposed to each other; which the *English* will not admit. I have chosen the best I could find, and wish they were better.

(*c*) It seems strange, that the Stoics generally put the *Assents* last: since both the Affections and Will should be governed by the Understanding; which, therefore, should be rectified, in order to do its Office well. *Epictetus* seems to be of this Opinion in B. I. c. 17. But, perhaps, they thought common Sense, or natural Logic, sufficient for this Purpose; and artificial Logic, which they meant, but did not express clearly, by the Word *Assents*, necessary as a Guard only against Sophistry. Yet their mentioning it, as a Guard also against being misled, when they were in Drink, and even in their Dreams, leaves but little Room for this Conjecture.

the ſecond was to produce a Security from Failure in Practice, *this* was to ſecure an Infallibility in Judgment, and to guard the Mind from ever either admitting a Falſhood, or diſſenting from Truth. A wiſe Man, in the Stoic Scheme, was never to be miſtaken, or to form any Opinion. Where Evidence could not be obtained, he was to continue in Suſpenſe. His Underſtanding was never to be miſled, even in Sleep, or under the Influence of Wine, or in a Delirium. In this laſt Particular, however, there is not a perfect Agreement: and ſome Authors are ſo very reaſonable, as to admit it poſſible for a Philoſopher to be miſtaken in his Judgment, after he hath loſt his Senſes (*d*).

Φαντασιαι. §. 7. The Subjects of theſe ſeveral Claſſes of philoſophic Exerciſe are, the *Appearances* of Things (*e*). By theſe *Appearances* the Stoics underſtood the Impreſſions (*f*) made on the Soul, by any Objects, preſented either to the Senſes, or to the Underſtanding. Thus a Houſe, an Eſtate, Life, Death, Pain, Reputation, *&c.* (conſidered in the View, under which they are preſented to the perceptive Faculties) in the Stoical Senſe are, *Appearances.* The Uſe of Appearances is common to Brutes, and Men; an *intelligent* Uſe of them belongs only to the latter: a Diſtinction, which is carefully to be obſerved in reading theſe Diſcourſes.

§. 8.

(*d*) Και μην την αρετην Χρυσιππος αποβλητην, Κλεανθης δε αναποβλητην· ὁ μεν, αποβλητην δια μεθην και μελαγχολιαν· ὁ δε, αναποβλητην, δια βεβαιους καταληψεις. DLOG. LAERT. *in* ZENO.

Nam ſi argumentaberis, ſapientem multo vino inebriari, et retinere rectum tenorem, etiamſi temulentus ſit: licet colligas, nec veneno poto moriturum, *&c.* SEN. *Epiſt.* 83.

(*e*) The original Word is of peculiar Signification among the Stoics: and I wiſh it could have been rendered into *Engliſh*, in a manner leſs ambiguous, and more expreſſive of its Meaning. But the Stoic Language periſhed with the Stoic Sect: and ſcarcely any of its technical Terms can now be rendered intelligible, except by a Paraphraſe, or a Definition.

(*f*) Τυπωσιν εν ψυχη. DIOG. LAERT. L. VII. §. 45.

§. 8. That Judgment, which is formed by the Mind concerning the *Appearances*, the Stoics termed *Principles*: and these Principles give a Determination to the Choice. Δογματα.

§. 9. The *Choice*, among the Stoics, signified, either the Faculty of Willing; or a deliberate Election made of some Action, or Course of Life. Προαιρεσις.

§. 10. As the Appearances respect particular Objects, the *Pre-conceptions* are general innate Notions, such as they supposed to take original Possession of the Mind, before it forms any of its own (*g*). To adapt these *Pre-conceptions* to particular Cases, is the Office of Reason: and is often insisted on by *Epictetus*, as a Point of the highest Importance. Προληψεις.

§. 11. By the Word, which throughout this Translation is rendered *Prosperity*, the Stoics understood the internal State of the Mind, when the Affections and active Powers were so regulated, that it considered all Events as happy: and, consequently, must enjoy an uninterrupted Flow of Success: since nothing could fall out contrary to its Wishes (*h*). Ευροια.

These, which have been mentioned, are the technical Terms of the greatest Consequence in the Stoic Philosophy: and which, for that Reason, are, except in a very few Places, always rendered by the same *English* Word. There are other Words used in a peculiar Sense by this Sect: but, as they are not of equal Importance, they are neither so strictly translated, nor need any particular Definition.

§. 12.

(*g*) Εςι δε 'η προληψις, εννοια φυσικη των καθ' ολου.
Diog. Laert. L. VII. §. 54.

(*h*) I am sensible, that *Prosperity*, in common Use, relates wholly to external Circumstances: but I could find no better Word to express the internal good Condition of Mind, which the Stoics meant by Ευροια. There is an Instance of the like Use 1 *John* iii. 2.

§. 12. The Stoics held Logic in the higheſt Eſteem: and often carried it to ſuch a trifling Degree of Subtilty, as rendered their Arguments very tedious and perplexed. The frequent References to logical Queſtions and the Uſe of ſyllogiſtical Terms, are the leaſt agreeable Part of the Diſcourſes of *Epictetus*: ſince, however well they might be underſtood by ſome of his Hearers, they are now unintelligible to the greateſt Part of his Readers. Indeed, with all his Strength and Clearneſs of Underſtanding, he ſeems to have been hurt by this favourite Science of his Sect. One is ſometimes ſurpriſed to find his Reaſoning incoherent and perplexed: and his Scholars rather ſilenced by Interrogatories, which they are unable to comprehend, than convinced by the Force of Truth; and then given up by him, as if they were hopeleſs and unteachable. Yet many a well-meaning Underſtanding may be loſt in a Wood by the Confuſion of dialectical Quibbles, which might have been led, without Difficulty, to the Point in view, if it had been ſuffered to follow the Track of common Senſe.

§. 13. The Stoic Scheme of Theology, as it is explained in *Cicero*, and other antient Writers, appears, in many Parts of it, ſtrangely perplexed and abſurd. Some however of this ſeeming Abſurdity may poſſibly ariſe from the Uſe of ſtrong Figures; and the infinite Difficulty of treating a Subject, for which no human Language can ſupply proper and adequate Terms (*i*). The Writings of the firſt Founders of the Stoic Philoſophy, who treated expreſly on Phyſiology and Metaphyſics, are now loſt: and all that can be known of their Doctrine is from Fragments, and the Accounts given of them by other

(*i*) Quidquid de Deo dixeris, quidquid tacitæ mentis cogitatione conceperis, in humanum tranſilit, et corrumpitur, ſenſum: nec habet propriæ ſignificationis notam, quod noſtris verbis dicitur, atque ad humana negotia compoſitis.

Arnob. *adv. gentes.* L. III. p. 111. Ed. *Ludg. Bat.* 1651.

other Authors. By what can be collected from these, and particularly by the Account which *Diogenes Laertius* gives of the Stoics, they appear to have held, that there is one supreme God, incorruptible, unoriginated (*k*), immortal, rational, and perfect in Intelligence and Happiness: unsusceptible of all Evil: governing the World, and every thing in it, by his Providence: not however of the human Form; but the Creator of the Universe: the Father likewise of all (*l*): and that the several Names of *Apollo*, *Minerva*, *Ceres*, &c. only denote different Exertions of his Power in the different Parts of the Universe (*m*). It would be well, if they had stopt here: but they plainly speak of the World, as God, or of God as the Soul of the World, which they call his Substance (*n*): and I do not recollect any Proof, that they believed Him to exist in the extramundane Space. Yet they held the World to be finite (*o*), and corruptible: and that, at certain Periods, it was to undergo successive Conflagrations, and then all Beings were to be resorbed into God, and again reproduced by Him (*p*). What they intended by being resorbed into God, as I do not comprehend, I will not attempt to explain: but I fear they understood by it, a Loss of separate personal Existence. Yet some of the later Stoics departed from this Doctrine of the Conflagration, and supposed the World to be immortal (*q*). Indeed

(*k*) Αφθαρτος και αγεννητος. Diog. Laert. L. VII. §. 137.

(*l*) Θεον δ' ειναι Ζωον αθανατον, λογικον, τελειον, η νοερον εν ευδαιμονια, κακου παντος ανεπιδεκτον, προνοητικον κοσμου τε και των εν κοσμω· μη ειναι μεντοι ανθρωπομορφον· ειναι δε τον μεν δημιουργον των ολων, ωσπερ και πατερα παντων. Ib. §. 147.

(*m*) Πολλαις προσηγοριαις προσονομαζεται κατα τας δυναμεις. Ib.

(*n*) Ουσιαν δε Θεου Ζηνων μεν φησι τον ολον κοσμον και τον ουρανον. Ib. §. 148.

(*o*) Ὁ μεν ουν κοσμος πεπερασμενος εστι. Ib.

(*p*) Κατα χρονων ποιας περιοδους αναλισκων εις εαυτον πασαν την ουσιαν, και παλιν εξ εαυτου γεννων. Ib. §. 137.

(*q*) See Philo Judæus, of the Incorruptibility of the World, p. 947. Ed. *Par.*

deed there is often ſo much Obſcurity, and Appearance of Contradiction, in their Expreſſions, that it is very difficult, if not impoſſible, to form any preciſe Idea of their Meaning. They who, with Impartiality, read what the ancient Philoſophers, of all Sects, have written on the Nature of God, will often find Cauſe to think, with the utmoſt Veneration and Gratitude, on the only Book, in which this important Article is explained, ſo far as is neceſſary to be known, in a manner perfectly agreeable to the Principles of ſimple, unperverted Reaſon. For what it graciouſly teaches more than Reaſon could, it confirms by ſuch Evidences of its Authority, as Reaſon muſt admit, or contradict itſelf.

§. 14. The Stoics ſometimes define God to be an intelligent, fiery Spirit, without Form, but paſſing into whatever Things it pleaſes, and aſſimilating itſelf to all (*r*): ſometimes an active, operative Fire (*s*). It might be hoped, that theſe were only metaphorical Phraſes, if they did not expreſsly ſpeak of God as corporal; which is objected to them by *Plutarch* (*t*). Indeed they defined all Eſſence to be Body (*u*). An Error of which, probably, they did not diſcover the ill Tendency, any more than *Tertullian*; who inconſiderately followed them in this very unphiloſophical Notion, that what is not Body, is nothing at all (*w*). His Chriſtian Faith

(*r*) Θεος εϛι πνευμα νοερον και πυρωδες, ουκ εχον μορφην, μεταϐαλλον δε εις α ϐουλεται και συνεξομοιουμενον πασι. POSIDONIUS.

(*s*) Πυρ τεχνικον. PLUT. *de Placit. Philoſoph.* L. I. c. 7.

(*t*) Ουτοι τον Θεον, αρχην οντα, Σωμα νοερον, και νουν εν ὑλη ποιουντες, ου καθαρον, ουδε απλουν ουδε ασυνθετον· αλλα εξ ἑτερου, και δι ἑτερου αποφαινουσι. PLUT. *de communibus notitiis adv. Stoicos.* p. 1085.

(*u*) Σωμα δε εϛι, κατά αυτους, ἡ ουσια. DIOG. LAERT. L. VII. §. 150.

(*w*) *Adv. Praxeam*, c 7. Yet, *De Anima*, c. 7. he ſays, Omne corporale paſſibile eſt; which he certainly did not think God was.

Faith ſecures him from the Imputation of Impiety: and the juſt and becoming Manner, in which the Stoics, in many Inſtances, ſpeak of God, ſhould incline one to form the ſame favourable Judgment of them: and thoſe Authors ſeem guilty of great Injuſtice, who repreſented them, as little better than Atheiſts.

§. 15. They held the Eternity of Matter, as a paſſive Principle; but that it was reduced into Form by God; and that the World was made, and is continually governed by Him (*x*). They ſometimes repreſent him, as modelling the Conſtitution of the World with ſupreme Authority (*y*): at others, as limited by the Materials, which He had not the Power to change (*z*). *Epictetus* may be thought to incline to this latter Opinion (*a*): yet his Words are capable of a different Turn. And there are, perhaps, more Arguments, in the Writings of the Stoics, to prove their Belief of the uncontroulable Power of the Deity in the Formation of Things, than thoſe, which ſome unguarded Expreſſions appear to furniſh againſt it.

§. 16. Of all the Philoſophers the Stoics were the cleareſt and moſt zealous Aſſertors of a particular Providence (*b*): a Belief, which was treated with the utmoſt Contempt by the *Epicureans* (*c*). As this

(*x*) Δοκει δ' αυτοις αρχας ειναι των ολων δυο, το ποιουν και το πασχον· το μεν ουν πασχον ειναι την αποιον ουσιαν, την υλην. Το δε ποιουν, τον εν αυτη λογον, τον Θεον. DIOG. LAER. L. VII. §. 134.

(*y*) Deus iſta temperat, quæ circumfuſa Rectorem ſequuntur et Ducem. Potentius autem eſt quod facit, quod eſt Deus, quam materia patiens Dei. SEN. *Epiſt.* 65.

Nulli igitur eſt naturæ obediens, aut ſubjectus Deus. Omnem ergo regit ipſe naturam. CIC. *de Nat. Deor.* L. II. §. 30. Ed. *Dav.*

(*z*) Non poteſt artifex mutare materiam. SEN. *de Provid.* c. 8.

(*a*) B. I. c. 1.

(*b*) Non univerſo Hominum Generi, ſolum, ſed etiam ſingulis, &c. CIC. *de Nat. Deor.* L. III.

(*c*) Anus fatidica. Ib. L. I.

this Principle is, of all others, the moſt conducive to the Intereſts of Virtue, and lays the Foundation of all true Piety, the Stoics are intitled to the higheſt Honour for their ſteady Defence of it; and their utter Rejection of the idle, and contemptible Notion of Chance (*d*).

§. 17. By *Fate* they ſeem to have underſtood a Series of Events, appointed by the immutable Counſels of God: or, that Law of his Providence, by which he governs the World (*e*). It is evident by their Writings, that they meant it in no Senſe, which interferes with the Liberty of human Actions. *Cicero* allows, that *Chryſippus* endeavoured to reconcile Fate with Free Will: and that it was contrary to his Intention, that, by a perplexed Way of arguing, he confirmed the Doctrine of Neceſſity (*f*). Whenever they ſpeak of God, as ſubject to *Fate*, which it muſt be owned they ſometimes do in a very ſtrong and unguarded manner, their Meaning ſeems to be, that his own eternal Will is his Law: that he cannot change; becauſe he always ordains what is beſt (*g*): and that, as Fate is no more than a connected Series of Cauſes, God is the Firſt Original Cauſe, on which all the reſt depend (*h*).

§. 18. They imagined the whole Univerſe to be peopled with Gods, Genii, and Demons: and among other inferior Divinities reckoned the Sun, Moon, and Stars, which they conceived to be animated and intelligent; or inhabited by particular Deities, as

(*d*) Nec ſine Ratione, quamvis ſubita, accidere. Sen. *de Provid.* c. 1.

(*e*) Λογος, καθ' ον ὁ κοσμ☉ διεξαγεται. Diog. Laer. L. VII. §. 149.

(*f*) *Chryſippus*——Applicat ſe ad eos potius, qui neceſſitate motus Animos [Animorum *Dav.*] liberatos volunt. Dum autem verbis utitur ſuis, delabitur in eas Difficultates, ut neceſſitatem Fati confirmet *invitus*. Cic. *de Fato*, §. 17. *Dav. Chryſippus* autem, cum et neceſſitatem improbaret, &c. §. 18.

(*g*) Sen. *de Beneficiis*. L. VI. c. 23.

(*h*) Ib. L. IV. c. 7.

as the Body is by the Soul, who presided over them, and directed their Motions (*i*).

§. 19. The Stoics held both the above-mentioned Intelligences, and the Souls of Men, to be Portions of the Essence of God (*k*), or Parts of the Soul of the World (*l*): and to be corporeal (*m*), and perishable (*n*). Some of them indeed maintained, that human Souls subsisted after Death: but that they were, like all other Beings, to be consumed at the Conflagration. *Cleanthes* taught, that all Souls lasted till that Time: *Chrysippus*, only those of the Good (*o*). *Seneca* is perpetually wavering: sometimes speaking of the Soul as immortal; and, at others, as perishing with the Body. And indeed there is nothing but Confusion, and a melancholy Uncertainty, to be met with among the Stoics, on this Subject.

§. 20. There is, I think, very little Evidence to be found, that they believed future Rewards or Punishments, compared with that which appears to the contrary (*p*): at least the Reader will observe, that *Epictetus* never asserts either. He strongly insists, that a bad Man hath no other Punishment, than being such; and a good Man, no other Reward (*q*): and he tells his Disciple, that, when Want of Necessaries obliges him to go out of Life,

(*i*) Cic. *de Natura Deorum* L. II. c. 15.

(*k*) Epic. B. I. c. 14, *&c.*

(*l*) Ἡς μερη ειναι τας εν τοις Ζωοις. Diog. Laert. L. VII. §. 156.

(*m*) Την δε ψυχην—και Σωμα ειναι. Ib.

(*n*) Την ψυχην μετα θανατον επιμενειν, φθαρτην δ' ειναι. Ib.

(*o*) Κλεανθης πασας, επιδιαμενειν φασι, μεχρι εκπυρωσεως. Χρυσιππος δε, τας των Σοφων μονων. Ib. §. 157.

(*p*) *Lactantius*, indeed, L. VII. c. 7. says: Esse inferos Zenon Stoicus docuit, et sedes piorum ab impiis esse discretas: et illos quidem quietas et delectabiles incolere Regiones; hos vero luere pœnas in tenebrosis locis, atque in cæni voraginibus horrendis. But I know not that any other Author relates this of him.

(*q*) See B. I. c. 12. p. 42. B. III. c. 7. p. 219. Id. c. 24. p. 280. B. IV. c. 9. §. 2, 3. Id. c. 10. §. 2. c. 12. §. 4.

he returns to the Four Elements, of which he was made: that there is no *Hades*, nor *Acheron*, nor *Pyriphlegethon* (r): and he clearly affirms, that personal Existence is lost in Death (s). Had *Epictetus* believed future Rewards, he must, of Course, have made frequent mention of them (t). *M. Antoninus*, upon a Supposition that Souls continue after Death, makes them to remain for some Time in the Air: and then to be changed, diffused, kindled and resumed into the productive Intelligence of the Universe (u). In another Place, he vindicates the Conduct of Providence, on the Hypothesis, that the Souls of the Good are extinguished by Death (w).

§. 21. The Stoics thought, that every single Person had a tutelary Genius assigned him by God, as a Guardian of his Soul, and a Superintendent of his Conduct (x): and that all Virtue and Happiness con-

(r) B. III. c. 13. p 233.

(s) Id. c. 24. p. 288.

(t) The only Passage, that I can recollect, in which any Intimation seems to be given of a future Reward, is in the XVth Chapter of the *Enchiridion*: and, probably, even there he means only a Happiness to be enjoyed in the present Life, after due Improvement in Philosophy; though he expresses it by the very strong Figures of partaking the Feasts and Empire of the Gods. For, doubtless, the wise Man, like his Kindred Deities, feasted upon every Thing that happened; and, by willing as *Jupiter* did, reigned along with Him. Besides, *Epictetus* says there, of *Diogenes*, and *Heraclitus*, or *Hercules*, not that they *are*, but that they *were* divine Persons: which must refer to something which had ceased when he wrote; and, consequently, to their Felicity before, not after their Deaths. At least, he doth not intimate any thing concerning their second Life: and if that was to be short, as it might be (and it could not reach beyond the Conflagration), and was not very certain neither, the Hope of it would be a very insufficient Counterbalance to vehement Appetites and Passions.

(u) L. 4. §. 21. These Expressions, *diffused* and *kindled*, allude to the Stoic Doctrine, that Souls are Portions of the Deity, separated for a Time, and that His Essence is Fire.

(w) L. 12. §. 5.

(x) Ειναι τινας δαιμονας ανθρωπων συμπαθειαν εχοντας, εποπτας των ανθρωπειων πραγματων. Diog. Laert. L. VII. §. 151.

Scit

consist in acting in concert with this Genius, with Reference to the Will of the supreme Director of the Whole (*y*). Sometimes, however, they make the Genius to be only the ruling Faculty of every one's own Mind (*z*).

§. 22. A very slight Examination of their Writings is sufficient to convince any impartial Reader, how little the Doctrines of this Sect were fitted to influence the Generality of Mankind. But indeed, about the Generality of Mankind, the Stoics do not appear to have given themselves any kind of Trouble. They seemed to consider All (except the Few, who were Students in the Intricacies of a philosophic System) as very little superior to Beasts: and, with great Tranquillity, left them to follow the Devices of their own ungoverned Appetites and Passions. How unlike was this to the diffusive Benevolence of the divine Author of the Christian Religion, who adapted his Discourses to the Comprehension, and extended the Means of Happiness, to the Attainment of all Mankind!

§. 23. There seem to be only two Methods, by which the present Appearances of Things are capable of being reconciled to our Ideas of the Justice, Wisdom, and Goodness, of God: the one is the Doctrine of a *future* State; the other, the Position, that Virtue alone is sufficient to human Happiness in *this* (*a*). The first, which was the Method cho-

Scit Genius, natale comes qui temperat Astrum,
Naturæ Deus humanæ, mortalis in unum
Quodcunque caput HOR. L. I. Ep. II. v. 186, &c.

See *Epict.* B. I. c. 14. p. 46.

(*y*) Ειναι δ᾽ αυτο τουτο του ευδαιμονος αρετην και την ευροιαν βιου, οταν παντα πραττηται κατα την Συμφωνιαν του παρ εκαστω δαιμονος, προς την του ολου Διοικητου βουλησιν. DIOG. LAERT. L. VII. §. 88.

(*z*) See *M. Antoninus*, L. II. c. 13. 17. L. III. c. 3. 5. L. V. c. 27.

(*a*) Condonanda tamen sententia, Stoice, vestra est.
Nam si post obitum, neque præmia sint, neque pœnæ,
Heu,

sen by *Socrates*, solves every Difficulty, without contradicting either Sense or Reason: the latter, which was unfortunately maintained by the Stoics, is repugnant to both.

§. 24. That there is an intrinsic Beauty and Excellency in moral Goodness; that it is the Ornament and Perfection of all rational Beings; and that, till Conscience is stifled by repeated Guilt, we feel an Obligation to prefer and follow, so far as we perceive it, in all Cases; and find an inward Satisfaction, and generally receive outward Advantages from so doing, are Positions, which no thinking Person can contradict: but it doth not follow from hence, that in such a Mixture, as Mankind, it is its own sufficient Reward. God alone, infinitely perfect, is happy in, and from Himself. The Virtue of *finite* Beings must be defective: and the Happiness of *created* Beings must be dependent. It is undeniable Fact, that the natural Consequences of Virtue in some, may be interrupted by the Vices of others. How much are the best Persons liable to suffer from the Follies of the Unthinking; from the Ill-nature, the Rage, the Scorn of the Malevolent; from the cold and the penurious Hard-heartedness of the Unfeeling; from Persecutions, for the sake both of Religion and Honesty; from ill Returns to conjugal, to parental, to friendly Affection; and from an innumerable Train of other Evils, to which the most amiable Dispositions are usually the most sensible. It is no less undeniable, that the natural Consequences of Virtue are interrupted by the

Heu, quo perventum est! Heu, quid jam denique restat!
Scilicet humanas gerit aut Res numen inique,
Aut nil curat iners, aut, si bene temperat orbem,
Nemo bonus miser est, nemo improbus esse beatus
In vita possit, Gens ut sibi Stoica fingit.

J. Hawkins Browne.

I have a singular Pleasure in quoting these Lines, from a Poem, which does Honour to our Country.

the Struggles of our own Passions; (which we may overcome rewardably, though very imperfectly; or, if we live to overcome more perfectly, we may not live to enjoy the Victory;) by Sickness, Pain, Languor, Want; and by what we feel from the Death, or the Sufferings of those, with whom we are most nearly connected. We are often indeed afflicted by many of these Things, more than we ought to be. But Concern for some, at least our own Failings, for Instance, is directly a Duty; for others, it is visibly the Instrument of moral Improvement; for more still, it is the unavoidable Result of our Frame: and they who carry it too far, may, on the whole, be good Characters; and even they who do not, in any considerable Degree, may however be extremely wretched. How then can Virtue be its own Reward to Mankind in general, or indeed a proportionable Reward to almost any Man? Or how, unless the View be extended beyond such a Scene of Things, the certain Means of Happiness? The originally *appointed* Means of Happiness it undoubtedly is: but that it should be an effectual and infallible Means to Creatures so imperfect, passing through such a disordered World, is impossible without a State of future Reward; and of this the Gospel alone gives us full Assurance.

§. 25. By rejecting the Doctrine of Recompences in another Life, the Stoics were reduced to the Extravagance of supposing Felicity to be enjoyed in Circumstances, which are incapable of it. That a good Man stretched on a Rack, or reposing on a Bed of Roses, should enjoy himself equally, was a Notion which could gain but few Proselytes: and a sad Experience, that Pain was an Evil, sometimes drove their own Disciples from the thorny Asperities of the Portico, to the flowery Gardens of *Epicurus*.

§. 26. The absolute Indifference of all Externals, and the Position, That Things independent on Choice are nothing to us, the grand Point on which their Arguments turned, every one, who feels, knows to be false: and the Practice of the Wisest and Best among them, proved it in Fact to be so. It is remarkable, that no Sect of Philosophers ever so dogmatically prescribed, or so frequently committed, Suicide, as those very Stoics, who taught that the Pains and Sufferings, which they strove to end by this Act of Rebellion against the Decrees of Providence, were no Evils. How absolutely this horrid Practice contradicted all their noble Precepts of Resignation and Submission to the divine Will, is too evident to need any Enlargement. They professed indeed in Suicide to follow the divine Will; but this was a lamentably weak Pretence. Even supposing Sufferings to be Evils, they are no Proof of a Signal from God to abandon Life; but to show an exemplary Patience, which he will reward: but, supposing them, as the Stoics did, not to be Evils, they afford not so much as the Shadow of a Proof.

§. 27. As the Stoics by the Permission of Suicide, plainly implied, that external Inconveniences were not indifferent in the Extremity; it follows, that they must proportionably be allowed not to be indifferent in the inferior Degrees: of which *Zeno* seemed to be perfectly well convinced, by hanging himself when his Finger aked. And where was the Use of taking so much Pains to say, and believe what they knew to be false? It might, perhaps, be thought to be of some Benefit, in the Time of the later Stoics, to the great Men of *Rome*, whom the Emperors frequently butchered at their Pleasure: and this is the Use, to which *Epictetus* is perpetually applying it. Yet, even in this Case, the Stoic Doctrine, where Men could bring themselves to act upon it, made them absurdly rough, as appears by the History of *Helvidius Priscus*: and hindered the Good, they might otherwise have done. And, if a Man, taught thus to despise Tortures and Death, should happen at the same time to be wrong-head-

ed,

ed, for which he had no ſmall Chance, he would, in one Reſpect, be a more terrible wild Beaſt, than an Enthuſiaſt of any other Sect; as he would not think his Sufferings Evils: though in another he would be leſs ſo, as he would not hope to be rewarded for them hereafter.

§. 28. The Stoics are frequently, and juſtly, charged with great Arrogance in their Diſcourſes, and even in their Addreſſes to God. They aſſert however the Doctrine of Grace, and the Duty of Praiſe and Thankſgiving for the divine Aſſiſtance in moral Improvements (*b*). But there doth not, I think, appear any Inſtance of a Stoic, or perhaps any other Heathen Philoſopher, addreſſing his Repentance to God, and begging Pardon for his Failings, or directing his Diſciples to do it. Indeed nothing can excuſe their Idolatry of human Nature: which they proudly, and inconſiſtently ſuppoſed perfect and ſelf-ſufficient. *Seneca* carried the Matter ſo far, as by an impious Antitheſis, to give his wiſe Man the Superiority to God (*c*). *Epictetus* indeed was attentive enough to the Voice of Conſcience to own himſelf not perfect (*d*): and he ſometimes tells his Hearers, that they cannot be perfect yet (*e*). But even He at other times informs them, that they are not inferior to the Gods (*f*). The Stoical Boaſting will, however, imply leſs of perſonal Arrogance, if we can ſuppoſe, that thoſe Speeches, which ſo ill become human Imperfection, were always uttered, as perhaps in part they often were, in the Character of their Idol, the per-

(*b*) B. II. c. 18. §. 3, 4. B. III. c. 21. p. 248. p. 331, 332. See likewiſe *M. Antoninus*, L. I. §. 17. L. IX. §. 4. L. XI. §. 14.

(*c*) Eſt aliquid, quo ſapiens antecedat Deum. Ille naturæ beneficio, non ſuo, ſapiens eſt: ecce res magna, habere imbecillitatem hominis, ſecuritatem Dei. SEN. *Epiſt.* 53.

(*d*) B. IV. c. 1. §. 17. B. IV. c. 8. p. 363.

(*e*) B. I. c. 15. p. 48. B. IV. c. 12. §. 4.

(*f*) B. I. c. 12. p. 43.

fectly wise and good Man, which they owned to be merely an ideal Being (g). At least, it may be affirmed with Truth, that they frequently mention themselves with Decency and Humility, and with an express Confession of their Deviation from this faultless Exemplar.

§. 29. But then where was the Use of their favourite Doctrine, that a wise Man must always be happy? Might not a Person, determined to follow his own Inclinations, very reasonably object, "What is that to me, if I am not, or to any body "else, if no one ever was, a *wise* Man? But, suppose I were one; which is the better grounded "Argument? *You must always be happy, and* "*therefore Externals are no Evils:* or, *These* "*Things are Evils, and therefore I am not happy.* "——But *Epictetus* will say, You have a Remedy: the Door is open; go, with great good "Humour and Thankfulness, and hang yourself: and there will be an End of your Pain and "you together.——A fine Scheme of Happiness "indeed! and much to be thankful for! Why, "is it not the shorter and merrier Way, instead of "studying this crabbed Philosophy, to indulge myself, in whatever I like, as long as I can, (it may "chance to be a good while) and hang myself "thankfully, when I feel Inconveniences from "that? The Door is just as open in one Case, as "in the other; and nothing beyond it, either "pleasing or terrible in either."——Such, alas! is the Conclusion too commonly drawn; and such must be the Consequence of every Doctrine, not built upon solid Foundations.

§. 30. *Epictetus* often lays it down as a Maxim, that it is impossible for one Person to be in Fault, and another to be the Sufferer. This, on the Supposition

(g) Quis sapiens sit, aut fuerit, nec ipsos Stoicos solere dicere. Cic. *Acad.* L. IV.

position of a future State, will certainly be made true at last; but in the Stoical Sense, and System, is an absolute Extravagance. Take any Person of plain Understanding, with all the Feelings of Humanity about him, and see whether the subtlest Stoic will ever be able to convince him, that while he is insulted, oppressed, and tortured, he doth not *suffer*. See what Comfort it will afford him, to be told, that, if he supports his Afflictions and ill Treatment with Fortitude and Patience, Death will set him free, and then he and his Persecutor will be equally rewarded; will equally lose all personal Existence, and return to the Elements. How different are the Consolations proposed by Christianity, which not only assures its Disciples, that they shall *rest from their Labours* in Death, but that *their Works shall follow them*: and, by allowing them to *rejoice in Hope*, teaches them the most effectual Way of becoming *patient in Tribulation*.

§. 31. The Stoical Doctrine, that human Souls are literally Parts of the Deity, was equally shocking, and hurtful: as it supposed Portions of his Being to be wicked and miserable; and, by debasing Mens Ideas of the divine Dignity, and teaching them to think themselves essentially as good as He, nourished in their Minds an irreligious and fatal Presumption. Far differently the Christian System, represents Mankind, not as a Part of the Essence, but a Work of the Hand of God: as created in a State of improveable Virtue and Happiness: Fallen, by an Abuse of Free Will, into Sin, Misery, and Weakness (*b*); but redeemed from them by an Almighty Saviour; furnished with additional Knowledge and Strength; commanded to use their best Endeavours; made sensible, at the same time, how wretchedly defective they are; yet assured of endless

(*b*) ——Cito nequitia subrepit: virtus difficilis inventu est, rectorem, ducemque desiderat. Etiam sine magistro vitia discuntur. SEN. *Natural. Quaest.* L. III. c. 30.

endless Felicity on a due Exertion of them. The Stoic Philosophy insults human Nature, and discourages all our Attempts, by enjoining and promising a Perfection in this Life, of which we feel ourselves incapable. The Christian Religion shows Compassion to our Weakness, by prescribing to us only the practicable Task of aiming continually at further Improvements; and animates our Endeavours, by the Promise of a divine Aid, equal to every Trial.

§. 32. Specifying thus the Errors and Defects of so celebrated a System, is an unpleasing Employment: but in an Age, fond of preferring the Guesses of human Sagacity before the unerring Declarations of God, it seemed on this Occasion necessary to observe, that the Christian Morality is agreeable to Reason and Nature: that of the Stoics, for the most part, founded on Notions, intelligible to Few; and which none could admit, without Contradiction to their own Hearts. They reasoned, many times, admirably well, but from false Principles: and the noblest of their practical Precepts, being built on a sandy Basis, lay at the Mercy of every strong Temptation.

§. 33. Stoicism is indeed, in many Points inferior to the Doctrine of *Socrates:* which did not teach, that all Externals were indifferent; which did teach a future State of Recompence; and, agreeably to that, forbad Suicide. It doth not belong to the present Subject to show, how much even this best System is excelled by Christianity. It is sufficient just to observe, that the Author of it died in a Profession, which he had always made, of his Belief in the popular Deities, whose Superstitions, and impure Worship was the great Source of Corruption in the Heathen World: and the last Words he uttered, were a Direction to his Friend, for the Performance of an idolatrous Ceremony. This melancholy Instance of Ignorance and Error, in the

most

most illustrious Character for Wisdom and Virtue, in all Heathen Antiquity, is not mentioned as a Reflexion on his Memory, but as a Proof of human Weakness in general. Whether Reason could have discovered the great Truths, which in these Days are ascribed to it, because now seen so clearly by the Light of the Gospel, may be a *Question*; but that it never did, is an undeniable *Fact*: and that is enough to teach us Thankfulness for the Blessing of a better Information. *Socrates*, who had, of all Mankind, the fairest Pretensions to set up for an Instructor and Reformer of the World, confessed, that he knew nothing, referred to Tradition, and acknowledged the Want of a superior Guide: and there is a remarkable Passage in *Epictetus*, in which he represents it, as the Office of his supreme God, or of One deputed by Him, to appear among Mankind, as a Teacher and Example (*g*).

§. 34. Upon the whole, the several Sects of Heathen Philosophy serve, as so many striking Instances of the Imperfection of human Wisdom; and of the extreme Need of a divine Assistance, to rectify the Mistakes of depraved Reason, and to replace natural Religion on its true Foundation. The Stoics every-where testify the noblest Zeal for Virtue, and the Honour of God: but they attempted to establish them on Principles, inconsistent with the Nature of Man, and contradictory to Truth and Experience. By a direct Consequence of these Principles, they were liable to be seduced, and in Fact often were seduced, into Pride, Hard-heartedness, and the last dreadful Extremity of human Guilt, Self-murder.

§. 35. But however indefensible the Philosophy of the Stoics in several Instances may be, it appears to have been of very important Use, in the Heathen World: and they are, on many Accounts, to be considered

(*g*) B. IV. c. 8. §. 6.

considered in a very respectable Light. Their Doctrine of Evidence and fixed Principles, was an excellent Preservative from the Mischiefs, that might have arisen from the Scepticism of the Academics and Pyrrhonists, if unopposed: and their zealous Defence of a particular Providence, a valuable Antidote to the atheistical Scheme of *Epicurus*. To this may be added, that their strict Notions of Virtue in most Points; (for they sadly failed in some) and the Lives of several among them, must contribute a good deal to preserve luxurious States from an absolutely universal Dissoluteness; and the Subjects of arbitrary Government, from a wretched and contemptible Pusilanimity.

§. 36. Even now, their Compositions may be read with great Advantage, as containing excellent Rules of Self-government, and of social Behaviour; of a noble Reliance on the Aid and Protection of Heaven, and of a perfect Resignation and Submission to the divine Will: Points, which are treated with great Clearness, and with admirable Spirit, in the Lessons of the Stoics; and though their Directions are seldom practicable on their Principles, in trying Cases, may be rendered highly useful in Subordination to Christian Reflections.

§. 37. If, among those, who are so unhappy as to remain unconvinced of the Truth of Christianity, any are prejudiced against it by the Influence of unwarrantable Inclinations: such Persons will find very little Advantage in rejecting the Doctrines of the New Testament for those of the Portico; unless they think it an Advantage to be laid under moral Restraints, almost equal to those of the Gospel, while they are deprived of its Encouragements and Supports. Deviations from the Rules of Sobriety, Justice and Piety, meet with small Indulgence in the Stoic Writings: and they, who profess to admire *Epictetus*, unless they pursue that severely virtuous Conduct which he every-where

pre-

prescribes, will find themselves treated by him, with the utmost Degree of Scorn and Contempt. An immoral Character is, indeed, more or less, the Out-cast, of all Sects of Philosophy: and *Seneca* quotes even *Epicurus*, to prove the universal Obligation of a virtuous Life (*b*). Of this great Truth, *God never left himself without Witness.* Persons of distinguished Talents and Opportunities seem to have been raised, from time to time, by Providence, to check the Torrent of Corruption, and to preserve the Sense of moral Obligations on the Minds of the Multitude, to whom the various Occupations of Life left but little Leisure to form Deductions of their own. But then they wanted a proper Commission to enforce their Precepts; they intermixed with them, through false Reasoning, many gross Mistakes; and their unavoidable Ignorance, in several important Points, entangled them with Doubts, which easily degenerated into pernicious Errors.

§. 38. If there are others, who reject Christianity, from Motives of Dislike to its peculiar Doctrines: they will scarcely fail of entertaining more favourable Impressions of it, if they can be prevailed on, with impartiality, to compare the holy Scriptures, from whence alone the Christian Religion is to be learned, with the Stoic Writings; and then fairly to consider, whether there is any thing to be met with in the Discourses of our blessed Saviour, in the Writings of his Apostles, or even in the obscurest Parts of the prophetic Books, by which, equitably interpreted, either their Senses, or their Reason are contradicted, as they are by the Paradoxes of these Philo-

(*b*) Eo libentius Epicuri egregia dicta commemoro, ut istis, qui ad illa confugiunt, spe mala inducti, qua velamentum seipsos suorum vitiorum habituros existimant, probem, quocunque ierint, honeste esse vivendum. SEN. *Epist.* 21. It was hard indeed to reconcile this with some of his other Doctrines.

Philosophers: and if not, whether Notices from above, of Things, in which, though we comprehend them but imperfectly, we are possibly much more interested, than at present we discern, ought not to be received with implicit Veneration; as useful Exercises and Trials of that Duty, which finite Understandings owe to infinite Wisdom.

§. 39. Antiquity furnishes but very few Particulars of the Life of *Epictetus*. He was born at *Hierapolis*, a City of *Phrygia*: but of what Parents, is unknown; as well as by what Means he came to *Rome*, where he was the Slave of *Epaphroditus*, one of *Nero*'s Courtiers *(i)*. It is reported, that when his Master once put his Leg to the Torture, *Epictetus*, with great Composure, and even smiling, observed to him; "You will certainly break my "Leg:" which accordingly happened; and he continued, in the same Tone of Voice—"Did "not I tell you, that you would break it *(k)*?" This Accident might, perhaps, be the Occasion of his Lameness: which, however, some Authors say he had from his early Years *(l)*; and others attribute to the Rheumatism *(m)*. At what Time he obtained his Liberty doth not appear. When the Philosophers, by a Decree of *Domitian*, were banished from *Rome*, *Epictetus* retired to *Nicopolis* *(n)*, a City of *Epirus*, where he taught Philosophy; from which he doth not seem to have derived any external Advantages, as he is universally said to have been extremely poor. At least, he was so when he lived at *Rome*: where his whole Furniture consisted of a Bed *(o)*, a Pipkin, and an Earthen Lamp *(p)*; which last was purchased for about a hundred

(i) Suidas in Voc.
(k) Orig. contra Cels. L. VII. §. 53.
(l) Suidas in Voc.
(m) Simplic. Com. p. 102.
(n) A. Gell. L. XV. c. 11.
(o) Simplic. Com. p. 102.
(p) Id. Ib.

hundred Pounds after his Death, by a Person whom *Lucian* ridicules for it, as hoping to acquire the Wisdom of *Epictetus* by studying over it. His only Attendant was a Woman, whom he took in his advanced Years, to nurse a Child, whom, otherwise, one of his Friends would have exposed to perish (*q*): an amiable Proof of the poor old Man's Good-nature, and Disapprobation, it is to be hoped, of that shocking, yet common Instance of Heathen Blindness and Barbarity.

In this extreme Poverty, a Cripple, unattended, and destitute of almost every Convenience of Life, *Epictetus* was not only obliged by the Rules of his Philosophy to think himself happy, but actually did so, according to the Distich of which *Aulus Gellius* affirms him to have been the Author (*r*).

A Slave, in Body maim'd, as Irus (*s*) *poor;*
Yet to the Gods was Epictetus *dear.*

He is said to have returned to *Rome* in the Reign of *Adrian*, and to have been treated by him with a high Degree of Familiarity (*t*). If this be true, he lived to a great Age. But that he should continue alive, to the Time of M. *Antoninus*, as *Themistius* (*u*), and *Suidas* (*w*) affirm, is utterly improbable (*x*), as the learned *Fabricius* observes; to whose Life of *Epictetus* (*y*) I am greatly indebted. When, or where, he died, is, I think, no-where mentioned. All Authors agree in bearing Testimony

(*q*) Id. p. 272.
(*r*) A. Gellius, L. II. c. 18
(*s*) The Name of a Beggar in *Homer*.
(*t*) Ælii. Spart. Adrian. c. 17.
(*u*) Orat. Conf. ad *Jovian.* Imp.
(*w*) In Voc.
(*x*) The Reign of *Nero* began *A. D.* 54. of *Adrian*, 117. of *M. Antoninus*, 161.
(*y*) *Bibl. Gr.* Vol. III. p. 257.

ny to the unblemiſhed Conduct of his Life, and the Uſefulneſs of his Inſtructions. The laſt-named Emperor expreſſes much Obligation to a Friend, who had communicated his Works to him (z): and in another Place, he ranks him, not only with *Chryſippus*, but with *Socrates* (a). *A. Gellius* calls him the greateſt of the Stoics (b): *Origen* affirms, that his Writings had done more Good than *Plato*'s (c): And *Simplicius* ſays, perhaps by way of indirect Oppoſition to an infinitely better Book, that he who is not influenced by them, is reclaimable by nothing but the Chaſtiſements of another World (d). In what manner he inſtructed his Pupils, will be ſeen in the following Treatiſe.

§. 40. There are ſo many of the Sentiments and Expreſſions of Chriſtianity in it, that one ſhould be ſtrongly tempted to think, that *Epictetus* was acquainted with the New Teſtament, if ſuch a Suppoſition was not highly injurious to his Character. To have known the Contents of that Book, and not to have been led by them into an Enquiry, which muſt have convinced him of their Truth, would argue ſuch an Obſtinacy of Prejudice, as one would not willingly impute to a Mind, which appears ſo well diſpoſed. And, even paſſing over this Conſideration, to have borrowed ſo much from Chriſtianity as he ſeems to have done, without making the leaſt Acknowlegement from whence he received it, would be an Inſtance of Diſingenuity, utterly unworthy of an honeſt Man, and inconſiſtent with his Practice in other Reſpects: for he often quotes, with great Applauſe, the Sentences of many Writers, not of his own Sect. Poſſibly indeed he might, like the other Heathens in general, have a peculiar Con-

(z) L. I. §. 7.
(a) L. VII. §. 19.
(b) *Noct. Att.* L. I. c. 2.
(c) Contra *Celſ.* L. VI. §. 2.
(d) Com. p. 2.

Contempt of, and Averſion to, Chriſtian Authors, as akin to the *Jews*, and Oppoſers of the eſtabliſhed Worſhip; notwithſtanding thoſe Parts of them, which he muſt approve. But ſtill I hope, his Conformity with the ſacred Writings may be accounted for, without ſuppoſing him acquainted with Chriſtianity, as ſuch. The great Number of its Profeſſors, diſperſed through the *Roman* Empire, had probably introduced ſeveral of the New Teſtament Phraſes into the popular Language: and the Chriſtian Religion might by that Time have diffuſed ſome Degree of general Illumination; of which many might receive the Benefit, who were ignorant of the Source, from whence it proceeded: and *Epictetus* I apprehend to have been of this Number. Several ſtriking Inſtances of this Reſemblance between him and the New Teſtament, have been obſerved in the Notes; and the attentive Reader will find many, which are not mentioned; and may perceive from them, either that the Stoics admired the Chriſtian Language, however they came to the Knowledge of it; or that treating a Subject practically, and with a Feeling of its Force, leads Men to ſuch ſtrong Expreſſions, as we find in Scripture, and ſhould find oftener in the Philoſophers, if they had been more in earneſt: but however, they occur frequently enough to vindicate thoſe, in which the Scriptures abound, from the Contempt and Ridicule of light Minds.

§. 41. *Arrian*, the Diſciple of *Epictetus*, to whom we are obliged for theſe Diſcourſes, was a *Greek* by Birth, but a Senator and Conſul of *Rome*; and an able Commander in War (*m*). He imitated *Xenophon*, both in his Life and Writings; and particularly, in delivering to Poſterity the Converſations of his Maſter. There were originally Twenty Books of them, beſides the *Enchiridion*, which ſeems to be taken out of them,

 and

(*m*) Fabricii *Bibl. Gr.* Vol. III. L. IV. c. 8. p. 269, &c.

and an Account of his Life and Death. Very little Order or Method is to be found in them, or was from the Nature of them to be expected. The Connexion is often ſcarcely diſcoverable: a Reference to particular Incidents, long ſince forgotten, at the ſame time that it evidences their Genuineneſs, often renders them obſcure in ſome Places; and the great Corruption of the Text, in others. Yet, under all theſe Diſadvantages, this immethodical Collection is perhaps one of the moſt valuable Remains of Antiquity; and they, who conſult it with any Degree of Attention, can ſcarcely fail of receiving Improvement. Indeed it is hardly poſſible to be inattentive to ſo awakening a Speaker as *Epictetus.* There is ſuch a Warmth and Spirit in his Exhortations; and his good Senſe is enlivened by ſuch a Keenneſs of Wit, and Gaiety of Humour, as render the Study of him, a moſt delightful as well as profitable Entertainment.

§. 42. For this Reaſon it was judged proper, that a Tranſlation of him ſhould be undertaken; there being none, I believe, but of the *Enchiridion*, in any modern Language, excepting a pretty good *French* one, publiſhed about a hundred and fifty Years ago, and ſo extremely ſcarce, that I was unable to procure it, till Mr. *Harris* obligingly lent it me, after I had publiſhed the Propoſals for printing this: which, notwithſtanding the Aſſiſtance given me in the Proſecution of it, hath ſtill, I am ſenſible, great Faults. But they, who will ſee them the moſt clearly, will be the readieſt to excuſe, as they will know beſt the Difficulty of avoiding them. There is one Circumſtance, which, I am apprehenſive, muſt be particularly ſtriking, and poſſibly ſhocking to many, the frequent Uſe of ſome Words in an unpopular Senſe: an Inconvenience, which, however, I flatter myſelf, the Introduction and Notes will, in ſome Degree, remove. In the Tranſlation of technical Terms, if the

the ſame *Greek* Word had not always been rendered in the ſame manner, at leaſt, when the Propriety of our Language will at all permit it, every new Expreſſion would have been apt to raiſe a new Idea. The Reader, I hope, will pardon, if not approve, the Uncouthneſs, in many Places, of a Tranſlation pretty ſtrictly literal: as it ſeemed neceſſary, upon the whole, to preſerve the original Spirit, the peculiar Turn and characteriſtic Roughneſs of the Author. For elſe, taking greater Liberties would have ſpared me no ſmall Pains.

I have been much indebted to Mr. *Upton*'s Edition: by which, many Paſſages, unintelligible before, are cleared up. His Emendations have often aſſiſted me in the Text; and his References furniſhed me with Materials for the Hiſtorical Notes.

TABLE OF CONTENTS.

BOOK I.

BOOK II.

Chap.

BOOK III.

Chap.

BOOK IV.

ARRIAN

TO

LUCIUS GELLIUS

Wisheth all Happiness.

I Neither composed the Discourses of *Epictetus* in such a manner, as Things of this Nature are commonly composed: nor did I myself produce them to public View, any more than I composed them. But whatever Sentiments I heard from his own Mouth, the very same I endeavoured to set down in the very same Words, as far as possible, and preserve as Memorials for my own Use, of his Manner of Thinking, and Freedom of Speech.

These Discourses are such as one Person would naturally deliver from his own Thoughts, *extempore*, to another; not such as he would prepare to be read by Numbers afterwards. Yet, notwithstanding this, I cannot tell how, without either my Consent or Knowledge, they have fallen into the Hands of the Public. But it is of little Consequence to me, if I do not appear an able Writer; and of none to *Epictetus*, if any one treats his Discourses (a) with Con-

(a) *His* means the Composition, not the Subject-matter of them.

Contempt; ſince it was very evident, even when he uttered them, that he aimed at nothing more than to excite his Hearers to Virtue. If they produce that one Effect, they have in them what, I think, philoſophical Diſcourſes ought to have. And ſhould they fail of it, let the Readers, however, be aſſured, that when *Epictetus* himſelf pronounced them, his Audience could not help being affected in the very Manner he intended they ſhould. If by themſelves they have leſs Efficacy, perhaps it is my Fault, or perhaps it is unavoidable.

Farewell.

SUBSCRIBERS NAMES.

His Grace the Duke of BEDFORD, Lord Lieut. of IRELAND, &c.
Her Grace the Dutchefs of BEDFORD

A.

THOMAS Adderley, Efq;
Mr. John Abernethy, Merchant
Mr. James Armftrong, Merchant
Mrs. Afhworth

B.

The Right Honourable the Lord Bowes, Lord High Chancellor of Ireland
John Bourke, jun. Efq;
Bellingham Boyle, Efq;
Richard Baldwin, junior, Efq;
Samuel Brooke, Efq;
Thomas Blair, Efq;
The Reverend Mr. John Brownlow
Mrs. Sarah Bradley
Mr. John Butler
Mafter Edward Bacon
Mifs Elizabeth Barret
The Reverend Mr. Robert Bryan
The Reverend Mr. Adam Blair
John Baily, A. B. T. C. D.
Oliver Bourk, Efq;
Chriftopher Bowen, Efq;
The Reverend Mr. Henry Blacker
Mr. Richard Branfon
——— Beaumont, Efq;
Edmond Blackal, M. D.
Conftantine Barber, M. D.
Mr. Randall Bourk, Apothecary

C.

The Hon. William Crofbie
The Honourable John Caulfeild

The

The Honourable Mrs. Crosbie
William Francis Crosbie, Esq;
John Cramer, Esq;
The Reverend Middleton Cornyn, D. D.
Captain Edward Corneile
Lieutenant John Corneile
The Reverend Dean Crowe
Mr. George Cottingham
Mr. Alexander Cunningham, Surgeon
Mr. David Courtney
Thomas Carter, junior, Esq;
The Reverend Thomas Carr, D. D.

D.

The Right Honourable Lady Doneraile
The Reverend Dean Delany, 6 Books
Mr. William Dennis, 6 Books

E.

George Evans, Esq; F. C. T. C. D.
John Evans, Esq; F. C. T. C. D.
Mr. John Exshaw, Bookseller
John Eyre, Esq;
Francis Evans, Esq;
Thomas Eyre, Esq;
Mr. Gasper Erck, Junior

F.

John Foster, Esq; F. C. T. C. D.
William Fairtlough, Esq;
Mr. John Fairtlough
The Reverend Alexander Fulton

G.

The Right Honourable Charles Gardiner
Richard Griffith, Esq;
James Gildea, of Partry, Esq;
James Gildea, of Cloonigashell, Esq;
The Reverend John Graves
Mr. Boulter Grierson, Bookseller, 6 Books
Mr. Ben. Gunne, Bookseller, 6 Books
George Gunne, Esq;

H.

The Honourable and Reverend Archdeacon Hamilton
The Reverend Dean Harman
Mr. John Holliday, 6 Books

I.

The Reverend Charles Jones

K.

The Right Reverend the Lord Bifhop of Kilmore
Mr. George Knox
Mrs. Jane King

L.

The Hon. Jofeph Leefon
The Rev. Tho. Leland, D. D. Fellow of T. C. D. 6 Books
The Reverend John Leland, D. D.
Thomas Litton, Efq;
Mr. James Lindfay

M.

The Right Hon. and Right Rev. the Lord Bifhop of Meath
Thomas Montgomery, Efq;
Henry Marcus Mafon, Efq;
Redmond Morris, Efq;
Mr. Folliot Magrath, Merchant
Mr. Robert Maxwell
The Reverend Mr. John Mears
Captain Manfergh
Mrs. M'Quay
Mr. David Melville
Mr. Alexander M' Mahon, Merchant

N.

The Hon. Lord Newbattle

O.

Richard Olpherts, Efq;

P.

His Grace the Lord Primate
The Right Hon. John Ponfonby, Speaker of the Hon. House of Commons
The Right Hon. Lord Vifcount Powerfcourt
Mr. Robert Pettigrew
John Piggot, Efq;
Kingfmill Penefather, Efq;
Marcus Patterfon, Efq;
Mr. Samuel Price, 6 Books
Narciffus Charles Proby, Efq; F. C. T. C. D.

R.

The Right Hon. Richard Rigby, 2 Books
Major John Rutter
Thomas Rutlidge, Efq;
Peter Rutlidge, Efq;

Andrew

Andrew Rutlidge, Eſq;
James Rutlidge, Eſq;
William Rutlidge, Eſq;
Mr. George Rogers, T. C. D.
Miſs Eſther Rogers, of Greenwood
Mr. John Rowlet, T. C. D.

S.

The Right Hon. the Earl of Shannon
The Honourable Hungerford Skeffington
James Semple, M. D.
Anthony Sterling, T. C. D.
Alexander Stewart, Eſq;
John Smith, Eſq;
Thomas Smyth, Eſq;
Charles Smith, Eſq;
William Smith, ſen. 6 Books
William Smith, jun. 6 Books
The Reverend Barlow Scott

T.

The Moſt Hon. the Marquis of Taviſtock
James Taylor, Eſq; Crooked-Staff
George Thwaites, Eſq;
Mr. Richard Thwaites
Mr. Joſeph Thwaites
Mr. Nat. Thwaites
Mr. Ephraim Thwaites
Mr. Edwin Thomas

V.

Richard Vernon, Eſq;
Mr. William Vance, Surgeon

W.

The Reverend John Wall, D. D.
Mr. Samuel Watſon, 6 Books
The Reverend Iſaac Weld, 6 Books
George Woods, Eſq;
Matthias Walker, A. M. 6 Books

Y.

Barry Yelverton, A. B. 6 Books.

THE

THE

DISCOURSES

OF

EPICTETUS.

BOOK I.

CHAPTER I.

Of the Things which are, and of those which are not, in our own Power.

§. 1. OF other Faculties, you will find no one that contemplates, or consequently approves or disapproves, itself. How far does the contemplative Power of Grammar extend?

As far as the Judging of Language.

Of Music?

As far as Judging of Melody.

Does either of them contemplate itself, then?

By no means.

Thus, for Inſtance, when you are to write to your Friend, Grammar will tell you what to write: but whether you are to write to your Friend at all, or no, Grammar will not tell you. Thus Muſic, with regard to Tunes: but whether it be proper or improper, at any particular Time, to ſing or play, Muſic will not tell you.

What will tell, then?

That which contemplates both itſelf and all other Things.

And what is that?

The *reaſoning Faculty*: for that alone is found to conſider both itſelf, its Powers, its Value, and likewiſe all the reſt. For what is it elſe that ſays Gold is beautiful? (for the Gold itſelf does not ſpeak) Evidently that Faculty, which judges of the Appearances of Things (*a*). What elſe diſtinguiſhes Muſic, Grammar, the other Faculties, proves their uſes, and ſhows their proper Occaſions?

Nothing but this.

§. 2. As it was fit then, this moſt excellent and ſuperior Faculty alone, a right Uſe of the Appearances of Things, the Gods have placed in our own Power; but all other Matters, not in our Power. Was it becauſe they would not? I rather think, that if they could, they had granted us theſe too: but they certainly could not. For, placed upon Earth, and confined to ſuch a Body, and to ſuch Companions, how was it poſſible that, in theſe Reſpects, we ſhould not be hindered by Things without us?

§. 3. But what ſays *Jupiter*? "O *Epictetus*, if "it were poſſible, I had made this little Body "and Property of thine free, and not liable to "Hindrance. But now do not miſtake: it is "not thy own, but only a finer Mixture of "Clay.

(*a*) See Introduction, §. 7.

"Clay (*b*). Since, then, I could not (*c*) give thee "this, I have given thee a certain Portion of my- "self: this Faculty of exerting the Powers of Pur- "suit and Avoidance (*d*), of Desire and Aversion; "and, in a Word, the Use of the Appearances of "Things. Taking Care of this Point, and making "what is thy own to consist in this, thou wilt ne- "ver be restrained, never be hindered; thou wilt "not groan, wilt not complain, wilt not flatter "any one. How then! Do all these Advantages "seem small to thee? Heaven forbid! Let them "suffice thee then, and thank the Gods."

§. 4. But now, when it is in our Power to take Care of *one* Thing, and to apply to *one*, we chuse rather to take Care of *many*, and to incumber ourselves with *many*; Body, Property, Brother, Friend, Child, and Slave; and, by this Multiplicity of Incumbrances, we are burdened and weighed down. Thus, when the Weather doth not happen to be fair for sailing, we sit screwing ourselves, and perpetually looking out,—Which Way is the Wind? —North.—What have we to do with that?— When will the West blow?—When itself, Friend, or *Æolus* pleases; for *Jupiter* has not made *You* Dispenser of the Winds, but *Æolus*.

§. 5. What then is to be done?

To make the best of what is in our Power, and take the rest as it naturally happens.

And how is that?

As it pleases God.

What, then, must *I* be the only one to lose my Head?

 Why,

(*b*) The Sacred Writers also mention Man as made of Clay, *Gen.* ii. 7. *Job* x. 9. xxxiii. 6. Η συ λαϐων γην πηλον, επλασας ζωον, xxxviii. 14.

(*c*) One would hope, from the Context, that *Epictetus* is here speaking only of a moral, not a natural Impossibility; an Impossibility arising merely from the present Constitution of Things. See Introduction, §. 17. See likewise B. II. chap. v. §. 5.

(*d*) See Introduction, §. 5.

Why, would you have all the World, then, lose their Heads for your Consolation? Why are not you willing to stretch out your Neck, like *Lateranus* (*e*), when he was commanded by *Nero* to be beheaded? For, shrinking a little, after receiving a weak Blow, he stretched it out again. And before this, when *Epaphroditus (f)*, the Freedman of *Nero*, interrogated him about the Conspiracy; "If "I have a Mind to say any thing, replied he, I "will tell it to your Master."

§. 6. What then should we have at hand upon such Occasions? Why what else but—what is *mine*, and what not *mine*; what is permitted me, and what not.—I must die: and must I die *groaning* too? —Be fetter'd. Must it be *lamenting* too?—Exiled. And what hinders me, then, but that I may go smiling, and chearful, and serene?—"Betray a secret"—I will not betray it; for this is in my own Power.—"Then I will fetter you." —What do you say, Man? Fetter *me?* You will fetter my *Leg*; but not *Jupiter* himself can get the better of my *Choice* (*g*). "I will throw you "into Prison: I will behead that paltry Body of "yours." Did I ever tell you, that I alone had a Head not liable to be cut off?——These Things ought Philosophers to study; these ought they

(*e*) *Plautius Lateranus*, a Consul elect, was put to Death by the Command of *Nero*, for being privy to the Conspiracy of *Piso*. His Execution was so sudden, that he was not permitted to take Leave of his Wife and Children; but was hurried into a Place appropriated to the Punishment of Slaves, and there killed by the Hand of the Tribune *Statius*. He suffered in obstinate Silence, and without making any Reproach to *Statius*, who was concerned in the same Plot for which he himself was punished. TACITUS, *L.* xv. *c.* 60.

(*f*) *Epaphroditus* was the Master of Requests and Freedman of *Nero*, and the Master of *Epictetus*. He assisted *Nero* in killing himself; for which he was condemned to Death by *Domitian*. SUETONIUS *in vitâ Neronis*, *c.* 49. *Domit. c.* 14.

(*g*) See Introduction, §. 9.

they daily to write; and in these to exercise themselves.

§. 7. *Thraseas* (*h*) used to say, "I had rather "be killed To-day, than banished To-morrow." But how did *Rufus* (*i*) answer him? "If you "prefer it as a heavier Misfortune, how foolish "a Preference! If as a lighter, who has put it "in your Power? Why do not you study to be "contented with what is allotted you?"

§. 8. Well, and what said *Agrippinus* (*k*), upon this Account? "I will not be a Hindrance to my-"self." Word was brought him, "Your Cause "is trying in the Senate."—"Good Luck attend "it.—But it is Eleven o'Clock" (the Hour when he used to exercise before bathing): "Let us go "to our Exercise." When it was over, a Messenger tells him, "You are condemned." To Banishment, says he, or Death? "To Banishment." —What of my Estate?—"It is not taken away." Well then, let us go as far as *Aricia* (*l*), and dine there.

§. 9. This it is to have studied (*m*) what

 ought

(*h*) *Thraseas Pætus*, a Stoic Philosopher, put to Death by *Nero*. He was Husband of *Arria*, so well known by that beautiful Epigram in *Martial*. The Expression of *Tacitus* concerning him is remarkable: *After the Murder of so many excellent Persons,* Nero *at last formed a Desire of cutting off Virtue itself, by the Execution of* Thraseas Pætus *and* Bareas Soranus. *L.* xvi. *c.* 21.

(*i*) *Rufus* was a *Tuscan* of the Equestrian Order, and a Stoic Philosopher. When *Vespasian* banished the other Philosophers, *Rufus* was alone excepted. UPTON.

(*k*) *Agrippinus* was banished by *Nero*, for no other Crime than the unfortunate Death of his Father, who had been causelessly killed by the Command of *Tiberius*: and this had furnished a Pretence for accusing him of hereditary Disloyalty. TACITUS, *L.* xvi. *c.* 28, 29.

(*l*) *Aricia*, a Town about sixteen Miles from *Rome*, which lay in his Road to Banishment.

(*m*) This chearful Readiness for Death, whenever appointed by Providence, is noble in a Christian, to whom dying is taking Possession of Happiness. But in Stoics, who seem to form no Hope beyond the Grave, it had surely more Insensibility than true Bravery, and was indeed contrary to Nature.

ought to be ſtudied; to have rendered our Deſires and Averſions incapable of being reſtrained, or incurred. I muſt die: if inſtantly, I will die inſtantly; if in a ſhort time, I will dine firſt; and when the Hour comes, then I will die. How? As becomes one who reſtores what is not his own.

CHAPTER II.

In what Manner, upon every Occaſion, to preſerve our Character.

§. 1. TO a reaſonable Creature, that alone is inſupportable which is unreaſonable: but every thing reaſonable may be ſupported. Stripes are not naturally inſupportable.—"How ſo?" —See how the *Spartans* (*a*) bear whipping, after they have learned that it is a reaſonable Thing. Hanging is not inſupportable: for, as ſoon as a Man has taken it into his Head that it is reaſonable, he goes and hangs (*b*) himſelf. In ſhort, we ſhall find by Obſervation, that no Creature is oppreſſed ſo much by any thing, as by what is unreaſonable; nor, on the other hand, attracted to any thing ſo ſtrongly, as to what is reaſonable.

§. 2. But it happens that different Things are *reaſonable* and *unreaſonable*, as well as good and bad, advan-

(*a*) The *Spartans*, to make a Trial of the Fortitude of their Children, uſed to have them publickly whipt at the Altar of *Diana*; and often with ſo much Severity, that they expired. The Boys ſupported this Exerciſe with ſo much Conſtancy, as never to cry out, nor even groan. Upton *from* Cicero, &c.

(*b*) The Suppoſition made by *Epictetus*, that it may be reaſonable, ſometimes, for Perſons to kill themſelves, is a ſtrong and alarming Inſtance of the great Neceſſity of being careful, not only in *general* to form juſt and diſtinct Ideas of reaſonable and unreaſonable, but to apply them properly to *particular* Subjects; ſince ſuch a Man as He, failed in ſo important a Caſe, at the very time when he was giving Cautions to others.

advantageous and disadvantageous, to different Persons. On this Account, chiefly, we stand in need of a liberal Education, to teach us, to adapt the Preconceptions of reasonable and unreasonable to particular Cases, conformably to Nature. But to judge of reasonable, and unreasonable, we make use not only of a due Estimation of Things without us, but of what relates to each Person's particular Character. Thus, it is reasonable for one Man to submit to a dirty (*c*) disgraceful Office, who considers this only, that if he does not submit to it, he shall be whipt, and lose his Dinner; but if he does, that he has nothing hard or disagreeable to suffer: Whereas to another it appears insupportable, not only to submit to such an Office himself, but to bear with any one else who does. If you ask me, then, whether you shall do this dirty Office or not, I will tell you, it is a more valuable Thing to get a Dinner, than not; and a greater Disgrace to be whipt, than not to be whipt: So that, if you measure yourself by these Things, go and do your Office.

"Ay, but this is not suitable to my Character."

It is *You* who are to consider that, not *I*: For it is you who know yourself, what Value you set upon yourself, and at what Rate you sell yourself: for different People sell themselves at different Prices.

§ 3. Hence *Agrippinus* (*d*), when *Florus* was considering whether he should go to *Nero*'s Shows, so as to perform some Part in them himself, bid him go.—"But why do not *you* go then?" says *Florus*. "Because, replied *Agrippinus*, *I* do not deliberate

(*c*) The Translation here gives only the general Sense, as a more particular Description would be scarcely supportable in our Language.

(*d*) *Nero* was remarkably fond of Theatrical Entertainments; and used to introduce upon the Stage the Descendants of noble Families, whom Want had rendered venal. Tacitus, *L.* xiv. *c.* 14.

" about it." For he who once sets himself about such Considerations, and goes to calculating the Worth of external Things, approaches very near to those who forget their own Character. For, why do you ask me whether Death or Life be the more eligible? I answer, Life, Pain or Pleasure? I answer, Pleasure.——" But if I do not act a Part, " I shall lose my Head."——Go and act it then, but *I* will not.——" Why?"——Because you esteem yourself only as one Thread of many that make up the Piece.——" What then?"——You have nothing to care for, but how to be like the rest of Mankind, as one Thread desires not to be distinguished from the others. But *I* would be the Purple (*e*), that small and shining Thing, which gives a Lustre and Beauty to the rest. Why do you bid me resemble the Multitude then? At that Rate, how shall I be the Purple?

§. 4. This *Priscus Helvidius* (*f*) too saw, and acted accordingly: For when *Vespasian* had sent to forbid his going to the Senate, he answered, " It is " in your Power to prevent my continuing a Senator; " but while I am one, I must go."——" Well " then, at least be silent there."——" Do not ask " my Opinion, and I will be silent."——" But I " must ask it."——" And I must speak what appears to me to be right."——" But if you do, I " will put you to Death."——" Did I ever tell " you that I was immortal? You will do your Part, " and I mine: It is yours to kill, and mine to die " intrepid; yours to banish me, mine to depart " untroubled."

§. 5.

(*e*) An Allusion to the Purple Border, which distinguished the Dress of the *Roman* Nobility.

(*f*) *Helvidius Priscus* was no less remarkable for his Learning and Philosophy, than for the Sanctity of his Manners and the Love of his Country. He behaved however with too much Haughtiness, on several Occasions, to *Vespasian*, who sentenced him to Death with great Reluctance, and even forbad the Execution, when it was too late. SUETON. *in Vesp.* §. 15.

§. 5. What Good, then, did *Priscus* do, who was but a single Person? Why, what good does the Purple do to the Garment? What, but the being a shining Character in himself (*g*), and setting a good Example to others? Another, perhaps, if in such Circumstances *Cæsar* had forbidden his Going to the Senate, would have answered, "I am obliged to you for excusing me." But such a one he would not have forbidden to go: well knowing, that he would either sit like a Statue; or, if he spoke, he would say what he knew to be agreeable to *Cæsar*, and would overdo it by adding still more.

§. 6. Thus acted even a Wrestler, who was in Danger of Death, unless he consented to an ignominious Amputation. His Brother, who was a Philosopher, coming to him, and saying, "Well, "Brother, what do you design to do? Let us cut "away this morbid Part, and return again to the "Field." He refused, and courageously died.

§. 7. When it was asked, whether he acted thus as a Wrestler, or a Philosopher? I answer, As a *Man*, said *Epictetus*; but as a Man who had been proclaimed a Champion at the Olympic Games; who had been used to such Places, and not exercised merely in the School of *Bato* (*h*). Another would have had his very Head cut off, if he could have lived without it. This is that Regard to Character, so powerful with those who are accustomed to introduce it, from their own Breasts, into their Deliberations.

§. 8. "Come now, *Epictetus*, take off your "Beard (*i*)."—If I am a Philosopher, I answer, I will

(*g*) Αυτω in the Original refers to ιματιω; but the Figure would have appeared harsh in the Translation.

(*h*) *Bato* was a famous Master of the Olympic Exercises. Upton.

(*i*) *Domitian* ordered all the Philosophers to be banished. To avoid this Inconvenience, those who had a Mind to disguise their Profession, took off their Beards. Upton.

will not take it off.——"Then I will take off "your Head."—If that will do you any good, take it off.

§. 9. It was asked, How shall each of us perceive what belongs to his Character? Whence, replied *Epictetus*, does a Bull, when the Lion approaches, perceive his own Qualifications *(k)*, and expose himself alone for the whole Herd? It is evident, that with the Qualifications, occurs, at the same time, the Consciousness of being indued with them. And in the same manner, whoever of Us hath such Qualifications, will not be ignorant of them. But neither is a Bull, nor a gallant-spirited Man, formed all at once. We are to exercise and qualify ourselves, and not to run rashly upon what doth not concern us.

§. 10. Only consider at what Price you sell your own Will and Choice, Man *(l)*: If for nothing else, that you may not sell it for a Trifle. Greatness indeed, and Excellence, perhaps belong to others, to such as *Socrates*.

Why then, as we are born with a like Nature, do not all, or the greater Number become such as he?

Why, are all Horses swift? Are all Dogs sagacious? What then, because Nature hath not befriended me, Shall I neglect all Care of myself? Heaven forbid! *Epictetus* is inferior to *Socrates* *(m)*; but if superior to ——— this is enough for me. I shall

(k) This Term was used, among the Stoics, to express the natural or acquired Powers necessary to the Performance of any Action.

(l) See Introduction, §. 9.

(m) This is a difficult Place. The Text, as it stands now, is Επικτητος κρεισσων Σωκρατου ουκ εστιν. ει δε μη, ου χειρων· τουτο μοι ικανον εστιν. Which must be translated, Epictetus *is not superior to* Socrates: *But if not, he is not inferior; and this is enough for me.* By a Change in the Pointing, it might perhaps be translated, *but if he is not inferior, this is enough for me.* And sometimes

I ſhall never be *Milo*, and yet I do not neglect my Body; nor *Crœſus*, and yet I do not neglect my Property: Nor, in general, do we omit the Care of any thing belonging to us, from a Deſpair of arriving at the higheſt Degree of Perfection.

CHAPTER III.

How, from the Doctrine that God is the Father of Mankind, we may proceed to its Conſequences.

§. 1. IF a Perſon could be perſuaded of this Principle as he ought, that we are all originally deſcended from God, and that he is the Father of Gods and Men; I conceive he never would think meanly or degenerately concerning himſelf. Suppoſe *Cæſar* were to adopt you, there would be no bearing your haughty Looks: And will you not be elated on knowing yourſelf to be the Son of *Jupiter?* Yet, in Fact, we are not elated. But having two Things in our compoſition, intimately united, a Body in Common with the Brutes, and Reaſon and Sentiment in common with the Gods; many incline to this unhappy and mortal Kindred, and only ſome few to the divine and happy one. And, as of Neceſſity every one muſt treat each particular Thing, according to the Notions he forms about it; ſo thoſe few, who think they are made for Fidelity, Decency, and a well-grounded Uſe of the Appearances of Things, never

times the Stoics conſidered themſelves as not inferior to the Deity. See lib. I. c. xii. §. 2. But neither of theſe Renderings makes a proper Connexion. I have therefore adventured to ſuppoſe, that κρεισσων and χειρων have changed Places; that ουκ hath ariſen from a caſual Repetition of the two laſt Letters of Σωκρατου; and that μη ου is the Remainder of ſome proper Name known: perhaps Μελιτου, as he was one of the Accuſers of *Socrates*: which cannot now be known. This will give the Senſe which I have expreſſed, and it is the only unexceptionable one that I can find.

ver think meanly or degenerately concerning themselves. But with the Multitude the Case is contrary: "For what am I? A poor contemptible "Man, with this miserable Flesh of mine!" Miserable indeed. But you have likewise something better than this paultry Flesh. Why then, overlooking *that*, do you pine away in Attention to *this?*

§. 2. By means of this [animal] Kindred, some of us, deviating towards it, become like Wolves, faithless, and insidious, and mischievous: others, like Lions, wild, and savage, and untamed: but most of us Foxes, and Wretches even among Brutes. For what else is a slanderous and ill-natured Man, than a Fox, or something yet more wretched and mean? See then, and take heed, that you do not become such Wretches.

CHAPTER IV.

Of Improvement.

§. 1. HE who is entering on a State of Improvement, having learnt from the Philosophers, that the Object of Desire is Good, of Aversion, Evil; and having learnt too, that Prosperity and Ease are no otherwise attainable by Man, than in not being disappointed of his Desire, nor incurring his Aversion: such an one, removes totally from himself and postpones Desire *(a)*, and applies Aversion only to things dependent on Choice. For if he should be averse to Things independent on Choice; he knows, that he must sometimes incur his Aversion, and be unhappy. Now if Virtue promises Happiness, Prosperity, and Ease; then, an Improvement in Virtue is certainly an Improvement in each of these. For to whatever Point the Per-

(a) See *Enchiridion*, c. ii. Note *(b)*.

Perfection of any thing absolutely brings us, Improvement is always an Approach towards it.

§. 2. How happens it then, that when we confess Virtue to be such, yet we seek, and make an ostentatious Show of Improvement in other Things? What is the Business of Virtue?

A prosperous Life.

Who is in a State of Improvement then? He who hath read the many Treatises of *Chrysippus* (b)? Why, doth Virtue consist in having read *Chrysippus* through? If it doth, Improvement is confessedly nothing else than understanding a great deal of *Chrysippus*: otherwise we confess Virtue to produce one Thing; and declare Improvement, which is an Approach to it, to be quite another Thing.

§. 3. This Person, says one [of you], is already able to read *Chrysippus*, by himself.——"Certainly, Sir, you have made a vast Improvement!" What Improvement? Why do you ridicule him? Why do you withdraw him from a Sense of his Misfortunes? Why do not you show him the Business of Virtue, that he may know where to seek Improvement?——Seek it there, Wretch, where your Business lies. And where doth your Business lie?

(b) *Chrysippus* is called, by *Cicero*, the most subtile Interpreter of the Stoic Dreams, and the Support of the Portico. He composed 705 Volumes; which is not very wonderful, as he was so fond of Quotations, that in one of his Pieces he transcribed almost an entire Play of *Euripides*. His chief Study was Logic, which he carried to a trifling Degree of Subtility. There is nothing now remaining of his Works but some of their Titles. He died about 200 Years before the Christian Æra, and was honoured by the *Athenians* with a Statue in the *Ceramicus*. His Death is said to have been occasioned by an immoderate Fit of Laughing, at seeing an Ass eat Figs. *Chrysippus* desired the Ass might have a Glass of Wine to wash them down; and was so diverted with his own Conceit, that it cost him his Life. He is said to have been a very copious and laborious Writer, but obscure and immoral; though one would be inclined to think, from the Respect with which he is mentioned by *Epictetus*, that this latter Accusation was groundless.

lie? In Desire and Aversion; that you may neither be disappointed of the one, nor incur the other; in exerting the Powers of Pursuit and Avoidance, that you may not be liable to fail; in Assent and Suspense, that you may not be liable to be deceived. The first and most necessary is the first Topic (*c*). But if you seek to avoid incurring your Aversion, trembling and lamenting all the while, at this rate how do you improve?

§. 4. Show me then your Improvement in this Point. As if I should say to a Wrestler, Show me your Shoulders; and he should answer me, "See "my Poisers."——Do you and your Poisers look to that: I desire to see the Effect of them.

"Take the Treatise on the Subject of *the active* "*Powers*, and see how thoroughly I have pe"rused it."

I do not enquire into this, Wretch: but how you exert those Powers; how you manage your Desires and Aversions, how your Intentions and Purposes; how you are prepared for Events, whether conformably or contrary to Nature. If conformably, give me Evidence of that, and I will say you improve: if contrary, go your way, and not only comment on these Treatises, but write such yourself; and what Service will it do you? Do not you know that the whole Volume is sold for Half a Crown? Doth he who comments upon it, then, value himself at more than Half a Crown? Never look for your Business in one Thing, and for Improvement in another.

Where is Improvement, then?

If any of you, withdrawing himself from Externals, turns to his own Faculty of Choice, to exercise, and finish, and render it conformable to Nature; elevated, free, unrestrained, unhindered, faithful, decent: if he hath learnt too, that whoever desires,

(*c*) See Introduction, §. 4, 5, 6.

desires, or is averse to, Things out of his own Power, can neither be faithful nor free, but must necessarily be changed and tossed up and down with them; must necessarily too be subject to others, to such as can procure or prevent what he desires or is averse to: if, rising in the Morning, he observes and keeps to these Rules; bathes and eats as a Man of Fidelity and Honour; and thus, on every Subject of Action, exercises himself in his principal Duty; as a Racer, in the Business of Racing; as a public Speaker, in the Business of exercising his Voice: this is he, who truly improves; this is he, who hath not travelled in vain. But if he is wholly intent on reading Books, and hath laboured that Point only, and travelled *(d)* for that: I bid him go home immediately, and not neglect his domestic Affairs; for what he travelled for, is nothing. The only real Thing is, studying how to rid his Life of Lamentation, and Complaint, and *Alas!* and *I am undone*, and Misfortune, and Disappointment; and to learn what Death, what Exile, what Prison, what Poison is: That he may be able to say in a Prison, like *Socrates*, "My dear "*Crito*; if it thus pleases the Gods, thus let it be;" and not ——"Wretched old Man, have I kept "my grey Hairs for this!" Who speaks thus? Do you suppose I will name some mean and despicable Person? Is it not *Priam* who says it? Is it not *Oedipus?* Nay, how many Kings say it? For what else is Tragedy, but the Sufferings of Men, struck by an Admiration of Externals, represented in that Kind of Poetry? If one was to be taught by Fictions, that Externals independent upon Choice are nothing to us; *I*, for my Part, should wish for such a Fiction, as that, by which I might

(d) An Allusion to the antient Custom among Philosophers, of travelling into foreign Countries, for Improvement.

might live prosperously and undisturbed. What *you* wish for, it is *your* Business to consider.

§. 5. Of what Service, then, is *Chrysippus* to us?

(*e*) To teach you, that those Things are not false, on which Prosperity and Ease depend. "Take "my Books, and you will see, how true and con-"formable to Nature those Things are, which "render me easy." How great a Happiness! And how great the Benefactor, who shows the Way! To *Triptolemus* all Men have raised Temples and Altars, because he gave us a milder Kind of Food: but to him who hath discovered, and brought to Light, and communicated, the Truth to all (*f*); the Means, not of living, but of living well; who among you ever raised an Altar or a Temple, or dedicated a Statue, or who worships God on that Account? We offer Sacrifices on the Account of those [Benefactors] who have given us Corn and the Vine; and shall we not give Thanks to God, for those who have produced that Fruit in the human Understanding, by which they proceed to discover to us the true Doctrine of Happiness?

CHAP-

(*e*) What ought to be our Dispositions towards Good and Evil, may be learned from Philosophy: but what that certainly-attainable Good, and that Evil which, without our own Faults, we need never incur, are, Christianity alone can teach. That alone can enable us to unite the Wisdom, Courage, Dignity, and Composure of the Stoics, with the Humility that belongs to our frail Nature, and the various Affections that are insepa-rable from Humanity.

(*f*) *Epictetus* speaks with great Thankfulness to Heaven on the Account of *Chrysippus*, a subtile and perplexed Writer, from whose Instructions, only a few studious abstracted Persons could derive any Benefit. How much stronger ought to be the Gratitude of those, who are blessed with the Knowledge of Him, who hath *brought Life and Immortality to Light* (the Word is the same in *Epictetus* and St. *Paul*); who hath ren-dered the Way to Virtue and to Happiness not only intelligible, but accessible, to all Mankind; and who is Himself *the Way, the Truth, and the Life.*

CHAPTER V.

Concerning the Academics (a).

§. 1. IF any one opposes very evident Truths, it is not easy to find a Reason which may persuade him, to alter his Opinion. This arises neither from his own Strength, nor from the Weakness of his Teacher: but when, after being driven upon an Absurdity, he becomes petrified, how shall we deal with him any longer by Reason?

§. 2. Now there are two Sorts of Petrifaction: The one, a Petrifaction of the Understanding; the other, of the Sense of Shame, when a Person hath obstinately set himself not to assent to evident Truths, nor to quit the Defence of Contradictions. We all dread a bodily Mortification; and would make use of every Contrivance to avoid it: but none of us is troubled about a Mortification in the Soul. And yet, indeed, even with regard to the Soul, when a Person is so affected, as not to apprehend or understand any thing, we think him in a sad Condition: but where the Sense of Shame and Modesty is under an absolute Mortification, we go so far, as even to call *this*, Strength of Mind (b).

§. 3. Are you certain that you are awake?——"I am not (replies such a Person): for neither am "I certain, when, in dreaming, I appear to my-"self to be awake."——Is there no Difference, then, between these Appearances?———"None."

 ——Shall

(a) The Academics held, that there is nothing to be known; that we have not Faculties to distinguish between Truth and Falshood; and their Custom was neither to affirm nor deny any thing.

(b) A Sceptic was held to be an *Esprit fort.*

——Shall I argue with this Man any longer? For what Steel or what Caustic can I apply, to make him sensible of his Mortification? He is sensible of it: and pretends not to be so. He is even worse than dead. Doth not he see the Repugnancy of contradictory Propositions? He sees it; and is never the better. He is neither moved, nor improves. Nay, he is in a yet worse Condition: his Sense of Shame and Modesty is utterly extirpated. His reasoning Faculty indeed is not extirpated; but turned wild and savage. Shall I call *this*, Strength of Mind? By no means: unless we allow it be such in the vilest Debauchées, publickly to speak and act whatever comes into their Heads.

CHAPTER VI.

Of Providence.

§. 1. FROM every Event that happens in the World, it is easy to celebrate Providence, if a Person hath but these two Circumstances in himself; a Faculty of considering what happens to each Individual, and a grateful Temper. Without the first, he will not perceive the Usefulness of Things which happen: and without the other, he will not be thankful for them. If God had made Colours, and had not made the Faculty of seeing them, what would have been their Use?

None.

On the contrary, if he had made the Faculty, without such Objects as fall under its Observation, what would have been the Use of that?

None.

Again: If he had formed both the Faculty and the Objects, but had not made Light?

Neither in that Case would they have been of any Use.

§. 2.

§. 2. Who is it then that hath fitted each of these to the other? Who is it that hath fitted the Sword to the Scabbard, and the Scabbard to the Sword? Is it no one? From the very Construction of a complete Work, we are used to declare positively, that it must be the Operation of some Artificer, and not the Effect of mere Chance. Doth every such Work, then, demonstrate an Artificer; and do not visible Objects, and the Sense of Seeing, and Light, demonstrate one? Doth not the Difference of the Sexes, and their Inclination to each other, and the Use of their several Powers; do not these Things, neither, demonstrate an Artificer?

Most certainly they do.

§. 3. But farther: This Constitution of Understanding, by which we are not simply impressed by sensible Objects; but take and substract from them; and add and compose something out of them; and pass from some to others absolutely remote (*a*): Is not all this, neither, sufficient to prevail on some Men, and make them ashamed of leaving an Artificer out of their Scheme? If not, let them explain to us what it is that effects each of these; and how it is possible that Things so wonderful, and which carry such Marks of Contrivance, should come to pass spontaneously, and without Design.

What, then, do these Things come to pass for *our* Service only?

Many for *ours* only; such as are peculiarly necessary for a reasonable Creature: but you will find many, common to us with mere Animals.

Then, do *they* too understand what is done?

Not at all: For Use is one Affair, and Understanding another. But God had Need of Animals,

(*a*) The Translation follows οὐδαμῶς in Mr. *Upton's Addenda*.

to make use of the Appearances of Things (*b*); and of Us to *understand* that Use. It is sufficient, therefore, for them to eat, and drink, and sleep, and continue their Species, and perform other such Offices as belong to each of them: but to *us*, to whom he hath given likewise a Faculty of Understanding, these Offices are not sufficient. For if we do not act in a proper and orderly Manner, and suitably to the Nature and Constitution of each Thing; we shall no longer attain our End. For where the Constitution of Beings is different, their Offices and Ends are different likewise. Thus where the Constitution is adapted only to Use, there Use is alone sufficient: But where understanding is added to Use, unless that too be duely exercised, the End of such a Being will never be attained.

§. 4. Well then: each of the Animals is constituted either for Food, or Husbandry, or to produce Milk; and the rest of them for some other like Use: and for these Purposes what need is there of *understanding* the Appearances of Things, and being able to make Distinctions concerning them? But God hath introduced *Man*, as a Spectator of Himself, and his Works; and not only as a Spectator, but an Interpreter of them. It is therefore shameful that *Man* should begin, and end, where irrational Creatures do. He is indeed rather to begin there, but to end where Nature itself hath fixt our End; and that is in Contemplation, and Understanding, and in a Scheme of Life conformable to Nature.

§. 5. Take care, then, not to die without Spectators of these Things. You take a Journey to *Olympia* to behold the Work (*c*) of *Phidias*, and each of you thinks it a Misfortune to die without a Knowledge of such Things: and will you have no

(*b*) See Introduction, §. 7.
(*c*) The famous Statue of *Jupiter Olympius*.

no Inclination to underſtand, and be Spectators of thoſe Works, for which there is no need to take a Journey; but which are ready and at hand, even to thoſe who beſtow no Pains (*d*)! Will you never perceive, then, either what you are, or for what you were born; nor for what Purpoſe you are admitted Spectators of this Sight?

But there are ſome Things unpleaſant and difficult, in Life.

And are there none at *Olympia*? Are not you heated? Are not you crouded? Are not you without good Conveniencies for bathing (*e*)? Are not you wet through, when it happens to rain? Do not you bear Uproar, and Noiſe, and other diſagreeable Circumſtances? But I ſuppoſe, by comparing all theſe with the Advantage of ſeeing ſo valuable a Sight, you ſupport and go through them. Well: and [in the preſent Caſe] have not you received Faculties by which you may ſupport every Event? Have not you received Greatneſs of Soul? Have not you received a manly Spirit? Have not you received Patience? What ſignifies to me any thing that happens, while I have a Greatneſs of Soul? What ſhall diſconcert or trouble or appear grievous to me? Shall I not make uſe of my Faculties, to that Purpoſe for which they were granted me; but lament and groan at what happens?

§. 6. Oh, but my Noſe (*f*) runs.

And what have you Hands for, Beaſt, but to wipe it?

(*d*) The Tranſlation follows a conjectural Emendation of Mr. *Upton*'s on this Paſſage.

(*e*) It was one Part of the Elegance of thoſe Times, to bathe every Day.

(*f*) *Epictetus* probably introduces this ridiculous Complaint, in order to intimate, that others commonly made are little leſs ſo. See *M. Antoninus*, l. viii. §. 50. of *Gataker*'s Edition and the *Glaſgow* Tranſlation.

But was there then any good Reason, that there should be such a dirty Thing in the World?

And how much better is it that you should wipe your Nose, than complain? Pray, what Figure do you think *Hercules* would have made, if there had not been such a Lion, and a Hydra, and a Stag, and unjust and brutal Men; whom he expelled and cleared away? And what would he have done, if none of these had existed? Is it not plain, that he must have wrapt himself up and slept? In the first place, then, he would never have become a *Hercules*, by slumbering away his whole Life in such Delicacy and Ease: or if he had, what Good would it have done? What would have been the Use of his Arm, and the rest of his Strength; of his Patience, and Greatness of Mind; if such Circumstances and Subjects of Action had not roused and exercised him?

What then, must we provide these Things for ourselves; and introduce a Boar, and a Lion, and a Hydra, into our Country?

This would be Madness and Folly. But as they were in being, and to be met with, they were proper Subjects to set off and exercise *Hercules*. Do *you* therefore likewise, being sensible of this, inspect the Faculties you have: and after taking a View of them, say, "Bring on me now, O *Jupiter*, what Difficulty thou wilt, for I have Faculties granted me by Thee, and Abilities by which I may acquire Honour and Ornament to myself."———No: but you sit trembling, for fear this or that should happen: and lamenting, and mourning, and groaning at what doth happen; and then you accuse the Gods. For what is the Consequence of such a Meanspiritedness, but Impiety? And yet God hath not only granted us these Faculties, by which we may bear every Event, without being depressed or broken by it; but, like a good Prince, and a true Father, hath rendered

them

them incapable of Reſtraint, Compulſion, or Hindrance, and intirely dependent on our own Pleaſure: nor hath he reſerved a Power, even to himſelf, of hindering or reſtraining them. Having theſe Things free, and your own, will you make no Uſe of them, nor conſider what you have received, nor from whom? But ſit groaning and lamenting, ſome of you, blind to him who gave them, and not acknowledging your Benefactor; and others, baſely turning yourſelves to Complaints and Accuſations of God? Yet I undertake to ſhow you, that you have Qualifications and Occaſions for Greatneſs of Soul, and a manly Spirit: but what Occaſions you have to find Fault, and complain, do *you* ſhow me.

CHAPTER VII.

Of the Uſe of convertible and hypothetical Propoſitions, and the like.

§. 1. IT (*a*) is a Secret to the Vulgar, that the Practice of convertible, and hypothetical, and interrogatory Arguments, and, in general, of all other logical Forms, hath any Relation to the Duties of Life. For, in every Subject of Action, the Queſtion is, how a wiſe and good Man may find a Way of extricating himſelf, and a Method of Behaviour conformable to his Duty upon the Occaſion. Let them ſay, therefore, either that the Man of Virtue will not engage in Queſtions and Anſwers; or that, if he doth, he will not think it worth his Care whether he behaves raſhly and at hazard in queſtioning and anſwering: or, if they allow neither of theſe; it is neceſſary to confeſs, that ſome Examination ought to be made of thoſe

 Topics,

(*a*) It is but fair to warn the Reader, that little Entertainment is to be expected from this Chapter, which is wholly logical.

Topics, in which the Affair of Question and Answer is principally concerned. For what is the Profession of Reasoning? To lay down true Positions; to reject false ones; and to suspend the Judgment in doubtful ones. Is it enough, then, to have learned merely this?——It is enough, say you.——Is it enough, then, for him who would not commit any Mistake in the Use of Money, merely to have heard, that we are to receive the good Pieces, and reject the bad?——This is not enough:——What must be added besides?——That Faculty which tries and distinguishes what Pieces are good, what bad.——Therefore, in Reasoning too, what hath been already said is not enough; but it is necessary that we should be able to prove and distinguish between the true, and the false, and the doubtful.——It is necessary.

§. 2. And what farther is professed in Reasoning?——To admit the Consequence of what you have properly granted.——Well: and here, too, is the mere Knowing this enough?——It is not; but we must learn how such a Thing is the Consequence of such another; and when one Thing follows from one Thing, and when from many Things in common. Is it not moreover necessary, that he, who would behave skilfully in Reasoning, should both himself demonstrate whatever he delivers, and be able to comprehend the Demonstrations of others; and not be deceived by such as sophisticate, as if they were demonstrating. Hence, then, the Employment and Exercise of concluding Arguments and Figures arises; and appears to be necessary.

§. 3. But it may possibly happen, that from the Premises which we have properly granted, there arises some Consequence, which, though false, is nevertheless a Consequence. What then ought I to do? To admit a Falsehood?——And how is that possible?——Well: or to say that my Conceſſions were not properly made?——But neither is this allowed——Or that the Conſequence doth not ariſe from the Premiſes?——Nor is even this allowed.——What then is to be done in the Caſe?——Is it not this? As the having once borrowed Money, is not enough to make a a Perſon a Debtor, unleſs he ſtill continues to owe Money, and hath not paid it: ſo the having granted the Premiſes, is not enough to make it neceſſary to grant the Inference, unleſs we continue our Conceſſions. If the Premiſes continue to the End, ſuch as they were when the Conceſſions were made, it is abſolutely neceſſary to continue the Conceſſions, and to admit what follows from them. But if the Premiſes do not continue ſuch as they were when the Conceſſion was made, it is abſolutely neceſſary to depart from the Conceſſion, and admit [rather the contrary: I mean] what doth not (*b*) follow from the Argument itſelf. For this Inference is no Conſequence of ours, nor belongs to us, when we have departed from the Conceſſion of the Premiſes. We ought then to examine theſe Kinds of Premiſes, and their Changes and Converſions, on which any one, by laying hold, either in the Queſtion itſelf, or in the Anſwer, or in the ſyllogiſtical Concluſion, or in any other thing of that ſort, gives an Occaſion to the Unthinking of being diſconcerted, not foreſeeing the Conſequence.——Why ſo?——That in this Topic we may not behave contrary to our Duty, nor with Confuſion.

§. 4. The ſame Thing is to be obſerved in Hypotheſes and hypothetical Arguments. For it is ſome-

(*b*) The Paſſage ſeems to require that ανακολυθον ſhould be ακολυθον; *We are to depart from the Conceſſion, and admit what follows from the Argument itſelf.* The Meaning I apprehend to be, that if, in the Courſe of an Argument, our Opponent ſophiſtically alters the State of the Queſtion on which our Conceſſions were founded, it is lawful to revoke thoſe Conceſſions; and admit no Conſequence but what is fairly drawn from the Argument itſelf.

sometimes necessary to require some Hypothesis to be granted, as a kind of Step to the rest of the Argument. Is every given Hypothesis then to be granted, or not every one; and if not every one, which? And is he who has granted an Hypothesis, for ever to abide by it? Or is he sometimes to depart from it, and admit only Consequences, but not to admit Contradictions?——Ay; but a Person may say, on your admitting the Hypothesis of a Possibility, I will drive you upon an Impossibility. With such a one as this, shall the Man of Prudence not engage; but avoid all Examination and Conversation with him?——And yet who, besides the Man of Prudence, is capable of treating an Argument, or who besides is sagacious in Questions and Answers, and incapable of being deceived and imposed on by Sophistry?——Or will he indeed engage, but without regarding whether he behaves rashly and at hazard in the Argument? ——Yet how then can he be such a one as we are supposing him? But, without some such Exercise and Preparation, is it possible for him to preserve himself consistent? Let them shew this: and all these Theorems will be superfluous and absurd, and unconnected with our Idea of the virtuous Man. Why then are we still indolent, and slothful, and sluggish, seeking Pretences of avoiding Labour? Shall we not be watchful to render Reason itself accurate?——"But suppose, after all, I should "make a Mistake in these Points: have I killed a Father?——Wretch! why, in this Case, where had you a Father to kill? What is it then that you have done? The only Fault that you could commit, in this Instance, you have committed. This very Thing I myself said to *Rufus*, when he reproved me, for not finding something that was omitted in some Syllogism. Why, said I, have I burnt the Capitol then? Wretch! answered he, was the Thing here omitted the Capitol? Or are there no other Faults, but burning the Capitol, or killing a Father? and is it no Fault to treat the Appearances presented to our Minds rashly, and vainly, and at hazard; not to comprehend a Reason, nor a Demonstration, nor a Sophism; nor, in short, to see what is for, or against one's self in a Question or Answer? Is nothing of all this any Fault?

CHAPTER VIII.

That Faculties are not safe to the Uninstructed.

§. 1. IN as many Ways as equivalent Syllogisms may be varied, in so many may the Forms of Arguments, and Enthymemas, be varied likewise. As for Instance: *If you had borrowed, and not paid, you owe me Money. But you have not borrowed, and not paid; therefore you do not owe me Money.* To perform this skilfully, belongs to no one more than to a Philosopher. For if an Enthymema be an imperfect Syllogism; he who is exercised in a perfect Syllogism, must be equally ready at an imperfect one.

(a) Why then do not we exercise ourselves and others, after this Manner?

Because, even now, though we are not exercised in these Things, nor diverted, by me, at least, from the Study of Morality; yet we make no Advances in Virtue. What is to be expected then if we should add this Avocation too? Especially, as it would not only be an Avocation from more necessary Studies, but likewise a capital Occasion of Conceit and Insolence. For the Faculty of arguing, and of persuasive Reasoning is great; and, particularly, if it be much laboured, and receive an additional Ornament from Rhetoric. For, in general,

(a) This is spoken by one of the Audience.

general, every Faculty is dangerous to weak and uninstructed Persons; as being apt to render them arrogant and elated. For by what Method can one persuade a young Man, who excells in these Kinds of Study, that he ought not to be an Appendix to *them*, but they to *him*? Will he not trample upon all such Advice; and walk about elated, and puffed up, not bearing any one should touch him, to put him in mind, where he is wanting, and in what he goes wrong.

What then, was not *Plato* a Philosopher?

Well, and was not *Hippocrates* a Physician? Yet you see [how elegantly] he expresses himself. But is it in Quality of Physician, then, that he expresses himself so? Why do you confound Things, accidentally united, from different Causes, in the same Men? If *Plato* was handsome and well-made, must I too set myself to endeavour at becoming handsome and well-made; as if this was necessary to Philosophy, because a certain Person happened to be at once handsome and a Philosopher? Why will you not perceive and distinguish what are the Things that make Men Philosophers, and what belong to them on other Accounts? Pray, if I *(b)* were a Philosopher, would it be necessary that you should be lame too?

§. 2.

(b) Epictetus, whenever he has Occasion to mention himself, speaks with remarkable Modesty; and in a Stile very different from that of many of the more ancient Philosophers: as appears by the several arrogant Speeches recorded of them by *Diogenes Laertius*, &c. It is probable he might improve in this humble Disposition, by the Character of *Socrates*, which he seems particularly to have studied, and admired. Yet other Philosophers had studied and admired the same Character, without profiting by it. Perhaps the sober and unassuming Temper of Christianity might, from the Example of its Professors in those Days, have produced this, and other good Effects, in the Minds of many who knew little, if any thing, of the Gospel itself.

§. 2. What then? Do I reject these Faculties? By no means. For neither do I reject the Faculty of Seeing. But if you ask me, what is the Good of Man; I have nothing else to say to you, but that it is a certain Regulation of the Choice, with regard to the Appearances of Things.

CHAPTER IX.

How from the Doctrine of our Kindred to God, we are to proceed to its Consequences.

§. 1. IF what Philosophers say of the Kindred between God and Man be true; what has any one to do, but, like *Socrates*, when he is asked what Countryman he is, never to say that he is a Citizen of *Athens*, or of *Corinth*; but of the World? For why do you say that you are of *Athens*: and not of that Corner only, where that paultry Body of yours was laid at its Birth? Is it not, evidently, from what is principal, and comprehends not only that Corner, and your whole House; but the general Extent of the Country, from which your Pedigree is derived down to you, that you call yourself an *Athenian*, or a *Corinthian*? Why may not he then, who understands the Administration of the World; and has learned that the greatest, and most principal, and comprehensive, of all Things, is this System, composed of Men and God: and that from Him the Seeds of Being are descended, not only to my Father or Grandfather, but to all Things that are produced and born on Earth; and especially to rational Natures, as they alone are qualified to partake of a Communication with the Deity, being connected with him by Reason: Why may not [such a one] call himself a Citizen of the World? Why not a Son of God? And, why shall he fear any thing that happens among Men? Shall Kindred to *Cæsar*, or any other of the Great

at

at *Rome*, enable a Man to live ſecure, above Contempt, and void of all Fear whatever: and ſhall not the having God for our Maker, and Father, and Guardian, free us from Griefs and Terrors?

§. 2. "But how ſhall I ſubſiſt? For I have nothing."

Why, how do Slaves, how do Fugitives? To what do they truſt, when they run away from their Maſters? Is it to their Eſtates? Their Servants? Their Plate? To nothing but themſelves. Yet they do not fail to get Neceſſaries. And muſt a Philoſopher, think you, when he leaves his own Abode, reſt and rely upon others; and not take care of himſelf? Muſt he be more helpleſs and anxious than the brute Beaſts; each of which is ſelf-ſufficient, and wants neither proper Food, nor any ſuitable and natural Proviſion? One would think, there ſhould be no Need for an old Fellow to ſit here contriving, that you may not think meanly, nor entertain low and abject Notions of yourſelves: but that his Buſineſs would be, to take care, that there may not happen to be [among you] young Men of ſuch a Spirit, that, knowing their Affinity to the Gods; and that we are as it were fettered by the Body and its Poſſeſſions, and by ſo many other Things as are neceſſary, upon theſe Accounts, for the Oeconomy and Commerce of Life; they ſhould reſolve to throw them off, as both troubleſome and uſeleſs, and depart to their Kindred.

§. 3. This is the Work, if any, that ought to employ your Maſter and Preceptor, if you had one: that you ſhould come to him, and ſay; "*Epictetus*, we can no longer bear being tied "down to this paultry Body: feeding and reſting, "and cleaning it, and hurried about with ſo many "low Cares on its Account. Are not theſe Things "indifferent, and nothing to us: and Death no "Evil? Are not we Relations of God; and did

"we

"we not come from him? Suffer us to go back "thither from whence we came: suffer us, at "length, to be delivered from these Fetters, that "chain and weigh us down. Here, Thieves and "Robbers, and Courts of Judicature, and those "who are called Tyrants, seem to have some "Power over us, on account of the Body and its "Possessions. Suffer us to show them, that they "have no Power."

§. 4. And in this Case it would be my Part to answer: "My Friends, wait for God, till he shall "give the Signal, and dismiss you from this Ser-"vice: then return to him. For the present, be "content to remain in this Post, where he has "placed you. The Time of your Abode here is "short, and easy to such as are disposed like you: "For what Tyrant, what Robber, what Thief, "or what Courts of Judicature are formidable to "those, who thus account the Body, and its Pos-"sessions, as nothing? Stay. Depart not incon-"siderately."

§. 5. Thus ought the Case to stand between a Preceptor and ingenuous young Men. But how stands it now? The Preceptor has no Life in him: you have none neither. When you have had enough To-day, you sit weeping about To-morrow, how you shall get Food. Why, if you have it, Wretch, you will have it: if not you will go out of Life. The Door is open: why do you lament? What room doth there remain for Tears? What Occasion for Flattery? Why should any one Person envy another? Why should he be struck with awful Admiration of those who have great Possessions, or are placed in high Rank, [as is common,]? Especially, if they are powerful and passionate? For what will they do to us? The Things which *they* can do, *we* do not regard: the Things which *we* are concerned about, *they* cannot do. Who then, after all, shall command a Person

Person thus disposed? How was *Socrates* affected by these Things? As it became one persuaded of his being a Relation of the Gods. "If you should "tell me (says he to his Judges), we will acquit "you, upon Condition that you shall no longer "discourse in the Manner you have hitherto done, "nor make any Disturbance either among our "young or our old People;" I would answer; "You are ridiculous in thinking, that if your Ge-"neral had placed me in any Post, I ought to "maintain and defend it, and chuse to die a thou-"sand times, rather than desert it: but if God "hath assigned me any Station or Method of Life, "that I ought to desert *that* for you." *(a)*

§. 6. This it is, for a Man to be truly a Relation of God. But we consider ourselves as a mere Assemblage of Stomach and Entrails, and bodily Parts. Because we fear, because we desire; we flatter those who can help us in these Matters; we dread the very same Persons.

§. 7. A Person desired me once to write for him to *Rome*. He was one vulgarly esteemed unfortunate, as he had been formerly illustrious and rich, and afterwards stript of all his Possessions, and reduced to live here. I wrote for him in a submissive Stile: but, after reading my Letter, he returned it to me, and said; "I wanted your Assistance, "not your Pity; for no Evil hath befallen me."

§. 8 (*b*) Thus *Rufus*, to try me, used to say, this or that you will have from your Master. When I answered him, these are [uncertain] human Affairs: Why then, says he, should I intercede with him

(a) Δει ὑμας should probably be δι ὑ'μας; and is so translated.

(b) This Passage has great Difficulties, which I know not how to solve, any otherwise than by supposing something after ανθρωπινα to be lost.

him (*c*), when you can receive these Things from yourself? For what one hath of his own, it is superfluous and vain to receive from another. Shall I then, who can receive Greatness of Soul and a manly Spirit from myself, receive an Estate, or a Sum of Money, or a Place, from you? Heaven forbid! I will not be so insensible of my own Possessions. But, if a Person is fearful and abject, what else is necessary, but to write Letters for him as if he was dead. "Pray oblige us with the "Corpse and Blood of such a one." For, in fact, such a one is Corpse and Blood; and nothing more. For, if he was any thing more, he would be sensible, that one Man is not rendered unfortunate by another.

CHAPTER X.

Concerning Those who strove for Preferments at Rome.

§. 1. IF we all applied ourselves as heartily to our proper Business, as the old Fellows at *Rome* do to their Schemes; perhaps *we* too might make some Proficiency. I know a Man older than I am, and who is now Superintendant of Provisions at *Rome*. When he past through this Place, on his Return from Exile, what an Account did he give me of his former Life! and how did he promise, that for the future, when he was got back, he would apply himself to nothing but how to spend the Remainder of his Days in Repose and Tranquillity. "For how few have I now remaining!"----- You will not do it, said I. When you are once got within the Smell of *Rome*, you will forget all this: and, if you can but once gain Admittance to Court,

(*c*) The Translator follows Mr. *Upton*'s Conjecture in this Place, and the *French* Version agrees with it.

you will (*a*) go in, heartily rejoiced, and thank God. "If you ever find me, *Epictetus*, said he, "putting one Foot into the Court, think of me "whatever you please." Now, after all, how did he act? Before he entered the City, he was met by a Billet from *Cæsar*. On receiving it, he forgot all his former Resolutions; and has ever since been heaping up one Incumbrance upon another. I should be glad now, to have an Opportunity of putting him in mind of his Discourse upon the Road; and of saying, how much more clever a Prophet am I than you!

§ 2. What then do I say? that Man is made for an inactive Life? No, surely. "But why is "not ours a Life of Activity?" For my own part, as soon as it is Day, I recollect a little what Things I am to read over again [with my Pupils], and then say to myself quickly, What is it to me how such a one reads? My chief Point is to get to sleep.

§ 3. But, indeed, what Likeness is there between the Actions of these [old Fellows at *Rome*] and ours? If you consider what it is they do, you will see. For about what are they employed the whole Day, but in calculating, contriving, consulting, about Provisions; about an Estate; or other Emoluments like these? Is there any Likeliness, then, between reading such a Petition from any one, as-----"*I* "*intreat you to give me a Permission to export Corn*;" and----"*I intreat you to learn from* Chrysippus, *of* "*what Nature the Administration of the World is*; "*and what Place a reasonable Creature holds in it.* "*Learn, too, what you yourself are; and wherein* "*your Good and Evil consists.*" Are these Things at all alike? Do they require an equal Degree of Appli-

(*a*) Ἐσεται probably should be Εἰσιεσαι, and the *French* Translator seems to have followed, and made the same Conjecture.

Application? And is it as ſhameful to neglect the one as the other (*b*)?

§ 4. Well, then, are we Preceptors the only idle Dreamers? No: but you young Men are ſo firſt, in a greater Degree. And ſo even we old Folks, when we ſee young ones trifling, are tempted to grow fond of trifling with them. Much more, then, if I was to ſee you active and diligent, I ſhould be excited to join with you in ſerious Induſtry.

CHAPTER XI.

Of Natural Affection.

§. 1. WHEN one of the great Men came to viſit him; *Epictetus*, having inquired into the Particulars of his Affairs, aſked him, Whether he had a Wife and Children? The other replying, that he had; *Epictetus* likewiſe inquired, In what Manner do you live with them? Very miſerably, ſays he----How ſo? For Men do not marry, and get Children, to be miſerable; but rather to make themſelves happy.——But, I am ſo very miſerable about my Children, that the other Day, when my Daughter was ſick, and appeared to be in Danger; I could not bear even to be with her; but ran away, till it was told me that ſhe was recovered.——And pray do you think this was acting right? It was acting naturally, ſaid he.——Well: do but convince *me* that it was acting naturally, and I will convince *you* that every thing natural is right.——All, or moſt of us Fathers are affected in the ſame Way.——I do not deny the Fact: but the Queſtion between us is, whether it be

(*b*) This Paſſage has a ſtriking Reſemblance to that in Scripture, where the Children of this World are ſaid to be wiſer in their Generation than the Children of Light.

be right. For, by this Way of Reaſoning, it muſt be ſaid, that Tumours happen for the Good of the Body, becauſe they do happen: and even that Vices are natural, becauſe all or the moſt Part of us are guilty of them. Do you ſhow me then how ſuch a Behaviour as yours, appears to be natural.

I cannot undertake that. But do you rather ſhow me, how it appears to be neither natural, nor right.

If we were diſputing about Black and White, what Criterion muſt we call in, to diſtinguiſh them?

The Sight.

If about Hot and Cold, and Hard and Soft, what?

The Touch.

Well then: when we are debating about Natural and Unnatural, and Right and Wrong; what Criterion are we to take?

I cannot tell.

And yet, to be ignorant of a Criterion of Colours, or of Smells, or Taſtes, might perhaps be no very great Loſs. But do you think, that he ſuffers only a ſmall Loſs, who is ignorant of what is Good and Evil, and Natural and Unnatural, to Man?

No. The very greateſt.

Well: tell me; Are all Things which are judged good and proper by ſome, rightly judged to be ſo? Is it poſſible, that the ſeveral Opinions of *Jews*, and *Syrians*, and *Egyptians*, and *Romans*, concerning Food, ſhould all be right?

How can it be poſſible?

I ſuppoſe then, it is abſolutely neceſſary, if the Opinions of the *Egyptians* be right, the others muſt be wrong: if thoſe of the *Jews* be good, all the reſt muſt be bad.

How can it be otherwiſe?

And

And where Ignorance is, there likewiſe is Want of Learning, and Inſtruction, in neceſſary Points.

It is granted.

Then, as you are ſenſible of this, you will for the future apply to nothing, and think of nothing elſe, but how to acquaint yourſelf with the Criterion of what is agreeable to Nature: and to uſe that in judging of each particular Caſe.

§. 2. At preſent the Aſſiſtance I have to give you, towards what you deſire, is this. Doth Affection ſeem to you to be a right and a natural Thing (*a*)?

How ſhould it be otherwiſe?

Well: and is Affection natural and right, and Reaſon not ſo?

By no means.

Is there any Oppoſition, then, between Reaſon and Affection?

I think not.

If there was, of two Oppoſites if one be natural, the other muſt neceſſarily be unnatural. Muſt it not?

It muſt.

What we find, then, at once affectionate, and reaſonable, *that* we may ſafely pronounce to be right and good.

Agreed.

Well, then: you will not diſpute, but that to run away, and leave a ſick Child, is contrary to Reaſon. It remains for us to conſider, whether it be conſiſtent with Affection.

Let us conſider it.

Did you, then, from an Affection to your Child, do right in running away, and leaving her? Hath her Mother no Affection for the Child?

 Yes,

(*a*) The Stoics ſay, that wiſe and good Men have the truly natural Affection towards their Children; and bad Perſons have it not. Diog. Laert. L. vii. §. 120.

Yes, ſurely, ſhe hath.

Would it have been right, then, that her Mother too ſhould leave her; or would it not?

It would not.

And doth not her Nurſe love her?

She doth.

Then ought not ſhe likewiſe to leave her?

By no means.

And doth not her Preceptor love her?

He doth.

Then ought not he alſo to have run away, and left her: and ſo the Child to have been left alone, and unaſſiſted, from the great Affection of her Parents, and her Friends; or to die in the Hands of People, who neither loved her, nor took care of her.

Heaven forbid!

But is it not unreaſonable and unjuſt, that what you think right in yourſelf, on the Account of your Affection; ſhould not be allowed to others, who have the very ſame Affection as you?

It is abſurd.

Pray, if you were ſick yourſelf, ſhould you be willing to have your family, and even your Wife and Children, ſo very affectionate, as to leave you helpleſs and alone?

By no means.

Or would you wiſh to be ſo loved by your Friends, as from their exceſſive Affection, always to be left alone when you were ſick? Or would you not rather wiſh, if it were poſſible, to have ſuch a Kind of Affection from your Enemies, as to make them always keep from you? If ſo, it remains, that your Behaviour was by no means affectionate. Well then: was it merely *nothing* that induced *you* to deſert your Child?

How is that poſſible?

No: but it was ſome ſuch Motive, as induced a Perſon at *Rome* to hide his Face while a Horſe was

running,

running, to which he earneſtly wiſhed Succeſs: and when, beyond his Expectation, it won the Race; he was obliged to have Recourſe to Spunges, to recover his Senſes.

And what was this Motive?

At preſent perhaps it cannot be accurately explained. It is ſufficient to be convinced, (if what Philoſophers ſay be true) that we are not to ſeek it from without: but that there is univerſally one and the ſame Cauſe, which moves us to do or forbear any Action; to ſpeak or not to ſpeak; to be elated or depreſſed; to avoid or purſue: that very Cauſe which hath now moved us two; you, to come, and ſit and hear me; and me, to ſpeak as I do.

And what is that?

Is it any thing elſe, than that it ſeemed right to us to do ſo?

Nothing elſe.

And if it had ſeemed otherwiſe to us, what ſhould we have done elſe than what we thought right? This, and not the Death of *Patroclus*, was the Cauſe of Lamentation to *Achilles*, (for every Man is not thus affected by the Death of a Friend) that it ſeemed right to him. This too was the Cauſe of your running away from your Child, that it ſeemed right: and if hereafter you ſhould ſtay with her, it will be becauſe *that* ſeemed right. You are now returning to *Rome*, becauſe it ſeems right to you: but if you ſhould alter your Opinion, you will not return. In a word neither Death, nor Exile, nor Pain, nor any thing of this Kind, is the Cauſe of our doing, or not doing, any Action: but our Opinions and Principles. Do I convince you of this, or not?

You do.

§. 3. Well then: ſuch as the Cauſe is, ſuch will be the Effect. From this Day forward, then, whenever we do any thing wrong, we will impute it only to the Principle from which we act: and we will endeavour to remove that, and cut it up by the

Roots, with greater Care than we would Wens and Tumours from the Body. In like manner, we will ascribe what we do right, to the same Cause: and we will accuse neither Servant, nor Neighbour, nor Wife, nor Children, as the Causes of any Evils to us; persuaded, that if we had not such Principles, such Consequences would not follow. Of these Principles we ourselves, and not Externals, are the Masters.

Agreed.

From this Day, then, we will neither consider nor enquire of what Sort, or in what Condition, any thing is; our Estate, or Slaves, or Horses, or Dogs, but only our *Principles.*

I wish to do it.

You see, then, that it is necessary for you to become a Scholar: that Kind of Animal which every one laughs at; if you really desire to make an Examination of your Principles. But this, as you are sensible, is not the Work of an Hour or a Day.

CHAPTER XII.

Of Contentment.

§. 1. CONCERNING the Gods, some affirm, that there is no Deity: others, that he indeed exists; but slothful, negligent, and without a Providence: a third Sort admit both his Being and Providence, but only in great and heavenly Objects, and in nothing upon Earth: a fourth, both in Heaven and Earth; but only in general, not Individuals: a fifth like *Ulysses* and *Socrates* (*a*):

O Thou, who, ever present in my Way,
Dost all my Motions, all my Toils survey.

POPE's Homer.

It

(*a*) It was the Opinion of *Socrates*, That the Gods know all Things that are either said or done, or silently thought on: that they are every where present, and give Significations to Mankind concerning all human Affairs. XEN. MEM. L. 1.

It is, before all things, neceſſary to examine each of theſe; which is, and which is not, rightly ſaid. Now, if there are no Gods, how is it our End to follow them? If there are, but they take no Care of any thing; how will it be right, in this Caſe, to follow them? Or, if they both are, and take Care; yet, if there is nothing communicated from them to Men, nor indeed to myſelf in particular, how can it be right even in this Caſe? A wiſe and good Man, after examining theſe Things, ſubmits his Mind to him who adminiſters the Whole, as good Citizens do to the Laws of the Commonwealth.

§. 2. He, then, who comes to be inſtructed, ought to come with this Intention: "How may I "in every thing follow the Gods? How may I ac-"quieſce in the divine Adminiſtration? And how "may I be free?" For He is free, to whom all happens agreeably to his Choice, and whom no one can reſtrain.

What! then, is Freedom Diſtraction?

By no means: for Madneſs and Freedom are incompatible.

But I would have whatever appears to me to be right, happen; however it comes to appear ſo.

You are mad: you have loſt your Senſes. Do not you know, that Freedom is a very beautiful and valuable Thing? But for me to chuſe at random, and for things to happen agreeably to ſuch a Choice, may be ſo far from a beautiful Thing, as to be, of all others, the moſt ſhocking. For how do we proceed in Writing? Do I chuſe to write the Name of *Dion* [for Inſtance] as I will? No: but I am taught to be willing to write it, as it ought to be writ. And what is the Caſe in Muſic? The ſame. And what in every other Art or Science? Otherwiſe, it would be to no Purpoſe to learn any thing; if it was to be adapted to each one's particular Humour. Is it then only in the greateſt and principal Point, that of Freedom, permitted me to will at random? By no means: but

but true Instruction is this: learning to will, that Things should happen as they do. And how do they happen? As the Appointer of them hath appointed. He hath appointed, that there should be Summer and Winter; Plenty and Dearth; Virtue and Vice; and all such Contrarieties, for the Harmony of the Whole (*a*). To each of us he hath given a Body, and its Parts, and our several Properties, and Companions. Mindful of this Appointment, we should enter upon a Course of Education and Instruction, not to change the Constitutions of things; which is neither put within our Reach, nor for our Good; but that, being as they are, and as their Nature is with regard to us, we may have our Mind accommodated to what exists. Can we, for Instance, fly Mankind? And how is that possible? Can we, by conversing with them, change them? Who hath given us such a Power? What then remains, or what Method is there to be found for such a Commerce with them, that while *they* act agreeably to the Appearances in their own Minds, *we* may nevertheless be affected conformably to Nature? But you are wretched and discontented. If you are alone, you term it a Desart; and if with Men, you call them Cheats and Robbers. You find Fault too with your Parents, and Children, and Brothers, and Neighbours. Whereas you ought, when you live alone, to call *that* a Repose and Freedom; and to esteem yourself as resembling the Gods: and when you are in Company, not to call it a Crowd and a Tumult, and a Trouble; but an Assembly, and a Festival: and thus to take all things contentedly. What, then, is the Punishment of those who do not? To be just as they are. Is any one discontented with being alone? Let him be in a Desart (*b*). Discontented with his Parents? Let him be a bad Son; and let him mourn. Discontented with his Children? Let him be a bad Father. Throw him into Prison. What Prison? Where he already

(*a*) See *Enchiridion*, c. xxvii. (*b*) See Introduction, §. 20.

already is: for he is in a Situation againſt his Will; and wherever any one is againſt his Willl, that is to him a Priſon: juſt as *Socrates* was *not* in Priſon; for he was willingly there. "What then muſt my Leg "be lame?"——And is it for one paultry Leg, Wretch, that you accuſe the World? Why will you not give it up to the Whole? Why will you not withdraw yourſelf from it? Why will you not gladly yield it to him who gave it? And will you be angry and diſcontented with the Decrees of *Jupiter*; which he, with the *Fates*, who ſpun in his Preſence the Thread of your Birth, ordained and appointed? Do not you know how very ſmall a Part you are of the Whole? That is, as to Body: for, as to Reaſon, you are neither worſe, nor leſs, than the Gods. For Reaſon is not meaſured by Length or Height; but by Principles. Will you not therefore place your Good there, where you are equal to the Gods (*d*)? "How "wretched am I in ſuch a Father and Mother!"—What, then, was it granted you to come before-hand, and make your own Terms, and ſay; "Let ſuch and "ſuch Perſons, at this Hour, be the Authors of my Birth?" It was not granted: for it was neceſſary that your Parents ſhould exiſt before you, and ſo you be born afterwards.—Of whom?—Of juſt ſuch as they were. What, then, ſince they are ſuch, is there no Remedy afforded you? Now, ſurely, if you were ignorant to what Purpoſe you poſſeſs the Faculty of Sight, you would be wretched and miſerable, in ſhutting your Eyes at the Approach of Colours: and are not you more wretched and miſerable, in being ignorant, that you have a Greatneſs of Soul, and a manly Spirit, anſwerable to each of the abovementioned Accidents? Occurrences proportioned to your Faculty [of Diſcernment] are brought before you: but you turn it away, at the very Time when you ought to have it the moſt open, and quick-ſighted.

Why

(*d*) One of the Stoic Extravagances; ariſing from the Notion, that human ſouls were literally Parts of the Deity.

Why do not you rather thank the Gods, that they have made you superior to whatever they have not placed in your own Power; and have rendered you accountable for that only, which is in your own Power? Of your Parents they acquit you; as not accountable: of your Brothers they acquit you: of Body, Possessions, Death, Life, they acquit you. For what, then, have they made you accountable? For that which is alone in your own Power; a right Use of the Appearances of Objects. Why, then, should you draw those Things upon yourself, for which you are not accountable? This is giving one's self Trouble, without need.

CHAPTER XIII.

How every Thing may be performed acceptably to the Gods.

WHEN a Person inquired, How any one might eat acceptably to the Gods: if he eats with Justice, says *Epictetus*, and Gratitude; and fairly and temperately, and decently, must he not also eat acceptably to the Gods? And when you call for hot Water, and your Servant doth not hear you; or, if he doth, brings it only warm; or perhaps is not to be found at home; then, not to be angry, or burst with Passion: is not this acceptable to the Gods?

But how, then, can one bear such Things?

Wretch, will you not bear with your own Brother, who hath God for his Father, as being a Son from the same Stock, and of the same high Descent [with yourself]? But, if you chance to be placed in some superior Station, will you presently set yourself up for a Tyrant? Will you not remember what you are, and over whom you bear Rule? That they are by Nature your Relations, your Brothers; that they are the Offspring of God? (*a*) But

(*a*) *If I did despise the Cause of my Man Servant, or my Maid Servant, when they contended with me: what then shall I do when God riseth up? And when he visiteth, what shall I answer him? Did not He who made me in the Womb, make him? And did not One fashion us in the Womb?* Job xxxi, 13, 14, 15.

But I have them by Right of Purchase, and not they me.

Do you see what it is you regard? That it is Earth and Mire, and these wretched Laws of dead (b) Men; and that you do not regard those of the Gods.

CHAPTER XIV.

That all Things are under the divine Inspection.

§. 1. WHEN a Person asked him, How any one might be convinced, that each of his Actions are under the Inspection of God? Do not you think, says *Epictetus*, that all Things are mutually bound together and united?

I do.

Well: and do not you think, that Things on Earth feel the Influence of the heavenly Bodies?

Yes.

Else how could the Trees so regularly, as if by God's express Command, bud, (a) blossom, bring forth Fruit, and ripen it: then let it drop, and shed their Leaves, and lie contracted within themselves in Quiet and Repose; all when He speaks the Word? Whence, again, are there seen, on the Increase and Decrease of the Moon, and the Approach and Departure of the Sun, so great Vicissitudes and Changes, to the direct contrary, in earthly Things? Have then the very Leaves, and our own Bodies, this Connection and Sympathy with the Whole; and have not our Souls much more? But our Souls are thus connected and intimately joined

(b) *i. e.* Deceased Legislators, who had in View low and worldly Considerations.

(a) There is a Beauty in the Original, arising from the different Terminations in the Verbs, which cannot be preserved in our Language.

joined to God, as being indeed Members, and distinct Portions, of his Essence: and must not He be sensible of every Movement of them, as belonging, and connatural to himself? Can even *you* think of the divine Administration, and every other divine Subject, and together with these of human Affairs also? Can *you* at once receive Impressions on your Senses and your Understanding from a thousand Objects? At once assent to some things, deny or suspend your Judgment concerning others, and preserve in your Mind Impressions from so many and various Objects, and whenever you are moved by [the Traces of] them, hit on Ideas similar to those which first impressed you? Can *you* retain a Variety of Arts, and the Memorials of ten thousand Things? And is not *God* capable of surveying all Things, and being present with all, and receiving a certain Communication from all? Is the Sun capable of illuminating so great a Portion of the Universe, and of leaving only that small Part of it unilluminated, which is covered by the Shadow of the Earth: and cannot *He* who made and revolves the Sun, a small Part of himself, if compared with the Whole; cannot *He* perceive all Things?

§. 2. "But *I* cannot (say you) attend to all "Things at once." Why, doth any one tell you, that you have equal Power with *Jupiter*? No: but nevertheless He has assigned to each Man a Director, his own good Genius, and committed him to his Guardianship: a Director, whose Vigilance no Slumbers interrupt, and whom no false Reasonings can deceive. For, to what better and more careful Guardian could he have committed us? So that when you have shut your Doors, and darkened your Room, remember, never to say that you are alone; for you are not: but God is within, and your Genius is within: and what need have

they

they of Light, to see what you are doing? To (*b*) this God you likewise ought to swear such an Oath as the Soldiers do to *Cæsar*. For do they, in order to receive their Pay, swear to prefer before all things, the Safety of *Cæsar*: and will not *you* swear, who have received so many and so great Favours: or, if you have sworn, will you not stand to it? And what must you swear? Never to disobey, nor accuse, nor murmur at any of the Things appointed by him: nor unwillingly to do or suffer any thing necessary. Is this Oath like the former? In the first, Persons swear not to honour any other beyond *Cæsar*; in the last, beyond all, to honour themselves.

CHAPTER XV.

What it is that Philosophy promises.

§. 1. WHEN one consulted him, How he might persuade his Brother to forbear treating him ill: Philosophy, answered *Epictetus*, doth not promise to procure any thing external to Man; otherwise it would admit something beyond its proper Subject-matter. For the Subject-matter of a Carpenter is Wood; of a Statuary, Brass: and so, of the Art of Living, the Subject-matter is each Person's own Life.

What, then, is my Brother's?

That, again, belongs to his own Art [of Living]; but to your's is external: like an Estate, like Health, like reputation. Now Philosophy promises none of these. In every Circumstance I will preserve the governing Part conformable to Nature. Whose governing Part? His in whom I exist.

But

(*b*) Perhaps the Και in this Line may have been misplaced; and it should be read τȣτω Και τω Θεω εδει υμας; and then the Translation will be——To this [Genius] and to God you ought to swear, &c.

But how, then, is my Brother to lay aside his Anger against me?

Bring him to me, and I will tell *him*; but I have nothing to say to *you* about his Anger.

§. 2. Well: but I still farther ask, How am I to keep myself in a State of Mind conformable to Nature, though he should not be reconciled to me?

No great Thing is brought to Perfection suddenly; when not so much as a Bunch of Grapes or a Fig is. If you tell me, that you would at this Minute have a Fig, I will answer you, that there must be Time. Let it first (*a*) blossom, then bear Fruit, then ripen. Is then the Fruit of a Fig-tree not brought to Perfection suddenly, and in one Hour; aud would you possess the Fruit of the human Mind in so short a Time, and without Trouble? I tell you, expect no such thing.

CHAPTER XVI.

Of Providence.

§. 1. BE not surprised, if other Animals have all Things necessary to the Body ready provided for them, not only Meat and Drink but Lodging: that they want neither Shoes, nor Bedding, nor Clothes: while we stand in need of all these. For they not being made for themselves, but for Service, it was not fit that they should be formed so as to need the Help of others. For, consider what it would be for us to take care, not only

(*a*) The Philosopher had forgot that Fig-trees do not blossom: and is less excusable than the *English* Translators of the Bible, *Hab.* iii. 17. to whom Fig-trees were not so familiar. But the *Hebrew* Word used there signifies rather in general to shoot out, thrive, than in particular to flower. The LXX have Καρποφορησει; reading, perhaps, תפרה for תפרח. This Note was given to the Translator by a Friend.

only for ourſelves, but for Sheep and Aſſes too: how they ſhould be clothed, how ſhod, and how they ſhould eat and drink. But as Soldiers are ready for their Commander, ſhod, clothed, and armed (for it would be a grievous thing for a Colonel to be obliged to go through his Regiment to put on their Shoes and Clothes): ſo Nature likewiſe has formed the Animals made for Service, ready provided, and ſtanding in need of no further Care. Thus one little Boy, with only a Crook, drives a Flock.

§. 2. But now we, inſtead of being thankful for this, complain of God, that there is not the ſame kind of Care taken of us likewiſe. And yet, good Heaven! any one Thing in the Creation is ſufficient to demonſtrate a Providence, to a modeſt and grateful Mind. Not to inſtance at preſent in great Things: but only in the very Production of Milk from Graſs, Cheeſe from Milk, and Wool from Skins: who formed and contrived theſe Things? No one, ſay you. O ſurpriſing Stupidity, and want of Shame! But come; let us omit the *Works* of Nature. Let us contemplate what ſhe hath done, as it were, by-the-bye. What is more uſeleſs than the Hairs which grow on the Chin? And yet hath ſhe not made uſe even of theſe, in the moſt becoming manner poſſible? Hath ſhe not by theſe diſtinguiſhed the Sexes? Doth not Nature in each of us call out, even at a Diſtance, I am a Man; approach and addreſs me as ſuch; enquire no farther; ſee the Characteriſtic. On the other hand, with regard to Women, as ſhe hath mixed ſomething ſofter in their Voice, ſo ſhe hath deprived them of a Beard. But no: to be ſure, the Animal ſhould have been left undiſtinguiſhed, and each of us obliged to proclaim, *I am a Man!* But why is not this Characteriſtic beautiful and becoming, and venerable? How much more beautiful than the Comb of Cocks; how much more noble than the

the Mane of Lions! Therefore, we ought to have preserved the divine Characteristics: we ought not to have rejected them; nor confounded, as much as in us lay, the distinct Sexes.

§. 3. Are these the only Works of Providence, with regard to us . . . . (*a*) And what Words can proportionably express our Applauses and Praise? For, if we had any Understanding, ought we not both, in public and in private, incessantly to sing Hymns, and speak well of the Deity, and rehearse his Benefits? Ought we not, whether we are digging, or ploughing, or eating, to sing the Hymn [due] to God? Great is God, who has supplied us with these Instruments to till the Ground: Great is God, who has given us Hands, a Power of Swallowing, a Stomach: who has given us to grow insensibly, to breathe in Sleep. [Even] these Things we ought upon every Occasion to celebrate; but to make it the Subject of the greatest and most divine Hymn, that he has given us the Faculty of apprehending them, and using them in a proper Way. Well then: because the most of you are blind and insensible, was it not necessary, that there should be some one to fill this Station, and give out, for all Men, the Hymn to God? For what else can I, a lame old Man, do, but sing Hymns to God? If I was a Nightingale, I would act the Part of a Nightingale: if a Swan (*b*), the Part of a Swan. But, since I am a reasonable Creature, it is my Duty to praise God. This is my Business. I do it. Nor will I ever desert this Post, as long as it is vouchsafed me: and I exhort you to join in the same Song (*c*).

(*a*) Something here seems to be lost.

(*b*) The Ancients imagined Swans could sing very melodiously.

(*c*) Beautiful and affecting Examples of such Praise and Exhortation, see in *Ps.* xxxiv. civ. cxlv. and other Parts of the sacred Writings.

CHAP.

CHAPTER XVII.

That the Art of Reasoning is necessary.

§. 1. SINCE it is Reaſon which ſets in order and finiſhes all other Things, it ought not itſelf to be left in Diſorder. But by what ſhall it be ſet in Order?

Evidently, either by itſelf, or by ſomething elſe. Well: either *that* too is Reaſon, or there is ſomething elſe ſuperior to Reaſon (which is impoſſible): and, if it be Reaſon, what, again, ſhall ſet that in Order? For, if Reaſon can ſet itſelf in Order in one Caſe, it can in another: and, if we will ſtill require any thing further, it will be infinite, and without End.

But, the more urgent Neceſſity is to cure [our Opinions, Paſſions], and the like (*a*).

Would you hear about theſe, therefore? Well: hear. But then, if you ſhould ſay to me, "I cannot tell whether your Arguments are true or "falſe;" and if I ſhould happen to expreſs myſelf doubtfully, and you ſhould ſay, "diſtinguiſh "[which Senſe you mean]," I will bear with you no longer; but will retort your own Words upon you; *the more urgent Neceſſity is*, &c. Therefore, I ſuppoſe, the Art of Reaſoning is firſt ſettled: juſt as, before the Meaſuring of Corn, we ſettle the Meaſure. For, unleſs we firſt determine what a Buſhel, and what a Balance, is, how ſhall we be able to meaſure or weigh? Thus, in the preſent Caſe: unleſs we have firſt learnt, and accurately examined, that which is the Criterion of other Things, and by which other Things are learnt, how ſhall we be able accurately to learn any thing

 elſe?

(*a*) The Senſe here is ſupplied from a Conjecture of *Wolfius*.

else? And how is it possible? Well: a Bushel, however, is only Wood, a Thing of no Value [in itself]: but it measures Corn. And Logic [you say] is of no Value in itself. That we will consider hereafter. Let us, for the present, then, make the Concession. It is enough that it distinguishes and examines, and, as one may say, measures and weighs all other Things. Who says this? Is it only *Chrysippus*, and *Zeno*, and *Cleanthes*? And doth not *Antisthenes* say it? And who is it, then, who has written, That the Beginning of a right Education is the Examination of Words? Doth not *Socrates* say it? Of whom, then, doth *Xenophon* write, That he began by the Examination of Words; what each signified *(b)*.

§. 2. Is this, then, the great and admirable Thing, to understand or interpret *Chrysippus*?

Who says that it is? But what, then, is the admirable Thing?

To understand the Will of Nature.

Well then: do you apprehend it of yourself? In that Case, what Need have you for any one else? For, if it be true, that Men never err but involuntarily; and you have learnt the Truth, you must necessarily act right.

But, indeed, I do not apprehend the Will of Nature.

Who, then, shall interpret *that*?

They say, *Chrysippus* *(c)*. I go and inquire what this Interpreter of Nature says. I begin not to understand his Meaning. I seek one to interpret that. Here explain how this is expressed, and as if it were put into *Latin*. How, then, doth a supercilious Self-opinion belong to the Interpreter! Indeed,

(b) The Stoics were remarkably exact in tracing the Etymology of Words: a Study, certainly, of very great Use: but, by too great Subtlety and Refinement, they were often led by it into much Trifling and Absurdity.

(c) See the *Enchiridion*, ch. xlix.

Indeed, it doth not justly belong to *Chrysippus* himself, if he only interprets the Will of Nature, and doth not follow it: and much less to his Interpreter. For we have no need of *Chrysippus*, on his own Account; but that, by his Means, we may apprehend the Will of Nature: nor do we need a Diviner on his own Account; but that, by his Assistance, we hope to understand future Events, and what is signified by the Gods: nor the Entrails of the Victims, on their own Account; but, on the Account of what is signified by them: neither is it the Raven, or the Crow, that we admire; but the God, who delivers his Significations by their Means. I come, therefore, to the Diviner and Interpreter of these Things; and say, "Inspect the Entrails for "me: what is signified to me?" Having taken, and laid them open, he thus interprets them. You have a Choice, Man, incapable of being restrained or compelled. This is written here in the Entrails. I will show you this first, in the Faculty of Assent. Can any one restrain you from assenting to Truth? —"No one."—Can any one compel you to admit a Falshood?—"No one."—You see, then, that you have in this Topic a Choice incapable of being restrained, or compelled, or hindered. Well: is it any otherwise with regard to *Pursuit* and *Desire*? What can conquer one Pursuit?——"Another "Pursuit."——"What, Desire and Aversion? "Another Desire and another Aversion." If you *set Death before me* (say you) *you compel me.* No: not what is set before you doth it: but your Principle, that it is better to do such or such a thing, than to die. Here, again, you see it is your own Principle which compels you: that is, Choice compels Choice. For, if God hath constituted that Portion which he hath separated from his own Essence, and given to us, capable of being restrained or compelled, either by himself, or by any other, he would not have been God; nor have taken care of us, in a due manner.

§. 3. These Things, says the Diviner, I find in the Victims. These Things are signified to you. If you please, you are free. If you please, you will have no one to complain of; no one to accuse. All will be equally according to your own Mind, and to the Mind of God.

§. 4. For the Sake of this Oracle, I go to the Diviner and the Philosopher: admiring not *him* merely on the Account of his Interpretation, but the *Things* which he interprets.

CHAPTER XVIII.

That we are not to be angry with the Errors of others.

§. 1. (*a*) IF what the Philosophers say be true, That all Mens Actions proceed from one Source: that, as they assent, from a Persuasion that a Thing is so, and dissent, from a Persuasion that it is not; and suspend their Judgment, from a Persuasion that it is uncertain; so, likewise, they exert their Pursuits, from a Persuasion that such a Thing is for their Advantage; and it is impossible to esteem one Thing advantageous, and desire another; to esteem one Thing a Duty, and pursue another: why, after all, should we be angry at the Multitude?

They are Thieves and Pilferers.

What do you mean by Thieves and Pilferers? They are in an Error concerning Good and Evil. Ought

(*a*) The most ignorant Persons often practise what they know to be evil: and they, who voluntarily suffer, as many do, their Inclinations to blind their Judgment, are not justified by following it. The Doctrine of *Epictetus*, therefore, here, and elsewhere, on this Head, contradicts the Voice of Reason and Conscience: nor is it less pernicious, than ill grounded. It destroys all Guilt and Merit, all Punishment and Reward, all Blame of ourselves or others, all Sense of Misbehaviour towards our Fellow-creatures, or our Creator. No wonder that such Philosophers did not teach Repentance towards God.

Ought you, then, to be angry, or to pity them? Do but shew them their Error, and you will see, that they will amend their Faults: but, if they do not see it, the Principles they form, are to them their supreme Rule.

What, then, ought not this Thief and this Adulterer to be destroyed?

By no means [ask that]: but say rather (b), "Ought not he to be destroyed, who errs and is "deceived in Things of the greatest Importance; "blinded, not in the Sight that distinguishes White "from Black, but in the Judgment, that distin- "guishes Good from Evil?" By stating your Question thus, you see how inhuman it is; and just as if you would say, "Ought not this blind, or that deaf "Man, to be destroyed?" For, if the greatest Hurt be a Deprivation of the most valuable Things, and the most valuable Thing to every one is a right Judgment of chusing; when any one is deprived of this, why, after all, are you angry? You ought not to be affected, Man, contrary to Nature, by the Ills of another. Pity (c) him rather. Do not be angry; nor say, as many do, What! shall these execrable and odious Wretches dare to act thus! Whence have you so suddenly learnt Wisdom? Because we admire those Things which such People take from us. Do not admire your Clothes, and you will not be angry with the Thief. Do not admire the Beauty of your Wife, and you will not be angry with an Adulterer. Know, that a Thief and an Adulterer have no place in the Things that are properly your own: but in those that belong to

 others;

(b) Several Words are wanting in different Places of some of the following Lines of the *Greek*; which are conjecturally supplied in the Translation from Mr. *Upton*'s Version.

(c) See *Gal.* vi. 1. and many other Parts of the New Testament, in which all the Humanity and Tenderness prescribed by the Stoics are enjoined; and the dangerous Notions, on which they found them, are avoided.

others; and which are not in your Power. If you give up these Things, and look upon them as nothing, with whom will you any longer be angry? But, while you admire them, be angry with yourself, rather than with others. Consider only: You have a fine Suit of Clothes; your Neighbour has not. You have a Window; you want to air them. He knows not in what the Good of Man consists; but imagines it is in a fine Suit of Clothes: the very Thing which you imagine too. Must not he, then, of course, come and take them away? When you show a Cake to greedy People, and are devouring it all yourself; would not you have them snatch it from you? Do not provoke them: Do not have a Window: Do not air your Clothes. I, too, the other Day, had an Iron Lamp burning before my Houshold Deities. Hearing a Noise at the Window, I ran. I found my Lamp was stolen. I considered, that he who took it away, did nothing unaccountable. What then? To-morrow, says I, you shall find an Earthen one: for a Man loses only what he hath. *I have lost my Coat.* Ay: because you had a Coat. *I have a Pain in my Head.* Why, can you have a Pain in your Horns (d)? Why, then, are you out of Humour? For Loss and Pain can be only of such Things as are possessed.

§. 2. But the Tyrant will chain——What? ——A Leg——He will take away——What? ——A Head.——What is there, then, that he can neither chain, nor take away?——The Will, and Choice. Hence the Advice of the Ancients——*Know thyself.*

What ought to be done, then?

Exercise

(d) This alludes to a famous Quibble among the Stoics. *What you have not lost, you have: but you have not lost a Pair of Horns; therefore you have a Pair of Horns.* UPTON.

Exercise yourself, for Heaven's sake, in little Things; and thence proceed to greater. "I have "a Pain in my Head."——Do not cry, alas! ——"I have a Pain in my Ear"——Do not cry, alas! I do not say, you may not groan; but do not groan inwardly: or, if your Servant is a long while in bringing you something to bind your Head, do not bawl, and distort yourself; and say; "Every body hates me." For, who would not hate such a one?

§. 3. Relying for the future on these Principles, walk upright, and free; not trusting to Bulk of Body, like a Wrestler: for one should not be unconquerable in the Sense that an Ass is.

Who then is unconquerable? He whom nothing, independent on Choice, disconcerts. Then I run over every Circumstance, and consider [such a one in each. As they say] of an athletic Champion. He has been victorious in the first Encounter: What will he do in the Second? What, if the Heat should be excessive? What, if he were to appear at *Olympia?* So I say in this Case. What, if you throw Money in his Way? He will despise it. What, if a Girl? What, if in the dark? What, if he be tried by popular Fame, Calumny, Praise, Death? He is able to overcome them all. What, then, if he be placed in the Heat, or in the Rain (*e*)? What, if

(*e*) Mr. *Upton* observes, That *Epictetus* here applies to the wise Man, what he had just been saying of the athletic Champion: and he proposes a Change in one Word; by which, instead of the Heat, or the Rain, the Translation will be, in a Fever, or in Drink. For the Stoics held their wise Man to be a perfect Master of himself in all these Circumstances. The Passages which Mr. *Upton* produces from L. ii. c. 17. towards the End, and L. iii. c. 2. towards the Beginning, makes the Conjecture of οινωμενος for ‘υομενος as probable as it is ingenious. But yet the τι ουν αν καυμα η one would imagine to have crept in by a Repetition of the Transcriber, from the Description, a few Lines before; as it is scarcely probable, that the same Word should be used by *Epictetus* in two different Senses, at so small a Distance, in the same Discourse.

if he be hypochondriac, or asleep? [Just the same.] This is my unconquerable athletic Champion.

CHAPTER XIX.

Of the Behaviour to be observed towards Tyrants.

§. 1. WHEN a Person is possessed of some either real or imaginary Superiority, unless he hath been well instructed, he will necessarily be puffed up with it. A Tyrant, for Instance, says; "I am supreme over All."——And what can you do for *Me?* Can you exempt my Desires from Disappointment? How should you? For do you never incur your own Aversions? Are your own Pursuits infallible? Whence should *You* come by that Privilege? Pray, on Ship-board, do you trust to yourself, or to the Pilot? In a Chariot, to whom but to the Driver? And to whom in all other Arts? Just the same. In what, then doth your Power consist?——" All Men pay Regard to me."

So do I to my Desk. I wash it, and wipe it; and drive a Nail, for the Service of my Oil Flask.—" What, then, are these Things to be valued be-" yond *Me?*"——No: but they are of some Use to *me*, and therefore I pay Regard to them. Why, Do not I pay Regard to an Ass? Do I not wash his Feet? Do not I clean him? Do not you know, that every one pays Regard to himself; and to you, just as he doth to an Ass? For who pays Regard to you as a Man? Show that. Who would wish to be like *You?* Who would desire to imitate *You*, as he would *Socrates?*—" But I can take off your Head?"——"You say right. I had forgot, that one is to pay Regard to you as to a Fever, or the Cholic; and that there should be an Altar erected to you, as there is to the Goddess *Fever* at *Rome*.

§. 2. What is it, then, that disturbs and strikes Terror into the Multitude? The Tyrant, and his Guards? By no means. What is by Nature free,

cannot

cannot be disturbed, or restrained, by any thing but itself. But its own Principles disturb it. Thus, when the Tyrant says to any one; "I will chain your "Leg:" he who values his Leg, cries out for Pity: while he, who sets the Value on his own Will and Choice, says; "If you imagine it for your own In-"terest, chain it."——"What! do not you care?" ——No: I do not care.——"I will show you "that I am Master."——*You?* How should *You?* *Jupiter* has set me free. What! do you think he would suffer his own Son to be enslaved? You are Master of my Carcase. Take it.——"So that, when "you come into my Presence, you pay no Regard "to me?"——No: but to myself: or, if you will have me say, to you also: I tell you; the same to you as to a Pipkin. This is not selfish Vanity: for every Animal is so constituted, as to do every thing for its own Sake. Even the Sun doth all for his own Sake: nay; and to name no more, even *Jupiter* himself. But, when he would be stiled the Dispenser of Rain and Plenty, and the Father of Gods and Men, you see that he cannot attain these Offices and Titles, unless he contributes to the common Utility. And he hath universally so constituted the Nature of every reasonable Creature, that no one can attain any of its own proper Advantages, without contributing something to the Use of Society. And thus it becomes not unsociable to do every thing for one's own Sake. For, do you expect, that a Man should desert himself, and his own Interest? How, then, can all Beings have one and the same original Instinct, Attachment to themselves? What follows, then? That where those absurd Principles, concerning Things independent on Choice, as if they were either good or evil, are at the Bottom, there must necessarily be a Regard paid to Tyrants: and I wish it were to Tyrants only, and not to the very Officers of their Bed-chamber too. And how wise doth a Man grow on a sudden, when *Cæsar* has made him Clerk of the Close-stool? How immediately we say, "*Fe-* "*licio* talked very sensibly to me!" I wish he were turned out of the Bed-chamber, that he might once more appear to you the Fool he is.

§. 3. *Epaphroditus* had [a Slave, that was] a Shoemaker; whom, because he was good for nothing, he sold. This very Fellow being, by some strange Luck, bought by a Courtier, became Shoemaker to *Cæsar*. Then you might have seen how *Epaphroditus* honoured him. "How doth good *Fe-* "*licio* do, pray?" And, if any of us asked, what the great Man himself was about, it was answered; "He "is consulting about Affairs with *Felicio*." Did not he sell him, as good for nothing? Who, then, hath, all on a sudden, made a wise Man of him? This it is to honour any thing, besides what depends on Choice.

§. 4. Is any one exalted to the Office of Tribune? All that meet him congratulate him. One kisses his Eyes, another his Neck, and the Slaves his Hands. He goes to his House; finds it illuminated. He ascends the Capitol. Offers a Sacrifice. Now, who ever offered a Sacrifice for having good Desires? For exerting Pursuits conformable to Nature? For we thank the Gods for that wherein we place our Good.

§. 5. A Person was talking with me To-day about the Priesthood (*a*) of *Augustus*. I say to him, Let the thing alone, Friend: you will be at great Expence for nothing. "But my Name, says he, will be writ- "ten in the Annals." Will you stand by, then, and tell those who read them; "*I am the Person whose Name* "*is written there?*" But, if you could tell every one so now, what will you do when you are dead?—— "My Name will remain."—Write it upon a Stone, and it will remain just as well. But, pray what Remembrance will there be of you out of *Nicopolis?* "But I shall wear a Crown (*b*) of Gold."—If your Heart

(*a*) When Temples began to be erected to the Emperors, as to Gods, the Office of Priest was purchased by vile Flatterers, at a very great Expence. UPTON *from* CASAUBON. (*b*) Which was the Ornament of the Priests, while they were offering Sacrifice. *Nicopolis* was built by *Augustus*, in memory of the Victory at *Actium*.

Heart is quite ſet upon a Crown, take and put on one of Roſes; for it will make the prettier Appearance.

CHAPTER XX.

In what manner Reaſon contemplates itſelf.

EVERY Art, and every Faculty, contemplates ſome Things as its principal Objects. Whenever, therefore, it is of the ſame Nature with the Objects of its Contemplations, it neceſſarily contemplates itſelf too. But, where it is of a different Nature, it cannot contemplate itſelf. The Art of Shoemaking, for Inſtance, is exerciſed upon Leather; but is itſelf intirely diſtinct from the Materials it works upon: therefore it doth not contemplate itſelf. Again: Grammar is exerciſed on articulate Speech. Is the Art of Grammar itſelf, then, articulate Speech?

By no means.

Therefore it cannot contemplate itſelf. To what Purpoſe, then, is Reaſon appointed by Nature?

To a proper Uſe of the Appearances of Things.

And what is Reaſon?

A Compoſition of certain Appearances to the Mind: and, thus, by its Nature, it becomes contemplative of itſelf too. Again: what Subjects of Contemplation belong to Prudence?

Good and Evil, and Indifferent.

What, then, is Prudence itſelf?

Good.

What, Imprudence?

Evil.

You ſee, then, that it neceſſarily contemplates both itſelf and its contrary. Therefore, the firſt and greateſt Work of a Philoſopher is, to try and diſtinguiſh the Appearances; and to admit none untried. Even in Money, where our Intereſt ſeems to be concerned, you ſee what an Art we have invented

vented; and how many Ways an Assayer uses to try its Value. By the Sight; the Touch; the Smell; and, lastly, the Hearing. He throws the Piece down, and attends to the Jingle; and is not contented with its Jingling only once; but, by frequent Attention to it, becomes quite musical. In the same manner, whenever we think it of Consequence, whether we are deceived or not, we use the utmost Attention to distinguish those Things which may possibly deceive us. But, yawning and slumbering over the poor miserable ruling Faculty, we admit every Appearance that offers. For here the Mischief does not strike us. When you would know, then, how very languidly you are affected by Good and Evil, and how vehemently by Things indifferent; consider how you are affected with regard to being blinded; and how with regard to being deceived; and you will find, that you are far from being moved, as you ought, in relation to Good and Evil.

But much previous Qualification, and much Labour, and Learning, are wanted.

What, then? Do you expect the greatest of Arts is to be acquired by slight Endeavours? And yet the principal Doctrine of the Philosophers, of itself, is short. If you have a mind to know it, read *Zeno*, and you will see (*a*). For what Prolixity

(*a*) *Zeno*, The Founder of the Stoic Sect, was born at *Cittium*, a Seaport Town, in the Island of *Cyprus*. He was originally a Merchant; and very rich. On a Voyage from *Tyre*, where he had been trading in Purple, he was shipwrecked, near the *Piræus*. During his Stay at *Athens*, he happened to meet, in a Bookseller's Shop, with the Second Book of *Xenophon*'s Memoirs; with which he was extremely delighted; and asked the Bookseller, where such kind of Persons, as the Author mentioned, were to be found. The Bookseller answered, pointing to *Crates*, the Cynic, who was luckily passing by; Follow him: which *Zeno* did, and became his Disciple. But his Disposition was too modest to approve of the Cynic Indecency: and, forsaking *Crates*, he applied himself to the Academics; whom he attended for ten Years, and then formed a School of his own. There was

ity is there in ſaying, *Our End is to follow the Gods?* And, *The Eſſence of Good conſiſts in the proper Uſe of the Appearances of Things.* Indeed, if you ſay, What, then, is *God?* What is *an Appearance?* What is particular, what univerſal Nature? Here the Affair becomes prolix. And ſo, if *Epicurus* ſhould come and ſay, that Good muſt be placed in Body; here, too, it will be prolix: and it will be neceſſary to hear, what is the principal, the ſubſtantial and eſſential Part in us. It is unlikely, that the Good of a Snail ſhould be placed in the Shell: and, is it likely, that the Good of a Man ſhould? You yourſelf, *Epicurus*, have ſomething ſuperior to this: What is That in you, which deliberates, which examines, which forms the Judgment, concerning Body itſelf, that it is the principal Part? And why do you light your Lamp, and labour for us, and write ſo many Books? That we may not be ignorant of the Truth? What are *We?* What are we to *You?* Thus the Doctrine becomes prolix.

CHAPTER XXI.

Of the Deſire of Admiration.

WHEN a Perſon maintains his proper Station in Life, he doth not gape after Externals. What would you have, Man?

" I am contented, if my Deſires and Averſions " are conformable to Nature: if I manage my " Powers

was a conſtant Severity, or, perhaps, Auſterity, in his Manners, his Dreſs, and his Diſcourſe; except at an Entertainment, when he uſed to appear with Chearfulneſs and Eaſe. His Morals were irreproachable: and he was preſented by the *Athenians* with a golden Crown; becauſe his Life was a public Example of Virtue, by its Conformity with his Words and Doctrines. He lived Ninety-eight Years, and then ſtrangled himſelf; becauſe, in going out of his School, he happened to fall down, and break his Finger. DIOG. LAERT. *in* ZENO.

"Powers of Purſuit and Avoidance, my Purpoſes, "and Intentions and Aſſent, in the manner I was "formed to do."

Why, then, do you walk, as if you had ſwallowed a Spit?

"I could wiſh moreover to have all who meet "me, admire me, and all who follow me, cry "out, What a great Philoſopher!"

Who are thoſe, by whom you would be admired? Are they not the very People, who, you uſed to ſay, were mad? What, then, would you be admired by Madmen?

CHAPTER XXII.

Of Pre-conceptions.

§. 1. PRe-conceptions (*a*) are common to all Men: and one Pre-conception doth not contradict another. For, who of us doth not lay it down as a Maxim, That Good is advantageous and eligible, and at all Events, to be purſued and followed: that Juſtice is fair and becoming? Whence, then, ariſes the Diſpute?——In adapting theſe Preconceptions to particular Caſes. As, when one cries; "Such a Perſon hath acted well: he is a gallant "Man:" and another; "No; he hath acted like a Fool." Hence ariſes the Diſpute among Men. This is the Diſpute between *Jews*, and *Syrians*, and *Egyptians*, and *Romans*: not whether Sanctity be preferable to all Things, and in every Inſtance to be purſued; but whether the eating Swine's Fleſh be conſiſtent with Sanctity, or not. This, too, you will find to have been the Diſpute between *Achilles* and *Agamemnon*. For, call them forth: What ſay you, *Agamemnon*? Ought not that to be done, which is fit and right?——Yes, ſurely.

(*a*) See Introduction, §. 10.

ſurely.——*Achilles*, what ſay you? Is it not agreeable to you, that what is right ſhould be done?——Yes: beyond every other thing. Adapt your Preconceptions, then. Here begins the Diſpute. One ſays; "It is not fit, that I ſhould reſtore *Chryſeis* "to her Father." The other ſays; "Yes; but "it is." One, or the other of them, certainly makes a wrong Adaptation of the Pre-conception of *Fitneſs*. Again: one ſays; "If it be fit, that I ſhould give "up *Chryſeis*; it is fit, too, that I ſhould take ſome "one of your Prizes." The other: "What, that "you ſhould take my Miſtreſs?" "Ay; yours." "What, *mine* only? Muſt *I* only, then, loſe my "Prize?"

§. 2. What, then, is it to be properly educated? To learn how to adapt natural Pre-conceptions to particular Caſes, conformably to Nature: and, for the future, to diſtinguiſh, that ſome Things are in our own Power; others not. In our own Power, are Choice, and all Actions dependent on Choice: not in our Power, the Body, the Parts of the Body, Property, Parents, Brothers, Children, Country; and, in ſhort, all with whom we are engaged in Society. Where, then, ſhall we place Good? To what kind of Things ſhall we adapt the Pre-conception of it? To that in our own Power.

§. 3. What, then, is not Health, and Strength, and Life, good? And are not Children, nor Parents, nor Country? Who will have Patience with you?

Let us transfer it, then, to the other Sort of Things. Can he who ſuffers Harm, and is diſappointed of good Things, be happy?

He cannot.

And can he preſerve a right Behaviour with regard to Society? How is it poſſible he ſhould? For I am naturally led to my own Intereſt. If, therefore, it is for my Intereſt, to have an Eſtate, it is for my Intereſt likewiſe to take it away from my

Neighbour. If it is for my Intereſt to have a Suit of Clothes; it is for my Intereſt likewiſe to ſteal it wherever I find it (*b*). Hence Wars, Seditions, Tyranny, unjuſt Invaſions. How ſhall I, if this be the Caſe, be able, any longer, to preſerve my Duty towards *Jupiter?* If I ſuffer Harm, and am diſappointed, he takes no care of me. And, what is *Jupiter* to me, if he cannot help me: or, again; what is he to me, if he chuſes I ſhould be in the Condition I am? Henceforward I begin to hate him. What, then, do we build Temples, do we raiſe Statues, to *Jupiter*, as to evil Demons, as to the Goddeſs *Fever?* How, at this rate, is he the Preſerver; and how the Diſpenſer of Rain and Plenty? If we place the Eſſence of Good any-where here, all this will follow.——What, then, ſhall we do?

§. 4. This is the Enquiry of him who philoſophizes in reality, and labours to bring forth [Truth]. "Do (*c*) not I now ſee what is good, and what is evil?" Surely I am in my Senſes. Ay: but ſhall I place Good any-where on this other Side; in Things dependent [only] on my own Choice? Why, every one will laugh at me. Some grey-headed old Fellow will come, with his Fingers covered with Gold Rings, and ſhake his Head, and ſay; "Hark "ye, Child, it is fit you ſhould learn Philoſophy; "but it is fit, too, you ſhould have Brains. This "is Nonſenſe. You learn Syllogiſms from Philo- "ſophers: but how you are to act, you know bet- "ter than they." "Then, why do you chide me, "Sir, if I do know." What can I ſay to this Wretch? If I make no Anſwer, he will burſt. I muſt e'en anſwer thus: "Forgive me, as they "do People in Love. I am not myſelf. I have "loſt my Senſes."

CHAP-

(*b*) *Wars and Fightings* are aſcribed to the ſame Cauſes, by St. *James*, iv. 1.

(*c*) This ſeems intended to expreſs the Perplexity of a Perſon convinced, that Good is not to be found in Externals; and afraid of popular Raillery, if he places it in ſuch Things only, as depend on our own Choice.

CHAPTER XXIII.

Against EPICURUS.

§. 1. EVEN *Epicurus* is ſenſible, that we are by Nature ſociable: but having once placed our Good in the mere Shell, he can ſay nothing afterwards different from that. For, again, he ſtrenuouſly maintains, that we ought not to admire, or receive, any thing ſeparated from the Nature of Good. And he is in the right to maintain it. But how, then, came (*a*) any ſuch Suſpicions [as your Doctrines imply, to ariſe], if we have no natural Affection towards an Offspring? Why do you, *Epicurus*, diſſuade a wiſe Man from bringing up Children? Why are you afraid, that, upon their Account, he may fall into Uneaſineſſes? Doth he fall into any for a Mouſe, that feeds within his Houſe? What is it to him, if a little *Mouſe* bewails itſelf there? But *Epicurus* knew, that, if once a *Child* is born, it is no longer in our Power not to love and be ſolicitous for it. For the ſame Reaſon, he ſays, a wiſe man will not engage himſelf in public Buſineſs: for he knew very well, what ſuch an Engagement would oblige him to do: For what ſhould reſtrain any one from Affairs, if we may behave among Men, as we would among a Swarm of Flies

§. 2. And doth He, who knows all this, dare to bid us not bring up Children? Not even a Sheep, or a Wolf, deſerts its Offspring; and ſhall Man? What would you have? That we ſhould be as ſilly as Sheep? Yet even theſe do not deſert their Offspring. Or as ſavage as Wolves? Neither do theſe deſert them. Pray, who would

(*a*) This Paſſage is obſcure; and variouſly read, and explained by the Commentators. It is here tranſlated conjecturally.

mind *you*, if he ſaw his Child fallen upon the Ground, and crying? For my part, I am of Opinion, that your Father and Mother, even if they could have foreſeen, that you would have been the Author of ſuch Doctrines, would not, however, have thrown you away.

CHAPTER XXIV.

How we are to ſtruggle with Difficulties.

§. 1. DIfficulties are the Things that ſhew what Men are. For the future, on any Difficulty, remember, That God, like a *(a)* Maſter of Exerciſe, has engaged you with a rough Antagoniſt.

For what End?

That you may be a Conqueror, like one in the Olympic Games: and it cannot be without Toil. No Man, in my Opinion, has a more advantageous Difficulty on his Hands than you have; provided you will but uſe it, as an athletic Champion doth his Antagoniſt. We are now ſending *(b)* a Spy to *Rome:* but no one ever ſends a timorous Spy, who, when he only hears a Noiſe, or ſees a Shadow, runs back, frighted out of his Wits, and ſays; "The Enemy is juſt at hand." So now, if you ſhould come and tell us; "Things are in a "fearful Way at *Rome:* Death is terrible; Baniſh-"ment, terrible; Calumny, terrible; Poverty,

"terrible:

(a) The *Greek* Word ſignifies, a Perſon who uſed to anoint the Body of the Combatants: and prepare them, by proper Exerciſes for the Olympic Games.

(b) Probably, according to Mr. *Upton*'s Conjecture γε ſhould be σε. *We ſend you.*

Wolfius imagines this Paſſage to allude to the Commotions after the Death of *Nero*; when there were many Competitors for the Empire; and every one was eager to take the Part of him who appeared to have the greateſt Probability of Succeſs.

"terrible: run, good People, the Enemy is at "hand:" we will answer; Get you gone, and prophesy for yourself; our only Fault is, that we have sent such a Spy. *Diogenes* (*c*) was sent a Spy before *you*: but he told us other Tidings. He says, That Death is no Evil; for it is nothing base: that Defamation is only the Noise of Madmen. And what Account did this Spy give us of Pain? Of Pleasure? Of Poverty? He says, that, to be naked is better than a Purple Robe: to sleep upon the bare Ground the softest Bed: and gives a Proof of all he says, by his own Courage, Tranquillity, and Freedom; and, moreover, by a healthy and robust Body. There is no Enemy near, says he. All is profound Peace.——How so, *Diogenes*? Look upon *me*, says he. Am *I* hurt? Am *I* wounded? Have *I* run away from any one? This is such a Spy as he ought to be. But you come, and tell us one Thing after another. Go back again, and examine Things more exactly, and without Fear.

§. 2. What shall I do, then?

What do you do when you come out of a Ship? Do you take away the Rudder, or the Oars, along with you? What do you take, then? Your own, your Bottle, and your Bundle. So, in the present Case, if you will but remember what is your own, you will not claim what belongs to others. Are you bid to put off your Consular Robe?—Well: I am in my Equestrian. Put off that too.—I have only

(*c*) *Diogenes*, passing through the Camp of *Philip*, at the Time that he was on his March against the *Greeks*, was taken, and brought before the King; who, not knowing him, asked, If he was a Spy. Yes, certainly, *Philip* (answered the Philosopher); I am a Spy of your Inconsiderateness, and Folly, in risquing your Kingdom and Person, without any Necessity, upon the Hazard of a single Hour. Upton. The Story is thus told by *Plutarch*; but is related something differently by other Authors.

only my Coat.—Put off that too.—Well: I am naked.—Still you raiſe my Envy.—Then e'en take my whole Body. If I can throw off a paultry Body, am I any longer afraid of a Tyrant (*d*)?

§. 5. But ſuch a one will not leave me his Heir. What, then, have I forgot, that none of theſe Things is mine? How, then, do we call them *mine*? As a Bed, in an Inn. If the Landlord when he dies, leaves you the Beds; well and good: but, if to another, they will be his; and you will ſeek one elſewhere: and, conſequently, if you do not find one, you will ſleep upon the Ground: only ſleep quiet, and ſnore ſoundly; and remember, that Tragedies have no other Subjects, but the Rich, and Kings, and Tyrants. No poor Man fills any other Place in one, than as Part of the Chorus: whereas Kings begin, indeed with Proſperity. "*Crown* "*the Palace with feſtive Garlands*.(*e*)."—But, then, about the third or fourth Act; "*Alas*, Citheron! "*why didſt thou receive me!*" Where are thy Crowns, Wretch; where is thy Diadem? Cannot thy Guards help thee?

Whenever you approach any of theſe then, remember, that you meet a Tragic Player; or, rather, not an Actor, but *Oedipus* himſelf.——But ſuch a one is happy. He walks with a numerous Train. Well: I join myſelf with the Croud, and I too walk with a numerous Train.

§. 4. But, remember the principal thing; That the Door is open. Do not be more fearful than Children; but, as they, when the Play doth not pleaſe them, ſay; "I will play no longer:" ſo do you, in the ſame Caſe, ſay; "I will play no longer;" and go: but, if you ſtay, do not complain.

CHAP.

(*d*) The Tranſlation follows Mr. *Upton's* Reading.

(*e*) An Alluſion to the *Oedipus* of *Sophocles*.

CHAPTER XXV.

On the same Subject.

§. 1. IF these Things are true; and we are not stupid, or acting a Part, when we say, that the Good or Ill of Man consists in Choice, and that all besides is nothing to us; why are we still troubled? Why do we still fear? What hath been *our* Concern, is in no one's Power: what is in the Power of others, *we* do not regard. What Embarassment have we left?

But direct me.

Why should *I* direct you? Hath not *Jupiter* directed you? Hath he not given you what is your *own*, incapable of Restraint, or Hindrance; and what is *not* your own, liable to both? What Directions, then, what Orders, have you brought from him? "By all Methods keep what is your own: "what belongs to others, do not covet. Honesty, "is your own: a Sense of virtuous Shame is your "own. Who, then, can deprive you of these? "Who can restrain you from making use of them, "but yourself? And how do you do it? When "you make that your Concern which is not your "own, you lose what is." Having such Precepts and Directions from *Jupiter*, what sort do you still want from me? Am *I* better than *He*? More worthy of Credit? If you observe these, what others do you need? Or are not these Directions *his*? Produce your natural Preconceptions: produce the Demonstrations of Philosophers: produce what you have often heard, and what you have said yourself; what you have read, and what you have studied.

How long is it right to observe these Things, and not break up the Game?

As long as it goes on agreeably. A King is chosen at the *Saturnalian* Festival (for it was agreed to play at that Game): he orders; "Do you drink: "you mix the Wine: you sing: you go: you "come." I obey; that the Game may not be broken up by my Fault.——"Well: but I bid "you think yourself to be unhappy." I do not think so: and who shall compel me to think so? Again: we agreed to play *Agamemnon* and *Achilles*. He who is appointed for *Agamemnon*, says to me; "Go to *Achilles*, and force away *Briseis*." I go. "Come." I come.

§. 2. We should converse in Life as we do in hypothetical Arguments. "Suppose it to be Night." ——Well: suppose it.——"Is it Day, then?" No: for I admitted the Hypothesis, that it is Night.——"Suppose, that you think it to be "Night."——Well: suppose it.——But think al"so, in reality, that it is Night."——That doth not follow from the Hypothesis. Thus, too, in the other Case. Suppose you have ill Luck.——Suppose it.——"Are you, then, unlucky?"——Yes. ——"Have you some cross Demon."——Yes. ——"Well: but think too [in earnest], that you "are unhappy."——This doth not follow from the Hypothesis: and there is one who forbids me [to think so].

How long, then, are we to obey such Orders? As long as it is worth while: that is, as long as I preserve what is becoming and fit.

§. 3. Further: some are peevish and fastidious; and say, I cannot dine with such a Fellow, to be obliged to hear him all Day recounting, how he fought in *Mysia*. "I told you, my Friend, how I "gained the Eminence. There I am besieged "again." But another says, "I had rather get "a Dinner, and hear him prate as much as he "pleases."

Do

Do you compare the Value of these Things, and judge for yourself: but do not let it be with Depression, and Anxiety; and with a Supposition, that you are unhappy: for no one compels you to that. Is the House in a Smoke? If it be a moderate one, I will stay: If a very great one, I will go out. For you must always remember, and hold to this, that the Door is open, "Well: "do not live at *Nicopolis*."—I will not live there. —"Nor at *Athens*."—Well: nor at *Athens*.— "Nor at *Rome*."—Nor at *Rome* neither.—"But "you shall live at *Gyaros* (*a*)."—I will live there. But living at *Gyaros* seems to me like living in a great Smoke. I will retire where no one can forbid me to live; (for that Abode is open to all) and put off my last (*b*) Garment, this paultry Body of mine: beyond this, no one hath any Power over me. Thus *Demetrius* said to *Nero*; "You sentence *me* to Death; and Nature, *you* (*c*);" If I place my Admiration on Body, I give myself up for a Slave: if on an Estate, the same: for I immediately betray myself, how I may be taken. Just as when a Snake pulls in his Head, I say strike that Part of him which he guards: and be you assured,

(*a*) An Island in the *Ægean* Sea, to which the *Romans* used to banish Criminals.

(*b*) The Body, which *Epictetus* here compares to a Garment, is, by the sacred Writers, represented under the Figure of a House, or Tabernacle, *Job* iv. 19. 2 *Pet.* i. 13, 14. St. *Paul* with a sublime Rapidity of Expression, joins the two Metaphors together, 2 *Cor.* v. 2——4. as, indeed, the one is but a looser, the other a closer Covering. The same Apostle hath made use of the Figure of Clothing, in another Place, in a strikingly beautiful Manner, 1 *Cor.* xv. 53, 54.

(*c*) *Anaxagoras* is said, by some, and *Socrates*, by others, to have made the same Speech, on receiving the News of his being condemned to Death by the Judges of *Athens*: and from one of them, probably, *Demetrius* borrowed it. *Demetrius* was a Cynic Philosopher; and is mentioned with high Approbation by *Seneca*.

ſured, that whatever you ſhew a Deſire to guard, there your Maſter will attack you. Remember but this, whom will you any longer flatter, or fear?

But I want to ſit where the Senators do.

Do not you ſee, that by this you ſtraiten yourſelf? You ſqueeze yourſelf?

Why, how elſe ſhall I ſee the Show, in the Amphitheatre cleverly?

Do not ſee it [at all], Man; and you will not be ſqueezed. Why do you give yourſelf Trouble? Or wait a little while; and when the Show is over, go ſit in the Senators Places, and ſun yourſelf. For remember, that this holds univerſally; we ſqueeze ourſelves; we ſtraiten ourſelves: that is; our own Principles ſqueeze and ſtraiten us. What is it to be reviled, for Inſtance? Stand by a Stone, and revile it; and what will you get? If you, therefore, would hear like a Stone, what would your Reviler be the better? But, if the Reviler hath the Weakneſs of the Reviled for an Advantage-ground, then he carries his Point.—"Strip him." "What "do you mean by *him*?" "Take my Clothes; "ſtrip off *them* [if you will]."—"I have put an "Affront upon you."—"Much Good may it do "you."

§. 4. Theſe Things were the Study of *Socrates*; and, by this means, he always preſerved the ſame Countenance. But *we* had rather exerciſe and ſtudy any thing, than how to become unreſtrained and free.

The Philoſophers talk Paradoxes.

And are there not Paradoxes in other Arts? What is more paradoxical, than the pricking any one's Eye, to make him ſee? If a Perſon was to tell this to one ignorant of Surgery, would not he laugh at him? Where is the Wonder then, if, in Philoſophy too, many Truths appear Paradoxes to the Ignorant?

CHAP-

CHAPTER XXVI.

What the Law of Life is.

§. 1. AS one [of his Scholars] was reading hypothetical Syllogiſms; it is likewiſe a Law in theſe, ſays *Epictetus*, to admit what follows from the Hypotheſis: but much more is it a Law in Life, to do what follows from Nature. For, if we deſire in every Subject of Action, and in every Circumſtance, to keep up to Nature; we muſt, on every Occaſion, evidently make it our Aim, neither to let Conſequences eſcape our Obſervation, nor to admit Contradictions. Philoſophers, therefore, firſt exerciſe us in Theory, which is the more eaſy Taſk, and then lead us to the more difficult: for in Theory, there is nothing to oppoſe our following what we are taught; but in Life, there are many Things to draw us aſide. It is ridiculous then, to ſay, we muſt begin from theſe: for it is not eaſy to begin from the moſt difficult: and this Excuſe muſt be made to thoſe Parents, who diſlike that their Children ſhould learn philoſophical Speculations.—"Am I to blame then, Sir, and ig-
"norant of my Duty, and of what is incumbent
"on me? If this is neither to be learnt, nor
"taught, why do you find fault with me? If it
"is to be taught, pray teach me yourſelf: or,
"if you cannot, give me Leave to learn it from
"thoſe who profeſs to underſtand it. Beſides:
"do you think that I voluntarily fall into Evil,
"and miſs of Good? Heaven forbid! What
"then, is the Cauſe of my Faults?" Ignorance.
"Are you not willing then, that I ſhould get
"rid of my Ignorance? Who was ever taught
"the

"the Art of Music, or Navigation, by Anger? "Do you expect then, that your Anger should "teach me the Art of Living?"——This however, is allowed to be said only by one who really hath that Intention. But he who reads these Things, and applies to the Philosophers, merely for the sake of shewing, at an Entertainment, that he understands hypothetical Syllogisms; what doth he do it for, but to be admired by some Senator, who happens to sit near him (a) .....

§. 2. .... I once saw a Person weeping and embracing the Knees of *Epaphroditus*; and deploring his hard Fortune, that he had not 50,000 *l.* left. What said *Epaphroditus*, then? Did he laugh at him, as we should do? No: but cried out with Astonishment, Poor Man! How could you be silent? How could you bear it?

§. 3. .... The first Step, therefore, towards becoming a Philosopher, is, being sensible in what State the ruling Faculty of the Mind is: for, when a Person knows it to be in a weak one, he will not immediately employ it in great Attempts. But, for want of this, some, who can scarce get down a Morsel, buy, and set themselves to swallow, whole Treatises; and so they throw them up again, or cannot digest them: and then come Cholics, Fluxes, and Fevers. Such Persons ought to consider what they can bear. Indeed, it is easy to convince an ignorant Person in Theory; but in Matters relating to Life, no one offers himself to Conviction; and we hate those who have convinced us. *Socrates* used to say, that we ought not to live a Life unexamined.

CHAP.

(a) The Text is so very corrupt in some Parts of this Chapter, that the Translation must have been wholly conjectural; and therefore is omitted.

CHAPTER XXVII.

Of the several Appearances of Things to the Mind: and what Remedies are to be provided for them.

§. 1. APPEARANCES to the Mind are of Four Kinds. Things are either what they appear to be: or they neither are, nor appear to be: or they are, and do not appear to be: or they are not, and yet appear to be. To form a right Judgment in all these Cases, belongs only to the completely Instructed. But whatever presses, to that a Remedy must be applied. If the Sophistries of *Pyrrhonism (a)*, or the Academy, press us, the Remedy must be applied *there*: if specious Appearances,

(a) *Pyrrho*, the Founder of the Sect of the *Pyrrhonists*, was born at *Elis*, and flourished about the Time of *Alexander*. He held, That there is no Difference between Just and Unjust, Good and Evil: that all Things are equally indifferent, uncertain, and undistinguishable: that neither our Senses or Understanding give us either a true or a false Information: therefore, that we ought to give them no Credit; but to remain without Opinion; without Motion; without Inclination; and to say of every thing, that it no more *is*, than it is *not*; that it is no more one thing than another; and that against one Reason, there is always an equal Reason to be opposed. His Life is said to have been conformable to his Principles; for that he never avoided any thing: and his Friends were obliged to follow him, to prevent his running under the Wheels of a Coach, or walking down a Precipice. But these Stories, perhaps, are nothing but mere Invention; formed to expose the Absurdities of his System. Once, when he saw his Master *Anaxarchus* fallen into a Ditch, he passed by him, without offering him any Assistance. *Anaxarchus* was consistent enough with his Principles, not to suffer *Pyrrho* to be blamed for this Tranquil Behaviour: which he justified, as a laudable Instance of Indifference, and Want of Affection. A fine Picture this, of sceptical Friendship!

For a more complete Account of the System of *Pyrrho*, see DIOG. LAERT. in his Life. And LIPSIUS *Manuduct. ad Stoic. Philosoph.* B. ii. Dis. 3.

pearances, by which Things seem to be good which are not so, let us seek for a Comedy *there*. If it be Custom which presses us, we must endeavour to find a Remedy against that.

What Remedy is to be found against Custom? A contrary Custom. You hear the Vulgar say, "Such a one, poor Soul! is dead."——Why, his Father died: his Mother died.——"Ay: but he "was cut off in the Flower of his Age, and in a "foreign Land."——Hear the contrary Ways of Speaking: withdraw yourself from these Expressions. Oppose to one Custom, a contrary Custom; to Sophistry, the Art of Reasoning, and the frequent Use and Exercise of it. Against specious Appearances, we must have clear Pre-conceptions, brightened up, and ready. When Death appears as an Evil, we ought immediately to remember, that Evils may be avoided, but Death is Necessity. For what can I do, or where can I fly from it? Let me suppose myself to be *Sarpedon*, the Son of *Jove*, that I may speak in the same gallant Way.

Brave tho' we die, and honour'd if we live;
Or let us Glory gain, or Glory give. POPE.

If I can atchieve nothing myself, I will not envy another the Honour of doing some gallant Action. But suppose this to be a Strain too high for *us*; are not we capable [at least] of arguing thus? ——Where shall I fly from Death? Shew me the Place; shew me the People, to whom I may have Recourse, whom Death doth not overtake. Shew me the Charm to avoid it. If there be none, what would you have me do? I cannot escape Death: but (*b*) cannot I escape the Dread of it? Must I die trembling, and lamenting? For the Origin of the Disease is, wishing for something that is not obtained.

(*b*) The Translation follows Mr. *Upton*'s Reading, τὸ φοβεῖσθαι.

tained. In conſequence of this, if I can bring over Externals to my own Inclination, I do it: if not, I want to tear out the Eyes of whoever hinders me. For it is the Nature of Man, not to bear the being deprived of Good; not to bear the falling into Evil. And ſo, at laſt, when I can neither bring over Things [to my own Inclination], nor tear out the Eyes of him who hinders me, I ſit down, and groan, and revile him whom I can; *Jupiter*, and the reſt of the Gods (*c*). For what are they to me, if they take no care of me?

Oh! but you will be guilty of Impiety.

What then? Can I be in a worſe Condition than I am now? In general, remember this, That, unleſs Piety and Intereſt be placed in the ſame Thing, Piety cannot be preſerved in any mortal Breaſt.

§. 2. Do not theſe Things ſeem to have Force (*d*)? Let a *Pyrrhoniſt*, or an Academic, come and oppoſe them. For my part, I am not at Leiſure; nor able to ſtand up as an Advocate for general Conſent. Even if Buſineſs were concerning an Eſtate, I ſhould call in another Advocate. With what Advocate, then, am I contented [in the preſent Caſe]? With any that may be upon the Spot. I may be at a Loſs, perhaps, to give a Reaſon, how Senſation is performed: whether it be diffuſed univerſally, or reſide in a particular Part: for I find Difficulties that ſhock me, in each Caſe: but, that you and I are not the ſame Perſon, I very exactly know.

How ſo?

Why,

(*c*) The blaſphemous Impatience, here introduced, reſembles that which is ſtrongly deſcribed, in a few Words, *Iſ.* viii. 21.——— *When they ſhall be hungry, they ſhall fret themſelves; and curſe their King, and their God, and look upward.*

(*d*) This is ſpoken in Oppoſition to the Sceptics, who are alluded to in the Beginning of the Chapter; and who ſay, that no Argument hath any Force.

Why, I never, when I have a mind to swallow any thing, carry it to *your* Mouth; but my *own*. I never, when I wanted to take a Loaf, took a Brush: but went directly to the Loaf, as fit to answer my Purpose. And do you yourselves, who deny all Evidence of the Senses, act any otherwise? Who of you, when he intended to go into a Bath, ever went into a Mill?

What, then, must not we, to the utmost, defend these Points? support the general Consent [of Mankind]? be fortified against every thing that opposes it (*e*)?

Who denies that? But it must be done by him who hath Abilities; who hath Leisure: but he, who is full of Trembling and Perturbation, and inward Disorders of Heart, must employ his Time about something else.

CHAPTER XXVIII.

That we are not to be angry with Mankind. What Things are little, what great, among Men.

§. 1. WHAT is the Cause of Assent to any thing?

Its appearing to be true.

It is not possible, therefore, to assent to what appears to be not true.

Why?

Because it is the very Nature of the Understanding to agree to Truth; to be dissatisfied with Fal-

(*e*) This seems to be said by one of the Hearers, who wanted to have the Absurdities of the Sceptics confuted, and guarded against, by regular Argument. *Epictetus* allows this to be right, for such as have Abilities and Leisure: but recommends to others, the more necessary Task, of curing their own moral Disorders: and insinuates, that the mere common Occurrences of Life are sufficient to overthrow the Notions of the *Pyrrhonists*.

Falſhood; and to ſuſpend its Belief, in doubtful Caſes.

What is the Proof of this?

Perſuade yourſelf, if you can, that it is now Night.

Impoſſible.

Unperſuade yourſelf that it is Day.

Impoſſible.

Perſuade yourſelf, that the Stars are, or are not, even.

Impoſſible.

§. 2. When any one, then, aſſents to what is falſe, be aſſured, that he doth not wilfully aſſent to it, as falſe (for, as *Plato* affirms, the Soul is never voluntarily deprived of Truth): but what is falſe, appears to him to be true. Well, then: Have we, in Actions, any thing correſpondent to True and Falſe, in Propoſitions?

Duty, and contrary to Duty: Advantageous, and Diſadvantageous: Suitable and Unſuitable; and the like.

A Perſon then, cannot think a Thing advantageous to him, and not chuſe it.

He cannot. But how ſays *Medea?*

" *I know what Evils wait my dreadful Purpoſe;*
" *But vanquiſh'd Reaſon yields to powerful Rage.*"

Becauſe ſhe thought, that very Indulgence of her Rage, and the puniſhing her Huſband, more advantageous than the Preſervation of her Children.

Yes: but ſhe is deceived.

Shew clearly to her, that ſhe is deceived, and ſhe will forbear: but, till you have ſhewn it, what is ſhe to follow, but what appears to herſelf?

Nothing.

Why, then, are you angry (*a*) with her, that the unhappy Woman is deceived, in the moſt important Points; and inſtead of a human Creature, becomes a Viper? Why do not you rather, as we pity the Blind and Lame, ſo likewiſe pity thoſe who

(*a*) See Note *a*, c. 18. §. 1.

are blinded and lamed, in their ſuperior Faculties? Whoever, therefore, duly remembers, that the Appearance of Things to the Mind is the Standard of every Action to Man: that this is either right or wrong: and, if right, he is without Fault; if wrong, he himſelf bears the Puniſhment: for that one Man cannot be the Perſon deceived, and another the Sufferer: will not be outrageous and angry at any one; will not revile, or reproach, or hate, quarrel with, any one.

§. 3. So then, Have all the great and dreadful Deeds, that have been done in the World, no other Original than *Appearance?*

Abſolutely, no other. The *Iliad* conſiſts of nothing but the Appearances [of Things to the Mind]; and the Uſe of thoſe Appearances. It *appeared* [right] to *Paris*, to carry off the Wife of *Menelaus*. It *appeared* [right] to *Helen*, to follow him. If, then, it had *appeared* [right] to *Menelaus*, to perſuade himſelf, that it was an Advantage to be robbed of ſuch a Wife, what would have happened? Not only the *Iliad* had been loſt, but the *Odyſſey* too.

Do theſe great Events then, depend on ſo ſmall a Cauſe?

What are theſe Events, which you call great?

Wars, and Seditions; the Deſtruction of Numbers of Men; and the Overthrow of Cities.

And what great Matter is there in all this? Nothing. What great Matter is there in the Death of Numbers of Oxen, Numbers of Sheep, or in the burning or pulling down Numbers of Neſts of Storks or Swallows?

Are theſe like Caſes, then?

Perfectly like. The Bodies of Men are deſtroyed, and the Bodies of Sheep and Oxen. The Houſes of Men are burnt, and the Neſts of Storks. What is there great or dreadful in all this? Pray, ſhew me what Difference there is between the Houſe of a Man, and the Neſt of a Stork, ſo far as it is a Habitation

bitation (*b*), excepting that Houſes are built with Beams, and Tiles, and Bricks; and Neſts, with Sticks and Clay?

What, then, is a Stork and a Man a like Thing? What do you mean?

With regard to Body, extremely like.

Is there no Difference, then, between a Man and a Stork?

Yes, ſurely: but not in theſe Things.

In what then?

Enquire; and you will find, that the Difference conſiſts in ſomething elſe. See whether it be not, in acting with Diſcernment: whether it be not, in a ſocial Diſpoſition; in Fidelity, Honour, Steadineſs, Judgment.

§. 4. Where then, is the great Good or Evil of Man?

Where his Difference is. If this is preſerved, and remains well fortified, and neither Honour, Fidelity, or Judgment, is deſtroyed, then he himſelf is preſerved likewiſe: but, when any of theſe is loſt and demoliſhed, he himſelf is loſt alſo. In this do all great Events conſiſt. *Paris*, they ſay, was undone, becauſe the *Greeks* invaded *Troy*, and laid it waſte; and his Family were ſlain in Battle. By no means: for no one is undone by an Action, not his own. All *that* was only laying waſte the Neſts of Storks. But his true Undoing was, when he loſt the modeſt, the faithful, the hoſpitable, and the decent Character. When was *Achilles* undone? When *Patroclus* died? By no means. But when he gave himſelf up to Rage; when he wept over a Girl; when he forgot, that he came there, not to get Miſtreſſes, but to fight. This is human Undoing; this is the Siege; this the Overthrow; when right Principles are ruined; when theſe are deſtroyed.

But, when Wives and Children are led away

(*b*) The Order of the following Words is diſturbed in the Original. The Tranſlation follows Mr. *Upton*'s Correction.

Captives, and the Men themselves killed, are not these, Evils?

Whence do you conclude them such? Pray inform me, in my Turn.

Nay: but whence do you affirm, that they are not Evils?

§. 5. Let us recur to the Rules. Produce the Preconceptions. One cannot sufficiently wonder at what happens, in this Respect. When we would judge of Light and Heavy, we do not judge by Guess: when of Strait and Crooked, not by Guess: and, in general, when it concerns us to know the Truth of any Particular, no one of us will do any thing, by Guess. But, where the first and principal Cause is concerned, of acting either right or wrong; of being prosperous or unprosperous, happy or unhappy; there only do we act rashly, and by Guess. No-where any thing like a Balance; no-where any thing like a Rule: but some Fancy strikes me, and I instantly act conformably to it. For am I better than *Agamemnon* or *Achilles*; that they, by following their Fancies, should do and suffer so many Things, and Fancy not suffice me? And what Tragedy hath any other Original? The *Atreus* of *Euripides*, what is it? Fancy. The *Oedipus* of *Sophocles?* Fancy. The *Phœnix?* The *Hippolytus?* All Fancy. To what Character, then, doth it belong, think you, to take no care of this Point? What are they called who follow every Fancy?

Madmen.

Do *we*, then, behave any otherwise?

CHAPTER XXIX.

Of Intrepidity.

§. 1. THE Essence of Good and Evil, is a certain Disposition of the Choice.

What are Externals, then?

Materials to the Faculty of Choice: in the Management of which, it will attain its own Good or Evil.

How,

How, then, will it attain Good?

If it doth not admire the Materials themſelves: for right Principles, concerning theſe Materials, conſtitute a good Choice: but perverſe and diſtorted Principles, a bad one. This Law hath God ordained, who ſays; "If you wiſh for Good, receive "it from yourſelf." You ſay, No: but from another.——"Nay; but from yourſelf." In conſequence of this, when a Tyrant threatens, and ſends for me; I ſay, Againſt what is your Threatning pointed? If he ſays, "I will chain you;" I anſwer, It is my *Hands* and *Feet* that you threaten. If he ſays, "I will cut off your Head;" I anſwer, It is my *Head* that you threaten. If he ſays, "I will "throw you into Priſon;" I anſwer, It is the Whole of this paultry *Body* that you threaten: and, if he threatens Baniſhment, juſt the ſame.

Doth not he threaten *you*, then?

If I am perſuaded, that theſe Things are nothing to me, he doth not: but, if I fear any of them, it is *me* that he threatens. Whom, after all, is it that I fear? The Maſter of what? Of Things in my own Power? Of theſe no one is the Maſter. Of Things not in my Power? And what are theſe to *me*?

§. 2. What, then! do you Philoſophers teach us a Contempt of Kings?

By no means. Who of us teaches any one to contend with them, about Things of which they have the Command? Take my Body; take my Poſſeſſions; take my Reputation; take thoſe who are about me. If I perſuade any one to contend for theſe Things, as his own, accuſe me, with Juſtice. ——"Ay: but I would command your *Principles* "too."——And who hath given you that Power? How can you conquer the Principle of another?—By applying Terror, I will conquer it.——Do not you ſee, that (*a*) what conquers itſelf, is not conquered

(*a*) The Senſe of this Paſſage ſeems to require that the firſt *αυτο* ſhould be read ὁ.

quered by another? And nothing but itself can conquer the Choice. Hence, too, the most excellent and equitable Law of God; that the Better should always prove superior to the Worse. Ten are better than One.

To what Purpose?

For chaining, killing, dragging where they please; for taking away an Estate. Thus Ten conquer One, in the Instance wherein they are better.

In what, then, are they worse?

When the one hath right *Principles*, and the others have not. For can they conquer in this Point? How should they? If we were weighed in a Scale, must not the Heavier outweigh?

§. 3. That ever *Socrates* should suffer such Things from the *Athenians*!

Wretch! what do you mean by (*b*) *Socrates*? Express the Fact as it is. That ever the poor paultry *Body* of *Socrates* should be carried away, and dragged to Prison, by such as were stronger [than itself]: that ever any one should give Hemlock to the *Body* of *Socrates*; and that it should expire! Do *these* Things appear wonderful to you? *These* Things unjust? Is it for such Things as *these* that you accuse God? Had *Socrates*, then, no Equivalent for them? In what, then, to him, did the Essence of Good consist? Whom shall we mind; you, or him? And what doth he say? "*Anytus* and *Melitus* (*c*) may indeed kill; but hurt me they cannot." And again: "If it so pleases God, so let it be."

§. 4.

(*b*) *Socrates*, being asked by *Crito*, in what manner he would be buried? answered, As you please; if you can lay hold on me, and I do not escape from you. Then, smiling, and turning to his Friends, I cannot, says he, persuade *Crito*, that I, who am now disputing, and ranging the Parts of my Discourse, am *Socrates*: but he thinks the Corpse, which he will soon behold, to be *me*; and, therefore, asks how he must bury *me*. PLATO, *in Phæd.* §. 64. FORSTER's *Edition*.

(*c*) The two principal Accusers of *Socrates*.

§. 4. But ſhew me, that he who hath the worſe Principles, gets the Advantage over him, who hath the better. You never will ſhew it, nor any thing like it: for the Law of Nature and of God, is this; Let the Better be always ſuperior to the Worſe.

In what?

In that, wherein it is better. One Body is ſtronger than another: Many than One; and a Thief, than one who is not a Thief. Thus I, too, loſt my Lamp; becauſe the Thief was better at keeping awake, than I. But he bought a Lamp, at the Price of being a Thief, a Rogue, and a wild Beaſt. This ſeemed to him a good Bargain: and much Good may it do him!

§. 5. Well: but one takes me by the Coat, and draws me to the Forum; and then all the reſt bawl out——"Philoſopher, what Good do your *Prin-* " *ciples* do you? See, you are dragging to Priſon: " ſee, you are going to loſe your Head!"—— And, pray what Rule of Philoſophy could I contrive, that, when a ſtronger than myſelf lays hold on my Coat, I ſhould not be dragged? Or that, when ten Men pull me at once, and throw me into Priſon, I ſhould not be thrown there? But have I learnt nothing, then? I have learnt to know, whatever happens, that, if it is not a Matter of Choice, it is nothing to *me.* Have my Principles, then, done me no Good *(d)*? What, then! do I ſeek for any thing elſe to do me Good, but what I have learnt? Afterwards, as I ſit in Priſon, I ſay: He, who makes this Outcry, neither hears what Signal is

 given,

(d) This is evidently a Continuation of the Philoſopher's Anſwer to thoſe who reproached him, that his Principles had done him no Good; and, therefore, is tranſlated in the firſt Perſon, though it is ωφιλησαι and ζητεις in the *Greek.* This ſudden Change of the Perſon, is very frequent in *Epictetus*; but would often diſturb the Senſe, if it was preſerved in a Tranſlation. Perhaps ωφιλησαι is a Miſtake, for ωφιλημαι; as M, Σ are the ſame Letters differently turned.

given, nor understands what is said; nor is it any Concern to him, to know what Philosophers say, or do. Let him alone.——[Well: but I am bid] to come out of Prison again.——If you have no further Need for me, in Prison, I will come out: if you want me again, I will return.——"For how long "[will you go on thus?]"——Just as long as (*e*) Reason requires I should continue in this paultry Body: when that is over, take it, and fare ye well. Only let not this be done inconsiderately; nor from Cowardice; nor upon every slight Pretence: for that, again, would be contrary to the Will of God: for he hath Need of such a World, and such [Creatures] to live on Earth. But, if he sounds a Retreat, as he did to *Socrates*, we are to obey him, when he sounds it, as our General.

§. 6. Well: but are these Things to be said to the World?

For what Purpose? Is it not sufficient to be convinced one's self? When Children come to us, clapping their Hands, and saying; "To-morrow is the good Feast of *Saturn*:" do we tell them, that *Good* doth not consist in such Things? By no means: but we clap our Hands along with them. Thus, when you are unable to convince any one, consider him as a Child, and clap your Hands with him: or, if you will not do that, at least hold your Tongue. These Things we ought to remember; and, when we are called to any Difficulty, know, that an Opportunity is come, of shewing whether

(*e*) The Meaning of *Epictetus* in this Passage is not clear. If he is speaking of a voluntary Death, which some of his Expressions plainly imply, the Instance of *Socrates* seems improperly chosen: for he did not kill himself; but was sentenced by the Laws of his Country: to which, indeed, he paid so great a Reverence, as to refuse all the Assistance which was offered by his Friends, in order to his Escape.

whether we have been well taught. For he who goes from a philoſophical Lecture to a difficult Point of Practice, is like a young Man who has been ſtudying to ſolve Syllogiſms. If you propoſe an eaſy one, he ſays; Give me rather a fine intricate one, that I may try my Strength. Even athletic Champions are diſpleaſed with a ſlight Antagoniſt. He cannot lift me, ſays one. This is a Youth of Spirit. No: but, I warrant you, when the Occaſion calls upon him, he muſt fall a crying, and ſay; "I wanted to learn a little longer firſt."—Learn what? If you did not learn theſe Things to ſhew them in Practice, why did you learn them at all? I am perſuaded there muſt be ſome one among you who ſit here, that feels ſecret Pangs of Impatience, and ſays; "When will ſuch a Difficulty come to "*my* Share, as hath now fallen to his? Muſt I ſit "waſting my Life in a Corner, when I might be "crowned at *Olympia*? When will any one bring the "News of ſuch a Combat, for *me*?" Such ſhould be the Diſpoſition of you all. Even among the Gladiators of *Cæſar*, there are ſome who bear it very ill, that they are not brought upon the Stage, and match'd; and who offer Vows to God, and addreſs the Officers, begging to fight. And will none among *you*, appear ſuch? I would willingly take a Voyage, on purpoſe to ſee how a Champion of mine acts; how he treats his Subject.—"I do not chuſe "ſuch a Subject," ſay you.—Is it in your Power, then, to take what Subject you chuſe? Such a Body is given you; ſuch Parents, ſuch Brothers, ſuch a Country, and ſuch a Rank in it; and, then, you come to me, and ſay, "Change my Subject." Beſides, have not you Abilities to manage that which is given you? It is your Buſineſs, [we ſhould ſay] to propoſe; mine, to treat the Subject well.—"No. "But do not propoſe *ſuch* an Argument to me; "but *ſuch* a one: do not offer *ſuch* an Objection "to me; but *ſuch* a one."—There will be a Time, I ſup-

I suppose, when Tragedians will fancy themselves to be mere Masks, and Buskins, and long Train. These Things are your Materials, Man, and your Subject. Speak something; that we may know, whether you are a Tragedian, or a Buffoon: for both have all the rest, in common. If any one, therefore, should take away his Buskins, and his Mask, and bring him upon the Stage, in his (f) common Dress, is the Tragedian lost, or doth he remain? If he hath a voice, he remains. "Here, "this Instant, take upon you the Command." I take it; and, taking it, I shew how a Person, who hath been properly instructed, behaves.——"Lay "aside your Robe; put on Rags, and come upon "the Stage in that Character."—What then? Is it not in my Power to bring a good Voice [and Manner] along with me?——"In what Character do "you now appear?" As a (g) Witness cited by God.——"Come you, then, and bear witness for "me; for you are a Witness worthy of being pro-"duced by me. Is any thing, external to the "Choice, either Good or Evil? Do I hurt any "one? Have I placed the Good of each individual "in any one, but in himself? What Evidence do "you give for God?"—*I am in a miserable Condition, O Lord (h); I am undone: no Mortal cares for me: no Mortal gives me any thing: all blame me; all*

(f) φαινόλη. Lord SHAFTESBURY.

(g) This imaginary Witness, first extolled, then failing in his Testimony, brings to one's Mind with unspeakable Advantage, that *true and faithful Witness,* who hath so fully attested the far more important Doctrines of Pardon, Grace, and everlasting Life: and taught Men, on this Foundation, not *to be afraid of them that kill the Body; and, after that, have no more that they can do.*

(h) It hath been observed, that this manner of Expression is not to be met with in the Heathen Authors before Christianity: and, therefore, it is one Instance of Scripture Language coming early into common Use.

all speak ill of me.—Is *this* the Evidence you are to give? And will you bring Disgrace upon his Citation, who hath conferred such an Honour upon you, and thought you worthy of being produced as a Witness in such a Cause?

§. 7. But he who hath the Power, hath given Sentence. "*I judge you to be impious and profane.*" —What hath befallen you?—I have been judged to be impious and profane—Any thing else?—Nothing.—Suppose he had pass'd his Judgment upon an hypothetical Proposition, and pronounced it to be a false Conclusion, that, if it be Day, it is light; what would have befallen the Proposition? In this Case, who is judged; who condemned; the Proposition, or he who is deceived, concerning it? Doth he, who hath the Power of pronouncing any thing, concerning you, know, what Pious, or Impious, mean? Hath he made it his Study, or learned it? Where? From whom? A Musician would not regard him, if he pronounced Bass to be Treble: nor a Mathematician, if he pass'd Sentence, that Lines drawn from the Center to the Circle, are not equal. And shall He, who is truly learned, regard an unlearned Man, when he pronounces upon Pious and Impious, Just and Unjust?

§. 8. "Oh the Injuries to which the Learned are exposed!" Is it *here* that you have learn'd this? Why do not you leave such pitiful Reasonings to idle pitiful Fellows (*i*); and let them sit in a Corner, and receive some little sorry Pay; or grumble, that nobody gives them any thing? But do *you* appear, and make use of what you have learn'd. It is not *Reasonings* that are wanted now. On the contrary, Books are stuffed full of Stoical Reasonings. What is wanted, then?

One to apply them; whose Actions may bear Testimony to his Doctrines. Assume me this Character,

(*i*) The mercenary Professors of Philosophy, at that time.

racter, that we may no longer make use of the Examples of the Ancients, in the Schools; but may have some Example of our own.

§. 9. To whom, then, doth the Contemplation of these [speculative Reasonings] belong?

To him, that hath Leisure. For Man is an Animal fond of Contemplation. But it is shameful to take a View of these Things, as run-away Slaves do of a Play: We are to sit quietly, and listen, sometimes to the Actor, and sometimes to the Musician: and not do like those, who come in and praise the Actor, and at the same time look round them every Way: then, if any one happens to name their Master, are frighted out of their Wits, and run off. It is shameful for a Philosopher, thus to contemplate the Works of Nature. Now, what, in this Case, is the Master? Man is not the Master of Man; but Death, and Life, and Pleasure, and Pain: for without these, bring *Cæsar* to me, and you will see how intrepid I shall be. But, if he comes thundering and lightening with *these*; and *these* are the Objects of my Terror; what do I else, but, like the run-away Slave, acknowledge my Master? While I have any Respite from these, as the Fugitive comes into the Theatre, so I bathe, drink, sing; but all, with Terror and Anxiety. But, if I free myself from my Masters, that is, from such Things as render a Master terrible, what Trouble, what Master have I remaining?

§. 10. What, then, are we to publish these Things to all Men?

No. But humour the Vulgar, and say; This poor Man advises me to what he thinks good for himself. I excuse him: for *Socrates*, too, excused the Jailer, who wept when he was to drink the Poison: and said, "How heartily he sheds Tears "for us." Was it to *him* that *Socrates* said, "For "this Reason we sent the Women out of the Way?" No: but to his *Friends*; to such, as were capable of hearing

hearing it; while he humoured the other, as a Child.

CHAPTER XXX.

What we ought to have ready, in difficult Circumstances.

WHEN you are going to any of the Great remember, that there is Another, who sees from Above, what passes; and whom you ought to please, rather than Man. He, therefore, asks you:

In the Schools, what did you use to call Exile, and Prison, and Chains, and Death, and Defamation?

I? Indifferent Things.

What, then, do you call them *now?* Are they at all changed?

No.

Are *you* changed, then?

No.

Tell me, then, what Things are indifferent.

Things independent on Choice.

Tell me the Consequence too.

Things independent on Choice, are nothing to *me*.

Tell me, likewise, what appeared to us, to be the Good of Man.

A right Choice, and a [right] Use of the Appearances of Things.

What his End?

To follow Thee.

Do you the same Things *now*, too?

Yes. I do the same Things, even now.

Well, go in, then, boldly, and mindful of these Things; and he [to whom you are going] will see, what a Youth, who hath studied what he ought, is among Men, who have not. I protest, I imagine you

you will have ſuch Thoughts as theſe: "Why do "we provide ſo many and great Qualifications, for "nothing? Is the Power, the Antechamber, the "Attendants, the Guards, no more than this? Is "it for theſe, that I have liſten'd to ſo many Diſ-"ſertations? Theſe are nothing: and I had qua-"lified myſelf as for ſome great Encounter."

END *of the* FIRST BOOK.

THE

DISCOURSES

OF

EPICTETUS.

BOOK II.

CHAPTER I.

That Courage is not inconſiſtent with Caution.

§. 1. WHAT is aſſerted by the Philoſophers may, perhaps, appear a Paradox to ſome: let us, however, examine, as well as we can, whether this be true; That it is poſſible in all Things, to act at once with Caution and Courage. For Caution ſeems, in ſome meaſure, contrary to Courage: and Contraries are by no means conſiſtent.

The

The Appearance of a Paradox to many, in the present Case, seems to me to arise from something like this: If, indeed, we assert, that Courage and Caution are to be used, in the same Instances, we should justly be accused of uniting Contradictions: but, in the Way that we affirm it, where is the Absurdity? For, if what hath been so often said, and so often demonstrated, be certain, that the Essence of Good and Evil consists in the Use of the Appearances; and that Things independent on Choice, are not of the Nature either of Good or Evil; what Paradox do the Philosophers assert, if they say: "Where Things are not dependent on "Choice, be courageous: where they are, be "cautious?" For in these only, if Evil consists in a bad Choice, is Caution to be used. And if Things independent on Choice, and not in our Power, are nothing to us, in these we are to make use of Courage. Thus we shall be at once cautious and courageous: and, indeed, courageous on the Account of this very Caution; for by using Caution with regard to things really evil, we shall gain Courage, with regard to what are not so.

§. 2. But we are in the same Condition as [hunted] Deer: when these, in a Fright, fly from the Feathers (*a*), where do they turn, and to what do they retire for Safety? To the Toils And thus they are undone, by inverting the Objects of Fear and Confidence. Thus we, too, In what Instances do we make use of Fear? In Things independent on Choice. In what, on the other hand, do we behave with Courage, as if there were nothing to be dreaded? In Things dependent on Choice. To be deceived then, or to act rashly or impudently, or to indulge an ignominious Desire, is of no Importance

(*a*) This was a Kind of Scare-crow, formed of different coloured Feathers, by which the Animal was terrified, and so driven into the Net: which was the ancient Manner of Hunting.

Importance to us, if we do but take a good Aim, in Things independent on Choice. But where Death, or Exile, or Pain, or Ignominy, are concerned, there is the Retreat, there, the Flutter and Fright. Hence, as it muſt be with thoſe who err in Matters of the greateſt Importance, what is naturally Courage, we render bold, deſperate, raſh, and impudent: and what is naturally Caution, timid and baſe, and full of Fears and Perturbations. For if a Perſon was to transfer Caution to Choice, and the Actions of Choice, by a Willingneſs to be cautious, he will, at the ſame time, have it in his Power to avoid [what he guards againſt:] but if he transfers it to Things not in our Power, or Choice, by fixing his Averſion on what is not in our own Power, but dependent on others, he will neceſſarily fear; he will be hurried; will be diſturbed. For it is not Death, or Pain, that is to be feared; but the *Fear* of Pain, or Death. Hence we commend him who ſays;

Death is no Ill, but ſhamefully *to die.*

Courage, then, ought to be oppoſed to Death, and Caution to the Fear of Death: whereas *we*, on the contrary, oppoſe to Death, Flight; and to our Principle concerning it, Careleſſneſs, and Deſperateneſs, and Indifference.

§. 3. *Socrates* uſed, very properly, to call theſe Things Vizards: for, as Maſks appear ſhocking and formidable to Children, from their Inexperience; we are affected in like manner, with regard to Things, for no other Reaſon, than as Children are, with regard to Vizards. For what is a Child? Ignorance. What is a Child? Want of Learning: for, ſo far as the Knowledge of Children extends, they are not inferior to us. What is Death? A Vizard. Turn it, and be convinced. See, it doth not bite. This little body and Spirit muſt be ſeparated (as they formerly were) either now, or hereafter: why, then, are you displeased if it be now? For if not *now*, it will be hereafter. Why? To complete the Revolution of the World: for that hath need of some Things present, others to come, and others already completed. What is Pain? A Vizard. Turn it, and be convinced.

This paultry Flesh is sometimes affected by harsh, sometimes by smooth Impressions. If suffering be not worth your while, the Door is open; if it be, bear it: for it was fit the Door should be open, against all Accidents. And thus we have no Trouble.

§. 4. What, then, is the Fruit of these Principles? What it ought to be; the most noble, and the most becoming the Truly Educated (*b*), Tranquillity, Security, Freedom. For in this Case, we are not to give Credit to the Many, who say, that none ought to be educated but the Free; but rather to the Philosophers, who say, that the Well-educated alone are free.

How so?

Thus: Is Freedom any thing else, than the Power of Living as we like?

Nothing else.

Well: tell me then, do you like to live in Error?

We

(*b*) Παιδεια, in *Greek*, means nearly the same Thing, as what we now call *liberal Education*. It was that Sort of Education peculiar to Gentlemen; that is, such as were free; and of which the Slaves, or lower Sort of People, were forbid to partake, according to the Systems of some Legislators. Such (as well as I can remember) was the Case among the *Lacedemonians*, and amongst the ancient *Persians*, till the Time of *Cyrus*.

It must be observed, that the Words Educated, Free, King, and many others, were taken by the Stoics from common Life; and by them applied solely to the Character of their wise, and perfect Man.

The Translator is obliged for this Note, as well as for many other valuable Hints, to Mr. HARRIS; so well known for many Works of Literature and Genius.

We do not. No one, sure, that lives in Error, (*c*) is free.

Do you like to live in Fear? Do you like to live in Sorrow? Do you like to live in Perturbation?

By no means.

No one, therefore, in a State of Fear, or Sorrow, or Perturbation, is free: but whoever is delivered from Sorrow, Fear, and Perturbation, by the same means is delivered likewise from Slavery. How shall we believe you, then, good Legislators, when you say; "We allow none to be educated, but "the Free?" For the Philosophers say; "We "allow none to be free, but the Liberally-edu-"cated:" that is, God doth not allow it.

What, then, when any Person hath turned his Slave (*d*) about before the Consul, hath he done nothing?

Yes, he hath.

What?

He hath turned his Slave about, before the Consul.

Nothing more?

Yes. He pays a (*d*) Fine for him.

Well then: is not the Man, who hath gone through this Ceremony, rendered free?

No more than [he is rendered] exempt from Perturbation. Pray, have you, who are able to give this Freedom to others, no Master of your own? Are not you a Slave to Money? To a Girl?

(*c*) *And ye shall know the Truth, and the Truth shall make you free.* John viii. 32. This is one, among many other Passages to the same Purpose, in that *perfect Law of Liberty,* the New Testament.

(*d*) When a Slave was to be presented with his Freedom, he was brought before the Consul; and his Master, taking him by the Hand, pronounced a certain Form of Words, and then turned the Slave about, who was thus rendered free. The Fine which the Master was to pay on this Occasion, was applied to the public Use. UPTON.

To a Boy? To a Tyrant? To ſome Friend of a Tyrant? Elſe, why do you tremble when *any* of theſe is in queſtion? Therefore, I ſo often repeat to you, Let this be your Study; have this always at hand; in what it is neceſſary to be courageous, and in what cautious: courageous, in what doth not depend on Choice; cautious, in what doth.

§. 5. *(e)* But have not I read my Papers to you? Do not you know what I am doing?

In what?

In my Eſſays.

Show me in what State you are, as to Deſire and Averſion. Whether you do not fail of what you wiſh, and incur what you would avoid: but, as to theſe common-place Eſſays, if you are wiſe, you will take them, and obliterate them.

Why, did not *Socrates* write?

Yes: who *(f)* ſo much? But how? As he had not always one at hand, to argue againſt his Principles, or be argued againſt in his Turn, he argued with, and examined, himſelf; and always treated, at leaſt, ſome one natural Notion, in a manner fitted for the Uſe of Life. Theſe are the Things which a Philoſopher writes: but for ſuch *(g)* common-

(e) This ſeems to be ſpoken by one of the Scholars.

(f) No other ancient Author mentions *Socrates*, as having written any Thing, except a Hymn to *Apollo*, and a Tranſlation of ſome Fables of *Æſop* into Verſe. Many Authors of Credit affirm, that he wrote nothing. Therefore *Wolfius* doubts, whether ſome other Name ſhould not be put here, inſtead of *Socrates*. Yet the Deſcription moſt properly belongs to him. And, perhaps, *Epictetus* doth not mean to intimate here, that *Socrates* had publiſhed any thing: but that he wrote, when he had no Opportunity of diſcourſing, for his own Improvement. But ſtill, living conſtantly at *Athens*, the Seat of philoſophical Diſputation, he cannot be ſuppoſed, often to have had that Reaſon for Writing.

(g) The Original here ſeems corrupt, or inaccurate. I hope the Tranſlation is not far from the true Senſe.

mon-place Essays as those I am speaking of, he leaves to the Insensible, or to the happy Creatures whom Idleness (*h*) furnishes with Leisure; or to such as are too weak to regard Consequences. And will you, when you are gone from hence (*i*), which the Time now calls for, be fond of showing, and reading, and be ridiculously conceited, of these Things?

Pray see, how I compose Dialogues.

Talk not of that, Man; but rather be able to say; See, how I avoid being disappointed of my Desire: see, how I secure myself against incurring my Aversion. Set Death before me; set Pain, set a Prison, set Ignominy, set Condemnation before me; and you will know me. This is the [proper] Ostentation of a young Man come out from the Schools. Leave the rest to others. Let no one ever hear you utter a Word about them: nor suffer it, if any one commends you for them: but think that you are nobody, and that you know nothing. Appear to know only this, how you may never be disappointed of your Desire; never incur your Aversion. Let others study Causes, Problems, and Syllogisms. Do *you* study Death, Chains, Torture, Exile (*k*): and all these,

 with

(*h*) The *Greek* is Αταραξια, Tranquillity: but it seems to be false Reading for Απραξια. Αταραξια is the very Thing which *Epictetus* had been recommending through the whole Chapter, and which makes the Subject of the next; and, therefore, cannot be well supposed to be the true Reading in a Place, where it is mentioned with Contempt.

(*i*) For επελθων, perhaps, the Reading should be απελθων; and it is so translated. The Person to whom *Epictetus* speaks, was a young Man just leaving the philosophical School.

(*k*) Some *English* Readers, too happy to comprehend how Chains, Torture, Exile, and sudden Executions, can be ranked among the common Accidents of Life, may be surprized to find *Epictetus* so frequently endeavouring to prepare his Hearers for them. But it must be recollected, that he addressed himself to Persons, who lived under the *Roman* Emperors; from whose Tyranny, the very best of Men were perpetually liable to such Kind of Dangers.

with Courage, and Reliance upon Him who hath called you to them, and judged you worthy a Post, in which you may show, what the rational governing Faculty can do, when set in Array, against Powers independent on the Choice. And thus, this Paradox becomes neither impossible, nor a Paradox, that we must be at once cautious and courageous: courageous, in what doth not depend upon Choice; and cautious, in what doth.

CHAPTER II.

Of Tranquillity.

CONSIDER, you who are going to take your Tryal, what you wish to preserve, and in what to succeed. For if you wish to preserve a Choice conformable to Nature, you are intirely safe: every thing goes well; you have no Trouble on your Hands. While you wish to preserve what is in your own Power, and which is naturally free, and are contented with that, whom have you longer to care for? For who is the Master of Things like these? Who can take them away? If you wish to be a Man of Honour and Fidelity, who shall prevent you? If you wish not to be restrained, or compelled, who shall compel you to Desires, contrary to your Principles; to Aversions, contrary to your Opinion? The Judge, perhaps, will pass a Sentence against you, which he thinks formidable: but how can he likewise make you receive it with Aversion? Since, then, Desire and Aversion are in your own Power, what have you else to care for? Let this be your Introduction; this your Narration; this your Proof; this your Victory; this your Conclusion; and this your Applause. Thus *Socrates*, to one who put him in mind to prepare himself for his Tryal; "Do not you think, says he, that I "have

"have been preparing myself for this very Thing "my whole Life?"—By what kind of Preparation?—"I have preserved what was in my own "Power."—What do you mean?—"I have done "nothing unjust, either in public, or in private "Life."

§. 2. But if you wish to preserve Externals too; your paultry Body, your Estate, or Dignity; I advise you immediately to prepare yourself by every possible Preparation; and besides, consider the Disposition of your Judge, and of your Adversary. If it be necessary to fall down at his Feet; fall down at his Feet: if to weep, weep: if to groan; groan. For when you have subjected what is in your own Power to Externals, submit to Slavery at once, and do not struggle; and at one time, be willing to be a Slave, and at another, not willing: but simply, and with your whole Intention, be one or the other; free, or a Slave; well-educated, or not; a Game Cock, or a Craven: either bear to be beat till you die, or give out at once; and do not be soundly beat first, and then give out at last. If both these be shameful, make the Distinction immediately.

§. 3. Where is the Nature of Good and Evil? Where Truth likewise is. Where Truth and where Nature are (*a*), there is Caution: where Truth and where Nature are not, there is Courage. Why, do you think, that if *Socrates* had wished to preserve Externals, that he would have said, when he appeared at his Trial, "*Anytus* and *Melitus* may indeed kill; but hurt me they cannot?" Was he so foolish, as not to see that this Way doth not

(*a*) This Passage is perplexed in the *Greek*, and the Translation conjectural. The Meaning seems to be, that where our moral Conduct is concerned, Caution is necessary; and Courage is necessary in Things not dependent on our own Choice; and with which, according to the Stoic Principle, Truth and Nature have nothing to do.

lead to that End, but the contrary? What, then, is the Reason, that he not only disregards, but provokes his Judges? Thus my Friend *Heraclitus*, in a trifling Suit, about a little Estate at *Rhodes*, after having proved to the Judges that his Cause was good, when he came to the Conclusion of his Speech; "I will not intreat you, says he; nor care "what Judgment you give: for it is rather *you* "who are to be judged, than *I*." And thus he lost his Suit. What need was there of this? Be content not to intreat: do not *tell* them too, that you will not intreat; unless it be a proper Time to provoke the Judges designedly; as in the Case of *Socrates*. But if you too are preparing for such a speech, what do you wait for? Why do you submit to be tried? For if you wish to be hanged, have Patience and the Gibbet will come. But if you chuse rather to submit, and make your Defence as well as you can, all the rest is to be ordered accordingly; with a due Regard, however, to the Preservation of your own Character.

§. 4. For this Reason it is ridiculous too to say, "Suggest to me what is to be done." How should I know what to suggest to you? [You should rather say] inform my understanding to accommodate itself to whatever may be the Event. The former is just as if an illiterate Person should say, "Tell "me what to write, when any Name is proposed to me;" and I direct him to write *Dion*; and then another comes, and proposes to him the Name not of *Dion*, but of *Theon*; what will be Consequence? What will he write? Whereas, if you had made Writing your Study, you would be ready prepared for whatever Word might occur: if not, how can I suggest to you? For, if the Circumstances of the Affair should suggest something else, what will you say, or how will you act? Remember, then, the general Rule, and you will need no Suggestion; but if you gape after Externals, you must necessarily

rily be toſs'd up and down, according to the Inclination of your Maſter.

And who is my Maſter?

He in whoſe Power, is placed whatever you ſtrive to acquire, or would avoid.

CHAPTER III.

Concerning ſuch as recommend Perſons to the Philoſophers.

§. 1. DIOGENES rightly anſwered one, who deſired Letters of Recommendation from him, "At firſt ſight he will know you to be a "Man; and whether you are a good or a bad Man, "if he hath any ſkill in diſtinguiſhing, he will "know likewiſe: and, if he hath not, he will never know it, though I ſhould write a thouſand "times (*a*)." Juſt as if you were a Piece of Coin, and ſhould deſire to be recommended to any Perſon as good, in order to be tried: if it be to an Aſſayer, he will know your Value; for you will recommend yourſelf.

§. 2. We ought, therefore, in Life alſo, to have ſomething analogous to this Skill in Gold; that one may be able to ſay, like the Aſſayer, Bring me whatever Piece you will, and I will find out its Value: or, as I would ſay with regard to Syllogiſms, Bring me whomever you will, and I will diſtinguiſh for you, whether he knows how to ſolve Syllogiſms, or not. Why? Becauſe I can ſolve Syllogiſms myſelf, and have that Faculty, which is neceſſary for one who knows how to find out Perſons ſkilled in the Solution of Syllogiſms. But how do I act in Life? I at ſometimes call a Thing good; at others, bad. What is the Cauſe of this? The contrary to what happens in Syllogiſms; Ignorance, and Inexperience. CHAP-

(*a*) This is one of the many extravagant Refinements of the Philoſophers; and might lead Perſons into very dangerous Miſtakes, if it was laid down as a Maxim, in ordinary Life.

CHAPTER IV.

Concerning a Person, who had been guilty of Adultery.

§. 1. AS he was ſaying, that Man is made for Fidelity; and that whoever ſubverts this, ſubverts the peculiar Property of Man; one of thoſe who paſs for Men of Literature happened to come in, who had been found guilty of Adultery, in that City. But, continues *Epictetus*, if, laying aſide that Fidelity for which we were born, we form Deſigns againſt the Wife of our Neighbour, what do we do? What elſe but deſtroy and ruin—What? Fidelity, Honour, and Sanctity of Manners.——Only theſe? And do not we ruin Neighbourhood? Friendſhip? Our Country? In what Rank do we place ourſelves? How am I to conſider you, Sir? As a Neighbour? A Friend? What Sort of one? As a Citizen? How ſhall I truſt you? Indeed, if you were ſome ſorry Veſſel, ſo noiſome that no Uſe could be made of you; you might be thrown on a Dunghill, and no Mortal would take the Trouble to pick you up: but if, being a *Man*, you cannot fill any one Place in human Society, what ſhall we do with you? For, ſuppoſe you cannot hold the Place of a Friend, can you hold even that of a Slave? And who will truſt you? Why, then, ſhould not you alſo be contented to be thrown upon ſome Dunghill, as a uſeleſs Veſſel, and indeed as mere Dung? Will you ſay, after this, Hath no one any Regard for *me*, a Man of Letters? Why, you are wicked, and fit for no Uſe. Juſt as if Waſps ſhould take it ill that no one hath any Regard for them; but all ſhun, and whoever can, beats them down. You have ſuch a Sting, that whoever you ſtrike with it, is thrown into Troubles and Pangs. What would you have us do with you? There is no-where to place you.

§. 2.

§. 2. What, then, are not Women, by Nature, common?

I admit it: and ſo is a Pig at Table common to thoſe who are invited. But, after it is diſtributed, go, if you think proper, and ſnatch away the Share of him who ſits next you; or ſlily ſteal it, or ſtretch out your Hand, and taſte; and, if you cannot tear away any of the Meat, dip your Fingers and lick them. A fine Companion! A *Socratic* Gueſt indeed! Again: Is not the Theatre common to all Citizens? Therefore come, when all are ſeated, if you think proper, and turn any one of them out of his Place. Thus Women are common by Nature: but when the Legiſlator, like the Maſter of an Entertainment, diſtributes them, will not you, like the reſt of the Company, be contented with deſiring a Share for yourſelf; but muſt you pilfer, and taſte what belongs to another?

But I am a Man of Letters, and underſtand *Archedemus* (*a*).

With all your Underſtanding of *Archedemus*, then, be an Adulterer, and a Rogue: And, inſtead of a Man, a Wolf, or an Ape. For where is the Difference?

CHAPTER V.

How Magnanimity may be conſiſtent with Care.

§. 1. THE *Materials* of Action are indifferent: but the *Uſe* of them is not indifferent.

How, then, ſhall one preſerve Intrepidity and Tranquillity; and at the ſame time be careful, and neither raſh, nor indolent.

By imitating thoſe who play at Tables. The Dice are indifferent; the Pieces are indifferent. How do I know what will fall out? But it is my Buſineſs, to manage carefully and dextrouſly whatever

(*a*) A Stoic Philoſopher, of *Tarſus*, in *Cilicia*. UPTON.

ever doth fall out. Thus in Life too, this is the chief Business: distinguish, and separate Things; and say, "Externals are not in my Power; Choice "is. Where shall I seek Good and Evil? Within; "in what is my own." But in what belongs to others, call nothing Good, or Evil, or Profit, or Hurt, or any thing of that Sort.

§ 2. What then, are we to treat these, in a careless Way?

By no means: for this, on the other hand, is an evil Exercise of the Faculty of Choice; and on that (*b*) account, against Nature. But we are to act with Care, because the *Use* of the Materials [of Action] is not indifferent; and at the same time with Intrepidity and Tranquillity, because the *Materials* themselves are indifferent. For where a Thing is not indifferent, there no one can restrain or compell me. Where I am capable of being restrained, or compelled, the Acquisition doth not depend upon me; nor is either good or evil. The *Use* of it, indeed, is either good or evil; but that *doth* depend upon me. It is difficult, I own, to blend and unite [in one Character] the Carefulness of one who is affected by the Materials of Action, and the Intrepidity of one who disregards them; but it is not impossible: if it be, it is impossible to be happy. How do we act in a Voyage? What is in my Power? To chuse the Pilot, the Sailors, the Day, the Time of Day. Afterwards comes a Storm. What have I to care for? My Part is performed. The Subject belongs to another, to the Pilot. But the Ship is sinking: What then have I to do? That which alone I can do; I am drowned, without Fear, without Clamour, or accusing God; but as one who knows, that what is born, must likewise die. For I am not Eternity, but a Man; a Part of the Whole, as an Hour is of the Day. I must come like an Hour, and like an Hour must pass away. What signifies it whether by

(*b*) The Translation follows Mr. *Upton*'s Conjecture.

by Drowning, or by a Fever? For, in ſome Way or other, paſs I muſt.

§. 3. This you may ſee to be the Practice of thoſe, who play ſkilfully at Ball. No one contends for the Ball [itſelf], as either a Good or an Evil; but how he may throw, and catch it again. Here lies the Addreſs, here the Art, the Nimbleneſs, the Sagacity; that I may not be able to catch it, even if I hold up my Lap for it; another may catch it, whenever I throw it. But if we catch or throw it, with Fear or Perturbation, what Kind of Play will this be? How ſhall we keep ourſelves ſteady; or how ſee the Order of the Game? One will ſay, Throw: another, Do not throw: a Third, You have thrown once already. This is a mere Quarrel; not a Play. Therefore *Socrates* well underſtood playing at Ball.

What do you mean?

Uſing Pleaſantry at his Trial. "Tell me, ſays "he, *Anytus*, how can you ſay, that I do not be-"lieve a God? What do you think Demons "are? (*c*) Are they not either the Offspring of "the Gods, or compounded of Gods and Men?" ——"Yes."——Do you think, then, that one "can believe there are Mules, and not believe, that "there are Aſſes?" This was juſt as if he had been playing at Ball. And what was the Ball he had

(*c*) *Socrates* profeſſed himſelf to have a good Demon; and argues here jocularly from thence, that he muſt believe the Exiſtence of a Deity: as he who believes there are Mules, muſt believe there are Aſſes; becauſe that Species enters into the Compoſition of the other. But there is a Play upon the Words in the Original, which cannot be preſerved in the Tranſlation. One cannot, I think, help regretting, that *Plato* ſhould relate, and *Epictetus* approve, a Witticiſm unworthy of the *Attic* Genius; and an Inſtance of Levity, on ſo awful a Subject, unbecoming the Character of the wiſe and pious *Socrates*. It may, however, be ſome Excuſe, that he thought neither his Accuſer, nor his Judges deſerved, or were likely to be influenced by, a more ſerious Anſwer.

had to play with? Life, Chains, Exile, a Draught of Poiſon, Separation from a Wife, and the Deſertion of Orphan Children. Theſe were what he had to play with; and yet, nevertheleſs, he did play, and threw the Ball with Addreſs. Thus we ſhould be careful how we play; but indifferent, as to the Ball itſelf. We are by all means to manage external Materials with Art; not taking them for ourſelves; but ſhowing our Art about them, whatever they may happen to be. Thus a Weaver doth not make the Wool: but employs his Art upon what is given him. It is another who gives you Food, and a Property: and may take them away, and your paultry Body too. Do you, however, work upon the Materials you have received; and then, if you come off unhurt, others, no doubt, who meet you, will congratulate you on your Eſcape. But he who hath a clearer Inſight into ſuch Things, if he ſees [indeed] you have behaved in a becoming Manner, will praiſe and congratulate you: but, if you owe your Eſcape to any unbecoming Action, the contrary. For where there is a reaſonable Cauſe of Rejoicing, there is likewiſe [a reaſonable Cauſe] of Congratulation.

§. 4. How, then, are ſome external Things ſaid to be according to Nature; others contrary to it?

When we are conſidered as unconnected Individuals. I will allow it is natural for the Foot, [for Inſtance,] to be clean. But if you take it as a Foot, and not as an unconnected individual Thing, it will be fit that it ſhould walk in the Dirt, and tread upon Thorns; and ſometimes that it ſhould even be cut off, for the Good of the Whole: otherwiſe it is no longer a Foot. We ſhould reaſon in ſome ſuch manner concerning ourſelves. What are you? A Man. If then, indeed, you conſider yourſelf, as an unconnected Individual, it is natural that you ſhould

ſhould live to old Age; be rich, and healthy: but if you conſider yourſelf as a Man, and as a Part of the Whole, it will be fit, on the Account of that Whole, that you ſhould at one time be ſick; at another, take a Voyage, and be expoſed to Danger: ſometimes be in Want; and poſſibly it may happen, die before your Time. Why, then, are you diſpleaſed? Do not you know, that elſe, as the other is no longer a Foot, ſo you are no longer a Man? For what is a Man? A Part of a Commonwealth; principally of that which conſiſts of Gods and Men; and next, of that to which you immediately belong, which is a Miniature of the univerſal City.

§. 5. What then, muſt I, at one Time, be called to a Trial; muſt another, at another Time, be ſcorched by a Fever; another be expoſed to the Sea; another die; and another be condemned?

Yes: for it is impoſſible, in ſuch a Body, in ſuch a World, and among ſuch Companions, but that ſome or other of us muſt fall into ſuch Circumſtances. (*d*) Your Buſineſs, when you come into them, is, to ſay what you ought, to order Things as you can. Then ſays one, "I decide that you have acted unjuſtly." Much Good may it do you; I have done *my* Part. You are to look to it, whether you have done *yours*: for there is ſome Danger of that too, let me tell you.

CHAPTER VI.

Of Indifference.

§. 1. A Hypothetical Propoſition is an indifferent Thing; but the Judgment concerning it, is not indifferent: but is either Knowledge, or Opinion,

(*d*) See p. 3. Note *c*.

Opinion, or Miſtake. Thus Life is indifferent; the *Uſe* of it not indifferent. When you are told, therefore, that theſe Things are indifferent, do not, upon that account, ever be careleſs; nor, when you are excited to Carefulneſs, be abject, and ſtruck by the Admiration of the Materials of Action. It is good to know your own Qualifications and Powers; that, where you are not qualified, you may be quiet, and not angry that others have the Advantage of you, in ſuch Things. For you too, [in your Turn,] will think it reaſonable, that you ſhould have the Advantage in the Art of Syllogiſms: and, if others ſhould be angry at it, you will tell them, by way of Conſolation, "*I* have learned it, and *you* have "not." Thus too, where-ever Practice is neceſſary, do not pretend to what can be attained no other Way; but leave the Matter to thoſe who are practiſed in it, and do you be contented with a compoſed Firmneſs of Mind. "Go, for Inſtance, "and pay your Compliments to ſuch a Perſon." "How?" "Not meanly."——"But I have "been ſhut out; for I have not learned to get in at "the Window: and, finding the Door ſhut, I muſt "neceſſarily either go back, or get in at the Win-"dow." "But ſpeak to him too." "I will ſpeak "to him." "In what manner?" "Not meanly." But you have not ſucceeded; for this was not *your* Buſineſs, but *his*. Why do you claim what belongs to another? Always remember what is your own, and what is another's; and you will never be diſturbed.

§. 2. Hence *Chryſippus* rightly ſays; While Conſequences are uncertain, I will keep to thoſe Things which are beſt adapted to the Attainment of what is conformable to Nature: for God himſelf hath formed me to chuſe this. If I knew, that it was now deſtined for me to be ſick, I would even exert my Purſuits towards it: for even the Foot, if it had Underſtanding, would exert itſelf to get into the Dirt.

For

For why are Ears of Corn produced, if it be not to ripen? and why do they ripen, if not to be reaped? For they are not separate Individuals. If they were capable of Senſe, do you think they would wiſh never to be reaped? It would be a Curſe upon Ears of Corn, not to be reaped: and we ought to know, that it would be a Curſe upon Man, not to die; like that of not ripening, and not being reaped. Since, then, it is neceſſary for us to be reaped, and we have, at the ſame time, Underſtanding to know it, are we angry at it? This is only becauſe we neither know what we are, nor have ſtudied what belongs to Man, as Jockies do, what belongs to Horſes. Yet *Chryſantas* when he was about to ſtrike an Enemy, on hearing the Trumpet ſound a Retreat, drew back his Hand: for he thought it more eligible to obey the Command of his General, than his own Inclination *(a)*. But not one of *us*, even when Neceſſity calls, is ready and willing to obey it: but we ſuffer, whatever Things we do ſuffer, weeping and groaning, and calling them our Circumſtances *(b)*. What Circumſtances, Man? For if you call what ſurrounds you, *Circumſtances*, every thing is a *Circumſtance*: but, if you apply this Name to Hardſhips, where is the Hardſhip, that whatever is born muſt die. The Inſtrument is either a Sword, or a Wheel, or the Sea, or a Tile, or a Tyrant. And what doth it ſignify to you, by what Way you deſcend to Hades? All are equal: but, if you would hear the Truth, the ſhorteſt is that by which a Tyrant ſends you. No Tyrant was ever ſix

(a) In a Speech which *Cyrus* made to his Soldiers, after the Battle with the *Aſſyrians*, he mentions *Chryſantas*, one of his Captains, with particular Honour, for this Inſtance of his Obedience. Xenoph. L. iv.

(b) Περιστασεις, in *Greek*, hath a double Meaning, which cannot be preſerved in a Tranſlation. It ſignifies both in general, Circumſtances, and in particular, hard Circumſtances, or Difficulties.

Months, in cutting any Man's Throat: but a Fever is often a Year [in killing.] All these Things are mere Sound, and the Pomp of empty Names.

My Life is in Danger from *Cæsar*.

And am not *I* in Danger, who dwell at *Nicopolis*, where there are so many Earthquakes? And when you yourself cross the *Adriatic* (c), what is then in Danger? Is not your Life?

Ay: but I am in Danger, with respect to Opinion.

What, your own? How so? Can any one compel you to have any Opinion, contrary to your own Inclination?

But the Opinions of others too.

And what Danger is it of *yours*, if others have false Opinions?

But I am in Danger of being banished.

What is it to be banished? To be some-where else than at *Rome*.

Yes: but what if I should be sent to *Gyaros*?

If it be worth your while, you will go: if not, you have another Place to go to; where he, who now sends you to *Gyaros*, must go likewise, whether he will or not (d). Why, then, do you come to these, as to great Trials? They are not equal to your Qualifications. So that an ingenuous young Man would say, It was not worth while for this, to have read, and writ, so much, and to have sat so long, listening to a good-for-nothing old Fellow. Only remember, that Division, by which your *own*, and *not* your own, is distinguished, and you will never claim

(c) *Epictetus* probably means, in the Way Home, from *Nicopolis* to *Rome*; whence this Person had come to hear him.

(d) How gloomy, how empty the Stoic Consolation! How differently would the Christian answer. "Well, and can he "banish you from the Presence of your true Sovereign, your "indulgent Father, your best Friend? And what, then, is "*Gyaros* worse than *Rome*? You, behaving well in Adversity, "are the Object of Almighty Protection and future Reward: "he, amidst his Tyranny, accountable to an offended Judge."

claim what belongs to others. A Tribunal, and a Prison, is, each of them, a Place; one high, the other low: but Choice is equal: and if you have a mind to keep it equal for both Places, it may be kept. We shall then become Imitators of *Socrates*, when, even in a Prison, we are able to write Hymns (*e*) of Praise: but, as we now are, consider whether we could bear, that even another should say to us in a Prison, "Shall I read you a Hymn of "Praise?"——"Why do you trouble me: do you "know in what a sad Situation I am?" In such "Circumstances, am I able to hear Hymns?"——"What Circumstances?"——"I am going to "die."——"And are all other Men to be im-"mortal?"

CHAPTER VII.

Of Divination.

§. 1. FROM an unseasonable Regard to Divination, we omit many Duties (*a*). For what can the Diviner see, besides Death, or Danger, or Sickness, or, in short, Things of this Kind? When it is necessary, then, to expose one's self to Danger for a Friend, or even a Duty to die for him, what Occasion have I for Divination? Have not I a Diviner within, who hath told me the Essence of Good and Evil; and who explains to me the Indications of both? What further Need, then, have I of the Entrails [of Victims], or [the Flight] of Birds? Can I bear with the other Diviner, when he says, "This is for your Interest?"

(*e*) *Socrates* writ a Hymn to *Apollo*, when he was in Prison; of which *Diogenes Laertius* recites the first Line. See the Behaviour of *Paul* and *Silas* on a parallel Occasion. *Acts* xvi. 25.

(*a*) The Stoics were Advocates for Divination; though they condemned, what they deemed, the Abuses of it. The 32d Chapter of the *Enchiridion* is on the same Subject.

For doth *he* know what is for my Intereſt? Doth he know what Good is? Hath he learned the Indications of Good and Evil, as he hath thoſe of the Victims? If ſo, he knows the Indications likewiſe of Fair and Baſe, Juſt and Unjuſt. Do you tell me, Sir, what is indicated to me? Life or Death; Riches or Poverty. But whether theſe Things are for my Intereſt, or not, I ſhall not inquire of *you*. "Why?" Becauſe you do not give your Opinion about Grammar [or any eſtabliſhed Point of Knowledge]; and do you give it here, in Things about which we all take different Ways, and diſpute with one another? Therefore the Lady, who was going to ſend a Month's Proviſion to *Gratilla (b)*, in her Baniſhment, made a right Anſwer to one, who told her *Domitian* would ſeize it: I had rather, ſays ſhe, that he ſhould ſeize it, than I not ſend it.

§. 2. What, then, is it that leads us ſo often to Divination? Cowardice; the Dread of Events. Hence we flatter the Diviners. "Pray, Sir, ſhall I "inherit my Father's Eſtate?"——"Let us ſee: "let us ſacrifice upon the Occaſion."——"Nay, "Sir, juſt as Fortune pleaſes." Then, if he ſays, "You ſhall inherit it, we give him Thanks, as if we received the Inheritance from *him*. The Conſequence of this is, that they play upon us.

§. 3. What, then, is to be done?

We ſhould come without previous Deſire or Averſion. As a Traveller inquires the Road of the Perſon he meets, without any Deſire for that which turns to the right Hand, more than to the Left: for he wiſhes for neither of theſe; but that only which leads him properly. Thus we ſhould come to God, as to a Guide. Juſt as we make uſe of our Eyes: not perſuading them to ſhow us one Object rather than another; but receiving ſuch as they preſent

(*b*) A Lady of high Rank at *Rome*, baniſhed from *Italy*, among many other noble Perſons, by *Domitian*.

present to us. But now we hold the Bird with Fear and Trembling: and, in our Invocations to God, intreat him; "Lord have Mercy upon me: suffer "me to come off safe." You, Wretch! would you have any thing then, but what is best? And what is best, but what pleases God? Why do you, as far as in you lies, corrupt your Judge, and seduce your Adviser?

CHAPTER VIII.

Wherein consists the Essence of Good.

§. 1. GOD is beneficial. Good is also beneficial. It should seem, then, that where the Essence of God is, there too is the Essence of Good. What then is the Essence of God? Flesh? ——By no means. An Estate?——Fame?——By no means. Intelligence? Knowledge? Right Reason?——Certainly. Here then, without more ado, seek the Essence of Good. For, do you seek it in a Plant?——No.——Or in a Brute?——No. ———If then you seek it only in a rational Subject, why do you seek it any where but in what is distinct from Irrationals? Plants have not the Use of the Appearances of Things; and therefore you do not apply the Term *Good* to them.———*Good*, then, requires the Use of these Appearances. And nothing else? If so, you may say, that Good, and Happiness, and Unhappiness, belong to mere Animals. But this you do not say; and you are right: for, how much soever they have the Use of the Appearances of Things, they have not the Faculty of understanding that Use; and with good Reason: for they are made to be subservient to others, and not Principals themselves. Why was an Ass made? Was it as a Principal? No: but because we had need of a Back able to carry Burthens. We had need too that he should walk;

therefore he had the Use of the Appearances of Things added; otherwise he could not have walked. But here his Endowments end: for, if an Understanding of that Use had been likewise added, he would not, in Reason, have been subject to us, nor have done us these Services; but would have been like, and equal to ourselves. Why will you not, therefore, seek the Essence of Good in that, without which, you will not say, there can be Good in any thing?

§. 2. What then? Are not these likewise the Works of the Gods? They are: but not Principals, nor Parts of the Gods. But you are a Principal. You are a distinct Portion of the Essence of God; and contain a certain Part of him in yourself (*a*). Why then are you ignorant of your noble Birth? Why do not you consider, whence you came? why do not you remember, when you are eating, who you are who eat; and whom you feed? When you are in the Company of Women; when you are conversing; when you are exercising; when you are disputing; do not you know, that it is a God you feed; a God you exercise? You carry a God about with you, Wretch, and know nothing of it. Do you suppose I mean some God without you of Gold or Silver? It is within yourself you carry him; and profane him, without being sensible of it, by impure Thoughts, and unclean Actions. If even the Image of God were present, you

(*a*) See Introduction, §. 19.
See 1 *Cor.* vi. 19. 2 *Cor.* vi. 16. 2 *Tim.* i. 14. 1 *John* iii. 24. iv. 12, 13. But though the simple Expression of carrying God about with us, may seem to have some nearly parallel to it in the New Testament, yet those represent the Almighty in a more venerable Manner; as taking the Hearts of Good Men for a Temple to dwell in. But the other Expressions here of Feeding and Exercising God, and the Whole of the Paragraph, and indeed of the Stoic System, shew the real Sense of even its more decent Phrases to be vastly different from that of Scripture.

you would not dare to act as you do: and when God himſelf is within you, and hears and ſees all, are not you aſhamed to think and act thus; inſenſible of your own Nature, and hateful to God?

§. 3. After all, why are we afraid, when we ſend a young Man from the School, into Action, that he ſhould behave indecently, eat indecently, converſe indecently with Women: that he ſhould either debaſe himſelf by a ſhabby Dreſs, or clothe himſelf too finely? Doth not he know the God within him? Doth not he know with whom he ſets out? Have we Patience to hear him ſay, "I "wiſh to have *you* with me."

Have you not *God?* Do you ſeek any other, while you have *him?* Or will He tell you any other than theſe things? If you were a Statue of *Phidias*, either *Jupiter* or *Minerva*, you would remember both yourſelf and the Artiſt; and, if you had any Senſe, you would endeavour to do nothing unworthy of him who formed you, or of yourſelf: nor to appear in an unbecoming Manner, to Spectators. And are you now careleſs how you appear, becauſe you are the Workmanſhip of *Jupiter?* And yet, what Compariſon is there, either between the Artiſts, or the Things they have formed? What Work of any [human] Artiſt contains in itſelf, thoſe Faculties which are ſhown, in forming it? Is it any thing but Marble, or Braſs, or Gold, or Ivory? And the *Minerva* of *Phidias*, when its Hand is once extended, and a *Victory* placed in it, remains in that Attitude, for ever. But the Works of God are indued with Motion, Breath, the Uſe of the Appearances of Things, Judgment. Being, then, the Formation of ſuch an Artiſt, will you diſhonour him; eſpecially, when he hath not only formed, but intruſted, and given the Guardianſhip of you, to yourſelf? Will you not only be forgetful of this, but, moreover, diſhonour the Truſt? If God had committed ſome Orphan to your Charge, would you have been thus careless of him? He hath delivered yourself to your Care; and says, "I "had no one fitter to be trusted than you: pre-"serve this Person for Me, such as he is by Na-"ture; modest, faithful, sublime, unterrified, dis-"passionate, tranquil:" And will you not preserve him?

§. 4. But it will be said; "Whence this superci-"lious Look, and Gravity of Face?" [in our young Philosopher]——"I have not yet so much Gra-"vity, as the Case deserves. I do not yet trust "to what I have learned, and assented to. I still "fear my own Weakness. Let me but take Cou-"rage a little, and then you shall see such a Look, "and such an Appearance, as I ought to have. "Then I will show you the Statue, when it is fi-"nished, when it is polished. Do you think I will "show you a supercilious Countenance? Heaven "forbid! For *Olympian Jupiter* doth not lift up "his Brow; but keeps a steady Countenance, as "becomes him who is about to say,

———*Th' immutable Decree*
No Force can shake: what is, that ought to be.
POPE.

"Such will I show myself to you: faithful, mo-"dest, noble, tranquil."——"What, and immor-"tal too, and exempt from Age and Sickness?" No. But sickening and dying as becomes a God. This is in my Power; this I can do. The other is not in my Power, nor can I do it. Shall I show you the (*b*) Nerves of a Philosopher?

"What Nerves are those?"

A Desire undisappointed; an Aversion unincurred; Pursuits duly exerted; a careful Resolution; an unerring Assent. These you shall see.

CHAP-

(*b*) An Allusion to the Combatants in the public Exercises, who used to show their Shoulders, Muscles, and Nerves, as a Proof of their Strength. See B. I. c. 4. §. 4. B. II. c. 18. §. 5. B. III. c. 22 §. 5.

CHAPTER IX.

That when we are unable to fulfil what the Character of a Man promises, we assume that of a Philosopher.

§. 1. IT is no common Attainment, merely to fulfil what the Nature of Man promises. For what is Man?

A rational and mortal Being.

Well: from what are we distinguished by Reason?

From wild Beasts.

From what else?

From Sheep, and the like.

Take care, then, to do nothing like a wild Beast; otherwise, you have destroyed the Man; you have not fulfilled what your Nature promises. Take care too, to do nothing like Cattle: for thus likewise the Man is destroyed.

In what do we act like Cattle?

When we act gluttonously, lewdly, rashly, sordidly, inconsiderately, into what are we sunk?

Into Cattle.

What have we destroyed?

The rational Being.

When we behave contentiously, injuriously, passionately, and violently, into what are we sunk?

Into wild Beasts.

§. 2. And farther; some of us are wild Beasts of a larger Size: others, little mischievous Vermin; whence there is room to say, Let me rather be eat by a Lion. By all these Means, is destroyed what the Nature of Man promises. For, when is a conjunctive Proposition preserved?

When it fulfils what its Nature promises.

So that the Preservation of such a Proposition consists in this; that its several Parts are a Conjunction of Truths.

When

When is a disjunctive Proposition preserved?

When it fulfils what its Nature promises.

When is a Flute, a Harp, a Horse, or a Dog, preserved?

When each fulfils what its Nature promises.

Where is the Wonder then, that Man should be preserved, and destroyed, in the same Manner? All are preserved and improved by Operations correspondent [to their several Faculties]; as a Carpenter, by Building; a Grammarian, by Grammar: but if he accustom himself to write ungrammatically, his Art will necessarily be spoiled and destroyed. Thus modest Actions preserve the modest Man, and immodest ones destroy him: faithful Actions, the faithful Man; and the contrary destroy him. On the other hand, contrary Actions heighten contrary Characters. Thus Impudence, an impudent one; Knavery, a knavish one; Slander, a slanderous one; Anger, an angry one; and unequitable Dealings, a covetous one.

§. 3. For this Reason, Philosophers advise us, not to be contented with mere Learning; but to add Meditation likewise, and then Practice. For we have been long accustomed to contrary Actions, and have practised upon wrong Opinions. If therefore, we do not likewise habituate ourselves to practise upon right Opinions, we shall be nothing more than Expositors of the Principles of others. For who among us is not already able to discourse, according to the Rules of Art, upon Good and Evil? *That some Things are good, some evil, and others indifferent: the Good, Virtue, and whatever partakes of Virtue; the Evil, the contrary; and the Indifferent, Riches, Health, Reputation:* and then, if, while we are saying all this, there should happen some more-than-ordinary Noise, or one of the By-standers should laugh at us, we are disconcerted. Philosopher, what is become of what you were

saying?

saying? Whence did it proceed? Merely from your Lips? Why then, do you pollute the Aids which others have provided? Why do you trifle on the most important Subjects? It is one thing to hoard up Provision in a Store-house, and another to eat it. What is eaten is concocted, digested, and becomes Nerves, Flesh, Bones, Blood, Colour, Breath. Whatever is hoarded up is ready indeed, whenever you have a Mind to show it; but of no further Use to you than the mere Notion, that you have it. For, what Difference is there, whether you explain *these* Doctrines, or those of Persons of opposite Principles? Sit down now, and comment, according to the Rules of Art, upon the Principles of *Epicurus:* and perhaps you may comment more practically than he could have done himself. Why then do you call yourself a *Stoic?* Why do you act a *Jew*, when you are a *Greek?* Do not you see on what Terms each is called a *Jew*, a *Syrian*, an *Egyptian?* And when we see any one wavering, we are wont to say, This is not a *Jew*; but acts one. But, when he assumes the Sentiments of one who hath been baptized and circumcised (*a*), then he both really is, and is called, a *Jew*. Thus we, falsifying our Profession, are *Jews* in Name, but in reality something else. Our Sentiments are inconsistent with our Discourse; far from practising what we teach, and what we pride ourselves in the Knowledge of. Thus, while we are unable to fulfil what the Character of a Man promises, we assume, besides, so vast a Weight as that of a Philosopher. As if a Person, incapable of lifting ten Pounds, should endeavour to heave the same Stone with *Ajax*.

CHAP-

(*a*) The Translation follows Mr. *Upton*'s Conjecture.

CHAPTER X.

How we may investigate the Duties of Life from the Names which we bear.

§. 1. EXAMINE who you are. In the first Place, a Man, that is, one who hath nothing superior to the Faculty of Choice; but all Things subject to this; and this itself uninslaved, and unsubjected, to any thing. Consider then, from what you are distinguished by Reason. You are distinguished from wild Beasts: you are distinguished from Cattle. Besides: you are a Citizen of the World, and a Part of it: not a subservient, but a principal, Part. You are capable of comprehending the divine Oeconomy; and of considering the Connexions of Things. What then doth the Character of a Citizen promise? To hold no private Interest; to deliberate of nothing as a separate Individual, but like the Hand or the Foot; which, if they had Reason, and comprehended the Constitution of Nature, would never pursue, or desire, but with a Reference to the Whole. Hence the Philosophers rightly say, That, if a wise and good Man could foresee what was to happen, he would help forward Sickness, and Death, and Mutilation, to himself; being sensible, that these Things are appointed from the Order of the Universe; and that the Whole is superior to a Part, and the City, to the Citizen. But, since we do not foreknow what is to happen, it becomes our Duty to adhere to what is more naturally adapted to our Option: for, amongst other Things, we were born for this.

§. 2. Remember next, that you are a Son: and what doth this Character promise? To esteem every thing that is his, as belonging to his Father: in every

every Inſtance to obey him: not to revile him to another: not to ſay or do any thing injurious to him: to give way and yield in every thing; co-operating with him to the utmoſt of his Power.

§. 3. After this, know likewiſe, that you are a Brother: and that to this Character it belongs, to make Conceſſions; to be eaſily perſuaded; to uſe gentle Language: never to claim, for yourſelf, any of the Things independent on Choice; but chearfully to give theſe, that you may have the larger Share of what is dependent on it. For conſider what it is, inſtead of a Lettuce, for Inſtance, or a Chair, to procure for yourſelf a good Temper? How great an Advantage gained!

§. 4. If, beſides this, you are a Senator of any City, conſider yourſelf as a Senator: if a Youth, as a Youth: if an old Man, as an old Man. For each of theſe Names, if it comes to be conſidered, always points out the proper Duties. But, if you go and revile your Brother, I tell you, you have forgot who you are, and what is your Name. For even if you were a Smith, and made an ill Uſe of the Hammer, you would have forgot the Smith: and, if you have forgot the Brother, and are become, inſtead of a Brother, an Enemy, do you imagine you have made no Change of one Thing for another, in that Caſe? If, inſtead of a Man, a gentle, ſocial Creature, you are become a wild Beaſt, miſchievous, inſidious, biting; have you loſt nothing? But muſt you loſe Money, in order to ſuffer Damage; and is there no other Thing, the Loſs of which endamages a Man? If you were to part with your Skill in Grammar, or in Muſic; would you think the Loſs of theſe a Damage? And, if you part with Honour, Decency, and Gentleneſs, do you think *that* no Matter? Yet the firſt are loſt by ſome Cauſe external, and independent on Choice; but the laſt, by our own Fault. There is no Shame either

either in not (*a*) having, or in loſing the one; but either not to have, or to loſe, the other, is equally ſhamefully, and reproachful, and unhappy. What doth the Pathic loſe? The Man. What doth the ſmooth effeminate Fellow loſe? (*b*) Many other Things? but however the Man alſo. What doth an Adulterer loſe? The modeſt, the chaſte Character; the Neighbour. What doth an angry Perſon loſe? Something elſe. A Coward? Something elſe. No one is wicked without ſome Loſs, or Damage. Now, if, after all, you have made the Loſs of Money the only Damage, all theſe [Wretches] are unhurt and undamaged. Nay, it may be, even Gainers; as, by ſuch Practices, their Money may poſſibly be increaſed. But conſider: if you refer every thing to *Money*, the Man who loſes his Noſe is not hurt. Yes, ſay you; he is maimed in his Body. Well: but doth he who loſes his Smell itſelf, loſe nothing? Is there, then, no Faculty of the Soul, which he who poſſeſſes it is the better for; and he who parts with it, the worſe?

What Sort do you mean?

Have we not a natural Senſe of Honour?

We have.

Doth he, who loſes this, ſuffer no Damage? Is he deprived of nothing? Doth he part with nothing that belongs to him? Have we no natural Fidelity? No natural Affection? No natural Diſpoſition to mutual Uſefulneſs, to mutual Forbearance? Is he, then, who careleſsly ſuffers himſelf to be damaged in theſe Reſpects, unhurt and undamaged?

§. 5. What, then, ſhall not I hurt him, who hath hurt me?

Conſider firſt what *Hurt* is; and remember what you

(*a*) The true Reading of the *Greek* is ουτ᾽ ουκ εχειν.

(*b*) It hath been ſuggeſted to me, that διατιλθεις, not διατιθεις, is the true Reading; and I have ventured ſo to tranſlate it. See L. III. c. 1. p. 352, 353. of Mr. *Upton*'s Edition.

you have heard from the Philosophers. For, if both Good and Evil consist in Choice, see whether what you say, doth not amount to this: "Since "he hath hurt himself, by injuring me; shall not "I hurt myself by injuring him?" Why do we not make some such Representation to ourselves, as this? Are we hurt, when any Detriment happens to our bodily Possessions; and are we not at all hurt, when any happens to our Faculty of Choice? He who is deceived, or hath done an Injury, hath no Pain in his Head; nor loses an Eye, a Leg, or an Estate: and we wish for nothing beyond these. Whether we have a modest and faithful, or a shameless and unfaithful, Will and Choice, we make not the smallest Difference; except only in the Schools, as far as a few Words go. Therefore all the Improvement we make, reaches only to Words; and beyond them is absolutely nothing.

CHAPTER XI.

What the Beginning of Philosophy is.

§. 1. THE Beginning of Philosophy, at least to such as enter upon it in a proper Way, and by the Door, is a Consciousness of our own Weakness, and Inability, in necessary Things. For we came into the World without any natural Idea of a right-angled Triangle; of a Diesis, or a Hemitone, in Music: but we learn each of these Things by some Instruction of Art. Hence, they who do not understand them, do not form any Conceit of understanding them. But who ever came into the World, without an innate Idea of Good and Evil; Fair and Base; Becoming and Unbecoming; Happiness and Misery; Proper and Improper; what ought to be done, and what not to be done? Hence we all make use of the Names, and endeavour to apply our Pre-conceptions to particular Cases. "Such a one hath acted well;

"not

"not well: right; not right: is unhappy; is hap-"py: is juſt; is unjuſt." Who of us refrains from theſe Names? Who defers the Uſe of them, till he had learnt it; as thoſe do, who are ignorant of Lines and Sounds? The Reaſon of this is, that we *(a)* come inſtructed, in ſome degree, by Nature upon theſe Subjects; and from this Beginning, we go on to add Self-conceit. "For why, ſay you, "ſhould not I know what Fair and Baſe is? Have "not I the Idea of it?" You have. "Do not I "apply this Idea to Particulars?" You do. "Do "not I apply it right, then?" Here lies the whole Queſtion; and here ariſes the Self-conceit. For, beginning from theſe acknowledged Points, Men proceed to what is in Diſpute, by means of their unſuitable Application. For, if they poſſeſt a right Method of Application, what would reſtrain them from being perfect? Now, ſince you think, that you make a ſuitable Application, of your Pre-conceptions, to particular Caſes, tell me whence you derive this.

From its ſeeming ſo to me.

But it doth not ſeem ſo to another: and doth not he too form a Conceit, that he makes a right Application?

He doth.

Is it poſſible, then, that each of you ſhould apply your Pre-conceptions right, on the very Subjects about which you have contradictory Opinions?

It is not.

Have you any thing to ſhow us, then, for this Application, preferable to its *ſeeming* ſo to you? And doth a Madman act any otherwiſe than ſeems to him, right? Is this then a ſufficient Criterion to him too?

It is not.

Come therefore, to ſomething preferable to what *ſeems*.

What

(*a*) For τινας in the *Greek*, the Senſe ſeems to require ἡμᾶς.

What is that?

§. 2. The Beginning of Philosophy is this: The being sensible of the Disagreement of Men with each other: an Inquiry into the Cause of this Disagreement; and a Disapprobation, and Distrust of what merely *seems*: a certain Examination into what seems, whether it seem rightly: and an Invention of some Rule, like a Balance, for the Determination of Weights; like a Square, for strait and crooked.

Is this the Beginning of Philosophy, that all Things, which seem right to all Persons, are so?

Why; is it possible, that Contradictions can be right?

Well then, not all Things; but all that seem so to *us*.

And why more to *you*, than to the *Syrians*, or *Egyptians*? Than to me, or to any other Man?

Not at all more.

§. 3. Therefore [merely] what *seems* to each Man, is not sufficient to determine the Reality of a Thing. For even in Weights or Measures we are not satisfied with the bare Appearance; but for every thing we find some Rule. And is there, in the present Case then, no Rule, preferable to what *seems*? Is it possible, that what is of the greatest Necessity in human Life, should be left incapable of Determination and Discovery?

There is, then, some Rule.

And why do we not seek, and discover it; and, when we have discovered, make use of it, without fail, ever after, so as not even to move a Finger, without it. For this, I conceive, is what, when found, will cure (*b*) those of their Madness, who make use of no other Measure, but their own perverted Way of Thinking. That afterwards,

(*b*) The Sense requires, that the Reading should be ἀπαλλάσσοι ἂν, or ἀπαλλάξει.

ning from certain known and determinate Points, we may make uſe of Preconceptions, properly applied to Particulars. What is the Subject that falls under our Inquiry?

Pleaſure.

Bring it to the Rule. Throw it into the Scale. Muſt Good be ſomething in which it is fit to confide? and to which we may truſt?

Yes.

Is it fit to truſt to any thing unſteady?

No.

Is Pleaſure then, a ſteady Thing?

No.

Take it, then, and throw it out of the Scale, and drive it far diſtant from the Place of good Things. But, if you are not quick-ſighted, and one Balance is inſufficient, bring another. Is it fit to be elated by Good?

Yes.

Is it fit, then, to be elated by a preſent Pleaſure? See that you do not ſay it is; otherwiſe I ſhall not think you ſo much as worthy to uſe a Scale. Thus are Things judged, and weighed, when we have the Rules ready. This is the Part of Philoſophy, To examine, and fix the Rules: and to make uſe of them, when they are known, is the Buſineſs of a wiſe and good Man.

CHAPTER XII.

Of Diſputation.

§. 1. WHAT Things are to be learn'd, in order to the right Uſe of Reaſon, the Philoſophers of our Sect have accurately taught: but we are altogether unpractiſed in the due Application of them. Only give any of us, that you pleaſe, ſome illiterate Perſon, for an Antagoniſt, and he will not find out, how to treat him. But when

when he hath a little moved the Man, if he happens to anſwer beſide the Purpoſe, he knows not how to deal with him any further ; but either reviles, or laughs at him ; and ſays, "He is an "illiterate Fellow : there is no making any thing "of him." Yet a Guide, when he perceives his Charge going out of the Way, doth not revile, and ridicule, and then leave him ; but leads him into the right Path. Do you alſo ſhow your Antagoniſt the Truth, and you will ſee, that he will follow. But till you do ſhow it, do not ridicule him ; but rather be ſenſible of your own Incapacity.

§. 2. How then, did *Socrates* uſe to act? He obliged his Antagoniſt himſelf to bear Teſtimony to him ; and wanted no other Witneſs. Hence he might well ſay, "I give up all the reſt ; and "am always ſatisfied with the Teſtimony of my "Opponent : and I call in no one to vote, but my "Antagoniſt alone." For he rendered the Arguments drawn from natural Notions ſo clear, that every one ſaw, and avoided the Contradiction.— "Doth an envious Man rejoice?"——"By no "means. He rather grieves." (This he moved him to ſay, by propoſing the contrary.)—"Well: "and do you think Envy to be a Grief, for "Miſery?"——And who ever envied Miſery?—— "(Therefore he makes the other ſay, that "Envy is a Grief, for Happineſs.)——Doth "any one envy thoſe who are nothing to him?" ——"No, ſurely." Having thus drawn [from his Opponent] a full and diſtinct Idea, he then left that Point ; and doth not ſay, "Define "to me what Envy is :" and after he had defined it ; "You have defined it wrong ; for the De- "finition doth not reciprocate to the Thing defin- "ed." Technical Terms, and therefore grievous, and ſcarcely to be made intelligible to the Illiterate, which yet *We*, it ſeems, cannot part with. But we have no Capacity at all to move them, by ſuch Arguments, as might induce them, in following the Track of the Appearances in their own Minds, to allow, or diſprove, any Point And, from a Conſciouſneſs of this Incapacity, thoſe among us, who have any Modeſty, give the Matter intirely up: but the greater Part, raſhly entering upon theſe Debates, mutually confound, and are confounded; and, at laſt, reviling, and reviled, walk off. Whereas it was the principal and moſt peculiar Characteriſtic of *Socrates*, never to be provoked, in a Diſpute; nor to throw out any reviling or injurious Expreſſion: but to bear patiently with thoſe who reviled him; and to put an End to the Controverſy. If you would know, how great Abilities he had in this particular, read *Xenophon*'s *Banquet*, and you will ſee, how many Controverſies he ended. Hence, even among the Poets, that Perſon is juſtly mentioned with the higheſt Commendation,

Whoſe lenient Art attentive Crowds await,
To ſtill the furious Clamours of Debate.

HESIOD.

But what then? This is no very ſafe Affair now, and eſpecially at *Rome*. For he who doth it, muſt not do it in a Corner; but go to ſome rich Conſular Senator, for Inſtance, and queſtion him. "Pray, "Sir, can you tell me to whom you intruſt your "Horſes?"——"Yes, certainly."——"Is it then, "to any one indifferently, though he be igno- "rant of Horſemanſhip?"——"By no means." ——"To whom do you intruſt your Gold, or your "Silver, or your Clothes?"——"Not to any one "indifferently."——"And did you ever conſider, "to whom you committed the Care of your Body?" ——"Yes, ſurely."——"To one ſkilled in Exer- "ciſe, or Medicine, I ſuppoſe."——"Without "doubt."

" doubt."——" Are these Things your chief " Good; or are you possess'd of some thing better " than all of them?"——" What do you mean?" ——" Something which makes use of these; and " proves, and deliberates about each of them?"—— " What then, do you mean the Soul?"——" You " have guess'd right; for indeed I do mean that." ——" I do really think it a much better Possession " than all the rest."——Can you show us, then, in " what manner you have taken care of this Soul? " For it is not probable, that a Person of your Wis- " dom, and approved Character in the State, should " carelessly suffer the most excellent Thing that be- " longs to you, to be neglected, and lost."—— " no certainly."——" But do you take care of it " yourself? And is it by the Instructions of another, " or by your own Discovery [how it ought to be " done?]"——Here, now, comes the Danger, that he may first say, Pray, good Sir, what Business is that of yours? What are you to me? Then, if you persist to trouble him, he may lift up his Hand, and give you a Box on the Ear. I myself was once a great Admirer of this Method of Instruction, till I fell into such kind of Adventures.

CHAPTER XIII.

Of Solicitude.

§. 1. WHEN I see any one solicitous, I say, What doth this Man mean? Unless he wanted something or other, not in his own Power, how could he still be solicitous? A Musician, for Instance, feels no Solicitude, while he is singing by himself: but when he appears upon the Stage he doth; even if his Voice be ever so good, or he plays ever so well. For what he wants is not only to sing well, but likewise to gain Applause. But this is not; in his own Power. In ſhort, where his Skill lies, there is his Courage. (Bring any ignorant Perſon, and he doth not mind him.) But in the Point which he neither underſtands, nor hath ſtudied, there he is ſolicitous.

What Point is that?

He doth not underſtand what a Multitude is; nor what the Applauſe of a Multitude. He hath learnt, indeed, how to ſtrike Baſs and Treble; but what the Applauſe of the many is, and what Force it hath in Life, he neither underſtands, nor hath ſtudied. Hence he muſt neceſſarily tremble, and turn pale. I cannot, indeed, ſay, that a Man is no Muſician, when I ſee him afraid; but I can ſay ſomething elſe; and that not one, but many Things. And, firſt of all, I call him a Stranger; and ſay, This Man doth not know in what Country he is: and though he hath lived here ſo long, he is ignorant of the Laws and Cuſtoms of the State; and what is permitted, and what not: nor hath he ever conſulted any Lawyer, who might tell and explain to him the Laws. Yet no Man writes a Will, without knowing how it ought to be written, or conſulting ſome one who doth know: nor doth he raſhly ſign a Bond, or give Security. But he uſes his Deſire and Averſion, exerts his Purſuits, Intentions, and Reſolutions, without conſulting any Lawyer about the Matter.

How do you mean, without a *Lawyer*?

He knows not, that he chuſes what is not allowed him; and doth not chuſe what is neceſſary: and he knows not what is his own, and what belongs to others: for if he did know, he would never be hindered; would never be reſtrained; would never be ſolicitous.

How ſo?

Why: doth any one fear Things that are not Evils?

No.

Doth

Doth any one fear Things, that are Evils indeed, but which it is in his own Power to prevent?

No, surely.

§. 2. If, then, the Things independent on Choice, are neither good nor evil; and all that do depend on Choice, are in our own Power, and can neither be taken away from us, or given to us, unless we please; what room is there left for Solicitude? But we are solicitous about this paultry Body, or Estate, of ours; or about the Determination of *Cæsar*; and not at all about any thing internal. Are we ever solicitous not to take up a false Opinion? No: for this is in our own Power. Or not to exert our Pursuits, contrary to Nature? No: nor this neither. When, therefore, you see any one pale with Solicitude, as the Physician pronounces from the Complexion, that such a Patient is disordered in the Spleen, another in the Liver; so do you likewise say, this Man is disordered in his Desires and Aversions: he cannot walk steady; he is in a Fermentation. For nothing else changes the Complexion, or causes a Trembling, or sets the Teeth a chattering.

No Force, no Firmness, the pale Coward shows;
He shifts his Place; his Colour comes and goes.
Terror and Death in his wild Eye-balls stare;
With chatt'ring Teeth he stands, and stiffen'd Hair.

POPE's Homer.

Therefore (*a*) Zeno, when he was to meet *Antigonus*,

(*a*) *Antigonus Gonatas*, King of *Macedon*, had so great an Esteem for *Zeno*, that he often took a Journey to *Athens* to visit him; and endeavoured, by magnificent Promises, to allure him to his Court; but without Success. He gave it as a Reason, for the distinguished Regard which he paid him, that, though he had made him many, and very considerable Offers, *Zeno* never appeared either mean or insolent.

gonus, felt no Solicitude. For over what he admired, *Antigonus* had no Power; and those Things of which he had the Power, *Zeno* did not regard. But *Antigonus* felt a Solicitude when he was to meet *Zeno*; and with Reason: for he was desirous to please him; and this was external. But *Zeno* was not desirous to please *Antigonus*: for no one skilful in any Art, is desirous to please a Person unskilful.

I am desirous [says one of his Scholars] to please *You*.

For what? Do you know the Rules, by which one Man judges of another? Have you studied to understand what a good, and what a bad Man is; and how each becomes such? Why then are not you yourself a good Man;

On what Account am I not?

Because no good Man laments, nor sighs, nor groans: no good Man turns pale, and trembles, and says, "How will such a one receive me; how "will he hear me?"——As he thinks fit, Wretch. Why do you trouble yourself about what belongs to others? Is it not *his* Fault, if he receives you ill?

Yes, surely.

And can one Person be in fault, and another the Sufferer (*b*)?

No.

Why then are you solicitous, about what belongs to others?

Well: but I am solicitous how I shall speak to him.

What then, cannot you speak to him as you will?

But I am afraid I shall be disconcerted.

If you were going to write the Name of *Dion*, should you be afraid of being disconcerted.

By no means.

What

(*b*) This is a Stoic Extravagance. The very Thing that constitutes the Fault of the one in this Case is, that he makes the other suffer. However, if, instead of vainly affecting Insensibility, we extend our View, to the future Rewards of those who bear ill Treatment as they ought, the Position is true and useful.

What is the Reaſon? Is it not becauſe you have ſtudied how to write?

Yes.

And if you were going to read, would it not be exactly the ſame?

Exactly.

What is the Reaſon?

Becauſe every Art hath a certain Aſſurance and Confidence, in the Subjects that belong to it.

Have you not ſtudied then, how to ſpeak? And what elſe did you ſtudy at School?

Syllogiſms, and convertible Propoſitions.

For what Purpoſe? Was it not in order to talk properly? And what is that, but to talk ſeaſonably, and cautiouſly, and intelligibly, and without Flutter and Heſitation; and, in conſequence of all this, with Courage?

Very true.

When, therefore, you go into the Field on Horſeback, are you ſolicitous about one, who is here now on Foot? Solicitous in a Point which you have ſtudied, and another hath not?

Ay, but the Perſon [with whom I am to talk] hath Power to kill me.

Then ſpeak the Truth, pitiful Wretch, and do not be arrogant; nor take the Philoſopher upon you; nor conceal from yourſelf who are your Maſters: but while you may thus be laid hold on by the Body, follow every one who is ſtronger than you. *Socrates*, indeed, had ſtudied how to ſpeak, who talked in ſuch a manner to Tyrants, and Judges, and in a Priſon. *Diogenes* (c) had ſtudied how to

(c) When *Diogenes* was ſailing to *Ægina*, he was taken by Pirates, and carried to *Crete*; and there ſet to Sale. Being aſked what he could do; he anſwered, *Govern Men*: and pointing to a well-dreſs'd *Corinthian*, who was paſſing by, *Sell me* (ſaid he) *to him; for he wants a Maſter.* The *Corinthian*, whoſe Name was *Xeniades*, bought him, and appointed him the Tutor to his Children; and *Diogenes* perfectly well diſcharged his Truſt.

to ſpeak, who talked in ſuch a manner to *Alexander*, to *Philip*, to the Pirates, to the Perſon who bought him. This belonged to them who had ſtudied the Point; who had Courage. But do *you* walk off about your own Affairs, and never ſtir from them. Retire into ſome Corner, and there ſit and weave Syllogiſms, and propoſe them to others. For there is not, in *you*, one able

To rule the ſacred Citadel within.

CHAPTER XIV.

Concerning NASO.

§. 1. WHEN a certain *Roman* came to him with his Son, and had heard one Leſſon, This, ſaid *Epictetus*, is the Method of Teaching; and ſtopt. When the other deſired him to go on; Every Art, anſwered he, is tedious, when it is delivered to a Perſon ignorant and unſkilful in it. Indeed the Things performed by the common Arts, quickly diſcover the Uſe for which they were made; and moſt of them have ſomething engaging and agreeable. Thus the Trade of a Shoemaker, if one would ſtand by, and endeavour to comprehend it, is an unpleaſant Thing: but the Shoe is uſeful; and beſides, not diſagreeable to ſee. The Trade of a Smith is extremely uneaſy to an ignorant Perſon that chances to be preſent (*a*): but the Work ſhows the Uſefulneſs of the Art. You will ſee this much more ſtrongly in Muſic: for if you ſtand by, while a Perſon is learning, it will appear to you of all Sciences the moſt unpleaſant: but the Effects are agreeable and delightful, even to thoſe who do not underſtand it.

(*a*) The Tranſlation follows Mr. *Upton*. Παρατυγχάνοντι.

§. 2.

§. 2. Now here, we imagine it to be the Work of one who studies Philosophy, to adapt his Will to whatever happens. So that none of the Things which happen, may happen against our Inclination; nor those which do not happen, be wished for by us. Hence they who have settled this Point, have it in their Power never to be disappointed of their Desire, or incur their Aversion; but to lead a Life exempt from Sorrow, Fear, and Perturbation, in themselves; and in Society, preserving all the natural and adventitious Relations of a Son, a Father, a Brother, a Citizen, a Husband, a Wife, a Neighbour, a Fellow-Traveller, a Ruler, or a Subject. Something like this, is what we imagine to be the Work of a Philosopher. It remains to inquire, how it is to be effected. Now we see, that a Carpenter, by learning certain Things, becomes a Carpenter; and a Pilot, by learning certain Things, becomes a Pilot. Probably, then, it is not sufficient, in the present Case, merely to be willing to be wise and good; but it is moreover necessary that certain Things should be learned. What these Things are, is the Question. The Philosophers say, that we are first to learn that there is a God; and that his Providence directs the whole; and that it is impossible to conceal from him, not only our Actions, but even our Thoughts and Emotions. We are next to learn, what the Gods are: for such as they are found to be, such must *he*, who would please and obey them, to the utmost of his Power, endeavour to be. If the Deity is faithful, *he* too must be faithful: if free, beneficent, and exalted, he must be free, beneficent, and exalted, likewise; and, in all his Words and Actions, behave as an Imitator of God.

§. 3. Whence, then, are we to begin?

If you will give me Leave, I will tell you. It is necessary, in the first place, that you should understand Words.

So

So then! I do not understand them now?

No. You do not.

How is it, then, that I use them?

Just as the Illiterate do written Expressions; and Brutes, the Appearances of Things. For Use is one Thing, and Understanding another. But if you think you understand them, bring whatever Word you please, and let us see whether we understand it, or not.

Well: but it is a grievous Thing for a Man to be confuted who is grown old; and perhaps arrived, through a regular Course of Military Service, to the Dignity of a Senator.

I know it very well: for you now come to me, as if you wanted nothing. And how can it enter into your Imagination, that there should be any thing in which you are defective? You are rich; and perhaps have a Wife and Children, and a great Number of Domestics. *Cæsar* takes Notice of you: you have many Friends at *Rome*: you render to all their Dues: you know how to requite a Favour, and revenge an Injury. In what are you deficient? Suppose then, I should prove to you, that you are deficient, in what is most necessary and important to Happiness; and that hitherto you have taken care of every Thing, rather than your Duty; and, to complete all, that you understand neither what God or Man, or Good or Evil, means? That you are ignorant of all the rest, perhaps, you may bear to be told: but if I prove to you, that you are ignorant even of *yourself*, how will you bear with me, and how will you have Patience to stay and be convinced? Not at all. You will immediately be offended, and go away. And yet what Injury have I done you; unless a Looking-Glass injures a Person not handsome, when it shows him to himself, such as he is? Or unless a Physician can be thought to affront his Patient, when he says to him; "Do "you think, Sir, that you ail nothing? You have

"a Fever.

"a Fever. Eat no Meat To-day, and drink Water." Nobody cries out here, "What an intolerable Affront!" But, if you say to any one, Your Desires are in a Fermentation; your Aversions are low; your Intentions, contradictory; your Pursuits, not conformable to Nature; your Opinions, rash, and mistaken; he presently goes away, and complains, he is affronted.

§. 4. This is the Nature of our Proceedings. As in a crowded Fair, the Horses and Cattle are brought to be sold, and the greatest Part of Men come either to buy or sell; but there are a few, who come only to look at the Fair, and inquire, How it is carried on; and why in that Manner; and who appointed it; and for what Purpose. Thus, in the Fair of the World, some, like Cattle, trouble themselves about nothing but Fodder. For, as to all you, who busy yourselves about Professions, and Farms, and Domestics, and public Posts, these Things are nothing else but mere Fodder. But there are some few Men, among the Crowd, who are fond of looking on, and considering: "What then, after all, is the World? Who governs it? Hath it no Governor? How is it possible, when neither a City nor a House can remain ever so short a Time, without some one to govern and take care of it, that this vast and beautiful System should be administered, in a fortuitous and disorderly Manner? Is there then a Governor? What sort of one is he? And how doth he govern; and what are we, who are under him? And for what designed? Have we some Connexion and Relation to him; or none?" In this manner are the Few affected; and apply themselves only to view the Fair, and then depart. Well: and are they laughed at by the Multitude? Why, so are the Lookers-on, by the Buyers and Sellers; and, if the Cattle had any Apprehension, they too would laugh at such, as admired any thing but Fodder.

CHAP-

CHAPTER XV.

Concerning Those who obstinately persevere in whatever they have determined.

§. 1. SOME, when they hear such Discourses as these, *That we ought to be steady; that Choice is by Nature, free and uncompelled; and that all else is liable to Restraint, Compulsion, Slavery, and belongs to others*; imagine, that they must remain immutably fixed to every thing which they have determined. But it is first necessary, that the Determination should be a sound one. I agree, that there should be a Tension of the Nerves, in the Body; but such as appears in a healthy, an athletic Body: for, if you show me, that you have the Tension of a Lunatic, and value yourself upon that, I will say to you, Get yourself to a Physician, Man: this is not a Tension of the Nerves; but a Relaxation, of another kind. Such is the Distemper of Mind, in those who hear these Discourses in a wrong Manner: like an Acquaintance of mine, who, for no Reason, had determined to starve himself to Death. I went the third Day, and inquired what was the Matter. He answered, "I am determined."——Well: but what is your Motive? For, if your Determination be right, we will stay, and assist your Departure: but, if unreasonable, change it.——"we ought to keep our Determinations."——What do you mean, Sir? Not all; but such as are right. Else, if you should just now take it into your Head, that it is Night, if you think fit, do not change; but persist, and say, *We ought to keep our Determinations*. What do you mean, Sir? Not all. Why do not you begin, by first laying the Foundation, in an Inquiry, whether your Determination be a sound one, or not; and

then

and then build your Firmneſs and Conſtancy, upon it. For, if you lay a rotten and crazy Foundation, you muſt not build (*a*): and the greater and more weighty the Superſtructure is, the ſooner will it fall. Without any Reaſon, you are withdrawing from us, out of Life, a Friend, a Companion, a Fellow-Citizen both of the ſame greater (*b*), and leſſer City: and while you are committing Murder, and deſtroying an innocent Perſon, you ſay, *We muſt keep our Determinations.* Suppoſe, by any means, it ſhould ever come into your Head to kill *me*; muſt you keep ſuch a Determination?

§. 2. With Difficulty this Perſon was, however, at laſt convinced: but there are ſome at preſent, whom there is no convincing. So that now I think I underſtand, what before I did not, the Meaning of that common Saying, That a Fool will neither bend nor break. May it never fall to my Lot to have a wiſe, that is an untractable Fool, for my Friend (*c*). "It is all to no Purpoſe: I am determined." So are Madmen too; but the more ſtrongly they are determined upon Abſurdities, the more Need have they of Hellebore. Why will you not act like a ſick Perſon, and apply yourſelf to a Phyſician? "Sir, I am ſick. Give me your Aſſiſtance: conſider what I am to do. It is my Part to follow your Directions." So, in the preſent Caſe: I know not what I ought to do; and I am come to learn.——"No: but talk to me about other Things: for upon *This* I am determined." What other Things? What is of greater Conſequence, than to convince you, that it is not ſufficient to be determined, and to perſiſt. This is the Tenſion of a Madman; not of one in Health. "I will

(*a*) Inſtead of οικοδομημα τι ον, the true Reading ſeems to be οικοδομητεον; and is ſo tranſlated.
(*b*) The World.
(*c*) The Tranſlation here follows Mr. *Upton*'s Copy.

"I will die, if you compel me to this." Why so, Man: what is the Matter?——"I am determin-"ed." I have a lucky Escape, that you are not determined to kill me. "I take no Money (*d*)." Why so? "I am determined." Be assured, that with that very Tension which you now make use of to refuse it, you may, very possibly, hereafter, have as unreasonable a Propensity to take it; and again to say, "I am determined." As, in a distempered and rheumatic Body, the Humour tends sometimes to one Part, sometimes to another; thus it is uncertain which Way a sickly Mind will incline. But if, to its Inclination and Bent, an obstinate Tension be likewise added, the Evil then becomes desperate and incurable.

CHAPTER XVI.

That we do not study to make use of the Principles concerning Good and Evil.

§. 1. WHERE lies Good? In Choice. Where Evil? In Choice. Where neither Good nor Evil? In Things independent on Choice. What then? Doth any of us remember these Lessons out of the Schools? Doth any of us study how to Answer for himself in Things, as in Questions? "Is it Day?" "Yes." "Is it Night, then?" "No." "Is the Number of Stars even?" "I cannot tell." When (*a*) Money is offered you, have you studied to make the proper Answer, That it is not a Good? Have you exercised yourself in such Answers as these; or only in Sophistries? Why do you wonder then, that you improve in Points which you have studied; and in those which you have not studied,

(*d*) This, probably, is spoken in the Person of one, who is offered Assistance necessary for his Support, and refuses it.

(*a*) As a Bribe for bad Purposes.

ſtudied, there you remain the ſame? When an Orator knows, that he hath written well; that he hath committed to Memory what he hath written; and that he brings an agreeable Voice with him; why is he ſtill ſolicitous? Becauſe he is not contented, with what he hath ſtudied. What doth he want, then? To be applauded by the Audience. He hath ſtudied the Power of ſpeaking, then; but he hath not ſtudied Cenſure and Applauſe. For when did he hear from any one, what Applauſe, what Cenſure, is? What is the Nature of each? What kind of Applauſe is to be ſought, and what kind of Cenſure to be ſhunned? And when did he ever apply himſelf, to ſtudy what follows from theſe Leſſons? Why do you wonder then, if, in what he hath learned, he excels others; but, where he hath not ſtudied, he is the ſame with the reſt of the World? Juſt as a Muſician knows how to play, ſings well, and hath the proper Dreſs of his Profeſſion; yet trembles when he comes upon the Stage. For the firſt he underſtands: but what the Multitude is, or what the Clamour and Laughter of the Multitude is, he doth not underſtand. Nor doth he even know, what Solicitude itſelf is: whether it be our own affair, or that of others; or whether it be poſſible to ſuppreſs it, or not. Hence, if he is applauded, he is puffed up, when he makes his Exit: but, if he is laughed at, the Tumour is pricked, and ſubſides.

§. 2. Thus are we too affected. What do we admire? Externals. For what do we ſtrive? Externals. And are we then in any Doubt how we come to fear, and be ſolicitous? What is the Conſequence then, when we eſteem the Things that are brought upon us, to be Evils? We cannot but fear; we cannot but be ſolicitous. And then we ſay, " O Lord God, how ſhall I avoid Solici-

"tude!" Have you not Hands, Fool? (*b*) Hath not God made them for you? (*c*) Sit down now, and pray, that your Nose may not run. Wipe it rather; and do not murmur. Well; and hath he given you nothing in the present Case? Hath not he given you Patience? Hath not he given you Magnanimity? Hath not he given you Fortitude? When you have such Hands as these, do you still seek for Somebody to wipe your Nose? (*d*) But we neither study nor regard these Things. For give me but one, who cares how he doth any thing, who doth not regard the Success of any thing, but his own Manner of acting. Who, when he is walking, regards his own Action? Who, when he is deliberating, the Deliberation itself, and not the Success that is to follow it? If it happens to succeed, he is elated; and cries, "How prudently "have we deliberated! Did not I tell you, my "dear Friend, that it was impossible, when we "considered about any thing, that it should not "happen right?" But, if it miscarries, the poor Wretch is dejected; and knows not what to say about the Matter. Who among us ever, upon this Account, consulted a Diviner? Who of us ever slept in a Temple, to be informed concerning his Manner of acting? (*e*) I say, who? Show me one

(*b*) The Order of this Passage should be——Sit down now, and pray, that your Nose may not run. Have you not Hands, Fool? Hath not God made them for you, &c. But *Epictetus*, probably, might speak extempore in this inverted manner: and *Arrian* proposes to deliver what he said, with the greatest Exactness.

(*c*) Sitting, probably some particular Sort of it, was anciently (see *Judges* xx. 26. 1 *Chr.* xvii. 16.) one Posture of Devotion. Our Ancestors, in Queen *Elizabeth*'s Time, called Kneeling, *Sitting* on their Knees. A mixed Posture of Sitting and Kneeling is now used, by some Nations in Prayer.

(*d*) See p. 21. Note *f*.

(*e*) The Heathen had certain Temples, in which it was usual for Persons to sleep, in order to receive Oracles by Dreams. One of the most celebrated Places, appropriated to this Purpose, was the Temple of *Amphiaraus*. See PHILOSTRATUS, p. 771.

one (that I may see what I have long sought) who is truly noble and ingenuous. Show me either a young or an old Man *(f)*.

§. 3. Why then are we still surprised, if, when we waste all our Attention on the Materials of Action, we are, in the Manner of Action itself, low, sordid, worthless, fearful, wretched, and a mere Heap of Disappointment and Misery? For we do not care about these Things, nor make them our Study. If we had feared, not Death or Exile, but Fear itself, we should have studied not to fall into what appears to us to be evil. But, as the Case now stands, we are eager and loquacious in the Schools; and, when any little Question arises about any of these Things, we are prepared to trace its Consequences: but drag us into Practice, and you will find us miserably shipwrecked. Let some alarming Appearance attack us; and you will perceive what we have been studying, and in what we are exercised. Besides this Negligence, we always accumulate somewhat else, and represent Things greater than the Reality. In a Voyage, for Instance, casting my Eyes down upon the Ocean below, and looking round me, and seeing no Land, I am out of my Wits; and imagine, that, if I should be shipwrecked, I must swallow all that Ocean: nor doth it once enter my Head, that three Pints are enough to do my Business What is it then, that alarms me? The Ocean? No: but my own *Principle.* Again: in an Earthquake, I imagine the City

(f) It is observable, that this most practical of all the Philosophers, owns his Endeavours met with little or no Success, among his Scholars. The Apostles speak a very different Language, in their Epistles, to the first Converts to Christianity: and the Acts of the Apostles, and all the Monuments of the primitive Ages, bear Testimony to the Reformation of Manners produced by the Gospel. This Difference of Success might indeed justly be expected, from the Difference of the two Systems.

City, is going to fall upon me: but is not one little Stone enough, to knock my Brains out? What is it then, that oppresses, and puts us out of our Wits? Why, what else, but our *Principles?* For what is it, but mere *Principle*, that oppresses him, who leaves his Country, and is separated from his Acquaintance, and Friends, and Place, and usual Manner of Life? When Children cry, if their Nurse happens to be absent for a little while, give them a Cake, and they forget their Grief. Shall we compare you to these Children then?

No, indeed. For I do not desire to be pacified by a Cake; but by right *Principles*. And what are they?

Such as a Man ought to study all Day long, so as not to be attached to what doth not belong to him; neither to a Friend, to a Place, an Academy; nor even to his own Body: but to remember the Law, and to have that constantly before his Eyes. And what is the divine Law? To preserve inviolate what is properly our own: not to claim what belongs to others: to use what is given us; and not desire what is not given us: and, when any thing is taken away, to restore it readily; and to be thankful for the Time you have been permitted the Use of it; and not cry after it, like a Child for its Nurse and its Mamma. For what doth it signify, what gets the better of you, or on what you depend? And in what are you superior to him, who cries for a Puppet, if you lament for a paultry Academy, and a Portico, and an Assembly of young People; and such-like Amusements? Another comes, lamenting, that he must no longer drink the Water of *Dircè* (*f*). Why, is not the *Marcian* Water as good? "But I was used to that." And in time you will be used to the other. And, when you

(*f*) A beautiful clear River in *Bœotia*, flowing into the *Ismenus*. The *Marcian* Water was conveyed by *Ancus Martius* to *Rome*. UPTON.

you are attached to this too, you may cry again, and set yourself in Imitation of *Euripides*, to celebrate, in Verse,

The Baths of Nero, *and the* Marcian *Water*.

Hence see the Origin of Tragedy, when trifling Accidents befal foolish Men. "Ah, when shall I "see *Athens*, and the Citadel, again!" Wretch, are not you contented with what you see every Day? Can you see any thing better than the Sun, the Moon, the Stars, the whole Earth, the Sea? But if, besides, you comprehend him who administers the Whole, and carry him about in yourself, do you still long after Pebbles, and a fine Rock *(g)*? What will you do then, when you are to leave even the Sun and Moon? Will you sit crying, like an Infant? What then have you been doing in the School? What did you hear? What did you learn? Why have you written yourself a Philosopher, instead of writing the real Fact? I have made some (*h*) Introductions [you may say]; and read over *Chrysippus*; but I have not so much as gone near the Door of a Philosopher *(i)*. For what Pretensions have I, to any thing of the same kind with *Socrates*, who died, and who lived, in such a Manner? Or with *Diogenes*? Do you observe either of these crying, or out of Humour, that he is not to see such a Man, or such a Woman; nor to live any longer at *Athens*, or at *Corinth*; but at *Susa*, for Instance, or *Ecbatana*? For doth he stay, and repine, who is at his Liberty, whenever he pleases, to quit the Entertainment, and play no longer? Why doth he not stay, as Children do, as long as he is amused? Such a one, no doubt, will bear perpetual Banishment, and a Sentence of Death, wonderful

(g) Mr. *Upton* conjectures this to be an Allusion to some poetical, or rhetorical Description.

(*h*) Brief Summaries of any Science, for the Use of Beginners, are often so called.

(i) Perhaps the true Reading should be Φιλοσοφιας, Philosophy.

wonderful well! Why will you not be weaned, as Children are; and take more solid Food? Will you never cease to cry after your Mammas and Nurses, whom the old Women about you have taught you to bewail? "But if I go away, I shall "trouble them."——*You* trouble them! No: it will not be *you:* but that which troubles you too, *Principle.* What have you to do then? Pluck out your [false] Principle; and, if they are wise, they will pluck out theirs too; or, if not, they will groan for themselves.

§. 4. Boldly make a desperate Push, Man, as the Saying is, for Prosperity, for Freedom, for Magnanimity. Lift up your Head, at last, as free from Slavery. Dare to look up to God, and say; "Make use of me for the future as thou wilt. I "am of the same Mind: I am equal with Thee. "I refuse nothing which seems good to Thee. "Lead me whither Thou wilt. Clothe me in "whatever Dress Thou wilt. Is it Thy Will, "that I should be in a public or a private Condi-"tion; dwell here, or be banished; be poor, or "rich? Under all these Circumstances I will make "Thy Defence to Men (*k*). I will show what the "Nature of every Thing is."——No. Rather sit alone, in a warm (*l*) Place, and wait till your Mamma comes to feed you. If *Hercules* had sat loitering at Home, what would he have been? *Eurystheus*, and not *Hercules*. Besides, by travelling through the

(*k*) There are innumerable Passages in St. *Paul*, which, in reality, bear that noble Testimony which *Epictetus* here requires in his imaginary Character. Such are those in which he *glories in Tribulation*; speaks with an heroic Contempt of Life, when set in Competition with the Performance of his Duty; rejoices in Bonds and Imprisonments, and the View of his approaching Martyrdom: and represents Afflictions as a Proof of God's Love. See *Acts* xx. 23, 24. *Rom.* v. 3. viii. 35—39. 2 *Tim.* iv. 6.

(*l*) The Sense of the original Phrase, an Ox's Belly, is obscure to me. The *French* Translation hath, *in your Cradle*.

the World, how many Acquaintance, and how many Friends, had he? But none more his Friend, than God: for which Reaſon he was believed to be the Son of God; and was ſo. In Obedience to him, he went about extirpating Injuſtice, and lawleſs Force. But you are not *Hercules*; nor able to extirpate the Evils of others: nor even *Theſeus*, to extirpate the Evils of *Attica*. Extirpate your own then. Expel, inſtead of *Procruſtes* and *Sciron* (*m*), Grief, Fear, Deſire, Envy, Malevolence, Avarice, Effeminacy, Intemperance, [from your Mind]. But theſe can be no otherwiſe expelled, than looking up to God alone, as your Pattern: by attaching yourſelf to him alone, and being conſecrated to his Commands. If you wiſh for any thing elſe, you will, with Sighs and Groans, follow what is ſtronger than you: always ſeeking Proſperity without, and never able to find it. For you ſeek it where it is not, and neglect to ſeek it where it is.

CHAPTER XVII.

How to adopt Pre-conceptions to particular Caſes.

§. 1. WHAT is the firſt Buſineſs of one who ſtudies Philoſophy? (*a*) To part with Self-Conceit. For it is impoſſible for any one to begin to learn what he hath a Conceit that he already knows. We all go to the Philoſophers, talking at all Adventures upon negative and poſitive Duties; Good and Evil; Fair and Baſe. We praiſe, cenſure, accuſe; we judge and diſpute about fair and baſe Enterpriſes. And for what do we go to the Philoſophers? To learn what we ſuppoſe ourſelves

(*m*) Two famous Robbers, who infeſted *Attica*, and were at laſt killed by *Theſeus*. UPTON.

(*a*) See B. II. c. 11. §. 1.

selves not to know. And what is this? Theorems. We are desirous to hear what the Philosophers say, for its Elegance and Acuteness; and some with a View only to Gain. Now it is ridiculous to suppose, that a Person will learn any thing, but what he desires to learn; or make an Improvement, in what he doth not learn. But most are deceived, in the same Manner as *Theopompus*, the Orator, when he blames *Plato*, for defining every thing. "For, "what, says he, did none of us, before you, use "the Words *Good* and *Just*: or did we utter them "as empty Sounds, without understanding what "each of them meant?" Why, who tells you, *Theopompus*, that we had not natural Ideas and Pre-conceptions of each of these? But it is not possible, to adapt Pre-conceptions to their correspondent Subjects, without having minutely distinguished them, and examined what is the proper Subject to each. You may make the same Objection to the Physicians. For who of us did not use the Words, Wholesome and Unwholesome, before *Hippocrates* was born: or did we utter them as empty Sounds? For we have some Pre-conception of Wholesome too; but we cannot adapt it. Hence, one says, Let the Patient abstain from Meat; another, Give it him: one says, Let him be bled; another, Cup him. And what is the Reason, but not being able to adapt the Pre-conception of Wholesome, to particular Cases? Thus, too in Life: who of us doth not talk of Good and Evil; Advantageous and Disadvantageous: for who of us hath not a Pre-conception of each of these? But is it then a distinct and perfect one? Show me this.

How shall I show it?

§. 2. Adapt it properly to particular Subjects. *Plato*, to go no farther, puts Definitions under the Pre-conception of Useful; but you, under that of Useless. Can both of you be right? How is it possible? Again: doth not one Man adapt the Pre-

conception

conception of Good, to Riches? Another, not to Riches, but to Pleasure, or Health? Upon the whole, if none of us, who use Words, either utter them without Meaning, or need to take any manner of Care in distinguishing our Pre-conceptions, why do we differ? Why do we wrangle? Why do we censure each other? But what Occasion have I to mention this mutual Contradiction? If you yourself adapt your Pre-conceptions properly, how comes it to pass, that you do not prosper? Why do you meet with any Hindrance? Let us for the present omit the second Topic, concerning the *Pursuits*, and the Duties relative to them: Let us omit the Third too, concerning *Assent*. I make you a Present of all these. Let us insist only on the First (*b*); which affords almost a sensible Proof, that you do not adapt your Pre-conceptions right. You desire what is possible in itself, and possible for you. Why then are you hindered? Why are not you in a prosperous Way? You do not decline what is necessary. Why then do you incur any thing [which is your Aversion?]. Why are you unfortunate? When you desire any thing, why doth it not happen? When you do not desire it, why doth it happen? For this is the greatest Demonstration of ill Success and Misery. I desire something; and it doth not happen: and what is more wretched than I? From an Impatience of this, *Medea* came to murder her own Children: an Action of a noble Spirit in this View; for she had a proper Impression of what it was to be disappointed of one's Desire. "Thus I shall punish him, who hath injured and "dishonoured me: and what is so wicked a Wretch "good for? But how is this to be effected? I will "murder the Children: but that will be punish-"ing myself. And what do I care?" This is the Error of a Soul indued with great Powers. For she knew

(*b*) *i. e.* The Topic of the *Desires* and *Aversions*.

knew not where the Completion of our Desires is to be found: that it is not to be had from without; nor by altering the Appointment of Things. Do *not* desire the Man for your Husband, and nothing which you *do* desire will fail to happen. Do not desire to keep him to yourself. Do not desire to stay at *Corinth*; and, in a Word, have no Will, but the Will of God; and who shall restrain you; who shall compel *you*, any more than *Jupiter*? When you have such a Guide, and conform your Will and Inclinations to his, what need you fear being disappointed? Yield up your Desire and Aversion [as Slaves] to Riches, or Poverty; the one will be disappointed, the other incurred. Yield them up to Health, Power, Honours, your Country, Friends, Children, in short, to any thing independent on Choice, you will be unfortunate. But yield them up to *Jupiter*, and the other Gods. Give yourself up to these: let these govern: let both be ranged on the same Side with these; and how can you be any longer unprosperous? But if, poor Wretch, you envy, and pity, and are jealous, and tremble, and never cease, a single Day, from complaining of yourself, and the Gods, why do you boast of your Education? What Education, Man? That you have learned convertible Syllogisms? Why do not you, if possible, unlearn all these, and begin again; convinced, that hitherto, you have not even touched upon the Point? And, for the future, beginning from this Foundation, proceed, in Order, to the Superstructure; that nothing may happen which you do not wish, and that every thing may happen which you do. Give me but one young Man, who brings this Intention with him to the School; who is a Champion for this Point; and says, "I yield up all the rest: it suffices "me, if once I become able to pass my Life, "free from Hindrance and Grief: to stretch out "my Neck to all Events, as free; and to look "up

" up to Heaven, as the Friend of God; fearing " nothing that can happen." Let any one of you ſhow himſelf of ſuch a Diſpoſition, that I may ſay, " Come into the Place, young Man, that " is of right your own; for you are deſtined to be " an Ornament to Philoſophy. Yours are theſe " Poſſeſſions; yours theſe Books; yours theſe Diſ- " courſes." Then, when he hath maſter'd, and got the better of this firſt Claſs, let him come to me again, and ſay; " I deſire indeed to be free " from Paſſion, and Perturbation; but I deſire too, " as a pious, a philoſophic, and a carefully atten- " tive Man, to know, what is my Duty to God, " to my Parents, to my Relations, to my Country, " and to Strangers." " Come into the ſecond " Claſs too; for this likewiſe is yours." " But I " have now ſufficiently ſtudied the ſecond Claſs too; " and I would willingly be ſecure, and (*c*) un- " ſhaken by Error and Deluſion, not only awake, " but even when aſleep; when warmed with Wine; " when diſeaſed with the Spleen." " You are a " God, Man: your Intentions are great."

§. 3. " No. But I, for my part, deſire to under- " ſtand what *Chryſippus* ſays, in his logical Treatiſe " of the (*d*) *Pſeudomenos*."—Go hang yourſelf, piti- ful Wretch, with ſuch an Intention as this. What Good will it do you? You will read the Whole la- menting all the while; and ſay to others, trembling, " Do as I do."——" Shall I read to you, my " Friend,

(*c*) There are ſeveral Readings and Conjectures. I have fol- lowed *Wolfius*; who reads, for ασιτως, ασειστως; as agreeing beſt with the Senſe.

(*d*) The *Pſeudomenos* was a famous Problem among the Stoics; and it is this. When a Perſon ſays, *I lie*; doth he lie, or doth he not? If he lies, he ſpeaks Truth: if he ſpeaks Truth, he lies. The Philoſophers compoſed many Books on this Difficul- ty. *Chryſippus* wrote ſix. *Philetas* waſted himſelf to Death in ſtudying to anſwer it. MENAGE *on* DIOG. LAERT. L. II. §. 108. BRUCKER *Hiſt. Crit. Philoſ.* vol. i. p. 613, 614.

"Friend, and you to me?——You write (*e*) surprisingly, Sir; and you very finely imitate the "Stile of *Plato*; and you, of *Xenophon*; and you, "of *Antisthenes*." And thus, having relating your Dreams to each other, you return again to the same State. Your Desires and Aversions, your Pursuits, your Intentions, your Resolutions, your Wishes and Endeavours, are just what they were. You do not so much as seek for one to advise you; but are offended when you hear such Things as these; and cry, "An ill-natured old Fellow! He "never wept over me, when I was setting out, nor "said; To what a Danger are you going to be exposed! If you come off safe, Child, I will illuminate my House." "This would have been the "Part of a good-natured Man." Truly, it will be a mighty Happiness, if you do come off safe: it will be worth while to make an Illumination. For you (*f*) ought to be immortal, and exempt from Sickness, to be sure.

§. 4. Throwing away then, I say, this Self-conceit, by which we fancy, we have gained some Knowledge of what is useful, we should come to philosophic Reasoning, as we do to Mathematics and Music: otherwise we shall be far from making any Improvement, even if we have read over all the Collections and Compositions, not only of *Chrysippus*, but of *Antipater* and *Archedemus* too.

CHAP-

(*e*) This is spoken by *Epictetus*, in the Person of one of his Scholars; to ridicule their complimenting each other on their Writings, while they neglected the more important Concern of moral Improvements.

(*f*) Σε δει should be σε ιδει.

CHAPTER XVIII.

How the Appearances of Things are to be combated.

§. 1. EVERY Habit and Faculty is preſerved, and increaſed, by correſpondent Actions: as the Habit of Walking, by walking; of Running, by running. If you would be a Reader, read: if a Writer, write. But if you do not read for a Month together, but do ſomewhat elſe; you will ſee what will be the Conſequence. So, after ſitting ſtill for ten Days, get up and attempt to take a long Walk; and you will find how your Legs are weakened. Upon the whole then, whatever you would make habitual, practiſe it: and, if you would not make a Thing habitual, do not practiſe it; but habituate yourſelf to ſomething elſe.

§. 2. It is the ſame with regard to the Operations of the Soul. Whenever you are angry, be aſſured, that it is not only a preſent Evil, but that you have increaſed a Habit, and added Fuel to a Fire. When you are overcome by the Company of Women, do not eſteem it as a ſingle Defeat, but that you have fed, that you have increaſed, your Diſſoluteneſs. For it is impoſſible, but that Habits and Faculties muſt either be firſt produced, or ſtrengthened and increaſed by correſpondent Actions. Hence the Philoſophers derive the Growth of all Infirmities. When you once deſire Money, for Example, if a Degree of Reaſoning ſufficient to produce a Senſe of the Evil be applied, the Deſire ceaſes; and the governing Faculty of the Mind regains its Authority; whereas if you apply no Remedy, it returns no more to its former State: but, being again excited by a correſponding Appearance, it kindles at the Deſire more quickly than before; and by frequent Repetitions, at laſt becomes callous (*a*): and by this Infirmity

(*a*) Hardened againſt proper Reflections.

firmity is the Love of Money fixed. For he who hath had a Fever, even after it had left him, is not in the ſame State of Health as before, unleſs he was perfectly cured: and the ſame thing happens in Diſtempers of the Soul likewiſe. There are certain Traces and Bliſters left in it; which, unleſs they are well effaced, whenever a new Hurt is received in the ſame Part, inſtead of Bliſters, become Sores.

§. 3. If you would not be of an angry Temper then, do not feed the Habit. Give it nothing to help its Increaſe. Be quiet at firſt, and reckon the Days in which you have not been angry. I uſed to be angry every Day; now every other Day; then every third and fourth Day: and if you miſs it ſo long as thirty Days, offer a ſacrifice of Thankſgiving to God. For Habit is firſt weakened, and then intirely deſtroy'd. "I was not vex'd "To-day (*b*); nor the next Day; nor for three or "four Months after; but took heed to myſelf, "when ſome provoking Things happened." Be aſſured, that you are in a fine Way. "To-day, "when I ſaw a handſome Perſon, I did not ſay to "myſelf, O that I could poſſeſs her! And, how "happy is her Huſband (for he who ſays this, ſays "too, how happy is her Gallant): nor do I go on "to repreſent her as preſent, as undreſs'd, as lying "down beſide me." On this I ſtroak my Head, and ſay, Well done, *Epictetus*; thou haſt ſolved a pretty Sophiſm, a much prettier than one very celebrated in the Schools (*c*). But, if even the Lady ſhould happen to be willing, and give me Intimations of it, and ſend for me, and preſs my Hand, and place herſelf next to me; and I ſhould then forbear,

(*b*) Theſe ſeveral Facts are here ſuppoſed, to be recollected at different Times.

(*c*) In this Place, and the following Lines, the Original mentions particular Forms of Argument, which are now little underſtood; and could not be at all inſtructive to the *Engliſh* Reader.

bear, and get the Victory; that would be a Sophism beyond all the Subtleties of Logic. This, and not disputing artfully, is the proper Subject for Exultation.

§. 4. How then is this to be effected? Be willing to approve yourself to yourself. Be willing to appear beautiful in the Sight of God: be desirous to converse in Purity with your own pure Mind, and with God: and then, if any such Appearance strikes you, *Plato* directs you: "Have Recourse "to Expiations: Go a Suppliant to the Temples "of the averting Deities." It is sufficient, however, if you propose to yourself the Example of wise and good Men, whether alive or dead; and compare your Conduct with theirs. Go to *Socrates*, and see him lying by *Alcibiades*, yet slighting his Youth and Beauty. Consider what a Victory he was conscious of obtaining! What an *Olympic* Prize! In what Number did he stand from *Hercules* (*d*)? So that, by Heaven, one might justly salute *Him* (*e*); Hail! incredibly (*f*) great, universal Victor! not those sorry Boxers and Wrestlers; nor the Gladiators, who resemble them.

§. 5. By placing such an Object over-against you, you will conquer any Appearance, and not be drawn away by it. But, in the first place, be not hurried along with it, by its hasty Vehemence: but say; *Appearance*, wait for me a little. Let me see what you

(*d*) *Hercules* is said to have been the Author of the Gymnastic Games; and the first Victor. Those who afterwards conquered in Wrestling, and the Pancratium, were numbered from him. UPTON.

(*e*) Mr. *Upton* inserts νικησεις, which he conjectures, should be νικησας, into the Text, from his Manuscript: where, probably, it was written merely by an Accident of the Transcriber's casting his Eye upon that Word in the next Line. The Sense needs not this Addition, and perhaps doth better without it.

(*f*) This pompous Title was given to those, who had been Victors in all the *Olympic* Games.

you are, and what you represent. Let me try you. Then, afterwards, do not suffer it to go on drawing gay Pictures of what will follow: if you do, it will lead you where-ever it pleases. But rather oppose to it some good and noble Appearance, and banish this base and sordid one. If you are habituated to this kind of Exercise, you will see what Shoulders, what Nerves, what Sinews, you will have. But now it is mere trifling Talk, and nothing more. He is the true Practitioner, who exercises himself against such Appearances as these. Stay, Wretch, do not be hurried away. The Combat is great, the Atchievement divine; for Empire, for Freedom, for Prosperity, for Tranquillity. Remember God. Invoke Him for your Aid, and Protector; as Sailors do *Castor* and *Pollux*, in a Storm. For what Storm is greater than that which arises from violent Appearances, contending to overset our Reason? Indeed, what is the Storm itself, but Appearance? For, do but take away the Fear of Death, and let there be as many Thunders and Lightnings as you please, you will find, that, in the ruling Faculty, all is Serenity and Calm: but if you are once defeated, and say, you will get the Victory another Time, and then the same thing over again; assure yourself, you will at last be reduced to so weak and wretched a Condition, that you will not so much as know when you do amiss; but you will even begin to make Defences for your Behaviour, and thus verify the Saying of *Hesiod*:

With constant Ills, the Dilatory *strive.*

CHAPTER XIX.

Concerning Those who embrace Philosophy only in Word.

§. 1. THE Argument, called The ruling one, concerning which Disputants questioned each other, appears to have its Rise from

hence

hence (*a*). Of the following Propositions, any Two imply a Contradiction to the Third. They are these. *That every thing past is necessarily true: That an Impossibility is not the Consequence of a Possibility*: And, *That something is a Possibility, which neither is nor will be true. Diodorus*, perceiving this Contradiction, made use of the Probability of the Two first, to prove, That nothing is possible, which neither is nor will be true. Some again hold the Second and Third; That *something is possible, which neither is nor will be true*; and, That *an Impossibility is not the Consequence of a Possibility*: and, consequently, assert, That *not every thing past is necessarily true*. This Way *Cleanthes* and his Followers, took; whom *Antipater* copiously defends. Others, lastly, maintain the First and Third; *That something is possible, which neither is nor will be true*: and That *every thing past is necessarily true*: but then, That *an Impossibility may be the Consequence of a Possibility*. But all these Three Propositions cannot be at once maintained, because of their mutual Contradiction. If any one should ask me then, which of them I maintain; I answer him, That I cannot tell. But I have heard it related, That *Diodorus* held one Opinion about them; the Followers of *Panthædes*, I think, and *Cleanthes*, another; and *Chrysippus* a third.

What then is *yours* (*b*)?

(*c*) None. Nor was I born to examine the Appearances of Things to my own Mind; to compare what is said by others, and thence to form some Principle of my own, as to the Topic [which you mention]. Therefore, [in respect to it,] I am no

M better

(*a*) The curious Reader may see this whole Matter explained, with the greatest Acuteness and Accuracy, by the very learned and ingenious Mr. Harris, in Mr. *Upton*'s Notes.

(*b*) This is spoken to *Epictetus* by one of his Hearers.

(*c*) With Mr. *Upton*, I read οὐδὲν: but it seems necessary, that οὐδὲ should likewise stand; and it is so translated.

better than a Grammarian [who repeats what he hath read]. Who was the Father of *Hector?* *Priam.* Who were his Brothers? *Paris* and *Deiphobus.* Who was his Mother? *Hecuba.* This I have heard related. From whom? From *Homer.* But I believe *Hellanicus*, and other Authors, have written on the same Subject. And what better Account have I of the ruling Argument? But, if I was vain enough, I might, especially at an Entertainment (*d*), astonish all the Company by an Enumeration of Authors, relating to it. *Chrysippus* hath written wonderfully, in his first Book of Possibilities. *Cleanthes* and *Archedemus* have each written separately on this Subject. *Antipater* too hath written, not only in his Treatise of Possibilities, but purposely in a Discourse on the ruling Argument. Have not you read the Work? "No." Read it then.——And what Good will it do him? He will be more trifling and impertinent than he is already. For what else have *you* gained by reading it? What Principle have you formed upon this Subject? But you tell us of *Helen*, and *Priam*, and the Isle of *Calypso*, which never was, nor ever will be. And here, indeed, it is of no great Consequence, if you retain the Story, without forming any Principle of your own. But it is our Misfortune to do so, much more in Morality than upon such Subjects as these.

§. 2. Talk to me concerning Good and Evil (*e*). Hear.

The Wind from Ilium *to the* Cicon's *Shore*
Hath driven me——

Of

(*d*) Some Philosophers affected to show their Learning at such Times; and it is against this idle Ostentation that *Epictetus* points his Discourse: for the Study of Logic itself, under proper Regulations, he often strongly recommends.

(*e*) This I apprehend to be spoken by one of the Scholars of *Epictetus*; who seeing the Contempt with which his Master treats logical Subtleties, in the foregoing Paragraph, desires him to discourse upon Ethics.

Of Things, ſome are good, ſome evil, and ſome indifferent. Now the good, are the Virtues, and whatever partakes of them; and the evil, Vices, and what partakes of Vice: the indifferent, lie between theſe, as Riches, Health, Life, Death, Pleaſure, Pain.

Whence do you know this?

Hellanicus ſays it, in his *Egyptian* Hiſtory *(f)*. For what doth it ſignify, whether one names the Hiſtory of *Hellanicus*, or the Ethics of *Diogenes*, or *Chryſippus*, or *Cleanthes*? Have you then examined any of theſe Things, and formed a Principle of your own? But ſhow me, how you are uſed to exerciſe yourſelf on Shipboard. Remember this Diviſion *(g)*, when the Maſt rattles, and ſome idle Fellow ſtands by you, while you are ſcreaming, and ſays, "For Heaven's ſake, talk as you did a "little while ago. Is it Vice to ſuffer Shipwreck? "Or doth it partake of Vice?" Would not you take up a Log, and throw it at his Head? "What "have we to do with you, Sir? We are periſh-"ing, and you come and jeſt." Again: if *Cæſar* ſhould ſummon you, to anſwer an Accuſation, Remember the Diviſion. If, when you are going in, pale and trembling, any one ſhould meet you, and ſay, "Why do you tremble, Sir? What is this "Affair you are engaged in? Doth *Cæſar* within, "give Virtue and Vice to thoſe who approach "him?"——"What do you too inſult me, and "add to my Evils?"———"Nay, but tell me, "Philoſopher, why you tremble? Is there any o-"ther Danger, but Death, or a Priſon, or bodily "Pain,

(f) *Epictetus* gives this abſurd Reply to ridicule the Fondneſs of his Scholars for quoting Authors, and making a Parade of their Reading: and inſinuates, that it is not at all material, whether a Perſon, who on ſuch Subjects, means nothing further than Talk, knows what he is talking of, or blunders about it ever ſo groſsly.

(g) Of Things into good, evil, and indifferent.

" Pain, or Exile, or Defamation?"——" Why " what should there be else?"——" Are any of " these Vice? Or do they partake of Vice? " What then, did you yourself use to say of these " Things?"——" What have you to do with me, " Sir? My own Evils are enough for me."—— " You say right. Your own Evils are indeed enough " for you; your Baseness, your Cowardice, and " that Arrogance, by which you were elated, as " you sat in the Schools. Why did you plume " yourself with what is not your own? Why did " you call yourself a Stoic?"

§. 3. Observe yourselves thus in your Actions, and you will find of what Sect you are. You will find, that most of you are *Epicureans*; a few Peripatetics, and those but loose ones (*b*). For, by what Action will you prove, that you think Virtue equal, and even superior, to all other Things? Show me a Stoic, if you have one (*i*). Where? Or how should you? You can show, indeed, a Thousand, who repeat the Stoic Reasonings. But do they repeat the *Epicurean* worse? Are they not just as perfect in the Peripatetic? Who then is a *Stoic?* as we call that a *Phidian* Statue, which is formed according to the Art of *Phidias*; so show me some one Person, formed according to the Principles which he professes. Show me one, who is sick, and happy; in Danger, and happy; dying, and happy; exiled, and happy; disgraced, and happy. Show him me; for, by Heaven, I long to see a Stoic. But you [will say] you have not one perfectly formed. Show me then one who is forming: one who is approaching towards this Character. Do me this Favour. Do not refuse an old Man a Sight which he hath never yet seen.

(*b*) The Peripatetics held other Things besides Virtue to be good; but not in near so high a Degree.

(*i*) See Note *e*. B. ii. c. 16.

ſeen. Do you ſuppoſe, that you are [aſked] to ſhow the *Jupiter* or *Minerva* of *Phidias*, a Work of Ivory or Gold? Let any of you ſhow me a human Soul, willing to have the ſame Sentiments with thoſe of God: not to accuſe either God or Man: not to be diſappointed of its Deſire, or incur its Averſion: not to be angry: not to be envious: not to be jealous: in a Word, willing from a Man to become a God; and, in this poor mortal Body, aiming to have Fellowſhip with *Jupiter*. Show him to me. But you cannot. Why then do you impoſe upon yourſelves, and play Tricks with others? Why do you put on a Dreſs not your own; and walk about in it, mere Thieves and Pilferers of Names and Things, which do not belong to you? Here, I am your Preceptor, and you come to be inſtructed by me. And indeed my Intention is to ſecure you from being reſtrained, compelled, hindered: to make you free, proſperous, happy; looking to God upon every Occaſion, great or ſmall. And you come to learn and ſtudy theſe Things. Why then do not you finiſh your Work, if you have the proper Intention; and I, beſides the Intention, the proper Qualifications? What is wanting? When I ſee an Artificer, and the Materials lying ready, I expect the Work. Now here is the Artificer; here are the Materials; what is it we want? Is not the Thing capable of being taught? It is. Is it not in our own Power then? The only Thing of all others that is ſo. Neither Riches, nor Health, nor Fame, nor, in ſhort, any thing elſe is in our Power, except a right Uſe of the Appearances of Things. This alone is, by Nature, not ſubject to Reſtraint, not ſubject to Hindrance. Why then do not you finiſh it? Tell me the Cauſe. It muſt be by my Fault, or yours, or from the Nature of the Thing. The Thing itſelf is practicable, and the only one in our Power. The Fault then muſt be either in me, or in you, or, more truly, in both. Well then, shall we now, at last, bring this Intention along with us? Let us lay aside all that is past. Let us begin. Only believe me, and you will see the Consequence.

CHAPTER XX.

Concerning the Epicureans, *and Academics.*

§. 1. TRUE and evident Propositions must, of Necessity, be used even by those, who contradict them. And, perhaps, one of the strongest Proofs, that there is such a Thing as Evidence, is the Necessity which those, who contradict it, are under, to make use of it. If a Person, for Instance, should deny, that any thing is universally true, he will be obliged to assert the contrary, that nothing is universally true. What, Wretch, not even this itself? For what is this, but to say, that every thing universal is false. Again: if any one should come, and say, "*Know* that there is nothing "to be *known*; but all Things are uncertain:" or another; "*Believe* me, and it will be the better "for you, no Man ought to be *believed* in any "thing:" or a Third, "*Learn* from me, that nothing is to be *learned*; I tell you this, and will "teach the Proof of it, if you please." Now what Difference is there between such as these, and those who call themselves Academics? Who say to us, "Be *convinced*, that no one ever is *convinced* "[on good Grounds]. Believe us, that no body "believes any body."

§. 2. Thus also, when *Epicurus* would destroy the natural Relation of Mankind to each other, he makes use of the very thing he is destroying. For what doth he say? "Be not deceived; be not seduced, and mistaken. There is no natural Re-

"lation

"lation between reaſonable Beings. Believe me. "Thoſe who ſay otherwiſe, miſlead and impoſe "upon you."——Why are *you* concerned for *us* then? Let us be deceived. *You* will fare never the worſe, if all the reſt of us are perſuaded, that there is a natural Relation between Mankind; and that it is by all means to be preſerved. Nay, it will be much ſafer and better. Why do you give yourſelf any Trouble about us, Sir? Why do you break your Reſt for us? Why do you light your Lamp? Why do you riſe early? Why do you compoſe ſo many Volumes? Is it that none of us ſhould be deceived, concerning the Gods; as if they took any Care of Men? Or that we may not ſuppoſe the Eſſence of Good conſiſts in any thing, but Pleaſure? For, if theſe Things be ſo, lie down and ſleep, and lead the Life of which you judge yourſelf worthy; that of a mere Reptile. Eat and drink, and ſatisfy your Paſſion for Women, and eaſe yourſelf and ſnore. What is it to you, whether others think right or wrong about theſe Things? For what have you to do with us? You take care of Sheep, becauſe they afford us their Milk, their Wool, and, at laſt, their Fleſh. And would it not be a deſirable Thing that Men might be ſo lulled and inchanted by the Stoics, as to give themſelves up to be milked and fleeced by you, and ſuch as you? Should not theſe Doctrines be taught to your Brother *Epicureans* only, and concealed from the reſt of the World; who ſhould by all means, above all things, be perſuaded, that we have a natural Relation to each other: and that Temperance is a good Thing, in order that all may be kept ſafe for *you*? Or is this Relation to be preſerved towards ſome, and not towards others? Towards whom then, is it to be preſerved? Towards ſuch as mutually preſerve, or ſuch as violate it? And who violate it more, than you, who teach ſuch Doctrines?

§. 3. What was it then, that waked *Epicurus* from his Sleep; and compelled him to write what he did? What else, but that which is of all others the most powerful in Mankind, Nature; which draws every one, however unwilling and reluctant, to its own Purposes. For since, says she, you think that there is no Relation between Mankind, write this Doctrine, and leave it for the Use of others; and break your Sleep upon that Account; and, by your own Practice, confute your own Principles. Do we say, that *Orestes* was roused from Sleep by the Agitation of the Furies; and was not *Epicurus* waked by Furies, more cruel and avenging, which would not suffer him to rest; but compelled him to divulge his own Evils, as Wine and Madness do the Priests of *Cybele*? So strong and unconquerable a Thing is human Nature! For how can a Vine have the Properties not of a Vine, but of an Olive Tree? Or an Olive Tree, not those of an Olive Tree, but of a Vine? It is impossible. It is inconceivable. Neither, therefore, is it possible for a human Creature intirely to lose human Affections. But even those who have undergone a Mutilation, cannot have their Inclinations also mutilated: and so *Epicurus*, when he had mutilated all the Offices of a Man, of a Master of a Family, of a Citizen, and of a Friend, did not mutilate the Inclinations of Humanity: for he could not, any more than the idle Academics can throw away, or blind their own Senses; though this be, of all others, the Point they labour most. What a Misfortune is it, when any one, after having received, from Nature, Standards and Rules for the Knowledge of Truth, doth not strive to add to these, and make up their Deficiencies; but, on the contrary, endeavours to take away, and destroy, whatever Truth may be known even by them?

§. 4.

§. 4. What say you, Philosopher? What do you think of Piety and Sanctity? If you please, I will prove, that they are good.——Pray do prove it; that our Citizens may be converted (*a*), and honour the Deity, and may no longer neglect what is of the highest Importance.——Have you the Proofs, then?——I have, and I thank you. Since you are so well pleased with this then, learn the contrary: That there are no Gods; or, if there are, that they take no Care of Mankind; neither have we any Concern with them: that this Piety and Sanctity, which is so much talked of by many, is only an Imposition of boasting and sophistical Men; or, perhaps, of Legislators, for a Terror and Restraint to Injustice.——Well done, Philosopher. Our Citizens are much the better for you. You have already brought back all the Youth, to a Contempt of the Deity.——What! doth not this please you, then? Learn next, that Justice is nothing: that Shame is Folly: that the paternal Relation is nothing; the filial, nothing.——Well said, Philosopher: persist; convince the Youth: that we may have many more, to think and talk like you. By such Doctrines as these, have our well-governed States flourished? Upon these was *Sparta* founded! *Lycurgus*, by his Laws, and Method of Education, introduced such Persuasions as these; That it is just as honourable, as it is dishonourable, to be Slaves; and just as dishonourable, as honourable, to be free! They who died at *Thermopylæ*, died from such Principles as these! And from what other Doctrines did the *Athenians* leave their City (*b*)?

§. 5.

(*a*) A New Testament Word.

(*b*) When the *Athenians* found themselves unable to resist the Forces of the *Persians*, they left their City; and, having removed their Wives and Children, and their moveable Effects, to *Træzen* and *Salamis*, went on board their Ships, and defended the Liberty of *Greece* by their Fleet. UPTON *from* CICERO, &c.

§. 5. And yet, they who talk thus, marry, and produce Children; and engage in public Affairs, and get themſelves made Prieſts and Prophets (of whom? Of Gods that have no Exiſtence); and conſult the *Pythian* Prieſteſs, only to hear Falſhoods, and interpret the Oracles to others. What monſtrous Impudence and Impoſture!

§. 6. (*c*) What are you doing, Man? You contradict yourſelf every Day; and yet you will not give up theſe paultry Cavils. When you eat, where do you carry your Hand? To your Mouth, or to your Eye? When you bathe, where do you go? Do you ever call a Kettle, a Diſh; or a Spoon, a Spit? If I were a Servant to one of theſe Gentlemen, were it at the Hazard of being flayed every Day, I would plague him. "Throw ſome Oil "into the Bath, Boy." I would take Pickle, and pour upon his Head. "What is this?" Really, Sir, an Appearance ſtruck me ſo perfectly alike, as not to be diſtinguiſhed from Oil. "Give me the "Soup." I would carry him a Diſh full of Vinegar. "Did not I aſk for the Soup?"——Yes, Sir, this is the Soup.—"Is not this Vinegar?" Why ſo, more than Soup? "Take it and ſmell to it, take it "and taſte it." "How do you know then, but our "Senſes deceive us?" If I had three or four Fellow-ſervants to join with me, I would make him either choke with Paſſion, and burſt, or change his Opinions. But now they inſult us, by making uſe of the Gifts of Nature, while in Words, they deſtroy them. Grateful and modeſt Men, truly! Who, if there were nothing elſe in the Caſe, while they are eating their daily Bread, dare to ſay, "We "do not know, whether there be any *Ceres*, or "*Proſerpine*, or *Pluto* (*d*)." Not to mention, that while

(*c*) What follows is againſt the Academics, who denied the Evidence of the Senſes.

(*d*) By theſe Terms, the Stoics meant intelligent Powers, joining, to bring the Fruits of the Earth to Maturity, and to carry on the Courſe of Nature.

while they enjoy the Night and Day, the Seaſons of the Year, the Stars, the Earth and Sea, they are not the leaſt affected by any of theſe Things; but only ſtudy to throw out ſome idle Problem; and, when they have cleared their Stomachs, go and bathe: but take not the leaſt Care what they ſay; nor on what Subjects; nor to whom; nor what may be the Conſequence of their Talk: whether any well-diſpoſed young Man, by hearing ſuch Doctrines, may not be affected by them, and ſo affected as intirely to loſe the Seeds of his good Diſpoſition: whether they may not furniſh an Adulterer with Occaſions of growing ſhameleſs in his Guilt: whether a public Plunderer may not find Excuſes from theſe Doctrines: whether he, who neglects his Parents, may not gain an additional Confidence from them——(*e*) "What then, in "*your* Opinion, is good and evil, fair and (*f*) baſe; "such Things, or ſuch Things?"——Why ſhould one ſay any more againſt ſuch Creatures as theſe, or give them any Account, or receive any from them, or endeavour to convince them? By *Jupiter*, one might ſooner hope to convince the moſt unnatural Debauchees, than thoſe, who are thus deaf and blind to their own Evils (*g*).

(*e*) Theſe ſeem to be the Words of the Academic, deſirous of begining a Diſpute with *Epictetus*, to revenge himſelf, by puzzling him, for the ſevere Things which he had been ſaying againſt that Sect. But *Epictetus* refuſes to enter into it; and gives his Reaſon.

(*f*) I have followed Mr. *Upton*'s Addition of αισχρον; but, perhaps, even καλον may be an Addition, firſt ariſing from writing η κακον twice over.

(*g*) This reſembles what our Saviour ſaith to the *Jewiſh* Rulers; *Verily I ſay unto you, that the Publicans and the Harlots go into the Kingdom of God before you.* Matt. xxi. 31.

CHAP-

CHAPTER XXI.

Of Inconsistency.

§. 1. THERE are some Things which Men confess, with Ease; others, with Difficulty. No one, for Instance, will confess himself a Fool or a Blockhead; but, on the contrary, you will hear every one say, "I wish my Fortune was "equal to my Mind." But they easily confess themselves fearful; and say, "I am somewhat "timorous, I confess: but in other respects you "will not find me a Fool." No one will easily confess himself intemperate in his Desires; upon no Account dishonest, nor absolutely very envious, or meddling: but many confess themselves to have the Weakness of being compassionate. What is the Reason of all this? The principal is, an Inconsistency and Confusion in what relates to Good and Evil. But different People have different Inducements. In general, whatever they imagine to be base, they do not absolutely confess. Fear and Compassion, they imagine to belong to a well-meaning Disposition; but Stupidity, to a Slave. Offences against Society they do not own: but, in most Faults, they are brought to a Confession, chiefly from imagining, that there is something involuntary in them; as in Fear and Compassion. And, though a Person (*a*) should in some measure confess himself intemperate in his Desires, he accuses his Passion, and expects Forgiveness, as for an involuntary Fault. But Dishonesty is not imagined to be, by any means, involuntary. In Jealousy too, there is something, they suppose, of involuntary; and this likewise, in some degree, they confess.

§. 2.

(*a*) Mr. *Upton*'s Copy.

§. 2. Conversing among such Men, therefore, thus confused, thus ignorant what they say, what are, or are not, their Evils, whence they have them, and how they may be delivered of them; it is worth while, I think, to ask one's self continually, "Am I too one of these? What do I imagine myself to be? How do I conduct myself? "As a prudent, as a temperate Man? Do I, too, "ever talk at this Rate, That I am sufficiently instructed for what may happen? Have I that "Persuasion, That I know nothing, which becomes "one who knows nothing? Do I go to a Master, "as to an Oracle, prepared to obey; or do I, as "well as others, like a stupid Driveller (*b*), enter "the School, only to learn the History [of Philosophy], and understand Books, which I did not "understand before; or, perhaps, to explain them "to others?" (*c*) You have been fighting at home, with your Servant, Sir: you have turned the House upside-down, and alarmed the Neighbourhood: and do you come to me, with a pompous Show of Wisdom, and sit and pass Judgment how I explain a Sentence? How I prate whatever comes into my Head? Do you come, envious and dejected, that nothing is brought you from home? And, in the midst of the Disputations, sit thinking on nothing, but how your Father or your Brother may behave to you? "What are they saying about me at home? Now they think I am improving: and say, He will come back with universal Knowledge. I wish I could learn every "thing before my Return: but this requires much "Labour; and nobody sends me any thing. The "Baths

(*b*) We have no Expression exactly like that in the *Greek*. The Translation comes the nearest to it, of any I could think on.

(*c*) This seems to be spoken by *Epictetus*, to one of his Scholars.

"Baths are very bad at *Nicopolis*; and Things go "very ill both at home, and here."

§. 3. After all this, it is ſaid, nobody is the better for the philoſophic School. Why, who comes to the School? I mean, who comes to be reformed? Who, to ſubmit his Principles to Correction? Who, with a Senſe of his Wants? Why do you wonder then, that you bring back from the School, the very Thing you carried there. For you do not come to lay aſide, or correct, or change, your Principles. How ſhould you? Far from it. Rather conſider this, therefore, whether you have not what you come for. You come to talk about Theorems. Well: and are not you more impertinently talkative than you were? Do not theſe paultry Theorems furniſh you with Matter for Oſtentation? Do not you ſolve convertible and hypothetical Syllogiſms? Why then, are you ſtill diſpleaſed, if you have the very Thing for which you came? ——"Very true: but, if my Child, or my Bro- "ther, ſhould die; or if I muſt die, or be tor- "tured myſelf, what Good will theſe Things do "me?"——Why, did you come for *this?* Did you attend upon me for *this?* Was it upon any ſuch Account, that you ever lighted your Lamp, or ſat up at Night? Or did you, when you went into the Walk, propoſe any Appearance to your own Mind to be diſcuſſed, inſtead of a Syllogiſm? Did any of you ever go through ſuch a Subject jointly? And, after all, you ſay, Theorems are uſeleſs. To whom? To ſuch as apply them ill. For Medicines for the Eyes are not uſeleſs to thoſe, who apply them when, and as, they ought. Fomentations are not uſeleſs: Poiſers are not uſeleſs: but they are uſeleſs to ſome; and, on the contrary, uſeful to others. If you ſhould aſk me now, Are Syllogiſms uſeful? I anſwer, that they are uſeful: and, if you pleaſe, I will ſhow you how (*d*).——"Will they be of Service to me, "then?"——Why: did you aſk, Man, whether they would be uſeful to *you*, or in general? If any one in a Dyſentery ſhould aſk me, whether Acids be uſeful; I anſwer, They are. "Are they "uſeful for *me*, then?——I ſay, No. Firſt try to get the Flux ſtopt, and the Exulceration healed. Do you too firſt get your Ulcers healed; your Fluxes ſtopt. Quiet your Mind, and bring it free from Diſtraction, to the School; and then you will know what is the Force of Reaſoning.

CHAPTER XXII.

Of Friendſhip.

§. 1. TO whatever Objects a Perſon devotes his Attention, theſe Objects he, probably, loves. Do Men ever devote their Attention then, to Evils?——By no means.——Or even to what doth not concern them?——No: nor this.——It remains then, that *Good* muſt be the ſole Object of their Attention; and, if of their Attention, of their Love too. Whoever, therefore, underſtands *Good*, is capable likewiſe of Love: and he who cannot diſtinguiſh Good from Evil, and Things indifferent from both, how is it poſſible, that he can love? The prudent Perſon alone then, is capable of loving.

How ſo? I am not this prudent perſon, yet I love my Child.

I proteſt it ſurprizes me, that you ſhould, in the firſt place, confeſs yourſelf imprudent. For in what are you deficient? Have not you the Uſe of your Senſes? Do not you diſtinguiſh the Appearances of Things? Do not you provide ſuch Food, and

(*d*) The *Greek* is pointed at αποδειξω; but the Senſe requires the Stop, at πως.

and Cloathing, and Habitation, as are suitable to you? Why then do you confess, that you want Prudence? In truth, because you are often struck, and disconcerted by Appearances, and their Speciousness gets the better of you; and hence you sometimes suppose the very same Things to be good, then evil, and, lastly, neither: and, in a word, you grieve, you fear, you envy, you are disconcerted, you change. Is it from hence, that you confess yourself imprudent? And are you not changeable too in Love? Riches, Pleasure, in short, the very same Things, you at some times esteem good, and at others, evil: and do not you esteem the same Persons too, alternately good and bad? And, at one time, treat them with Kindness, at another, with Enmity? One time, commend, and at another, censure them?

Yes. This too is the Case, with me.

Well then, can he who is deceived in another, be his Friend, think you?

No, surely.

Or doth he, who loves him with a changeable Affection, bear him genuine Good-will?

Nor he, neither.

Or he, who now vilifies, then admires him?

Nor he.

Do you not often see little Dogs caressing, and playing with each other, that you would say, nothing could be more friendly: but, to learn what this Friendship is, throw a Bit of Meat between them, and you will see. Do you too throw a Bit of an Estate, betwixt you and your Son, and you will see, that he will quickly wish *you* under Ground, and you *him*: and then you, no doubt, on the other hand, will exclaim; What a Son have I brought up! He would bury me alive! Throw in a pretty Girl, and the old Fellow and the young one will, both, fall in Love with her:

or

or let Fame or Danger intervene, the Words of the Father of *Admetus* will be yours *a)*:

You hold Life dear: Doth not your Father too?

Do you suppose, that he did not love his own Child, when he was a little one? That he was not in Agonies, when he had a Fever; and often wished to undergo that Fever in his stead? But, after all, when the Trial comes home, you see what Expressions he uses. Were not *Eteocles* and *Polynices* born of the same Mother, and of the same Father? Were they not brought up, and did they not live, and eat, and sleep, together? Did not they kiss and fondle each other? So that any one, who saw them, would have laughed at all the Paradoxes, which Philosophers utter about Love.

(a) Admetus, King of *Thessaly*, being destined to die, *Apollo* obtained a Reversal of his Sentence from the Fates, on Condition, that some Person could be found to die in his stead. *Admetus* tried all his Friends, and, among the rest, his Father, *Pheres*; but no one chose to be his Representative, but his Wife, *Alcestis*. After her Death, *Pheres* is introduced preparing Honours for her Funeral, and condoling with his Son, on her Loss. *Admetus* rejects his Presents, with great Indignation; and makes him the severest Reproaches, on his Cowardice and Mean-spiritedness, in not parting with a few remaining Years of Life, to save his Son from an untimely Death; and in suffering *Alcestis* to descend to the Grave for him, in the Bloom of Youth. The Quotation made by *Epictetus*, is Part of the Answer of *Pheres*, to the Reproaches of his Son.

Some of the finest and most touching Parts of the Dialogue, in *Edward* and *Eleonora*, are taken from the *Alcestis*; but Mr. *Thomson* is much happier, in the Conduct of his Story, than *Euripides*. *Eleonora* exposes herself to Death, against the Consent, and without the Knowledge, of her Husband; which by no means appears to have been the Case of *Alcestis*. This Circumstance renders *Admetus*, a most despicable Character, throughout the Play; and the Reproaches which he throws upon *Pheres* appear absurd, and shocking. It is a little remarkable, that *Epictetus* should treat the Father with so much Contempt, and bestow none on the Son, to whom it was, at least equally, due. See B. III. c. 20. §. 1.

And yet, when a Kingdom, like a Bit of Meat, was thrown betwixt them, see what they say, and how eagerly they wish to kill each other (*b*). For universally, be not deceived, no Animal is attached to any thing so strongly, as to its own Interest. Whatever therefore, appears a Hindrance to that, be it Brother, or Father, or Child, or Mistress, or Friend, is hated, abhorred, execrated; for, by Nature, it loves nothing like its own Interest. This is Father, and Brother, and Family, and Country, and God (*c*). Whenever therefore, the Gods seem to hinder this, we vilify even them, and throw down their Statues, and burn their Temples; as *Alexander* ordered the Temple of *Esculapius* to be burnt, because he had lost the Man he loved.

§. 2. Whenever therefore, any one makes his Interest to consist in the same thing with Sanctity, Virtue, his Country, Parents, and Friends, all these are secured: but, where-ever they are made to interfere, Friends, and Country, and Family, and Justice itself, all give way, borne down by the Weight of Self-interest. For wherever *I* and *mine* are placed, thither must every Animal gravitate. If in Body, that will sway us; if in Choice, that; if in Externals, these. If therefore, *I* be placed in a right Choice, then only, I shall be a Friend, a Son, or a Father, such as I ought. For, in that Case, it will be for my Interest to preserve the faithful, the modest, the patient, the abstinent, the beneficent, Character; to keep the Relations of Life inviolate. But, if I place my *self* in one Thing, and Virtue in another, the Doctrine of *Epicurus* will stand

(*b*) The Original quotes some Verses from *Euripides*, of a Dialogue between *Eteocles* and *Polynices*, before the Walls of *Thebes*; of which the Translation gives the general Sense.

(*c*) See *Matt.* xii. 50.

ſtand its Ground, That Virtue is nothing, or mere Opinion (*d*).

§. 3. From this Ignorance it was, that the *Athenians* and *Lacedemonians* quarrelled with each other; and the *Thebans* with both: the *Perſian* King, with *Greece*; and the *Macedonians*, with both: and now the *Romans*, with the *Getes*. And, in ſtill remoter Times, the *Trojan* War aroſe from the ſame Cauſe. *Paris* was the Gueſt of *Menelaus*; and whoever had ſeen the mutual Proofs of Good-will, that paſſed between them, would never have believed, that they were not Friends. But a tempting Bit, a pretty Woman, was thrown in between them; and for this they went to War. At preſent, therefore, when you ſee dear Brothers have, in Appearance, but one Soul, do not immediately pronounce upon their Friendſhip; not though they ſhould ſwear it, and affirm it was impoſſible to live aſunder. (For the governing Faculty of a bad Man is faithleſs, unſettled, injudicious; ſucceſſively vanquiſhed by different Appearances). But inquire, not as others do, whether they were born of the ſame Parents, and brought up together, and under the ſame Preceptor; but this Thing only, in what they place their Intereſt; in Externals, or in Choice. If in Externals, no more call them Friends, than faithful, or conſtant, or brave, or free; nay, not even Men, if you are wiſe. For it is no Principle of Humanity, that makes them bite and vilify each other; and take Poſſeſſion of public Aſſemblies, as wild Beaſts do of Solitudes and Mountains;

 and

(*d*) By *ſelf* is here meant the proper Good, or, as *Solomon* expreſſes it, *Eccl.* xii. 13. *The Whole of Man.* The Stoic proves excellently, the Inconvenience of placing this, in any thing but a right Choice (a right Diſpoſition and Behaviour): but how it is the Intereſt of each Individual, in every Caſe, to make that Choice, in Preference to preſent Pleaſure, and in Defiance of preſent Sufferings, appears only from the Doctrine of a future Recompence.

and convert Courts of Justice into Dens of Robbers: nor that prompts them to be intemperate, Adulterers, Seducers; or leads them into other Offences, that Men commit against each other, from the one single Principle, by which they place themselves, and their own Concerns, in Things independent on Choice.

§. 4. But, if you hear, that these Men, in reality suppose Good to be placed only in Choice, and in a right Use of the Appearances of Things; no longer take the trouble of inquiring, if they are Father and Son, or old Companions and Acquaintance; but as boldly pronounce, that they are Friends, as that they are faithful and just. For where else can Friendship be met, but with Fidelity and Modesty, and a Communication (*e*) of Virtue; and of no other Thing?

Well: but such a one paid me the utmost Regard, for so long a Time; and did not he *love* me?

How can you tell, Wretch, if that Regard be any other than he pays to his Shoes, or his Horse, when he cleans them? And, how do you know, but when you cease to be a necessary Utensil, he may throw you away, like a broken Stool?

Well: but it is my Wife; and we have lived together many Years.

And how many did *Eriphyle* live with *Amphiaraus*; and was the Mother of Children, and not a few? But a Bracelet fell in between them. What was this Bracelet? The Principle [she had formed] concerning such Things. This turned her into a savage Animal: this cut asunder all Love; and suffered neither the Wife, nor the Mother, to continue such (*f*).

§. 5.

(*e*) Perhaps δοσις, in the *Greek*, should be διαδοσις.

(*f*) *Amphiaraus* married *Eriphyle*, the Sister of *Adrastus*, King of *Argos*. He was an excellent Soothsayer; and, by his Skill,

§. 5. Whoever therefore, among you, studies to be, or to gain a Friend, let him cut up all these Principles by the Root; hate them; drive them utterly out of his Soul. Thus, in the first place, he will be secure from inward Reproaches, and Contests; from Change of Mind, and Self-torment. Then, with respect to others; to every one, like himself, he will be unreserved. To such as are unlike, he will be patient, mild, gentle, and ready to forgive them, as failing in Points of the greatest Importance: but severe to none; being fully convinced of *Plato's* Doctrine, that the Soul is never willingly deprived of Truth. Without all this, you may, in many Respects, live as Friends do; and drink, and lodge, and travel together, and be born of the same Parents; and so may (g) Serpents too: but neither they, nor you, can ever be Friends, while you have these brutal and execrable Principles.

CHAPTER XXIII.

Of the Faculty of Speaking.

§. 1. A BOOK will always be read with the greater Pleasure, and Ease too, if it be written in a fair Character: therefore every one will the more easily attend to Discourses likewise, ornamented with proper and beautiful Expressions. It (a) ought not then to be said, that there is no such Thing

Skill, foresaw, that it would prove fatal to him, if he engaged himself in the *Theban* War. Wherefore, to avoid inevitable Destruction, he hid himself: but was discovered by his Wife *Eriphyle*, whom *Polynices* had corrupted, with a Present of a golden Chain. STATIUS's *Thebais*, L. VI.

(g) Mr. *Upton's* Copy.

(a) These are the Words of *Epictetus*; to which there are others equivalent afterwards. His Meaning, probably, is, that

Thing as the Faculty of Elocution: for this would be at once the Part of an impious and fearful Person (*b*). Impious; because he dishonours the Gifts of God; just as if he should deny any Use in the Faculty of Sight, Hearing, and Speech itself. Hath God then given you Eyes in vain? Is it in vain, that he hath infused into them, such a strong and active Spirit, as to be able to represent the Forms of distant Objects (*c*)? What Messenger is so quick and diligent? Is it in vain, that he hath made the intermediate Air, so yielding, and elastic, that the Sight penetrates through it? And is it in vain, that he hath made the Light; without which all the rest would be useless? Man, be not ingrateful; nor, on the other hand, unmindful of your superior Advantages (*d*): but for Sight, and Hearing, and indeed for Life itself and the Supports of it, as Fruits, and Wine, and Oil, be thankful to God: but remember, that he hath given you another Thing, superior to them all; which makes use of them, proves them, estimates the Value of each (*e*). For what is it that pronounces upon the Value of each of these Faculties? Is it the Faculty itself? Did you ever perceive the Faculty of Sight or Hearing, to say any thing concerning itself? Or Wheat, or Barley, or Horses, or Dogs? No. These Things are appointed as Instruments and Servants, to

that the Value and Usefulness of the Faculty of Elocution ought not to be denied: in Opposition to the Doctrine of *Epicurus*, who declared all the liberal Arts and Sciences to be useless and mischievous. See DIOG. LAERT. L. X. §. 6. and MENAGE's Notes there.

(*b*) He proves the Timidity at the Beginning of §. 3.

(*c*) It was an old Notion, that Vision was performed by the Emission of Rays from the Eye to the Object, not the Admission of Rays from the Object into the Eye; and to this *Epictetus* here refers.

(*d*) Mr. *Upton* gives a different Sense to κρεισσονων; but I think, that both παλιν, and what afterwards follows, justifies the *English* Translation.

(*e*) See B. I. c. 1.

to obey that which is capable of uſing the Appearances of Things. If you inquire the Value of any thing; of *what* do you inquire? What is it that anſwers you *(f)*? How then can any Faculty be ſuperior to this; which both uſes all the reſt as Inſtruments, and tries and pronounces concerning each of them? For which of them knows, what itſelf is; and what is its own Value? Which of them knows, when it is to be uſed, and when not? Which is it, that opens and ſhuts the Eyes, and turns them away from improper Objects? Is it the Faculty of Sight? No: but that of *Choice*. Which is it, that opens and ſhuts the Ears? What is it, by which they are made curious and inquiſitive; or, on the contrary, deaf, and unaffected by what is ſaid? Is it the Faculty of Hearing? No: but that of *Choice*. Will this then, perceiving itſelf to exiſt in [Man amidſt] the other Faculties, [which are] all blind and deaf, and unable to diſcern any thing, but thoſe Offices, in which they are appointed to miniſter, and be ſubſervient to it; and that itſelf alone ſees clearly, and diſtinguiſhes the Value of each of the reſt; will this, I ſay, inform us, that any thing is ſupreme, but itſelf? What doth the Eye, when it is opened, do more, than ſee? But whether we ought to look upon the Wife of any one, and in what manner, what is it that tells us? The Faculty of *Choice*. Whether we ought to believe, or to diſbelieve what is ſaid; or whether, if we do believe, we ought to be moved by it, or not; what is it that tells us? Is it not the Faculty of *Choice?* Again: the very Faculty of Elocution, and that which ornaments Diſcourſe, if there be any ſuch peculiar Faculty, what doth it more, than merely ornament and arrange Expreſſions, as

(f) The Hearer is underſtood in this Place to ſay, The Faculty of Choice. It is not improbable, however, that the *Greek* Word προαιρετικη, may have been omitted in tranſcribing.

Curlers do the Hair? But whether it be better to ſpeak, or to be ſilent; or better to ſpeak in this, or in that Manner; whether this be decent, or indecent; and the Seaſon and Uſe of each; what is it that tells us, but the Faculty of *Choice?* What then, would you have it appear, and bear Teſtimony againſt itſelf? What means this? If the Caſe be thus, that which ſerves, may be ſuperior to that to which it is ſubſervient; the Horſe to the Rider; the Dog, to the Hunter; the Inſtrument, to the Muſician; or Servants to the King. What is it that makes uſe of all the reſt? *Choice.* What takes care of all? *Choice.* What deſtroys the whole Man, at one time, by Hunger; at another, by a Rope, or a Precipice? *Choice.* Hath Man, then, any thing ſtronger than this? And how is it poſſible, that what is liable to Reſtraint ſhould be ſtronger, than what is not? What hath a natural Power of hindering the Faculty of Sight? Both Choice, and what depends on Choice. And it is the ſame of the Faculties of Hearing and Speech. And what hath a natural Power of hindering Choice? Nothing independent on itſelf, only its own Perverſion. Therefore *Choice* alone is Vice: *Choice* alone is Virtue.

§. 2. Since, then, Choice is ſuch a Faculty, and placed in Authority over all the reſt, let it come forth and ſay to us, that the Body is, of all Things, the moſt excellent. If even the Body itſelf pronounced itſelf to be the moſt excellent, it could not be borne. But now, what is it, *Epicurus*, that pronounces all this? What was it, that compoſed Volumes, concerning (*g*) the End of [Being], the (*g*) Nature of Things, the (*g*) Rule [of Reaſoning]; that aſſumed a philoſophic Beard; that, as it was dying, wrote, that it was *then ſpending its laſt*

(*g*) Celebrated Treatiſes on theſe Subjects, compoſed by *Epicurus.*

last and happiest Day (h)? Was this, Body, or was it the Faculty of Choice? And can you then, without Madneſs, confeſs any thing ſuperior to *this?* Are you in reality ſo deaf and blind? What then, doth any one, diſhonour the other Faculties? Heaven forbid! Doth any one deny, that the Faculty of Sight (*i*) is uſeful, and preferable [to the Want of it]? Heaven forbid! It would be ſtupid, impious, and ungrateful to God. But we render to each its Due. There is ſome Uſe of an Aſs, tho' not ſo much as of an Ox; and of a Dog, though not ſo much as of a Servant; and of a Servant, though not ſo much as of the Citizens; and of the Citizens, though not ſo much as of the Magiſtrates. And, though ſome are more excellent than others, thoſe Uſes, which the laſt afford, are not to be deſpiſed. The Faculty of Elocution hath its Value, though not equal to that of Choice. When therefore I talk thus, let not any one ſuppoſe, that I would have you neglect Elocution, any more than your Eyes, or Ears, or Hands, or Feet, or Clothes, or Shoes. But if you aſk me, what is the moſt excellent of Things, what ſhall I ſay? I cannot ſay, *Elocution*; but a right *Choice*: for it is that which makes uſe of this, and all the other Faculties, whether great or ſmall. If this be ſet right, a bad Man becomes good; if it be wrong, a good Man becomes wicked. By this we are unfortunate, fortunate; we diſapprove, or approve each other. In a word, it is this, which, neglected, forms Unhappineſs; and, well cultivated, Happineſs.

§. 3. But to take away the Faculty of Elocution; and to ſay, that it is in reality nothing, is not only ingrateful

(*h*) Theſe Words are Part of a Letter written by *Epicurus*, when he was dying, to one of his Friends. See DIOG. LAERT. L. X. §. 22.

(*i*) Probably for προαιρετικης ſhould be read ορατικης; which Word is uſed by *Epictetus*, but a little more than a Page before.

ingrateful to those who gave it, but cowardly too. For such a Person seems to me to be afraid, that, if there be any such Faculty, we may not, on occasion, be able to treat it with Contempt. Such are they too, who deny any Difference between Beauty, and Deformity. Was it possible then, to be affected in the same Manner by seeing *Thersites*, as *Achilles*; or *Helen*, as any (*k*) other Woman? These also are the foolish and clownish Notions of those, who are ignorant of the Nature of Things; and afraid, that, whoever perceives a Difference, must presently be carried away, and overcome. But the great Point is to leave to each Thing its own proper Faculty; and then to see what the Value of that Faculty is, and to learn what is the principal Thing, and, upon every Occasion, to follow that, and to make it the chief Object of our Attention: to consider other Things as trifling in Comparison of this; and yet, as far as we are able, not to neglect even these. We ought, for Instance, to take care of our Eyes; but not as of the principal Thing; but only on account of the Principal: because *that* will no otherwise preserve its own Nature, than by making a due Estimation of the rest, and preferring some to others. What is the usual Practice then? That of a Traveller, who returning into his own Country, and meeting on the Road with a good *Inn*, being pleased with the *Inn*, should remain at the *Inn*. Have you forgot your Intention, Man? You were not travelling *to* this Place, but only *through* it. "But this is a fine Place." And how many other fine Inns are there, and how many pleasant Fields? But only to be past through in your Way. The Business is, to return to your Country; to relieve the Anxieties of your Family; to perform the Duties of a Citizen; to marry; have Children; and go through the public Offices. For you

(*k*) Mr. *Upton*'s Reading ἣν ἔτυχε.

you did not set out, to chuse the finest Places; but to return, to live in that where you were born, and of which you are appointed a Citizen.

§. 4. Such is the present Case. Because by Speech, and verbal Precepts, we are to arrive at Perfection; and purify our own Choice; and rectify that Faculty, of which the Office is, the Use of the Appearances of Things: and, because, for the Delivery of Theorems, a certain Manner of Expression, and some Variety and Subtilty of Discourse, becomes necessary; many, captivated by these very Things, one, by Expression, another, by Syllogisms, a third, by convertible Propositions, just as our Traveller was by the good Inn, go no further: but sit down and waste their Lives shamefully there, as if amongst the Sirens. Your Business, Man, was to prepare yourself for such an Use of the Appearances of Things, as Nature demands: Not to be frustrated of your Desires, or incur your Aversions: never to be disappointed, or unfortunate: but free, unrestrained, uncompelled; conformed to the Administration of *Jupiter*; obedient to that; finding fault with nothing: but able to say, from your whole Soul, the Verses which begin,

Conduct me, Jove; *and thou*, O Destiny.

While you have such a Business before you, will you be so pleased with a pretty Form of Expression, or a few Theorems, as to chuse to stay and live with them, forgetful of your Home; and say, "They are fine Things!" Why, who says they are not fine Things; But only as a Passage; as an Inn. For, could you speak like *Demosthenes*, what hinders, but that you might be a disappointed Wretch? Could you resolve Syllogisms like *Chrisippus*, what hinders, but that you might be miserable, sorrowful, envious, in short, disturbed, unhappy? Nothing. You see then, that these are mere Inns, of small Value; and that your Point

in-

in View, is quite another Thing. When I talk thus to ſome, they ſuppoſe, that I am overthrowing all Care about Speaking, and about Theorems: but I do not overthrow that; only the reſting in theſe Things without End, and placing our Hopes there. If any one, by maintaining this, hurts an Audience, place me amongſt thoſe hurtful People: for I cannot, when I ſee one Thing to be the principal and moſt excellent, call another ſo, to gain your Favour.

CHAPTER XXIV.

Concerning a Perſon whom he treated with Diſregard.

§. 1. WHEN a certain Perſon ſaid to him; "I have often come to you, with a "Deſire of hearing you; and you have never given "me any Anſwer; but now, if poſſible, I intreat "you to ſay ſomething to me:" Do you think, replied *Epictetus*, that, as in other Things, ſo in Speaking, there is an Art, by which he, who underſtands it, ſpeaks ſkilfully, and he, who doth not, unſkilfully?

I do think ſo.

He then, who, by ſpeaking, both benefits himſelf, and is able to benefit others, muſt ſpeak ſkilfully; but he who rather hurts, and is hurt, muſt be unſkilful in this Art of ſpeaking. For you may find ſome Speakers hurt, and others benefited. And are all Hearers benefited by what they hear? Or will you find ſome benefited, and ſome hurt (*a*)?

Both.

Then thoſe who hear ſkilfully are benefited, and thoſe who hear unſkilfully, hurt.

Granted.

Is

(*a*) 2 *Cor.* ii. 16.

Is there an Art of Hearing, then, as well as of Speaking?

It ſeems ſo.

If you pleaſe, conſider it thus too. To whom, do you think, the Practice of Muſic belongs?

To a Muſician.

To whom the proper Formation of a Statue?

To a Statuary.

And do not you imagine ſome Art neceſſary, to view a Statue ſkilfully?

I do.

If, therefore, to *ſpeak* properly belongs to one who is ſkilful, do not you ſee, that to *hear* with Benefit belongs likewiſe to one who is ſkilful? For the preſent, however, if you pleaſe, let us ſay no more of doing Things perfectly, and with Benefit, ſince we are both far enough, from any thing of that Kind: but this ſeems to be univerſally confeſſed, that he, who would hear Philoſophers, needs ſome Kind of Exerciſe in Hearing. Is it not ſo? Tell me then, on what I ſhall ſpeak to you? On what Subject are you able to hear me (*b*)?

On Good and Evil.

The Good and Evil of what? Of a Horſe?

No.

Of an Ox.

No.

What then, of a Man?

Yes.

Do we know, then, what *Man* is? What is his Nature; what our Idea of him is; and how far our Ears are open in reſpect to this Matter (*c*). Nay, do you underſtand what Nature is; or are you able, and in what Degree, to comprehend me, when

(*b*) See *John* viii. 43.

(*c*) Κατα ποσον, περι του, ſhould be κατα ποσον περι τουτου. There is no Need of altering τα ωτα τετρημενα. *Opening the Ear*, is a Phraſe of Scripture. *Job* xxxiii. 16. xxxvi. 10. *Iſ.* lii. 20. *Mark* vii. 34, 35. And even digging open the Ear. *Pſ.* xl. 6. in the *Hebrew*.

when I come to say; "But I must use Demonstration to you?" How should you? Do you comprehend what Demonstration is; or, how a Thing is demonstrated; or by what Methods; or, what resembles a Demonstration, and yet is not a Demonstration? Do you know what True, or False is? What is consequent to a Thing, and what contradictory? Or unsuitable, or dissonant? But I must excite you to Philosophy. How shall I show you that Contradiction, among the Generality of Mankind, by which they differ, concerning Good and Evil, Profitable and Unprofitable, when you know not what *Contradiction* means? Show me then, what I shall gain, by discoursing with you? Excite an Inclination in me, as a proper Pasture excites an Inclination to eating, in a Sheep: for if you offer him a Stone, or a Piece of Bread, he will not be excited. Thus we too have certain natural Inclinations to speaking, when the Hearer appears to be somebody; when he gives us Encouragement: but if he sits by, like a Stone, or a Tuft of Grass, how can he excite any Desire in a Man? Doth a Vine say to an Husbandman, "Take care of me?" No: but invites him to take care of it, by showing him, that, if he doth, it will reward him for his Care. Who is there, whom engaging sprightly Children do not invite to play, and creep, and prattle, with them? But who was ever taken with an Inclination to divert himself, or bray, with an Ass? for, be the Creature ever so little, it is still a little Ass.

§. 2. Why do you say nothing to me, then?

I have only this to say to you: That, whoever is ignorant what he is, and wherefore he was born, and in what kind of a World, and in what Society; what Things are good, and what evil; what fair, and what base: who understands neither Discourse, nor Demonstration; nor what is true, nor what is false; nor is able to distinguish between them: such

a one

a one will neither exert his Desires, nor Aversions, nor Pursuits, conformably to Nature: he will neither intend, nor assent, nor deny, nor suspend, his Judgment, conformably to Nature: but will wander up and down, intirely deaf and blind, supposing himself to be somebody *(d)*; while he is in reality, nobody. Is there any thing new, in all this? Is not this Ignorance the Cause of all the Errors that have happened, from the very Original of Mankind? Why did *Agamemnon* and *Achilles* differ? Was it not for want of knowing what is advantageous, what disadvantageous? Doth not one of them say, It is advantageous to restore *Chryseis* to her Father; the other, That it is not? Doth not one say, That he ought to take away the Prize of the other; the other, that he ought not? Did they not, by these means, forget who they were, and for what Purpose they had come there? Why, what did you come for, Man: to gain a Mistress, or to fight? ——"To fight."——With whom? With the *Trojans*, or *Greeks*?——"With the *Trojans*."—— Leaving *Hector*, then, do you draw your Sword upon your own King? And do you, good Sir, forgetting the Duties of a King,

Intrusted with a Nation, and its Cares,

go to squabbling, about a Girl, with the bravest of your Allies; whom you ought, by every Method, to conciliate and preserve? And will you be inferior to a subtle Priest, who pays his Court, with the utmost Care, to you fine Gladiators?——You see the Effects, which Ignorance of what is advantageous, produces.——"But I am rich [you may "say], as well as other People."——What, richer than *Agamemnon*?——"But I am handsome "too."

(d) Δοκων μεν τις ειναι, ων δ'ουδεις, is very near to δοκει ειναι τι, μηδεν ων, *Gal.* vi. 3. There is a similar Expression of *Plato*, at the End of the Apology of *Socrates*.

"too."——What, handsomer than *Achilles?*——"But I have fine Hair too."——Had not *Achilles* finer and brighter? Yet he neither combed it nicely, nor curled it.——"But I am strong too."——Can you lift such a Stone then, as *Hector*, or *Ajax?*——"But I am of a noble Family too."——Is your Mother a Goddess, or your Father descended from *Jupiter?* And what Good did all this do *Achilles*, when he sat crying for a Girl?—"But I am an Orator."——And was not he? Do not you see how he treated the most eloquent of the *Greeks*, *Phœnix* and *Ulysses?* How he struck them dumb? This is all I have to say to you; and even this, against my Inclination.

Why so?

Because you have given me no Encouragement. For what can I see in you, to encourage me, as spirited Horses do their Riders? Your Person? That you disfigure. Your Dress? That is effeminate. Your Behaviour? Your Look? Absolutely nothing. When you would hear a Philosopher, do not say to him, "You tell me nothing;" but only show yourself worthy, or fit, to *hear*; and you will find, how you will move him to *speak*.

CHAPTER XXV.

That Logic is necessary.

WHEN one of the Company said to him, "Convince me that Logic is necessary;" Would you have me demonstrate it to you, says he?——"Yes."——Then I must use a demonstrative Form of Argument.——"Granted."——And how will you know then, whether I argue sophistically? On this, the Man being silent; You see, says he, that, even by your own Confession, Logic

is

is necessary; since, without its Assistance, you cannot learn so much as whether it be necessary, or not.

CHAPTER XXVI.

What is the Property of Error in Life.

§. 1. EVERY Error in Life implies a Contradiction: for, since he who errs, doth not mean to err, but to be in the Right, it is evident, that he acts contrary to his Meaning. What doth a Thief mean? His own Interest. If, then, Thieving be against his Interest, he acts contrary to his own Meaning. Now every rational Soul is naturally averse to Self-contradiction: but so long as any one is ignorant, that it is a Contradiction, nothing restrains him from acting contradictorily: but, whenever he discovers it, he must as necessarily renounce and avoid it, as any one must dissent from a Falshood, whenever he perceives it to be a Falshood: but, while this doth not appear, he assents to it, as to a Truth.

§. 2. He then is an able Speaker, and excels at once in Exhortation and Conviction, who can discover, to each Man, the Contradiction by which he errs, and prove clearly to him, that what he would, he doth not; and what he would not do, that he doth (*a*). For, if that be shown, he will depart from it, of his own accord: but, till you have shown it, be not surprised that he remains where he is: for he doth it on the Appearance, that he acts rightly (*b*). Hence *Socrates*, relying on this Faculty, used to say, "It is not my Custom to cite "any other Witness of my Assertions; but I am "always contented with my Opponent. I call and

(*a*) *For that which I do, I allow not: for what I would, that do I not; but what I hate, that I do.* Rom. vii. 15.

(*b*) See B. I. c. 18. Note *a*.

"summon him for my Witness; and his single "Evidence is instead of all others (*c*)." For he knew, that, if a rational Soul be moved by any thing, the Scale must turn, whether it will or no (*d*). Show the governing Faculty of Reason a Contradiction, and it will renounce it: but, till you have shown it, rather blame yourself, than him who is unconvinced.

(*c*) See c. 12. §. 2.

(*d*) Something here is lost in the Original. The Translation hath connected the Sense in the best and shortest Manner it could.

End *of the* Second Book.

THE DISCOURSES OF *EPICTETUS.*

BOOK III.

CHAPTER I.

Of Finery in Dress.

§. 1. A Certain young Rhetorician coming to him, with his Hair too curiously ornamented, and his Dress very fine; Tell me, says *Epictetus*, whether you do not think some Horses and Dogs beautiful; and so of all other Animals?

I do.

Are some Men then likewise beautiful, and others deformed?

Certainly.

Do we call each of theſe beautiful then in its Kind, on the ſame Account, or on ſome Account, peculiar to itſelf? You will judge of it, by this: ſince we ſee a Dog naturally formed for one thing, a Horſe for another, and a Nightingale, for Inſtance, for another; in general, it will not be abſurd to pronounce each of them beautiful, ſo far as it is in the Condition moſt ſuitable to its own Nature: but, ſince the Nature of each is different, I think each of them muſt be beautiful, in a different Way. Is it not ſo?

Agreed.

Then, what makes a Dog beautiful, makes a Horſe deformed; and what makes a horſe beautiful, a Dog deformed; if their Natures are different.

So it ſeems probable.

For, I ſuppoſe, what makes a good Pancratiaſt (*a*) makes no good Wreſtler, and a very ridiculous Racer; and the very ſame Perſon who appears beautiful as a Pentathlete (*a*), would appear very deformed, in Wreſtling.

Very true.

What then, makes a Man beautiful? Is it the ſame, in general, that makes a Dog or a Horſe ſo?

The ſame.

What is it then, that makes a Dog beautiful?

That Excellency which belongs to a Dog.

What, a Horſe?

The Excellency of a Horſe.

What,

(*a*) Theſe are the Names of Combatants in the *Olympic* Games. A Pancratiaſt was one who united the Exerciſes of Wreſtling and Boxing. A Pentathlete, one who contended in all the Five Games of Leaping, Running, Throwing the Diſcus, Darting, and Wreſtling. See POTTER's *Grecian Antiquities*, Vol. I. ch. 21.

What, a Man? Must it not be the Excellency belonging to a Man? If then you would appear beautiful, young Man, strive for human Excellency.

What is that?

Consider, when you praise, without partial Affection, whom you praise: Is it the Honest, or the Dishonest?

The Honest.

The Sober, or the Dissolute?

The Sober.

The Temperate, or the Intemperate?

The Temperate.

Then, if you make yourself such a Character, you know that you will make yourself beautiful: but, while you neglect these Things, though you use every Contrivance to appear beautiful, you must necessarily be deformed.

§. 2. I know not how to say any thing further to you: for if I speak what I think, you will be vexed, and perhaps go away, and return no more. And, if I do not speak, consider how I shall act: if you come to me to be improved, and I do not improve you; and you come to me as to a Philosopher, and I do not speak like a Philosopher. (*b*) Besides: how could it be consistent with my Duty towards yourself, to overlook, and leave you uncorrected? If hereafter you should come to have Sense, you will accuse me, with Reason: "What did *Epictetus* observe in me, that, when "he saw me come to him, in such a shameful Con-"dition, he overlooked it, and never said so much "as a Word of it? Did he so absolutely despair "of me? Was not I young? Was not I able to

(*b*) *Epictetus* had been before considering the Propriety of his own Character as a Philosopher: but, according to Mr. *Upton*'s very probable Conjecture, the Translation must be—would it not be cruel, *&c.*

"hear Reaſon? How many young Men, at that "Age, are guilty of many ſuch Errors? I am told "of one *Polemo*, who, from a moſt diſſolute Youth, "became totally changed (*c*). Suppoſe he did not "think I ſhould become a *Polemo*; he might how-"ever have ſet my Locks to rights: he might "have ſtript off my Bracelets and Rings: he might "have prevented my picking off the Hairs from "my Perſon. But when he ſaw me dreſſed like a "——what ſhall I ſay?——he was ſilent." I do not ſay like what; when you come to your Senſes, you will ſay it yourſelf, and will know what it is, and who they are who ſtudy ſuch a Dreſs.

§. 3. If you ſhould hereafter lay this to my Charge, what Excuſe could I make;——Ay: but if I do ſpeak, he will not regard me. Why, did *Laius* regard *Apollo*? Did not he go and get drunk, and bid Farewel to the Oracle? What then? Did this hinder *Apollo*, from telling him the Truth? Now, I am uncertain, whether you will regard *me*, or not; but *Apollo* poſitively knew, that *Laius* would not regard *him*, and yet he ſpoke (*d*). "And "why did he ſpeak?" You may as well aſk, Why is he *Apollo*; why doth he deliver Oracles; why hath he placed himſelf in ſuch a Poſt as a Prophet, and the Fountain of Truth, to whom the Inhabi-tants

(*c*) *Polemo* was a profligate young Rake of *Athens*, and even diſtinguiſhed by the Diſſoluteneſs of his Manners. One Day, after a riotous Entertainment, he came reeling, with a Chaplet on his Head, into the School of *Xenocrates*. The Audience were greatly offended at his ſcandalous Appearance: but the Philoſopher went on, without any Emotion, in a Diſcourſe upon Temperance and Sobriety. *Polemo* was ſo ſtruck by his Arguments, that he ſoon threw away his Chaplet; and, from that Time, became a Diſciple of *Xenocrates*; and profited ſo well by his Inſtructions, that he afterwards ſucceeded him in the *Socratic* School.

(*d*) *Laius*, King of *Thebes*, petitioned *Apollo* for a Son. The Oracle anſwered him, That, if *Laius* became a Father, he ſhould periſh by the Hand of his Son. The Prediction was ful-filed by *Oedipus*. UPTON.

tants of the World should resort? Why is KNOW THYSELF inscribed on the Front of his Temple, when no one minds it?

§. 4. Did *Socrates* prevail on all who came to him, to take care of themselves? Not on the thousandth Part: but however, being, as he himself declares, divinely appointed to such a Post, he never deserted it. What doth he say, even to his Judges? "If you would acquit me, on Condition, "that I should no longer act as I do now, I will "not accept it, nor desist: but I will accost all I "meet, whether young or old, and interrogate "them just in the same Manner: but particularly "you, my Fellow-citizens; as you are more nearly "related to me."——"Are you so curious and "officious, *Socrates?* What is it to you, how we "act?——What do you say? While you are of "the same Community, and the same Kindred, "with me, shall you be careless of yourself, and "show yourself a bad Citizen to the City, a bad "Kinsman to your Kindred, and a bad Neighbour "to your Neighbourhood?"——"Why, who are "*you?*"——Here it is a great Thing to say, "I "am He, who ought to take care of Mankind;" for it is not every little paultry Heifer that dares resist the Lion: but if the Bull should come up, and resist him, say to *him*, if you think proper, *Who are you? What Business is it of yours?* In every Species, Man, there is some one Part which by Nature excells; in Oxen, in Dogs, in Bees, in Horses. Do not say to what excells, *Who are you?* If you do, it will, some-how or other, find a Voice to tell you; "I am like the purple Thread in a Garment (*e*). Do not expect me to be like the rest; "or find fault with my Nature, which hath distinguished me from others."

§. 5. What then, am *I* such a one? How should *I*? Indeed, are *you* such a one as to be able to

(*e*) See P. 8. §. 3.

hear the Truth? I wish you were. But, however, since I am condemned to wear a grey Beard and a Cloke, and you come to me as to a Philosopher, I will not treat you cruelly, nor as if I despaired of you; but will ask you——Who is it, young Man, whom you would render beautiful? Know, first, who you are; and then adorn yourself accordingly. You are a Man; that is, a mortal Animal, capable of a rational Use of the Appearances of Things. And what is this rational Use? A perfect Conformity to Nature. What have you then, particularly excellent? Is it the animal Part? No. The mortal? No. That which is capable of the (*f*) Use of the Appearances of Things? No. The Excellence lies in the rational Part. Adorn and beautify this; but leave your Hair to him who formed it, as he thought good. Well; what other Denominations have you? Are you a Man, or a Woman? A Man. Then adorn yourself as a Man, not a Woman. A Woman is naturally smooth and delicate; and, if hairy, is a Monster, and shown among the Monsters at *Rome*. It is the same in a Man, not to be hairy; and, if he is by Nature not so, he is a Monster. But, if he clips and picks off his Hairs, what shall we do with him? Where shall we show him; and how shall we advertise him? *A Man to be seen, who would rather be a Woman.* What a scandalous Show! Who would not wonder at such an Advertisement? I believe indeed, that these very Pickers themselves would; not apprehending, that it is the very Thing of which they are guilty.

§. 6. Of what have you to accuse your Nature, Sir? That it hath made you a Man? Why; were all to be born Women then? In that Case, what would have been the Use of your Finery? For whom would you have made yourself fine, if all

(*f*) The bare *Use* of Objects belongs to all Animals; a *rational* Use of them is peculiar to Man. See Introduction, §. 7.

all were Women? But the whole Affair displeases you. Go to work upon the Whole then. Remove what is the Cause of these Hairs; and make yourself a Woman entirely, that we may be no longer deceived, nor you be half Man, half Woman? To whom would you be agreeable? To the Women? Be agreeable to them as a Man.

Ay; but they are pleased with smooth pretty Fellows.

Go hang yourself. Suppose they were pleased with Pathics, would you become one? Is this your Business in Life? Were you born to please dissolute Women? Shall we make such a one as you, in the *Corinthian* Republic, for Instance, Governor of the City, Master of the Youth, Commander of the Army, or Director of the public Games? Will you pick your Hairs, when you are married? For whom, and for what? Will you be the Father of Children, and introduce them into the State, picked, like yourself? O what a fine Citizen, and Senator, and Orator! For Heaven's sake, Sir, ought we to pray for a Succession of young Men, disposed and bred like you!

§. 7. Now, when you have once heard this Discourse, go home, and say to yourself; It is not *Epictetus* who hath told me all these Things (for how should he?) but some propitious God, by him (*g*); for it would never have entered the Head of *Epictetus*, who is not used to dispute with any one. Well; let us obey God then, that we may not incur the divine Displeasure. If a Crow had signified any thing to you, by his Croaking; it is not the Crow that signifies it, but God, by him. And, if you have any thing signified to you by the human Voice, doth he not cause the Man to tell it you; that you may know the divine Efficacy, which declares

(*g*) *For it is not ye that speak, but the Spirit of your Father which speaketh in you.* Matt. x. 20.

declares its Significations to different Persons in different Manners; and signifies the greatest and principal Things, by the noblest Messengers (*b*). What else does the Poet mean, when he says,

Hermes *I sent, his Purpose to restrain.*

Hermes, descending from Heaven, was to warn *Him*; and the Gods now, likewise, send a *Hermes* to warn *You*, not to invert the well-appointed Order of Things; nor be curiously trifling: but suffer a Man to be a Man; and a Woman, a Woman: a beautiful Man, to be beautiful, as a Man; a deformed Man, to be deformed, as a Man: for you do not consist of Flesh and Hair, but of the Faculty of Choice. If you take care to have *this* beautiful, you will be beautiful. But all this while, I dare not tell you, that you are deformed; for I fancy you would rather hear any thing than this. But consider what *Socrates* says to the most beautiful and blooming of all Men, *Alcibiades*: "Endeavour to make yourself beautiful. What doth he "mean to say to him; Curl your Locks, and pick "the Hairs from your Legs?" Heaven forbid! But, Ornament your Choice: Throw away your wrong Principles.

What is to be done with the poor Body then?

Leave it to Nature. Another hath taken care of such Things. Give them up to Him.

What! then, must one be a Sloven?

By no means: but be neat, conformably to your Nature. A Man should be neat, as a Man; a Woman, as a Woman; a Child, as a Child. If not, let us pick out the Mane of a Lion, that he may not be slovenly; and the Comb of a Cock; for he ought to be neat too. Yes; but let it be as a Cock; and a Lion, as a Lion; and a Hound, as a Hound.

CHAP-

(*b*) This Passage hath a remarkable Likeness to *Heb.* i. 1, 2. *God, who, at sundry Times and in diverse Manners, spake in Times past unto the Fathers by the Prophets, hath, in these last Days, spoken unto us by his Son*——

CHAPTER II.

In what a Proficient ought to be exercised; and that we neglect the principal Things.

§. 1. THERE are Three Topics in Philosophy, in which he, who would be wise and good, must be exercised (*a*). That of the *Desires*, and *Aversions*; that he may not be disappointed of the one, nor incur the other. That of the *Pursuits*, and *Avoidances*; and, in general, the Duties of Life; that he may act with Order and Consideration, and not carelessly. The Third Topic belongs to Circumspection, and a Freedom from Deception; and, in general, whatever belongs to the Assent.

§. 2. Of these Topics, the principal and most urgent, is that of the Passions: for Passion is produced no otherwise, than by a Disappointment of the Desires, and an incurring of the Aversions. It is this which introduces Perturbations, Tumults, Misfortunes, and Calamities: this is the Spring of Sorrow, Lamentation, and Envy: this renders us envious, and emulous; and incapable of hearing Reason.

§. 3. The next Topic regards the Duties of Life. For I am not to be undisturbed by Passions, in the same Sense as a Statue is; but as one who preserves the natural and acquired Relations; as a pious Person, as a Son, as a Brother, as a Father, as a Citizen.

§. 4. The Third Topic belongs to those who are now making a Proficiency; and is a Security to the other Two, that no unexamined Appearance may surprize us, either in Sleep, or Wine, or in the Spleen. This, say you, is above us. But our present

(*a*) See Introduction, §. 3, 4, 5, 6.

ſent Philoſophers, leaving the Firſt and Second Topics [the Affections, and moral Duties], employ themſelves wholly about the Third; Convertible, definitive, hypothetical Propoſitions [and other logical Subtilties]. For, they ſay, that we muſt, by engaging even in theſe Subjects, take care to guard againſt Deception. Who muſt? A wiſe and good Man. Is this Security from Deception, then, the Thing you want? Have you maſtered the other Subjects? Are you not liable to be deceived by Money? When you ſee a fine Girl, do you oppoſe the Appearance which is raiſed in your Mind? If your Neighbour inherits an Eſtate, do you feel no Vexation? Do you, at preſent, want nothing more, than Perſeverance? You learn even theſe very Things, Wretch, with Trembling, and a ſolicitous Dread of Contempt; and are inquiſitive to know, what is ſaid of you; and, if any one comes and tells you, that, in a diſpute which was the beſt of the Philoſophers, one of the Company ſaid, that ſuch a one was the only Philoſopher, that little Soul of yours grows to the Size of two Cubits, inſtead of an Inch: but if another ſhould come, and ſay, "You are miſtaken, he is not worth hearing; for what doth he know? He hath the firſt Rudiments, but nothing more;" you are Thunderſtruck; you preſently turn pale, and cry out, "I will ſhow him; what a Man, and how great a Philoſopher I am." It is evident [what you are], by theſe very Things; why do you aim to ſhow it by others? Do not you know, that *Diogenes* ſhowed ſome Sophiſt in this Manner, by extending his middle Finger (*b*); and, when he was mad with Rage, This, ſays *Diogenes*, is *He*: I have ſhowed him to you. For a Man is not ſhowed in the ſame Senſe as a Stone, or a Piece of Wood, by the Finger;

(*b*) Extending the middle Finger, with the Antients, was a Mark of the greateſt Contempt.

ger; but whoever shows his Principles, shows him as a Man.

§. 5. Let us see *your* Principles too. For is it not evident, that you consider your own Choice as nothing; but look out for something external, and independent on it? As, what such a one will say of you, and what you shall be thought; whether a Man of Letters; whether to have read *Chrysippus*, or *Antipater*; for, if *Archedemus* too, you have every thing you wish. Why are you still solicitous, lest you should not show us what you are? Will you let me tell you, what you have showed us, that you are? A mean, discontented, passionate, cowardly Fellow; complaining of every thing; accusing every body; perpetually restless; good for nothing. This you have showed us. Go now and read *Archedemus*: and then, if you hear but the Noise of a Mouse, you are a dead Man; for you will die some such Kind of Death as——Who was it? *Crinis* (*c*); who valued himself extremely too, that he understood *Archedemus*.

§. 6. Wretch, why do not you let alone Things, that do not belong to you? These Things become such as are able to learn them, without Perturbation; who can say, "I am not subject to Anger, or "Grief, or Envy. I am not restrained; I am not "compelled. What remains for me to do? I am "at Leisure; I am at Ease. Let us see how convertible Propositions are to be treated: Let us "consider, when an Hypothesis is laid down, how "we may avoid a Contradiction." To such Persons do these Things belong. They who are safe may light a Fire; go to Dinner, if they please; and sing, and dance: but you come and hoist a Flag, when your Vessel is just sinking.

(*c*) *Crinis* was a Stoic Philosopher. The Circumstances of his Death are not now known.

CHAP.

CHAPTER III.

What is the Subject-matter of a good Man; and in what we chiefly ought to be Practitioners.

§. 1. THE Subject-matter of a wise and good Man is, his own governing Faculty. The Body is the Subject-matter of a Physician, and of a Master of Exercise; and a Field, of the Husbandman. The Business of a wise and good Man is, an Use of the Appearances of Things, conformable to Nature. Now, every Soul, as it is naturally formed for an Assent to Truth, a Dissent from Falshood, and a Suspence with regard to Uncertainty; so it is moved by a Desire of Good, an Aversion from Evil, and an Indifference to what is neither good nor evil. For, as a Money-changer, or a Gardener, is not at Liberty to reject *Cæsar*'s Coin; but when once it is shown, is obliged, whether he will or not, to deliver what is sold for it; so is it in the Soul. Apparent Good at first Sight attracts, and Evil repells. Nor will the Soul any more reject an evident Appearance of Good, than [they will] *Cæsar*'s Coin.

§. 2. Hence depends every Movement, both of God and Man; and hence *Good* is preferred to every Obligation, however near. My Connexion is not with my Father; but with Good.——Are you so hard-hearted?——Such is my Nature, and such is the Coin which God hath given me. If, therefore, *Good* is made to be any thing but Fair and Just, away go Father, and Brother, and Country, and every thing. What! Shall I overlook my own Good, and give it up to *you?* For what? "I "am your Father." But not my *Good.* "I am "your Brother." But not my *Good.* But, if we place it in a right Choice, *Good* will consist in an Obser-

Obſervance of the ſeveral Relations of Life; and then, he who gives up ſome Externals, acquires *Good.* Your Father deprives you of your Money; but he doth not hurt you. Your Brother will poſſeſs as much larger a Portion of Land than you, as he pleaſes; but will he poſſeſs more Honour? More Fidelity? More fraternal Affection? Who can throw you out of this Poſſeſſion? Not even *Jupiter:* for, indeed, it is not his Will; but he hath put this Good into my own Power, and given it me, like his own, uncompelled, unreſtrained, and unhindered. But, when any one hath a Coin different from this, [for his Coin,] whoever ſhows it to him, may have whatever is ſold for it, in return. A thieviſh Proconſul comes into the Province: What Coin doth he uſe? Silver. Show it him, and carry off what you pleaſe. An Adulterer comes: What Coin doth he uſe? Women. Take the Coin, ſays one, and give me this Trifle. "Give " it me, and it is yours." Another is addicted to Boys: give him the Coin, and take what you pleaſe. Another is fond of hunting: give him a fine Nag, or a Puppy; and, though with Sighs and Groans, he will ſell you for it, what you will; for he is inwardly compelled by another, who hath conſtituted this Coin.

§. 3. In this manner, ought every one chiefly to exerciſe himſelf. When you go out in a Morning, examine whomſoever you ſee, or hear: anſwer, as to a Queſtion. What have you ſeen? A handſome Perſon? Apply the Rule. Is this dependent, or independent, on Choice? Independent. Throw it away. What have you ſeen? One grieving for the Deceaſe of a Child? Apply the Rule. Death is independent on Choice. Throw it by. Hath a Conſul met you? Apply the Rule. What Kind of thing is the Conſular Office? dependent, or independent, on Choice? Independent.

Throw

Throw aside this too. It is not Proof. Cast it away. It is nothing to *you*.

§. 4. If we acted thus, and practised in this manner, from Morning till Night, by Heaven, something would be done. Whereas now, on the contrary, we are caught by every Appearance, half-asleep; and, if we ever do awake, it is only a little in the School: but, as soon as we go out, if we meet any one grieving, we say, "He is undone." If a Consul, "How happy is he!" If an Exile, "How miserable." If a poor Man, "How wretch-"ed; he hath nothing to eat!"

§. 5. These vicious Principles then are to be lopped off: and here is our whole Strength to be applied. For what is Weeping and Groaning? Principle. What is Misfortune? Principle. What is Sedition, Discord, Complaint, Accusation, Impiety, Trifling? All these are Principles, and nothing more; and Principles concerning Things independent on Choice, as if they were either good or evil. Let any one transfer these Principles to Things dependent on Choice, and I will engage, that he will preserve his Constancy, whatever be the State of Things about him.

§. 6. The Soul resembles a Vessel filled with Water: the Appearances of things resemble a Ray falling upon its Surface. If the Water is moved, the Ray will seem to be moved likewise, though it is in reality without Motion. Whenever therefore any one is seized with a Swimming in his Head, it is not the Arts and Virtues that are confounded, but the Mind, in which they are: and, if this recover its Composure, so will they likewise.

CHAP-

CHAPTER IV.

Concerning one who exerted himſelf, with indecent Eagerneſs in the Theatre.

§. 1. WHEN the Governor of *Epirus* had exerted himſelf indecently, in favour of a Comedian, and was, upon that Account, publicly railed at; and, when he came to hear it, was highly diſpleaſed with thoſe who railed at him: Why: what Harm, ſays *Epictetus*, have theſe People done? They have favoured a Player; which is juſt what you did.

Is this a proper Manner then, of expreſſing their Favour?

Seeing you, their Governor, and the Friend and Vicegerent of *Cæſar*, expreſs it thus, was it not to be expected, that they would expreſs it thus too? For, if it is not right to expreſs Favour, in this Manner, to a Player, be not guilty of it yourſelf; and, if it is, why are you angry at them, for imitating you? For whom have the Many to imitate, but *you*, their Superiors? From whom are they to take Example, when they come into the Theatre, but from *you*? "Do but look how *Cæſar*'s Vice-" gerent ſees the Play? Hath he cried out? I will " cry out too. Hath he leaped up from his Seat? " I too will leap up from mine. Do his Slaves ſit " in different Parts of the Houſe, making an Up-" roar? I indeed have no Slaves; but I will make " as much Uproar as I can myſelf, inſtead of ever " ſo many."

§. 2. You ought to conſider then, that when you appear in the Theatre, you appear as a Rule and Example to others, how they ought to ſee the Play. Why is it, that they have railed at you? Becauſe every Man hates what hinders him. *They* would have one Actor crowned; *you*, another. They hindered you; and you, them. You proved the stronger. They have done what they could: they have railed at the Person who hindered them. What would you have then? Would you *do* as you please, and not have them even *talk* as they please? Where is the Wonder of all this? Doth not the Husbandman rail at *Jupiter*, when he is hindered by him? Doth not the Sailor? Do Men ever cease railing at *Cæsar*? What then, is *Jupiter* ignorant of this? Are not the Things that are said, reported to *Cæsar*? How then doth he act? He knows, that, if he was to punish all Railers, he would have nobody left to command.

§. 3. When you enter the Theatre then, ought you to say, "Come, let *Sophron (a)* be crowned?" No. But, "Come, let me preserve my Choice, in "a Manner conformable to Nature, upon this "Occasion. No one is dearer to me than my-"self. It is ridiculous then, that, because another "Man gains the Victory as a Player, *I* should be "hurt. Whom do I wish to gain the Victory? "Him who doth gain it; and thus he will always "be victorious, whom I wish to be so."——But I would have *Sophron* crowned.——Why, celebrate as many Games as you will, at your own House; *Nemean*, *Pythian*, *Isthmian*, *Olympic*; and proclaim him Victor in all: but, in public, do not arrogate more than your Due, nor seize to yourself what lies in common; otherwise, bear to be railed at: for, if you act like the Mob, you reduce yourself to an Equality with them.

(a) The Name of a Player. UPTON.

CHAP-

CHAPTER V.

(b) Concerning those who pretend Sickness, as an Excuse to return home.

§. 1. I Am sick here, said one of the Scholars. I will return home.

Were you never sick at home then? Consider, whether you are doing any thing here, conducive to the Regulation of your Choice: for, if you make no Improvement, it was to no Purpose that you came. Go home. Take care of your domestic Affairs. For, if your ruling Faculty cannot be brought to a Conformity to Nature, your Land may. You may increase your Money, support the old Age of your Father, mix in the public Assemblies, and make a bad Governor, as you are a bad Man, and do other Things of that sort. But, if you are conscious to yourself, that you are casting off some of your wrong Principles, and taking up different ones in their room, and that you have transferred your Scheme of Life from Things not dependent on Choice, to those which are; and that, if you do sometimes cry *alas*, it is not upon the Account of your Father, or your Brother, but yourself; why do you any longer plead Sickness (*c*)? Do not you know, that both Sickness and Death must overtake us? At what Employment? The Husbandman, at his Plow; the Sailor, on his Voyage. At what Employment would you be taken? For, indeed, at what Employment ought you to be taken? If there is any better Employment, at which

(*b*) The *Greek* Title to this Chapter is defective. Νοσον seems to be the Word wanting. Or, if Διαπλαττω signifies, to pretend, as πλαττω doth, the true Reading of the Text may be, προς τους νοσον διαπλαττομενους.

(*c*) Εμε. Ετι, probably, should be, Εμε. Τι ετι.

which you can be taken, follow that. For my own Part, I would be taken engaged in nothing, but in the Care of my own Faculty of Choice; how to render it undisturbed, unrestrained, uncompelled, free. I would be found studying this, that I may be able to say to God, "Have I transgressed thy Commands? Have I perverted the Powers, the Senses, the Pre-conceptions, which thou hast given me? Have I ever accused Thee, or censured Thy Dispensations? I have been sick, because it was Thy Pleasure; and so have others; but *I* willingly. I have been poor, it being thy Will; but with Joy. I have not been in Power; because it was not thy Will; and Power I have never desired. Hast thou ever seen me out of Humour, upon this Account? Have I not always approached Thee, with a chearful Countenance; prepared to execute Thy Commands, and the Significations of thy Will? Is it Thy Pleasure, that I should depart from this Assembly? I depart. I give Thee all Thanks, that Thou hast thought me worthy to have a Share in it, with Thee; to behold Thy Works, and to join with Thee, in comprehending Thy Administration." Let Death overtake me while I am thinking, while I am writing, while I am reading, such Things as these.

§. 2. But I shall not have my Mother, to hold my Head, when I am sick.

Get home then to your Mother; for you are fit to have your Head held, when you are sick.

But I used at home, to lie on a fine Couch.

Get to this Couch of yours; for you are fit to lie upon such a one, even in Health: so do not lose the doing what you are qualified for. But what says *Socrates*? "As one Man rejoices in the Improvement of his Estate, another of his Horse, so do I daily rejoice in apprehending myself to grow better."

In what? In pretty Speeches?

Good Words, I intreat you.

In trifling Theorems? In what doth he employ himſelf? For indeed I do not ſee, that the Philoſophers are employed, in any thing elſe.

Do you think it nothing, never to accuſe or cenſure any one, either God or Man? Always to carry abroad, and bring home, the ſame Countenance? Theſe were the Things which *Socrates* knew; and yet he never profeſſed to know, or to teach any thing; but if any one wanted pretty Speeches, or little Theorems, he brought him to *Protagoras*, to *Hippias*: juſt as if any one had come for Pot-herbs, he would have taken him to a Gardener. Who of you then hath ſuch an [earneſt] Intention as this? If you had, you would bear Sickneſs, and Hunger, and Death, with Chearfulneſs. If any of you hath been in Love, he knows that I ſpeak Truth.

CHAPTER VI.

Miſcellaneous.

§. 1. WHEN he was aſked, How (*a*) it came to paſs, that, though the Art of Reaſoning is more ſtudied now, yet the Improvements were greater, formerly? In what Inſtance, anſwered he, is it more ſtudied *now*; and in what were the Improvements greater, *then*? For in what is ſtudied, at preſent, in that will be found likewiſe the Improvements, at preſent. The preſent Study is the Solution of Syllogiſms; and in this, Improvements are made. But formerly, the Study was to preſerve the governing Faculty conformable to Nature;

(*a*) By changing των into πως, and, as Mr. *Upton* propoſes, ποτερον into προτερον, the whole Difficulty of this corrupted Paſſage is removed.

ture; and Improvement was made in that. Therefore do not confound Things; nor when you study one, expect Improvement in another; but see whether any of us, who applies himself to think and act conformably to Nature, ever fails of Improvement. Depend upon it, you will not find one.

§. 2. A good Man is invincible; for he doth not contend, where he is not superior. If you would have his Land, take it: take his Servants; take his public Post; take his Body. But you will never frustrate his Desire, nor make him incur his Aversion. He engages in no Combat, but what concerns the Objects of his own Choice. How can he fail then to be invincible?

§. 3. Being asked, what common Sense was? he answered; As that may be called a common Ear, which distinguishes only Sounds; but that, which distinguishes Notes, an artificial one: so there are some Things, which Men, not totally perverted, discern by their common natural Powers; and such a Disposition is called common Sense.

§. 4. It is not easy to gain the Attention of effeminate young Men; for you cannot take Custard by a Hook: but the Ingenuous, even if you discourage them, are the more eager for Learning. Hence *Rufus*, for the most part, did discourage them; and made use of that, as a Criterion of the Ingenuous and Disingenuous. For he used to say, As a Stone, even if you throw it up, will, by its own Propensity, be carried downward; so an ingenuous Mind, the more it is forced from its natural Bent, the more strongly will it incline towards it.

CHAP.

CHAPTER VII.

Concerning a Governor of the Free States, who was an Epicurean.

§. 1. WHEN the Governor, who was an *Epicurean*, came to him; It is fit, says he, that we ignorant People should enquire of you Philosophers, what is the most valuable Thing, in the World; as those who come into a strange City do of the Citizens, and such as are acquainted with it; that, after this Enquiry, we may go and take a View of it, as they do in Cities. Now, scarcely any one denies, but that there are three Things belonging to Man; Soul, Body, and Externals. It remains for you to answer which is the best. What shall we tell Mankind? Is it Flesh?

And was it for this, that *Maximus* took a Voyage in Winter as far as *Cassiope*, to accompany his Son? Was it to gratify the Flesh?

No, surely.

Is it not fit then, to employ our chief Study on what is best?

Yes, beyond all other Things.

What have we, then, better than Flesh?

The Soul.

Are we to prefer the Good of the Better, or of the Worse?

Of the Better.

Doth the Good of the Soul consist in what is dependent, or independent, on Choice?

In what is dependent on it.

Doth the Pleasure of the Soul then, depend on Choice?

It doth.

And whence doth this Pleasure arise? From itself? This is unintelligible. For there must subſiſt ſome principal Eſſence of Good, in the Attainment of which, we ſhall enjoy this Pleaſure of the Soul.

This too is granted.

In what then conſiſts this Pleaſure of the Soul? For if it be in mental Objects, the Eſſence of Good is found (*a*). For it is impoſſible, that we ſhould be reaſonably elated with Pleaſure, unleſs by Good; or that, if the leading Cauſe is not good, the Effect ſhould be good. For, to make the Effect reaſonable, the Cauſe muſt be good. But this, if you are in your Senſes, you will not allow; for it would be to contradict both *Epicurus*, and the reſt of your Principles. It remains then, that the Pleaſures of the Soul muſt conſiſt in bodily Objects; and that *there* muſt be the leading Cauſe, and the Eſſence of Good. *Maximus* therefore did fooliſhly, if he took a Voyage for the Sake of any thing but Body; that is, for the Sake of what is beſt. He doth fooliſhly too, if he refrains from what is another's, when he is a Judge, and able to take it. But let us conſider only this, if you pleaſe, how it may be done ſecretly, and ſafely, and ſo that no one may know it. For *Epicurus* himſelf doth not pronounce Stealing to be evil, only the being found out in it: and ſays, "Do not ſteal;" for no other Reaſon, but becauſe it is impoſſible to inſure ourſelves againſt a Diſcovery. But I ſay to you, That, if it be done dextrouſly and cautiouſly, we ſhall not be diſcovered. Beſides: we have powerful Friends, of both Sexes, at *Rome*; and the *Greeks* are weak; and nobody will dare to go up to *Rome*, on ſuch an Affair. Why do you refrain from your own proper Good? It is Madneſs; it is Folly. But if you were to tell me, that you do refrain, I would not believe you. For, as it is impoſſible to aſſent to an apparent

(*a*) The Tranſlation follows Lord *Shafteſbury*'s Correction of ψυχικοις, for αγαθοις; which ſeems abſolutely neceſſary to the Senſe of the Paſſage.

apparent Falſhood, or to deny an apparent Truth, ſo it is impoſſible to abſtain from an apparent Good. Now, Riches are a Good; and, indeed, the chief Inſtrument of Pleaſures. Why do not you acquire them? And why do not we corrupt the Wife of our Neighbour, if it can be done ſecretly? And, if the Huſband ſhould happen to be impertinent, why not cut his Throat too? if you have a mind to be ſuch a Philoſopher as you ought to be, a complete one, to be conſiſtent with your own Principles. Otherwiſe you will not differ from us, who are called Stoics. For we too ſay one Thing, and do another: we talk well, and act ill: but you will be perverſe in a contrary Way; teach bad Principles, and act well.

§. 2. For Heaven's ſake repreſent to yourſelf a City of *Epicureans* (*b*). "I do not marry." "Nor "I. For we are not to marry, nor have Children; "nor to engage in public Affairs." What will be the Conſequence of this? Whence are the Citizens to come? Who will educate them? Who will be the Governor of the Youth? Who, the Maſter of their Exerciſes? What then, will he teach them? Will it be what uſed to be taught at *Athens*, or *Lacedemon?* Take a young Man; bring him up, according to your Principles. Theſe Principles are wicked; ſubverſive of a State; pernicious to Families; nor becoming, even to Women. Give them up, Sir. You live in a capital City. You are to govern, and judge uprightly, and to refrain from what belongs to others. No one's Wife, or Child, or Silver or Gold Plate, is to have any Charms for you; but your own. Provide yourſelf with Principles, conſonant to theſe Truths; and, ſetting out from thence, you will with Pleaſure refrain from Things ſo perſuaſive to miſlead, and get the better. But, if to their own perſuaſive Force, we

(*b*) The Tranſlation follows the Reading of *Wolfius*. Εκεῖνοι.

we add ſuch a Philoſophy, as hurries us upon them, and confirms us in them, what will be the Conſequence?

§. 3. In a ſculptured Vaſe, which is the beſt; the Silver, or the Workmanſhip? In the Hand, the Subſtance is Fleſh: but its Operations are the principal Thing. Accordingly, the Duties, relative to it, are likewiſe threefold; ſome have reſpect to mere Exiſtence; others, to the manner of Exiſtence; and a third Sort are the leading Operations themſelves. Thus likewiſe, do not ſet a Value on the Materials of Man, mere paultry Fleſh; but on the principal Operations belonging to him.

What are theſe?

Engaging in public Buſineſs; Marrying; the Production of Children; the Worſhip of God; the Care of our Parents; and, in general, the having our Deſires and Averſions, our Purſuits and Avoidances, ſuch as each of them ought to be, conformable to our Nature.

What is our Nature?

To be free, noble ſpirited, modeſt. (For what other Animal bluſhes? What other hath the Idea of Shame?) But Pleaſure muſt be ſubjected to theſe, as an Attendant and Handmaid, to call forth our Activity, and to keep us conſtant in natural Operations.

But I am rich, and want nothing.

Then why do you pretend to philoſophize? Your Gold and Silver Plate is enough for you. What need have you of Principles?

Beſides, I am Judge of the *Greeks*.

Do you know how to judge? Who hath imparted this Knowledge to you?

Cæſar hath given me a Commiſſion.

Let him give you a Commiſſion to judge of Muſic; and what Good will it do you? But how were you made a Judge? Whoſe Hand have you kiſſed?

That

That of *Symphorus*, or *Numenius* (*c*)? Before whose Bed-chamber have you slept? To whom have you sent Presents? After all, do you perceive, that the Office of Judge is of the same Value as *Numenius*?

But I can throw whom I please into Prison.

As you may a Stone.

But I can beat whom I will too.

As you may an Ass. This is not a Government over Men. Govern us like reasonable Creatures: Show us what is for our Interest, and we will pursue it: show us what is against our Interest, and we will avoid it. Like *Socrates*, make us Imitators of yourself. He was properly a Governor of Men, who subjected their Desires and Aversions, their Pursuits, their Avoidances, to himself. "Do this; "do not do that, or I will throw you into Prison." Going thus far only, is not governing Men, like reasonable Creatures. But——"Do as *Jupiter* "hath commanded, or you will be punished. You will be a Loser."

What shall I lose?

Nothing more, than the not doing what you ought. You will lose your Fidelity, Honour, Decency. Look for no greater Losses, than these.

CHAPTER VIII.

How we are to exercise ourselves, against the Appearances of Things.

§. 1. IN the same manner, as we exercise ourselves, against sophistical Questions, we should exercise ourselves likewise, in relation to such Appearances, as every Day occur: for these too offer Questions to us.——Such a one's Son is dead.

(*c*) Of *Symphorus* and *Numenius* there is no Account; and their Names serve only to show, that Persons once of such Power are now totally forgot.

dead. What do you think of it? Anſwer: it is independent on Choice: it is not an Evil.——Such a one is diſinherited by his Father. What do you think of it? It is independent on Choice: it is not an Evil.——*Cæſar* hath condemned him.——This is independent on Choice: it is not an Evil.——He hath been afflicted by it.——This is dependent on Choice: it is an Evil.——He hath ſupported it bravely.——This is dependent on Choice: it is a Good.

§. 2. If we accuſtom ourſelves in this manner, we ſhall make an Improvement; for we ſhall never aſſent to any thing, but what the Appearance itſelf comprehends. A Son is dead.——What hath happened?——A Son is dead.——Nothing more?——Nothing.——A Ship is loſt.——What hath happened?——A Ship is loſt. He is carried to Priſon.——What hath happened?——He is carried to Priſon. That he is *unhappy*, is an Addition, that every one makes of his own.——"But *Jupiter* doth not order theſe Things right."——Why ſo? Becauſe he hath made you patient? Becauſe he hath hath made you brave? Becauſe he hath made them to be no Evils? Becauſe it is permitted you, while you ſuffer them, to be happy? Becauſe he hath opened you the Door, whenever they do not ſuit you? Go out, Man, and do not complain (*a*).

§. 3. If you would know how the *Romans* treat Philoſophers, hear. *Italicus*, eſteemed one of the greateſt Philoſophers among them, being in a Paſſion

(*a*) It is plain, the Stoics could not deny many of thoſe Things to be very ſeverely painful, which they maintain to be no Evils; ſince they ſo continually point at Self-murder as the Remedy. The lenient reviving Medicine, Future Hope, they knew nothing of; and their only Alternative, was an unfeeling Contempt, or a blind Deſpair. To feel tenderly the Loſs of a Son, and yet with meek Piety ſupport it, and *give Thanks always, for all Things, unto God, and the Father,* in humble Faith of their *working together for our Good*, was an Effort, beyond Stoiciſm to teach.

ſion with his own People, as if he had ſuffered ſome intolerable Evil, ſaid once when I was by, "I can-"not bear it; you are the Ruin of me; you will "make me juſt like *him*;" pointing to me.

CHAPTER IX.

Concerning a certain Orator, who was going to Rome *on a Law Suit.*

§. 1. WHEN a Perſon came to him, who was going to *Rome*, on a Law Suit, in which his Dignity was concerned; and, after telling him the Occaſion of his Journey, aſked him, what he thought of the Affair? If you aſk me, ſays *Epictetus*, what will happen to you at *Rome*, and whether you ſhall gain, or loſe your Cauſe, I have no Theorem for *this*. But if you aſk me, how you ſhall fare; I can anſwer, If you have right Principles, well; if wrong ones, ill. For Principle is to every one, the Cauſe of Action. For what is the Reaſon, that you ſo earneſtly deſired to be voted Governor of the *Gnoſſians*? Principle. What is the Reaſon, that you are now going to *Rome*? Principle. And in Winter too; and with Danger, and Expence? Why: becauſe it is neceſſary. What tells you ſo? Principle. If then, Principles are the Cauſes of all our Actions, where-ever any one hath bad Principles, the Effect will be anſwerable to the Cauſe. Well then: are all our Principles ſound? Are both yours, and your Antagoniſts? How then do you differ? Or are yours better than his? Why? You think ſo; and ſo doth he, that his are better; and ſo do Madmen. This is a bad Criterion. But ſhow me, that you have made ſome Examination, and taken ſome Care of your Principles. As you now take a Voyage to *Rome*, for the Government of the *Gnoſſians*, and are not contented to ſtay at home, with the Honours you before enjoyed, but deſire ſomething greater, and more illuſtrious; did you

you ever take ſuch a Voyage, in order to examine your own Principles; and to throw away the bad ones, if you happened to have any? Did you ever apply to any one, upon this Account? What Time did you ever ſet yourſelf? What Age? Run over your Years. If you are aſhamed of me, do it to yourſelf. Did you examine your Principles, when you were a Child? Did you not *then* do every thing, juſt as you do every thing, *now*? When you were a Youth, and frequented the Schools of the Orators, and made Declamations yourſelf, did you ever imagine, that you were deficient in any thing? And when you became a Man, and entered upon public Buſineſs, pleaded Cauſes, and acquired Credit, who, any longer, appeared to be equal to you? How would you have borne, that any one ſhould examine, whether your Principles were bad? What, then, would you have me ſay to you?

Aſſiſt me in this Affair.

I have no Theorem for that. Neither are you come to me, if it be upon that Account you came, as to a Philoſopher; but as you would come to an Herb-ſeller, or a Shoe-maker.

To what Purpoſes then, have the Philoſophers Theorems?

For preſerving and conducting the ruling Faculty conformably to Nature, whatever happens. Do you think this a ſmall Thing?

No: but the greateſt.

Well: and doth it require but a ſhort time? And may it be taken, as you paſs by? If you can, take it then: and ſo you will ſay, "I have viſited "*Epictetus*."——Ay: juſt as you would a Stone, or a Statue. For you have *ſeen* me, and nothing more. But he viſits a Man, as a Man, who learns his Principles; and, in return, ſhows his own. Learn my Principles. Show me yours. *Then* ſay, you have viſited me. Let us confute each other. If I have

have any bad Principle, take it away. If you have any, bring it forth. This is viſiting a Philoſopher. No. But "It lies in our Way; and, while we are "about hiring a Ship, we may call on *Epictetus.* "Let us ſee what it is he ſays." And then, when you are gone, you ſay, "*Epictetus* is nothing. His "Language was inaccurate, was barbarous." For what elſe did you come to judge of? "Well: "but if I employ (*a*) myſelf in theſe Things, I "ſhall be without an Eſtate, like you; without Plate, "without Equipage, like you."—Nothing perhaps is neceſſary to be ſaid to this, but that I do not want them. But, if you poſſeſs many Things, you ſtill want others: ſo that, whether you will or not, you are poorer than I.

§. 2. What then do I want?

What you have not: Conſtancy; a Mind conformable to Nature; and a Freedom from Perturbation. Patron, or no Patron, what care *I*? But *you* do. I am richer than you. I am not anxious what *Cæſar* will think of me. I flatter no one, on that Account. This I have, inſtead of Silver and Gold Plate. You have your Veſſels, of Gold; but your Diſcourſe, your Principles, your Aſſents, your Purſuits, your Deſires, of mere Earthen Ware. When I have all theſe conformable to Nature, why ſhould not I beſtow ſome Study upon my Reaſoning too? I am at Leiſure. My Mind is under no Diſtraction. In this Freedom from Diſtraction, what ſhall I do? Have I any thing more becoming a Man, than this? You, when you have nothing [to do], are reſtleſs; you go to the Theatre, or perhaps to bathe (*b*). Why ſhould not the Philoſopher

(*a*) The firſt ως I apprehend ſhould be ὣ, and is ſo tranſlated.

(*b*) I can find no Senſe of αναλυετε, which ſuits this Place. Perhaps the Reading ſhould be ἢ παραλουεσθε; and it is ſo tranſlated. Bathing was a common Amuſement of idle People. See B. III. c. 24. p. 495. of Mr. *Upton*'s Edition.

sopher polish his Reasoning? You have fine (*c*) crystal and myrrhine Vases; I have acute Forms of Reasoning. To *you*, all you have appears, little; to *me*, all I have, great. Your Appetite is unsatiable; mine is satisfied. When Children thrust their Hand into a narrow Jar of Nuts and Figs, if they fill it, they cannot get it out again; then they fall a crying. Drop a few of them, and you will get out the rest. And do you too drop your Desire: do not covet many Things, and you will get [some].

CHAPTER X.

In what Manner we ought to bear Sickness.

§. 1. WE should have all our Principles ready, to make use of, on every Occasion. At Dinner, such as relate to Dinner; in the Bath, such as relate to the Bath; and in the Bed, such as relate to the Bed.

Let not the stealing God of Sleep surprise,
Nor creep in Slumbers, on thy weary Eyes,
Ere ev'ry Action of the former Day
Strictly thou dost, and righteously survey,
What have I done? In what have I transgress'd?
What Good, or Ill, has this Day's Life express'd?
Where have I fail'd, in what I ought to do?
If Evil were thy Deeds, repent and mourn,
If Good, rejoice——————

ROWE's Pythagoras.

We should retain these Verses, so as to apply them to our Use: not merely to repeat them aloud, as

(*c*)—————— *and how they quaff in Gold,*
Crystal *and* myrrhine *Cups, imboss'd with Gems.*
Paradise Regained, B. IV. v. 118.

as we do the Verſes in Honour of *Apollo*, [without minding what we are about] (*a*).

§. 2. Again: In a Fever, we ſhould have ſuch Principles ready, as relate to a Fever; and not, as ſoon as we are taken ill, to loſe and forget all. Provided I do but act like a Philoſopher, let what will happen. Some Way or other depart I muſt, from this frail Body, whether a Fever comes, or not (*b*). What is it to be a Philoſopher? Is it not to be prepared againſt Events? Do not you comprehend, that you ſay, in Effect, if I am but prepared to bear all Events with Calmneſs, let what will happen; otherwiſe, you are like a Pancratiaſt, who, after receiving a Blow, ſhould quit the Combat. In that Caſe indeed you may allowably leave off, and not [run the Hazard] of being whipt (*c*). But what ſhall we get by leaving off Philoſophy? What then ought each of us to ſay upon every difficult Occaſion? "It was for this, that I exerciſed: it was "for this, that I prepared myſelf." God ſays to you, give me a Proof if you have gone through the preparatory Combats, according to Rule (*d*): if you have followed a proper Diet; a proper Exerciſe: if you have obeyed your Maſter: and, after this, do you faint, at the very Time of Action? Now is

(*a*) This Place is either corrupt, as Mr. *Upton* thinks; or alludes to ſome antient Cuſtom not ſufficiently underſtood now.

(*b*) This is a corrupt Paſſage, and the Tranſlation conjectural. Perhaps the true Reading might be πȣ ποτ' απελθοντα τȣ σωματιȣ δει απελθειν με; and it is ſo tranſlated. There is a ſimilar Turn of Expreſſion, in the fifth Chapter of the ſecond Book, which ſeems to favour this Notion. See Page 189. L. 1. of Mr. *Upton*'s Edition.

(*c*) Which was the Puniſhment of thoſe, who preſented themſelves, as Candidates at the *Olympic* Games, and did not comply with the Rules, which were to be obſerved, upon that Occaſion. *Epictetus* is here ſpeaking of the preparatory Exerciſes, which laſted for ten Months before the Combat.

(*d*) St. *Paul* hath made uſe of this very Expreſſion, νομιμως αθλειν, 2 *Tim.* ii. 5.

the proper Time for a Fever. Bear it well: for Thirst: bear it well: for Hunger: bear it well. Is it not in your Power? Who shall restrain you? A Physician may restrain you from drinking; but he cannot restrain you from bearing your Thirst, well. He may restrain you from eating; but he cannot restrain you from bearing Hunger, well.— But I cannot follow my Studies.——And for what End do you follow them, Wretch? Is it not that you may be prosperous? That you may be constant? that you may think and act conformably to Nature? What restrains you, but that in a Fever, you may preserve your ruling Faculty conformable to Nature? Here is the Proof of the Matter. Here is the Trial of the Philosopher: for a Fever is a Part of Life, just as a Walk, a Voyage, or a Journey. Do you read, when you are walking? No: nor in a Fever. But when you walk well, you have every thing belonging to a Walker: so, if you bear a Fever well, you have every thing belonging to one in a Fever. What is it to bear a Fever well? Not to blame either God or Man: not to be afflicted at what happens: to expect Death in a right and becoming Manner; and to do what is to be done. When the Physician enters, not to dread what he may say; nor, if he should tell you, that you are in a fair Way, to be too much rejoiced: for what good hath he told you? When you were in Health, what Good did it do you? Not to be dejected, when he tells you, that you are very ill: for what is it to be very ill? To be near the Separation of Soul and Body. What Harm is there in this, then? If you are not near it now, will you not be near it hereafter? What, will the World be quite overset when you die? Why then, do you flatter your Physician? Why do you say, "If "you please, Sir, I shall do well (*e*)?" Why do you

(*e*) See *Matth.* viii. 2. Κυριε, εαν θελης, δυνασαι με καθαρισαι. UPTON.

you furnish an Occasion to his Pride? Why do not you treat a Physician, with regard to an insignificant Body, which is not yours, but by Nature mortal, as you do a Shoemaker, about your Foot; or a Carpenter, about a House? These are the Things necessary, to one in a Fever. If he fulfils these, he hath what belongs to him. For it is not the Business of a Philosopher to take care of these mere Externals; of his Wine, his Oil, or his Body; but his ruling Faculty: And how, with regard to Externals? So as not to behave inconsiderately, about them. What Occasion then, is there for Fear? What Occasion for Anger *(f)*, about what belongs to others, and what is of no Value? For, two Rules we should always have ready: That nothing is good or evil, but Choice: and, That we are not to lead Events, but to follow them. "My Brother ought not to "have treated me so." Very true; but *he* must see to that. However he treats me, I am to act right, with regard to him; for the one is my own Concern; the other is not: the one cannot be restrained; the other may.

CHAPTER XI.

Miscellaneous.

§. 1. THERE are some Punishments appointed, as by a Law, for such as disobey the divine Administration. Whoever shall esteem any thing good, except what depends on Choice, let him envy, let him covet, let him flatter, let him be full of Perturbation. Whoever esteems any thing else to be evil, let him grieve, let him mourn, let him lament, let him be wretched.——And yet, though thus severely punished, we cannot desist.

(f) Φόβον, in the *Greek*, seems to have crept in from the preceding φοβεῖσθαι: Therefore it is omitted in the Translation.

Remember what the Poet says, of a Stranger.

A worse than Thou might enter here secure:
No rude Affront shall drive him from my Door;
For Strangers come from Jove——

HOMER.

§. 2. This too you should be prepared to say, with regard to a Father: It is not lawful for me to affront you, Father; even if a worse than you should have come: for all are from paternal *Jove.* And so of a Brother; for all are from kindred *Jove.* And thus we shall find *Jove* to be the Inspector of all the other Relations.

CHAPTER XII.

Of Ascetic Exercise.

§. 1. WE are not to carry our Exercises beyond Nature; nor merely to attract Admiration: for thus we, who call ourselves Philosophers, shall not differ from Jugglers. For it is difficult too, to walk upon a Rope; and not only difficult, but dangerous. Ought *we* too, for that Reason, to make it our Study to walk upon a Rope, or set up a Palm-Tree (*a*) or grasp a Statue (*b*)? By no means.

(*a*) A Tree remarkable for its being strait and high. I should imagine therefore, that to *set up the Palm-Tree* meant some Act of Dexterity, not unlike, perhaps, to that of our modern Ballance-masters: and that the Artist not only set up, but ascended to its Top, and there exhibited himself in various Attitudes. What confirms me in this Notion is, that these Palm-Tree Artists are joined with the Rope-dancers; their Professions being alike formed on the Difficulty and Danger. In LUCIAN's *Treatise de Syria Dea,* we meet with these Men, under the Name of the Φοινικοβατεοντες; who, it seems, were frequent in *Arabia* and *Syria;* Countries where the Palm is known to flourish. See the new Edition of LUCIAN. Tom. III. p. 475. I am obliged for this Note to Mr. HARRIS.

(*b*) *Diogenes* used, in Winter, to grasp Statues, when they were covered with Snow, as an Exercise, to enure himself to Hardship. DIOGENES LAERTIUS.

means. It is not every thing difficult, or dangerous, that is a proper Exercife; but fuch Things as are conducive, to what lies before us to do.

And what is it that lies before us to do?

To have our Defires and Averfions free from Reftraint.

How is that?

Not to be difappointed of our Defire, nor incur our Averfion. To this ought our Exercife to be turned. For, without ftrong and conftant Exercife, it is not poffible to preferve our Defire undifappointed, and our Averfion unincurred; and therefore, if we fuffer it to be externally employed on Things independent on Choice, be affured, that your Defire will neither gain its Object, nor your Averfion avoid it.

§. 2. And, becaufe Habit hath a powerful Influence, and we are habituated to apply our Defire and Averfion to Externals only, we muft oppofe one Habit to another; and, where the Appearances are moft flippery, there oppofe Exercife. I am inclinable to Pleafure. I will (*c*) bend myfelf beyond a due Proportion to the other Side, for the fake of Exercife. I am averfe to Pain. I will break and exercife the Appearances [which ftrike my Mind], that I may withdraw my Averfion from every fuch Object. For who is the Practitioner in Exercife? He who endeavours totally to reftrain Defire, and to apply Averfion only to Things dependent on Choice; and endeavours it moft in the moft difficult Cafes. Hence different

 Perfons

(*c*) Ανατυχησω is varioufly read. Perhaps the right Word may be ανατοιχησω derived from τοιχος; which fignifies, among other Things, the Side of a Ship, or Boat. It appears from *Julius Pollux*, and *Phrynicus*, in *Stephens*'s Lexicon, and *Scot*'s Appendix, that ἀνατοιχειν is a Word ufed by the Vulgar, to fignify being fometimes on one Side of the Veffel, and fometimes on the other; which agrees very well here: *I will lean to the oppofite Side*, &c. *i. e.* to keep the Veffel even. I am obliged for this Note to a Friend.

Persons are to be exercised, in different Ways. What signifies it, to this Purpose, to set up a Palm-Tree, or carry about a Tent (*d*) of Skins, or a Pestle and Mortar (*d*)? If you are hasty, Man, let it be your Exercise, to bear ill Language patiently; and, when you are affronted, not to be angry. Thus, at length, you may arrive at such a Proficiency, as, when any one strikes you, to say to yourself, "Let me suppose this, to be grasping "a Statue." Next, exercise yourself to make a decent Use of Wine: not to drink a great deal; for even in this, there are some so foolish as to exercise themselves: but at first to abstain from it; and to abstain from a Girl, and from Delicacies in Eating. Afterwards you will venture into the Lists, at some proper Season, by Way of Trial, if at all, to see whether Appearances get the better of you, as much as they used to do. But at first, fly from what is stronger than you. The Contest of a fine Girl, with a young Man, just initiated into Philosophy, is unequal. The Brass Pot and the Earthen Pitcher, as the Fable says, are an unsuitable Match.

§. 3. Next to the Desires and Aversions, is the Second Class, of the Pursuits and Avoidances; that they may be obedient to Reason; that nothing may be done improperly in Point of Time or Place, or in any other Respect.

§. 4. The Third Class relates to Assent, and what is plausible and persuasive. As *Socrates* said, that we are not to lead an unexamined Life; so neither are we to admit an unexamined Appearance; but to say, "Stop: let me see what you are, "and whence you come." (As the Watch say,

Show

(*d*) These Particulars are not now understood; but show, in general, that the antient Philosophers had their absurd and ostentatious Austerities, and Mortifications, as well as the Monks, and *Indian* Philosophers since.

Show me the Ticket.) "Have you that Signal "from Nature, which is neceſſary to the Admiſſion "of every Appearance?"

§. 5. In ſhort, whatever Things are applied to the Body, by thoſe who exerciſe it, if they any way affect Deſire or Averſion, they may be uſed in aſcetic Exerciſe. But, if this be done for mere Oſtentation, it belongs to one who looks out and hunts for ſomething external, and ſeeks for Spectators to exclaim, "What a great Man!" Hence *Apollonius* ſaid well. "If you have a mind to exerciſe yourſelf, for your own Benefit, when you "are choaking with Heat, take a little cold Water "in your Mouth; and ſpirt it out again, and tell "nobody."

CHAPTER XIII.

What Solitude is; and what a ſolitary Perſon.

§. 1. SOLITUDE is the State of a helpleſs Perſon. For not he who is alone, is therefore *ſolitary*, any more than one in a Crowd, the contrary. When therefore we loſe a Son, or a Brother, or a Friend, on whom we have been uſed to repoſe, we often ſay, we are left *ſolitary*, even in the midſt of *Rome*, where ſuch a Crowd is continually meeting us; where we live among ſo many, and when we have, perhaps, a numerous Train of Servants. For he is underſtood to be *ſolitary*, who is helpleſs and expoſed to ſuch as would injure him. Hence, in a Journey eſpecially, we call ourſelves ſolitary, when we fall among Thieves: for it is not the Sight of a *Man* that removes our Solitude, but of an *honeſt* Man; a Man of Honour, and a helpful Companion. If merely being alone is ſufficient for Solitude, *Jupiter* may be ſaid to be ſolitary at the Conflagration, and bewail himſelf, that he hath neither *Juno* nor *Pallas*, nor *Apollo*, nor Brother, nor Son, nor Descendant, nor Relation. This, some indeed say, he doth, when he is alone at the Conflagration (*a*). Such as these, moved by some natural Principle, some natural Desire of Society, and mutual Love, and by the Pleasure of Conversation, do not rightly consider the State of a Person who is alone. We ought, however, to be prepared in some manner for this also, to be self-sufficient, and able to bear our own Company. For as *Jupiter* converses with himself, acquiesces in himself, and contemplates his own Administration, and is employed in Thoughts worthy of himself; so should we too be able to talk with ourselves, and not to need the Conversation of others; nor be at a Loss [for Employment]: to attend to the divine Administration; to consider our Relation to other Beings: how we have formerly been affected by Events; how we are affected now: what are the Things that still press upon us: how these too may be cured; how removed: if any thing wants completing, to complete it, according to Reason. You see, that *Cæsar* hath procured us a profound Peace: there are neither Wars, nor Battles, nor great Robberies, nor Piracies; but we may travel at all Hours, and sail from East to West. But can *Cæsar* procure us Peace from a Fever too? From a Shipwreck? From a Fire? From an Earthquake? From a Thunder Storm? Nay, even from Love? He cannot. From Grief? From Envy? No: not from any one of these. But the Doctrine of Philosophers promises to procure us Peace, from these too. And what doth it say? "If you will attend to me, "O Mortals, where-ever you are, and whatever "you are doing, you shall neither grieve, nor be "angry, nor be compelled, nor restrained: but you

shall

(*a*) The Stoics held, successive Conflagrations at destined Periods; in which all Beings were resorbed into the Deity.

"shall live impassive, and free from all." Shall not he who enjoys this Peace, proclaimed, not by *Cæsar* (for how should *he* have it to proclaim?) but by God, through Reason, be contented, when he is alone reflecting, and considering; "To me there "can now no Ill happen: there is no Thief, no "Earthquake. All is full of Peace, all full of "Tranquillity; every Road, every City, every "Assembly. My Neighbour, my Compa- "nion, unable to hurt me." Another, whose Care it is, provides you with Food, with Clothes, with Senses, with Pre-conceptions. Whenever he doth not provide what is necessary, he sounds a Retreat: He opens the Door, and says to you; "Come." Whither? To nothing dreadful; but to that, whence you were made; to what is friendly and congenial, to the Elements *(b)*. What in you was Fire, goes away to Fire; what was Earth, to Earth; what Air, to Air; what Water, to Water. There is no *Hades*, nor *Acheron*, nor *Cocytus*, nor *Pyriphlegethon*; but all is full of Gods and Demons. He who can have such Thoughts; and can look upon the Sun, Moon, and Stars, and enjoy the Earth and Sea, is no more solitary, than he is helpless.——Well: but suppose any one should come and murder me, when I am alone.—— Fool: not *you*; but that insignificant *Body* of yours.

§. 2. What Solitude is there then left? What Destitution? Why do we make ourselves worse than

(b) What a melancholy Description of Death, and how gloomy the Ideas, in this *consolatory* Chapter! All Beings reduced to mere Elements, in successive Conflagrations! A noble Contrast to the Stoic Nations upon this Subject, may be produced from several Passages in the Scriptures.——*Then shall the Dust return to the Earth, as it was; and the Spirit shall return to God, who gave it.* Eccles. xii. 7. *For, if we believe, that* Jesus *died, and rose again, even so them also, which sleep in* Jesus, *will God bring with him.* 1 Thess. iv. 14. See *Jo.* vi. 39, 40. xi. 25, 26. 1 *Cor.* vi. 14. xv. 53. 2 *Cor.* v. 14, &c.

than Children? What do they do, when they are left alone? They take up Shells and Dust: they build Houses; then pull them down: then build something else: and thus never want Amusement. Suppose you were all to sail away; am I to sit, and cry, because I am left alone, and solitary? Am I so unprovided with Shells and Dust? But Children do this from Folly; and *we* are wretched from Wisdom.

§. 3. Every great Faculty is dangerous to a Beginner (*c*). Study first how to live like a Person in Sickness; that in time you may know how to live like one in Health. Abstain from Food. Drink Water. Totally repress your Desire, for some time, that you may at length use it according to Reason; and, if according to Reason, [as you may,] when you [come to] have some Good in you, you will use it well. No: but we would live immediately as Men already wise; and be of Service to Mankind.——Of what Service? What are you doing? Why: have you been of Service to yourself? but you would exhort them. *You* exhort! Would you be of Service to them, show them, by your own Example, what kind of Men Philosophy makes; and be not impertinent. When you eat, be of Service to those who eat with you; when you drink, to those who drink with you. Be of Service to them, by giving way to all, yielding to them, bearing with them; and not by throwing out your own ill Humour upon them.

(*c*) The *Greek*, from φερειν αν δει to φθισικω, is so corrupted and unintelligible, that it is totally rejected. Indeed, the Connexion of this Paragraph with what proceeds, is by no means clear.

CHAP-

CHAPTER XIV.

Miscellaneous.

§. 1. AS bad Performers cannot sing alone, but in a Chorus; so some Persons cannot walk alone. If you are any thing,* walk alone; talk by yourself; and do not skulk in the Chorus. Think a little at last: look about you: sift yourself, that you may know what you are.

§. 2. If a Person drinks Water, or doth any thing else, for the sake of Exercise, upon every Occasion he tells all he meets; "I drink Water." Why: do you drink Water merely for the sake of drinking it? If it doth you any Good to drink it, drink it; if not, you act ridiculously. But, if it is for your Advantage, and you drink it, say nothing about it before those who are apt to take Offence. What then? These are the very People you wish to please.

§. 3. Of Actions some are performed on their own Account; others occasioned by Circumstances: some proceed from Motives of Prudence: some from Complaisance to others; and some are done in pursuance of a Manner of Life, which we have taken up.

§. 4. Two Things must be rooted out of Men; Conceit and Diffidence. Conceit lies in thinking you want nothing: and Diffidence, in supposing it impossible, that, under such adverse Circumstances, you should ever succeed. Now, Conceit is removed by Confutation: and of this *Socrates* was the Author. And [in order to see] that the Undertaking is not impracticable, consider and enquire. The Enquiry itself will do you no Harm: and it is almost being a Philosopher, to enquire, How it is possible

possible to make use of our Desire and Aversion, without Hindrance.

§. 5. I am better than you; for my Father hath been Consul. I have been a Tribune, says another, and not you. If we were Horses, would you say, My Father was swifter than yours? I have Abundance of Oats and Hay, and fine Trappings? What now, if, while you were saying this, I should answer; "Be it so. Let us run a Race then." Is there nothing in Man analogous to a Race in Horses, by which it may be known, which is better or worse? Is there not Honour, Fidelity, Justice? Show yourself the better in these; that you may be the better, as a Man. But if you tell me, you can kick violently; I will tell you gain, that you value yourself on the Property of an Ass.

CHAPTER XV.

That every Thing is to be undertaken with Circumspection.

§. 1. (*a*) IN every Affair consider what precedes and follows; and then undertake it. Otherwise you will begin with Spirit; but, not having thought of the Consequences, when some of them appear, you will shamefully desist. "I would "conquer at the *Olympic* Games." But consider what proceeds and follows, and then, if it be for your Advantage, engage in the Affair. You must conform to Rules; submit to a Diet; refrain from

(*a*) This XVth Chapter makes the XXIXth of the *Enchiridion*; but with some Varieties of Reading. Particularly, for εν τω αγωνι παρορυσσεσθαι here, is εις τον αγωνα παρερχεσθαι there.

This Chapter hath a great Conformity to *Luke* xiv. 28, &c. But it is to be observed, that *Epictetus*, both here, and elsewhere, supposes some Persons incapable of being Philosophers; that is, virtuous and pious Men: but Christianity requires and enables all, to be such.

from Dainties; exercise your Body, whether you chuse it or not, at a stated Hour, in Heat and Cold: you must drink no cold Water; nor, sometimes, even Wine *(b)*. In a word, you must give yourself up to your Master, as to a Physician. Then, in the Combat, you may be thrown into a Ditch, dislocate your Arm, turn your Ankle, swallow Abundance of Dust, be whipt *(c)*; and, after all, lose the Victory. When you have reckoned up all this, if your Inclination still holds, set about the Combat. Otherwise, take notice, you will behave like Children, who sometimes play Wrestlers, sometimes Gladiators; sometimes blow a Trumpet, and sometimes act a Tragedy; when they happen to have seen and admired these Shows. Thus you too will be, at one Time, a Wrestler; at another, a Gladiator; now, a Philosopher; then, an Orator: but, with your whole Soul, nothing at all. Like an Ape, you mimick All you see; and one thing after another is sure to please you; but is out of Favour, as soon as it becomes familiar. For you have never entered upon any thing considerately, nor after having viewed the whole Matter on all Sides, or made any Scrutiny into it; but rashly, and with a cold Inclination. Thus some, when they have seen a Philosopher, and heard a Man speaking like *Euphrates (d)*, (though, indeed, who can speak like him,) have a Mind to be Philosophers too. Consider first, Man, what the Matter is, and what your own Nature is able to bear. If you would

(b) St. *Paul* hath a similar Allusion to the public Games. 1 *Cor.* ix. 25. Both Writers have them frequently in view.

(c) Which was the Case, in any Violation of the Laws of the Games.

(d) The Translation doth not follow the Pointing of Mr. *Upton*'s Edition in this Place.

Euphrates was a Philosopher of *Syria*, whose Character is described, with the highest Encomiums, by *Pliny*. See L. I. Ep. x.

would be a Wrestler, consider your Shoulders, your Back, your Thighs: for different Persons are made for different Things. Do you think, that you can act as you do, and be a Philosopher? That you can eat (*e*), and drink, and be angry, and discontented, as you are now? You must watch; you must labour; you must get the better of certain Appetites: must quit your Acquaintance; be despised by your Servant; be laughed at by those you meet: come off worse than others, in every thing; in Magistracies; in Honours; in Courts of Judicature. When you have considered all these Things round, approach, if you please: if, by parting with them, you have a Mind to purchase Apathy, Freedom, and Tranquillity. If not, do not come hither: do not, like Children, be one while a Philosopher, then a Publican, then an Orator, and then one of *Cæsar*'s Officers. These Things are not consistent. You must be one Man, either good or bad. You must cultivate either your own ruling Faculty, or Externals; and apply yourself either to Things within or without you; that is, be either a Philosopher, or one of the Vulgar (*f*).

CHAPTER XVI.

That Caution is necessary in Condescension and Complaisance.

§. 1. HE who frequently converses with others, either in Discourse, or Entertainments, or in any familiar Way of Living, must necessarily either become like his Companions, or bring them over.

(*e*) Τά υτα in this Place should be ταὐτά.

(*f*) What is omitted at the End of this Chapter, is placed at the End of the XVIIth; to which Lord *Shaftesbury* thinks it belongs, or to one of the Miscellaneous Chapters; which is the more probable Opinion.

over to his own Way. For, if a dead Coal be applied to a live one, either the first will quench the last, or the last kindle the first. Since then, the Danger is so great, Caution must be used in entering into these Familiarities with the Vulgar; remembering, that it is impossible to touch a Chimney-Sweeper, without being Partaker of his Soot. For what will you do, if you are to talk of Gladiators, of Horses, of Wrestlers, and what is worse, of Men? "Such a one is good; another, bad: "this was well, that ill done." Besides: what if any one should sneer, or ridicule, or be ill-natured? Is any of you prepared, like a Harper; who, when he takes his Harp, and tries the Strings, finds out which Notes are discordant, and knows how to put the Instrument in Tune? Hath any of you such a Faculty as *Socrates* had; who, in every Conversation, could bring his Companions to his own Purpose? Whence should you have it? You must therefore be carried along by the Vulgar. And why are they more powerful than you? Because they utter their corrupt Discourses, from Principle, and you your good ones, only from your Lips. Hence they are without Strength, or Life; and it would turn one's Stomach to hear your Exhortations, and poor miserable Virtue, celebrated up-hill and down. Thus it is, that the Vulgar get the better of you: for Principle is always strong, always invincible. Therefore, before these good Opinions are fixed in you, and you have acquired some Faculty for your Security, I advise you to be cautious, in your Familiarity with the Vulgar: otherwise, if you have any Impressions made on you in the Schools, they will melt away daily, like Wax before the Sun. Get away then, far from the Sun, while you have these waxen Opinions.

§. 2. It is for this Reason, that the Philosophers advise us to leave our Country; because inveterate Manners draw the Mind aside, and prevent the Beginning

ginning of a new Habit. We cannot bear those, who meet us, to say, "Hey-day! such a one is "turned Philosopher; who was so and so." Thus Physicians send Patients, with lingering Distempers, to another Place, and another Air: and they do right. Do you too import other Manners, instead of those you carry out. Fix your Opinions, and exercise yourselves in them. No: but from hence to the Theatre, to the Gladiators, to the Walks, to the *Circus*; then hither again; then back again; just the same Persons all the while. No good Habit, no Attention, no Animadversion, upon ourselves. No Observation what Use we make of the Appearances presented to our Minds; whether it be conformable, or contrary, to Nature; whether we answer them right, or wrong; (*a*) whether we say to Things independent on Choice, "You are nothing to me." If this be not (*b*) yet your Case, fly from your former Habits: fly from the Vulgar, if you would ever begin to be any thing.

CHAPTER XVII.

Of Providence.

§. 1. WHENEVER you lay any thing to the Charge of Providence, do but reflect; and you will find, that it hath happened agreeably to Reason.

Well: but a dishonest Man hath the Advantage.

In what?

In Money.

Why:

(*a*) The Translation follows Mr. *Upton*'s Conjecture, δει. Εɩ επιλεγω, &c.

(*b*) Μηπω, Mr. *Upton*'s Manuscript.

Why: he is better [qualified] for it *(c)* than you: becauſe he flatters, he throws away Shame, he keeps awake: and where is the Wonder? But look whether he hath the Advantage of you in Fidelity, or in Honour. You will find he hath not: but, that where-ever it is beſt for you to have the Advantage of him, there you have it. I once ſaid to one who was full of Indignation, at the good Fortune of *Philoſtorgus*, "Why: would you be "willing to ſleep with *Sura (d)*? Heaven forbid, ſaid he, that Day ſhould ever come!——Why then are you argry, that he is paid for what he ſells: or how can you call him happy, in Poſſeſſions acquired by Means, which you deteſt? Or what Harm doth Providence do, in giving the beſt Things to the beſt Men? Is it not better to have a Senſe of Honour, than to be rich?——Granted. ——Why then are you angry, Man, if you have what is beſt? Always remember then, and have it ready, That a better Man hath the Advantage of a worſe, in that Inſtance, in which he is better; and you will never have any Indignation.

But my Wife treats me ill.

Well: if you are aſked, what is the Matter: anſwer; "My Wife treats me ill."

Nothing more?

Nothing.

My Father gives me nothing.——What is the Matter?——My Father gives me nothing. To denominate this an Evil, ſome external and falſe

(c) *"But ſometimes Virtue ſtarves, while Vice is fed."*
What then? Is the Reward of Virtue, Bread?
That, Vice may merit; 'tis the Price of Toil:
The Knave deſerves it, when he tills the Soil;
The Knave deſerves it, when he tempts the Main.
Eſſay on Man, L. IV.

(d) This Perſon is not known. One of his Name is mentioned in the *Acts of Ignatius*, as being Conſul at the Time, when he ſuffered Martyrdom.

Addition muſt be made. We are not therefore to get rid of Poverty; but of our Principle concerning it; and we ſhall do well.

When *Galba* was killed, ſomebody ſaid to *Rufus*, "Now, indeed, the World is governed by Providence." I never thought, anſwered *Rufus*, of bringing the ſlighteſt Proof, that the World was governed by Providence, from *Galba*.

CHAPTER XVIII.

That we ought not to be alarmed, by any News that is brought us.

§. 1. WHEN any alarming News is brought you, always have it at Hand, that no News can be brought you, concerning what is in your own Choice. Can any one bring you News, that your Opinions or Deſires are ill conducted? By no means: but that ſomebody is dead. What is that to *you* then? That ſomebody ſpeaks ill of you. And what is that to *you* then? That your Father is forming ſome Contrivance, or other. Againſt what? Againſt your Choice? How can he? Well: but againſt your Body; againſt your Eſtate? You are very ſafe: this is not againſt *you*. ——But the Judge [perhaps] hath pronounced you guilty of Impiety. And did not the Judges pronounce the ſame of *Socrates?* Is his pronouncing a Sentence, any Buſineſs of yours? No. Then why do you, any longer, trouble yourſelf about it? There is a Duty incumbent on your Father; which, unleſs he performs, he loſes the Character of a Father, of natural Affection, of Tenderneſs. Do not want him to loſe any thing elſe, by this: for no Perſon is ever guilty in one Inſtance, and a Sufferer in another. Your Duty, on the other hand, is to make your Defence, with Conſtancy, Modeſty,

ſty, and Mildneſs: otherwiſe you loſe the Character of filial Piety; of Modeſty, and Generoſity of Mind. Well: and is your Judge free from Danger? No. He runs an equal Hazard. Why then, are you ſtill afraid of his Deciſion? What have you to do with the Evil of another? Making a bad Defence would be your own Evil. Let it be your only Care to avoid that: but whether Sentence is paſſed on you, or not, as it is the Buſineſs, ſo it is the Evil, of another. "Such a one threa- "tens you."——*Me?* No.——"He cenſures "you."——Let him look to it, how he doth his own Buſineſs——"He will give an unjuſt Sentence againſt you.——Poor Wretch!

CHAPTER XIX.

What is the Condition of the Vulgar; and what of a Philoſopher.

§. 1. THE firſt Difference between one of the Vulgar, and a Philoſopher, is this: the one ſays, I am undone, on the Account of my Child, my Brother, my Father: but the other, if ever he be obliged to ſay, I am undone! reflects, and adds, on Account of myſelf. For Choice cannot be reſtrained, or hurt, by any thing to which Choice doth not extend; but only by itſelf. If therefore we always would incline this Way, and, whenever we are unſucceſsful, would lay the Fault on ourſelves, and remember, that there is no Cauſe of Perturbation and Inconſtancy, but Principle, I engage we ſhould make ſome Proficiency. But we ſet out in a very different Way, from the very Beginning. In Infancy, for Example, if we happen to ſtumble, our Nurſe doth not chide *us*, but beats the Stone. Why: what Harm hath the Stone done? Was it to move out of its Place, for the

Folly of your Child? Again: if we do not find ſomething to eat, when we come out of the Bath, our Governor doth not try to moderate our Appetite, but beats the Cook. Why: did we appoint you Governor of the Cook, Man? No: but of our Child. It is he whom you are to correct and improve. By theſe Means, even when we are grown up, we appear Children. For an unmuſical Perſon is a Child in Muſic; an illiterate Perſon, a Child in Learning; and an untaught one, a Child in Life.

CHAPTER XX.

That ſome Advantage may be gained, from every external Circumſtance.

§. 1. IN Appearances that are merely Objects of Contemplation, almoſt all Perſons have allowed Good and Evil to be in ourſelves, and not in Externals. No one ſays, it is good, to be Day; evil, to be Night; and the greateſt Evil, that Three ſhould be Four: but what? That Knowlege is good, and Error evil. So that, concerning Falſhood itſelf, there exiſts one *(a)* good Thing; the Knowledge, that it is Falſhood. Thus then, ſhould it be, in Life alſo. Health is a Good; Sickneſs, an Evil. No, Sir. But what? A right Uſe of Health is a Good; a wrong one, an Evil. So that, in truth, it is poſſible to be a Gainer, even by Sickneſs. And is it not poſſible, by Death too? By Mutilation? Do you think *(b)* *Menæceus* an inconſiderable Gainer by Death?——"May whoever

(a) The Paſſage, as it now ſtands in the *Greek*, is ſcarcely intelligible. The Difficulty is removed, by reading αγαθον for απατην, and the Tranſlation follows this Conjecture.

(b) The Son of *Creon*, who killed himſelf, after he had been informed, by an Oracle, that his Death would procure a Victory to the *Thebans*. APOLLODORUS. UPTON.

"ever talks thus, be such a Gainer as he was!"— Why: pray, Sir, did not he preserve his Patriotism, his Magnanimity, his Fidelity, his gallant Spirit? And, if he had lived on, would he not have lost all these? Would not Cowardice, Mean-spiritedness, and Hatred of his Country, and a wretched Love of Life, have been his Portion? Well, now: do not you think him a considerable Gainer, by dying? No: but I warrant you, (c) the Father of *Admetus* was a great Gainer, by living on, in so mean-spirited and wretched a Way, as he did! Why: did not he die at last? For Heaven's sake, cease to be thus struck, by the mere Materials, [of Action.] Cease to make yourselves Slaves; first of Things, and then, upon their Account, of the Men who have the Power, either to bestow, or take them away. Is there any Advantage then to be gained from these Men? From all; even from a Reviler. What Advantage doth a Wrestler gain from him, with whom he exercises himself, before the Combat: the greatest. Why: just in the same manner I exercise myself with this Man. (d) He exercises me in Patience, in Gentleness, in Meekness. No: but, I suppose, I gain an Advantage from him who manages my Neck, and sets my Back and Shoulders in order; and the best Thing a Master of Exercise can say, is, "Lift him up with both Hands," and the heavier he is, the greater is my Advantage: and yet, it is no Advantage to me, when I am exercised in Gentleness of Temper! This is not knowing, how to gain an Advantage from Men. Is my Neighbour a bad one? He is so, to himself; but a good one, to me. He exercises my good Temper, my Moderation. Is my Father bad? To himself; but not to me. "This is the Rod of "*Hermes*. Touch with it whatever you please,

(c) See P. 177: Note *a*.
(d) Ὁυτος for ὁυτως. Wolfius.

"and it will become Gold." No: but bring whatever you pleaſe, and I will turn it into *Good*. Bring Sickneſs, Death, Want, Reproach, capital Trial. All theſe, by the Rod of *Hermes*, ſhall turn to Advantage.——"What will you make of Death?"—Why: what but an Ornament to you; what but a Means of your ſhowing, by (*e*) Action, what the Man is, who knows, and follows the Will of Nature. "What will you make of Sickneſs?"——I will ſhow its Nature. I will make a good Figure in it; I will be compoſed and happy. I will not flatter my Phyſician. I will not wiſh to die. What need you aſk further? Whatever you give me, I will make it happy, fortunate, reſpectable, and eligible. No.——"But, take care not to be ſick." Juſt as if one ſhould ſay, "Take care, that the "Appearance of Three being Four, doth not pre-"ſent itſelf to you." "It is an Evil." How an Evil, Man? If I think as I ought about it, what Hurt will it any longer do me? Will it not rather be even an Advantage to me? If then I think as I ought, of Poverty, of Sickneſs, of being out of Power, is not that enough for me? Why then muſt I any longer ſeek Good or Evil, in Externals? But what is the State of the Caſe? Theſe Things are allowed here; but nobody carries them home; but immediately every one is in a State of War with his Servant, his Neighbours, with thoſe who ſneer and ridicule him. Well fare (*f*) *Leſbius*, for proving every Day, that I know nothing.

(*e*) For δειξη σε εργω, δειξης εργω ſeems the true Reading.

(*f*) Mr. *Upton* conjectures this *Leſbius* to have been ſome Buffoon.

CHAP-

CHAPTER XXI.

Concerning those who readily ſet up for Sophiſts.

§. 1. (*a*) THEY who have received bare Propoſitions, are preſently inclined to throw them up, as a ſick Stomach doth its Food. Firſt concoct it, and then you will not throw it up; otherwiſe it will be crude and impure, and unfit for Nouriſhment. But ſhow us, from what you have digeſted, ſome Change in your ruling Faculty; as Wreſtlers do in their Shoulders, from their Exerciſe, and their Diet: as Artificers, in their Skill, from what they have learnt. A Carpenter doth not come and ſay, "Hear me diſcourſe on "the Art of Building:" but he hires a Houſe, and fits it up, and ſhows himſelf Maſter of his Trade. Let it be your Buſineſs likewiſe to do ſomething like this: eat like a Man; drink, dreſs, marry, have Children, perform the Duty of a Citizen; bear Reproach; bear with an unreaſonable Brother; bear with a Father; bear with a Son, a Neighbour, a Companion; as becomes a Man. Show us theſe Things, that we may ſee that you have really learnt ſomewhat, from the Philoſophers. No: "But "come and hear me repeat Commentaries." Get you gone, and ſeek ſomebody elſe, to throw them

 out

(*a*) The Tranſlation follows the Conjecture of *Wolfius*, ακαθαρτον.

There are other Difficulties in the Text, as it now ſtands. Εξεμεσης, perhaps, ſhould be εξεμεσεις; or, probably, there ſhould be no μη before εξεμησης; and then the Meaning of *Epictetus* will be, That the Perſons whom he is ſpeaking of, ought firſt to concoct Propoſitions for their own Uſe, and then throw them up (*i. e.* utter them in Diſcourſe), for the Uſe of others. But the Figure he makes uſe of is ſo dirty, that it is not to be enlarged upon, though taken from the Practice of the *Greek* and *Roman* Phyſicians.

out upon. "Nay, but I will explain the Doctrines "of *Chrysippus* to you, so as no other Person can: "I will elucidate his Diction, in the clearest Man-"ner." And is it for this then, that young Men leave their Country, and their own Parents, that they may come and hear you explain *Words?* Ought they not to return patient, active, free from Passion, free from Perturbation; furnished with such a Provision for Life, that, setting-out with it, they will be able to bear all Events well, and derive Ornament from them? But how should you impart what you have not? For have you yourself done any Thing else, from the Beginning, but spent your Time in solving Syllogisms, and convertible Propositions, and interrogatory Arguments. ——"But such a one hath a School, and why should not I have one?"——Wretch, these Things are not effected, in a careless and fortuitous Manner. But there must be Age, and a Method of Life, and a guiding God. Is it not so? No one quits the Port, or sets Sail, till he hath sacrificed to the Gods, and implored their Assistance: nor do Men sow, without first invoking *Ceres.* And shall any one who hath undertaken so great a Work, undertake it safely, without the Gods? And shall they, who apply to such a one, apply to him with Success? What are you doing else, Man, but divulging the Mysteries? And you say, "There is "a Temple at *Eleusis*; and here is one too. *There* "is a (*b*) Priest; and *I* will make a Priest *here:* "*there* is a Herald; and *I* will appoint a Herald "too: *there* is a Torch-bearer; and *I* will have a "Torch-

(*b*) The Priest who presided over the *Eleusinian* Mysteries was called *Hierophantes*; *i. e.* a Revealer of sacred Things. He was obliged to devote himself to divine Service, and lead a chaste and single Life. He was attended by three Officers; a Torch-bearer, a Herald, and One who assisted at the Altar. For a fuller Account of the *Eleusinian* Mysteries, see POTTER's *Grecian* Antiquities, Vol. I. c. 20.

"Torch-bearer: *there* are Torches; and so shall "there be *here*. The Words said, the Things "done, are the same. Where is the Difference "betwixt one and the other?" Most impious Man! is there no Difference? Are these Things of Use out of Place, and out of Time? A man should come with Sacrifices and Prayers, previously purified, and his Mind affected with a Sense, that he is approaching to sacred and ancient Rites. Thus the Mysteries become useful: thus we come to have an Idea, that all these Things were appointed by the Ancients, for the Instruction and Correction of Life. But you divulge and publish them, without Regard to Time and Place; without Sacrifices, without Purity: you have not the Garment that is necessary for a Priest, nor the Hair, or the Girdle (*c*), that is necessary; nor the Voice, nor the Age: nor have you purified yourself, like him. But, when you have got the Words by Heart, you say, "The Words are sacred of them-"selves." These Things are to be approached, in another Manner. It is a great, it is a mystical Affair; not given by Chance, or to every one indifferently. Nay, mere Wisdom, perhaps, is not a sufficient Qualification for the Care of Youth. There ought to be likewise a certain Readiness and Aptitude for this, and indeed a particular Constitution of Body; and, above all, a Counsel from God to undertake this Office, as he counselled *Socrates* to undertake the Office of Confutation; *Diogenes*, that of authoritative Reproof; *Zeno*, that of dogmatical Instruction. But *you* set up for a Physician, provided with nothing but Medicines, and without knowing, or having studied, where, or how, they are to be applied. "Why: such a one had Me-"dicines for the Eyes; and I have the same." Have

(*c*) The Girdle is mentioned among the holy Garments of the Levitical Priests. *Exod.* xxviii. 4. 39, 40, &c.

Have you then, a Faculty too of making use of them? Do you, at all, know when, and how, and to whom, they will be of Service? Why then do you act at Hazard? Why are you careless, in Things of the greatest Importance? Why do you attempt a Matter unsuitable to you? Leave it to those who can perform it, and do it Honour. Do not you too bring a Scandal upon Philosophy, by your Means; nor be one of those, who cause the Thing itself to be calumniated. But, if Theorems delight you, sit quiet, and turn them every Way by yourself; but never call yourself a Philosopher; nor suffer another to call you so; but say, "He is "mistaken: for my Desires are not different from "what they were; nor my Pursuits directed to o-"ther Objects; nor my Assent otherwise given; nor "have I at all made any Change in the Use of the "Appearances, from my former Condition." Think and speak thus of yourself, if you would think as you ought: if not, act at all Hazards, and do as you do; for it becomes you.

CHAPTER XXII.

Of the Cynic Philosophy (*a*).

§. 1. WHEN one of his Scholars, who seemed inclined to the Cynic Philosophy, asked him, what a Cynic must be, and what was the general Plan of that Sect? Let us examine it, says he, at our Leisure. But thus much I can tell you now, that

(*a*) The Cynics owed their Original to *Antisthenes*, a Disciple of *Socrates*. They held Virtue to be the highest Good, and the End of Life; and treated Riches, Honours, and Power, with great Contempt. They were Enemies to Science, and polite Literature; and applied themselves wholly to the Study of Morality. There was, in many Respects, great Conformity between them and the Stoics: but the Stoics selected what seemed laudable, in their Principles, without imitating the Roughness

that he who (*b*) attempts ſo great an Affair without God, is an Object of divine Wrath, and would only bring public Diſhonour upon himſelf. For, in a well regulated Houſe, no one comes, and ſays to himſelf, "I ought to be the Manager here." If he doth, and the Maſter (*c*) returns, and ſees him inſolently giving Orders, he drags him out, and hath him whipt. Such is the Caſe likewiſe in this great City [of the World.] For here too is a Maſter of the Family, who orders every thing. "*You* "are the Sun: you can, by making a Circuit, form "the Year, and the Seaſons, and increaſe and nou-"riſh the Fruits; raiſe and calm the Winds, and "give a moderate Warmth to the Bodies of Men. "Go: make your Circuit, and thus intimately "move every thing, from the greateſt to the leaſt. "*You* are a Calf: when the Lion appears, do your "(*d*) Part, or you will ſuffer for it. *You* are a "Bull: come and fight; for that is incumbent "on *you*, and becomes you, and you can do it. "*You* can lead an Army to *Troy*: be you *Aga-*"*memnon.* You can engage in ſingle Combat with "*Hector*: be you *Achilles*." But, if *Therſites* had come

neſs of their Addreſs, and the deteſtable Indecency of their external Behaviour. The Stoics were indeed a reformed Branch of the Cynics, and thence, perhaps, ſpoke of them ſomewhat more favourably, than they might otherwiſe have done. The Cynics are ſaid to have derived their Name from *Cynoſarges*, a *Gymnaſium*, without the Walls of *Athens*, where *Antiſthenes* taught; and which was ſo called from the Accident of a white Dog ſtealing Part of a Victim, which *Diomus* was ſacrificing to *Hercules*: and their barking at every body, and their Want of Shame, helped to confirm the Appellation. In this *Cynoſarges* was a celebrated Temple of *Hercules*; which, very poſſibly, gave the Cynics the original Hint of comparing themſelves to that Hero; which they ſo much affected.

(*b*) *And no Man taketh this Honour unto himſelf, but he that is called of God.*——*Heb.* v. 4.

(*c*) This hath a remarkable Likeneſs to *Matth.* xxiv. 50, 51. eſpecially in the Originals.

(*d*) *i. e.* run away.

come and claimed the Command, either he would not have obtained it; or, if he had, he would have disgraced himself, before the more Witnesses.

§. 2. Do you too, carefully deliberate upon this Matter: it is not what you think it. "I wear an "old Cloke now; and I shall have one then. I "sleep upon the hard Ground now; and I shall "sleep so then. I will moreover take a Wallet "and a Staff, and go about, and will beg of those "I meet, and begin by (*e*) abusing them: and, if "I see any one using Means to take off the Hair "from his Face, or Body; or setting his Curls, or "walking in Purple, I will rebuke him." If you imagine this to be the Thing, avaunt; come not near it: it doth not belong to you. But, if you imagine it to be what it really is, and do not think yourself unworthy of it, consider how great a thing you undertake. First, with regard to yourself: you must no longer, in any Instance, appear like what you do now. You must accuse neither God nor Man. You must totally suppress Desire; and must transfer Aversion to such Things only as are dependent on Choice. You must have neither Anger, nor Resentment, nor Envy, nor Pity. Neither Boy, nor Girl, nor Fame, nor Delicacies in Eating, must have Charms for you. For you must know, that other Men indeed fence themselves with Walls, and Houses, and Darkness, when they do any thing of this kind, and have many Concealments: a Man shuts the Door, places somebody before the Apartment; "Say, He is gone out; "say, He is not at Leisure." But the Cynic, instead of all this, must fence himself with virtuous Shame; otherwise *He* will act indecently, naked, and in the open Air. This is *his* House; this, *his* Door; this, *his* Porter; this, *his* Darkness. He must not wish to conceal any thing relating to himself:

(*e*) For λοιδορεῖν read λοιδορῶν. UPTON.

ſelf; for, if he doth, he is gone; he hath loſt the Cynic; the open, the free Character: he hath begun to fear ſomething external: he hath begun to need a Concealment; nor can he get it when he will. For where ſhall he conceal himſelf, or how? For if this Tutor, this Pedagogue of the Public, ſhould happen to ſlip, what muſt *he* ſuffer? Can he then, who dreads theſe Things, be thoroughly bold within, and preſcribe to other Men? Impracticable; impoſſible.

§. 3. In the firſt place then, you muſt purify your own ruling Faculty, conformably *(f)* to this Method of Life. Now the Subject-matter for me to work upon, is my own Mind; as Wood is for a Carpenter, or Leather for a Shoemaker: and my Buſineſs is, a right Uſe of the Appearances of Things. But Body is nothing to me; its Parts nothing to me. Let Death come when it will; either of the Whole, or of a Part. "Go into Exile." And whither? Can any one turn me out of the World? He cannot. But where-ever I go, there is the Sun, the Moon, the Stars, Dreams, Auguries, Communication with God. And even this Preparation is, by no means, ſufficient for a true Cynic. But it muſt farther be known, that he is a Meſſenger ſent from *Jupiter* to Men, concerning Good and Evil; to ſhow them, that they are miſtaken, and ſeek the Eſſence of Good and Evil where it is not; but do not obſerve it where it is: that He is a Spy, like *Diogenes*, when he was brought to *Philip*, after the Battle of *Chæronea* (*g*). For, in effect, a Cynic is a Spy, to diſcover what Things are friendly, what hoſtile, to Man: and he muſt, after making an accurate Obſervation, come and tell them the Truth: not be ſtruck with Terror, ſo as to point out

(f) The Senſe ſeems to require, that καὶ ſhould be κατα; and it is ſo tranſlated.

(g) See P. 69. Note (*c*).

out to them Enemies, where there are none; nor, in any other Instance, disconcerted or confounded by Appearances.

§. 4. He must then, if it should so happen, be able to lift up his Voice, come upon the Stage, and say, like *Socrates*, "O Mortals, whither are you "hurrying? What are you about? Why do you "tumble up and down, Wretches, like blind "Men? You are going a wrong Way, and have "forsaken the right. You seek Prosperity and "*(h)* Happiness in a wrong Place, where it is not; "nor do you give Credit to another, who shows "you where it is. Why do you seek it without? "It is not in Body: if you do not believe me, "look upon *(i) Myro*; look upon *Ofellius*. It is "not in Wealth: if you do not believe me, look "upon *Crœsus*; look upon the Rich of the present "Age, how full of Lamentation their Life is. It "is not in Power: for, otherwise, they, who have "been twice and thrice Consuls, must be happy: "but they are not. To whom shall we give Cre-"dit in this Affair? To you who look only upon "the Externals of their Condition, and are dazled "by Appearances, or to themselves? What do "they say? Hear them, when they groan, when "they sigh, when they think themselves more "wretched, and in more Danger, from these very "Consulships, this Glory, and Splendor. It is not "in Empire: otherwise *Nero* and *Sardanapalus* had "been happy. But not even *Agamemnon* was hap-"py, though a better Man than *Sardanapalus*, or "*Nero*. But, when others are snoring, what is "*He* doing?"

He rends his Hairs——

And what doth he say himself?

Scarce

(*h*) The Translation follows Lord *Shaftesbury*'s Conjecture.

(*i*) Unknown Persons, probably of great bodily Strength.

Scarce can my Knees these trembling Limbs sustain;
And scarce my Heart support its Load of Pain.

POPE.

Why: which of your Affairs goes ill, poor Wretch? Your Possessions? No. Your Body? No. But you have Gold and Brass in Abundance. What then goes ill? That Part of you, whatever it be called, is neglected and corrupted, by which we desire, and are averse; by which we pursue, and avoid.——How neglected?——It is ignorant of that for which it was naturally formed, of the Essence of Good, and of the Essence of Evil. It is ignorant what is its own, and what another's. And, when any thing belonging to others goes ill it says, "I am undone; the *Greeks* are in danger!" (Poor ruling Faculty! which alone is neglected, and hath no Care taken of it.) "They will die by the "Sword of the *Trojans!*"——And, if the *Trojans* should not kill them, will they not die?—"Yes: "but not all at once."——Why: where is the Difference? For, if it be an Evil to die, whether it be all at once, or singly, it is equally an Evil. Will any thing more happen, than the Separation of Soul and Body (*k*)?——"Nothing"——And, when the *Greeks* perish, is the Door shut against *you?* Is it not in your own Power to die?——"It is."——Why then do you lament, while you are a King, and hold the Sceptre of *Jove?* A King is no more to be made unfortunate than a God. What are you then? You are a Shepherd (*l*), truly so called: for you weep, just as Shepherds do, when

(*k*) Were Conquerors deeply to consider, how much more happens than the mere Separation of Soul and Body, they would not, for Increase of Dominion, or a Point of false Honour, push Thousands at once into an unknown Eternity.

(*l*) We find this Phrase often used by the inspired Writers, to describe the Office and Duty of a King, or Ruler. And the most tender and affectionate Compassion is implied in it, *Isaiah* xl.

when the Wolf seizes any of their Sheep: and they who are governed by you are mere Sheep. But why did you come hither? Was your Desire in any Danger? Your Aversion? Your Pursuits? Your Avoidances? "No," says he: "but my "Brother's Wife hath been stolen."——Is it not great good Luck then, to be rid of a sorry adulterous Wife?——"But must we be held in Con-"tempt by the *Trojans*?"——What are they? Wise Men, or Fools? If wise, why do you go to war with them? If Fools, why do you mind them?

§. 5. Where then doth our Good lie, since it doth not lie in these Things? Tell us, Sir; you who are our Messenger and Spy.——Where you do not think, nor are willing to seek it. For, if you were willing, you would find it in yourselves: nor would you wander abroad, nor seek what belongs to others, as your own. Turn your Thoughts into yourselves. Consider the Pre-conceptions which you have. What do you imagine Good to be?——What is prosperous, happy, unhindered.——Well: and do not you naturally imagine it great? Do not you imagine it valuable? Do not you imagine it incapable of being hurt? In what Materials then must you seek Prosperity, and Exemption from Hindrance?

In

xl. 11. where it is said of the KING of Kings, *He shall feed his Flock, like a Shepherd: He shall gather the Lambs with his Arm, and carry them in his Bosom; and shall gently lead those that are with young.* He accordingly applies this distinguishing Character to himself, in several Places of the New Testament; especially *John* x. 11. 14, 15, 16.

Homer speaks of *Agamemnon* by this Name (which we see was not unusual in the East) to express his Authority and Care: but *Epictetus* applies it as a Term of Reproach, to imply Ignorance, and Meanness of Spirit. One cannot help observing, on what is here said of *Agamemnon*, the Selfishness of the Stoic Doctrine; which, as it all along forbids Pity and Compassion, will have even a King to look upon the Welfare of his People, and a General on the Preservation of his Soldiers, as Matters quite foreign and indifferent to him.

In that which is inslaved, or free?—In the Free?—Is your Body then inslaved, or free?——We do not know.———Do not you know, that it is the Slave of Fever, Gout, Defluxion, Dysentery: of a Tyrant; of Fire, Steel; of every thing stronger than itself?——Yes, it is a Slave——How then can any thing belonging to the Body be unhindered? And how can that be great, or valuable, which is, by Nature, lifeless, Earth, Clay? What then, have you nothing free?—Possibly nothing.—Why: who can compel you to assent to what appears false?——No one.——Or who, not to assent to what appears true?——No one.——Here then you see, that there is something in you, by Nature, free. But who of you can desire or be averse, or use his active Powers of Pursuit or Avoidance, or concert, or purpose, unless he hath been impressed by an Appearance of its being for his Advantage, or his Duty?——No one.——You have then, in these too, something unrestrained and free. Cultivate this, Wretches; take care of this; seek for Good here.——"But how is it possible, that a "Man, worth nothing, naked, without House or "Home, squalid, unattended, who belongs to no "Country, can lead a prosperous Life?"——See: God hath sent us One, to show, in fact, that it is possible (*m*). "Take Notice of me, that I am

(*m*) It is observable, that *Epictetus* seems to think it a necessary Qualification in a Teacher, sent from God, for the Instruction of Mankind, to be destitute of all External Advantages, and a *suffering* Character. Thus doth this excellent Man, who, had carried human Reason to so great a Height, bear Testimony to the Propriety of that Method which the Divine Wisdom hath thought fit to follow, in the Scheme of the Gospel; whose Great Author had not *where to lay his Head:* and which some, in later Ages, have inconsiderately urged as an Argument against the Christian Religion. The infinite Disparity between the Proposal of the Example of *Diogenes*, in *Epictetus*, and of our Redeemer, in the New Testament, is too obvious to need any Enlargement.

"without a Country, without a House, without an "Estate, without a Servant: I lie on the Ground: "no Wife, no Children, no Coat (*n*); but only "Earth, and Heaven, and one sorry Cloke. And, "what do I want? Am not I without Sorrow, "without Fear? Am not I free? Did any of you "ever see me disappointed of my Desire, or in-"curring my Aversion? Did I ever blame God or "Man? Did I ever accuse any one? Hath any "of you seen me look discontented? How do I "treat those whom *you* fear, and of whom you are "struck with Awe? Is it not like sorry Slaves? "Who that sees me, doth not think, that he sees "his own King and Master?" This is the Language, this the Character, this the Undertaking, of a Cynic. No: I warrant you; but the Wallet, and the Staff, and the great Jaws: swallowing, or treasuring up, whatever is given you; abusing unseasonably those you meet; or showing a brawny Arm. Do you consider, how you shall attempt so important an Affair? First take a Mirror. View your Shoulders, examine your Back, your Thighs. You are going to be enrolled a Combatant at the Olympic Games, Man; not in a poor slight Contest. In the Olympic Games, a Champion is not allowed merely to be conquered, and depart: but must first be disgraced, in the View of the whole World; not only of the *Athenians*, or *Spartans*, or *Nicopolitans*: and then he, who hath rashly departed, must be whipt too; and, before that, must suffer Thirst, and Heat; and swallow an Abundance of Dust.

§. 6. Consider carefully; know yourself; consult the Divinity: attempt nothing without God: for, if he counsels you, be assured, that it is his Will, that you should be a great Man; or, [which comes to

(*n*) The Translation follows Mr. *Upton*'s Conjecture, of χιτωνάριον, instead of τριχιτώριδιον.

to the ſame thing,] ſuffer many a Blow. For there is this very fine Circumſtance connected with the Character of a Cynic, that he muſt be beat like an Aſs; and, when he is beat, muſt love thoſe who beat him; as the Father, as the Brother of All (*o*). No, to be ſure: but, if any body beats you, ſtand publicly and roar out, "O, *Cæſar*, am I to ſuffer "ſuch Things, in breach of your Peace? Let us "go before the Proconſul."———But what is *Cæſar* to a Cynic, or what is the Proconſul, or any one elſe, but *Jupiter?* Who hath deputed him, and Whom he ſerves. Doth he invoke any other but Him? And is he not perſuaded, that whatever he ſuffers of this Sort, it is *Jupiter*, who doth it to exerciſe him? Now *Hercules*, when he was exerciſed by *Euryſtheus*, did not think himſelf miſerable; but executed, with Alacrity, all that was to be done. And ſhall *he* who is appointed to the Combat, and exerciſed by *Jupiter*, cry out, and take Offence at things? A worthy Perſon, truly, to bear the Scepter of *Diogenes!* Hear what *He*, in a Fever, ſaid to thoſe who were paſſing by (*p*). "Sorry Wretches, why do not you ſtay? Do you "take ſuch a Journey to *Olympia*, to ſee the De-"ſtruction, or Combat, of the Champions; and "have you no Inclination to ſee the Combat be-

 "tween

(*o*) Compare this with the Chriſtian Precepts, of Forbearance, and Love to Enemies, *Matth.* v. 39——44. The Reader will obſerve, that Chriſt ſpecifies higher Injuries and Provocations than *Epictetus* doth; and requires of *all* his Followers, what *Epictetus* deſcribes only as the Duty of one or two *extraordinary* Perſons, as ſuch.

(*p*) St. *Jerom*, cited by Mr. *Upton*, gives the following, ſomewhat different, Account of this Matter. *Diogenes*, as he was going to the Olympic Games, was taken with a Fever, and laid himſelf down in the Road: his Friends would have put him into ſome Vehicle; but he refuſed it, and bid them go on to the Show. "This Night," ſaid he, "I will either con-"quer, or be conquered. If I conquer the Fever, I will "come to the Games; if it conquers me, I will deſcend to "Hades."

" tween a Man and a Fever?" Such a one, who took a Pride in difficult Circumstances, and thought himself worthy to be a Spectacle to those who passed by, was a likely Person, indeed, to accuse God, who had deputed him, as treating him unworthily! For what Subject of Accusation shall he find? That he preserves a Decency of Behaviour? With what doth he find fault? That he sets his own Virtue in a clearer Light?——Well: and what doth he say of Poverty? Of Death? Of Pain? How did he compare his Happiness with that of the *Persian* King; or rather thought it beyond Comparison. For, amidst Perturbations, and Griefs, and Fears, and disappointed Desires, and incurred Aversions, how can there be any Entrance for Happiness? And, where there are corrupt Principles, there must all these Things necessarily be.

§. 7. The same young Man enquiring, Whether, if a Friend should be willing to come to him, and take care of him when he was sick, he should comply? And where, says *Epictetus*, will you find me the Friend of a *Cynic*? For to be worthy of being numbered among his Friends, a Person ought to be such another as himself: he ought to be a Partner of the Scepter and the Kingdom, and a worthy Minister, if he would be honoured with his Friendship; as *Diogenes* was the Friend of *Antisthenes*; as *Crates*, of *Diogenes*. Do you think, that he who only comes to him, and salutes him, is his *Friend*; and that he will think him worthy of being entertained as such? If such a Thought comes into your Head, rather look round you, for some clever Dunghill, to shelter you in your Fever, from the North Wind, that you may not perish by taking Cold. But you seem to me, to want [only] to get into somebody's House, and to be well fed there a while. What Business have *you* then, even to attempt so important an Affair as this?

§. 8.

§. 8. But (ſaid the young Man) will a Cynic engage himſelf in Marriage, and the Production of Children, as a principal Point (*q*)?

If you will allow me a Republic of Sages, no one there, perhaps, will readily apply himſelf to the Cynic Philoſophy. For on whoſe Account ſhould he embrace that Method of Life? However, ſuppoſe he doth, there will be nothing to reſtrain him from marrying, and having Children. For his Wife will be ſuch another as himſelf; his Father-in-Law ſuch another as himſelf; and his Children will be brought up in the ſame manner. But as the State of Things now is, like that of an Army prepared for Battle, is it not neceſſary that a Cynic ſhould be without (*r*) Diſtraction; intirely attentive to the Service of God: at Liberty to walk about among Mankind: not tied down to vulgar Duties, nor entangled in Relations; which, if he tranſgreſſes, he will no longer keep the Character of a wiſe and good Man; and which, if he obſerves, there is an End of him, as the Meſſenger, and Spy, and Herald of the Gods? For, conſider, there are ſome Offices due to his Father-in-Law; ſome to the other Relations of his Wife; ſome to his Wife herſelf: beſides, after this, he is (*s*) confined to the

(*q*) The Stoics directed this; and the *Epicureans* forbad it.

(*r*) It is remarkable, that *Epictetus* here uſes the ſame Word (απεριςπαςως) with St. *Paul*, 1 *Cor.* vii. 35. and urges the ſame Conſideration, of applying wholly to the Service of God, to diſſuade from Marriage. His Obſervation too, that the State of Things was then (ως εν παραταξει) like *that of an Army prepared for Battle*, nearly reſembles the Apoſtle's (ενεςωσα αναγκη) *preſent Neceſſity.* St. *Paul* ſays, 2 *Tim.* ii. 4. (ουδεις ςρατευομενος εμπλεκεται, &c.) *no Man that warreth* entangleth *himſelf with the Affairs of this Life.* So *Epictetus* ſays here, that a Cynic muſt not be (εμπεπλεγμενον) entangled *in Relations*, &c. From theſe and many other Paſſages of *Epictetus*, one would be inclined to think, that he was not unacquainted with St. *Paul*'s Epiſtles; or, that he had heard ſomething of the Chriſtian Doctrine. Yet ſee Introduction, § 40.

(*s*) Εκκλειεται ſhould be εγκλειεσθαι; and is ſo tranſlated.

Care of his Family when ſick, and making Proviſion for their Support. Not to ſpeak of other Things, he muſt have a Veſſel, to warm Water in, to bathe his Child. There muſt be Wool, Oil, a Bed, a Cup, for his Wife, after her Delivery; and thus the Furniture increaſes: more Buſineſs, more Diſtraction. Where, for the future, is this King, whoſe Time is devoted to the public Good?

To whom its Safety, a whole People owes.

Who ought to overſee others; married Men, Fathers of Children: [to obſerve] who treats his Wife well; who, ill: who quarrels: which Family is well regulated; which, not: like a Phyſician, who goes about, and feels the Pulſe of his Patients: "*You* have a Fever; *you* the Head-ach; *you*, the "Gout. Do *you* (*t*) abſtain from Food: do *you* "eat: do *you* omit Bathing: *you* muſt have an In-"ciſion made: *you* muſt be cauteriſed. Where ſhall He have Leiſure for this, who is tied down to vulgar Duties? Muſt not he provide Clothes for his Children; and ſend them with Pens, and Ink, and Paper, to a Schoolmaſter? Muſt not he provide a Bed for them? (For they cannot be Cynics from their very Birth) Otherwiſe, it would have been better to expoſe them, as ſoon as they were born, than to kill them thus. Do you ſee to what we bring down our Cynic? How we deprive him of his Kingdom?——"Well: but *Crates* (*u*) was "married."

(*t*) Ασιτησον. Upton. Wolfius.

(*u*) *Crates* was a *Theban* of Birth and Fortune, who was ſo charmed by the Appearance of *Telephus*, in the Character of a dirty, ragged Beggar, upon the Stage, that he gave away all his Eſtate, aſſumed the Wallet and Staff, and turned Cynic. *Hipparchia*, a *Thracian* Lady, was ſo affected by the Diſcourſes and Manners of this polite Philoſopher, that ſhe fell deſperately in love with him, and neither the Riches, Beauty, or Diſtinction, of others, who paid their Addreſſes to her, were able to rival him, in her Heart. Her Relations vainly endeavoured to oppoſe

"married." The Case of which you speak was a particular one, arising from Love; and the Woman, another *Crates*. But we are enquiring about ordinary and (*v*) common Marriages: and in this Enquiry we do not find the Affair mightily suited to the Condition of a Cynic.

§. 9. How then shall he keep up Society?

For Heaven's sake, do they confer a greater Benefit upon the World, who leave two or three sniveling Children in their stead, than those, who, as far as possible, oversee all Mankind; what they do; how they live; what they attend to; what they neglect, contrary to their Duty. Did all they, who left Children to the *Thebans*, do them more Good than *Epaminondas*, who died childless? And did *Priam*, who was the Father of fifty Profligates, or *Danaus* (*w*) or *Æolus*, conduce more to the Advantage

oppose her Inclination: she was deaf to all their Remonstrances; and even threatened to kill herself, unless she was suffered to marry *Crates*. At the Desire of her Family, he tried, himself, to dissuade her from this Scheme. He pointed out to her the Deformity of his Person; and, throwing down his Wallet and Staff before her, told her, these were all the Riches she was to expect; and that his Wife must pursue the same Course of Life, as he did: and desired her to consider of it. But no Consideration was able to shake her Resolution. She married him, and became as absolute a Cynic as himself; utterly disregarding all external Propriety and Decency. See DIOG. LAERTIUS, in their Lives.

(*v*) Mr. *Upton*'s Reading.

(*w*) *Danaus* and *Egyptus* were the Sons of *Belus*. *Danaus* had fifty Daughters, who, from their Grandfather, were called *Belides*; and *Egyptus*, fifty Sons. After a Quarrel between the two Brothers, a Reconciliation was agreed, upon Condition of a Marriage between their Children. But *Danaus*, having learnt from an Oracle, that he was to be killed by one of his Sons-in-Law, commanded his Daughters to murder their Husbands, and furnished them with Daggers for that Purpose. They all, except one, executed this cruel Order. The Poets represent them, as punished, in the infernal Regions, by an everlasting unavailing Attempt, to fill a Sieve with Water.

Æolus was the Father of *Sisyphus*; who, for his infamous Rob-

vantage of Society, than *Homer?* Shall a military Command, or any other Post, then, exempt a Man from marrying, and becoming a Father, so that he shall be thought to have made sufficient Amends for the Want of Children: and shall not the Kingdom of a Cynic be a proper Compensation for it? Perhaps we do not understand his Grandeur, nor duly represent to ourselves the Character of *Diogenes*; but consider Cynics as they are now; who stand like Dogs watching at Tables, and who imitate the others in nothing, unless, perhaps, in breaking wind; but absolutely in nothing besides: else this [which you have objected] would not move us; nor should we be astonished, that a Cynic will not marry, nor have Children. Consider, Sir, that he is the Father of Human-kind: that all Men are his Sons, and all Women his Daughters. Thus he attends; thus takes Care of All. What! do you think it is from Impertinence, that he rebukes those he meets? He doth it as a Father, as a Brother, as a Minister of the common Parent, *Jove*.

§. 10. Ask me, if you please, too, Whether a Cynic will engage in the Administration of the Commonwealth. What Commonwealth do you enquire after, Blockhead, greater than what he administers? Whether *he* will harangue among the *Athenians*, about Revenues and Taxes, whose Business it is to debate with all Mankind; with the *Athenians*, *Corinthians*, and *Romans*, equally; not about Taxes and Revenues, or Peace and War, but about Happiness and Misery, Prosperity and Adversity, Slavery and Freedom. Do you ask me, whether a Man engages in the Administration of the Commonwealth, who administers such a Commonwealth as this? Ask me too, whether he will accept any Command? I will answer you again, What

Robberies, was killed by *Theseus*, and, after his Death, condemned, in *Tartarus*, to roll continually a vast Stone up a Hill.

What Command, Fool, greater than that which he now exercises?

§. 11. A Cynic, however, hath need of a Constitution duly qualified: for, if he should appear consumptive, thin, and pale, his Testimony hath no longer the same Authority. For he must not only give a Proof to the Vulgar, by the Constancy of his Mind, that it is possible to be a Man of Figure and Merit, without those Things that strike *them* with Admiration: but he must show too, by his Body, that a simple and slender Diet, under the open Air, doth no Injury to the Constitution. "See, I and "my Body are a Witness to this." As *Diogenes* did: for he went about fresh, and plump; and gained the Attention of the Many, by the very Appearance of a healthy Body. But a pitiable Cynic seems a mere Beggar: all avoid him; all are offended at him: for he ought not to appear slovenly, so as to drive People from him; but even his rough Negligence should be neat and engaging.

§. 12. Much natural Agreeableness and Acuteness are likewise necessary in a Cynic, (otherwise he becomes a mere Driveller, and nothing else); that he may be able to give an Answer readily, and pertinently, upon every Occasion. Like *Diogenes*, to one who asked him, "Are you that *Diogenes*, who "do not believe, there are any Gods?" "How "so, replied he, when I think *you* odious to them?" Again: when *Alexander* surprised him sleeping, and repeated,

To waste long Nights in indolent Repose
Ill fits a Chief, who mighty Nations guides,

before he was quite awake, he answered,

Directs in Council, and in War presides.
Pope's Homer. B. II. V. 27.

§. 13. But, above all, the ruling Faculty of a Cynic must be purer than the Sun: otherwise he must

must necessarily be a common Cheat, and a Rascal; if, while he is guilty of some Vice himself, he reproves others. For, consider how the Case stands. Arms and Guards give a Power to common Kings and Tyrants of reproving, and of punishing Delinquents, though they are wicked themselves: but to a Cynic, instead of Arms and Guards, Conscience gives this Power; when he knows, that he hath watched and laboured for Mankind: that he hath slept pure, and waked still purer: and that he hath regulated all his Thoughts as the Friend, as the Minister of the Gods, as a Partner of the Empire of *Jupiter:* that he is ready to say, upon all Occasions,

Conduct me Jove, *and thou,* O Destiny.

And, "if it thus pleases the Gods, thus let it be." Why should he not dare to speak boldly to his own Brethren, to his Children? in a word, to his Kindred? Hence he, who is thus qualified, is neither impertinent, nor a busy Body: for he is not busied about the Affairs of others, but his own, when he oversees the Transactions of Men. Otherwise say, that a General is a busy Body, when he oversees, examines, and watches his Soldiers; and punishes the Disorderly. But, if you reprove others, at the very Time that you have a Cake [concealed] under your own Arm, I will ask you; Had you not better, Sir, go into a Corner, and eat up what you have stolen? But what have you to do with the Concerns of others? For what are *you*? Are you the Bull in the Herd, or the Queen of the Bees? Show me such Ensigns of Empire, as she hath from Nature. But, if you are a Drone, and arrogate to yourself the Kingdom of the Bees, do not you think, that your fellow Citizens will drive you out, just as the Bees do the Drones?

§. 14. A Cynic must, besides, have so much Patience, as to seem insensible, and a Stone, to the Vulgar.

Vulgar. No one reviles, no one beats, no one affronts *him*; but he hath surrendered his Body to be treated at pleasure, by any one who will. For he remembers, that the Inferior, in whatever Instance it is the inferior, must be conquered by the Superior: and the Body is inferior to the Multitude, the Weaker to the Stronger. He never therefore, enters into a Combat where he can be conquered; but immediately gives up what belongs to others: he doth not claim what is slavish and dependent: but, where Choice, and the Use of the Appearances, are concerned, you will see, that he hath so many Eyes, you would say *Argos* was blind to him. Is his Assent ever precipitate? His Pursuits, ever rash? His Desire, ever disappointed? His Aversion, ever incurred? His Intention, ever fruitless? Is he ever querulous, ever dejected, ever envious? Here lies all his Attention and Application. With regard to other Things, he snores supine. All is Peace. There is no Robber, no Tyrant of the Choice.——But of the Body?——Yes.—— The Estate?——Yes.——Magistracies and Honours?——Yes. And what doth he care for these? When any one therefore would frighten him with them, he says, "Go, look for Children: Vizards "are frightful to *Them*; but *I* know they are "only Shell, and have nothing withinside."

§. 15. Such is the Affair about which you are deliberating: therefore, if you please, for Heaven's sake, defer it; and first consider how you are prepared for it. Mind what *Hector* says to *Andromache*.

No more——but hasten to thy Tasks at home,
There guide the Spindle, and direct the Loom.
Me, Glory summons, to the Martial Scene,
The Field of Combat is the Sphere for Men.

POPE's Homer.

Thus conscious he was of his own Qualifications, and of her Weakness.

CHAP-

CHAPTER XXIII.

Concerning such as read and dispute, ostentatiously.

§. 1. FIRST say to yourself, what you would be; and then do, what you have to do. For, in almost every thing else, we see this to be the Practice. Olympic Champions first determine what they would be, and then act accordingly. To a Racer, in a longer Course, there must be one kind of Diet, Walking, Anointing, and Exercise: to one in a shorter, all these must be different; and to a Pentathlete (*a*), still more different. You will find the Case the same in the manual Arts. If a Carpenter, you must have such and such Things: if a Smith, such other. For, if we do not refer each of our Actions to some End, we shall act at random: if to an improper one, we shall miss our Aim. Further: there is a general and a particular End. First, to act as a Man. What is comprehended in this? Not to be, though gentle, like a Sheep; nor mischievous, like a wild Beast. But the particular End relates to the Study, and Choice of each Individual. A Harper is to act as a Harper; a Carpenter, as a Carpenter; a Philosopher, as a Philosopher; an Orator, as an Orator. When therefore you say, "Come, and hear me read:" observe first, not to do this at random; and, in the next place, after you have found to what End you refer it, consider whether it be a proper one. Would you be useful, or be praised? You presently hear him say, "What do I value the Praise "of the Multitude?" And he says well: for this is nothing to a Musician, or a Geometrician, as such. You would be useful then. In what? Tell us, that we too may run, to make Part of your Audience.

(*a*) See Note *a*. p. 196.

Audience. Now, is it poſſible for any one to benefit others, who hath received no Benefit himſelf? No: for neither can he, who is not a Carpenter, or a Shoemaker, benefit any, in reſpect to thoſe Arts. Would you know then, whether you have received Benefit? Produce your Principles, Philoſopher: What is the Aim and Promiſe of Deſire? Not to be diſappointed. What of Averſion? Not to be incurred. Come: do we fulfil this Promiſe? Tell me the Truth: but, if you falſify, I will tell it *you.* The other Day, when your Audience came but coldly together, and did not receive what you ſaid, with Acclamations of Applauſe, you went away dejected. Again: the other Day, when you were praiſed, you went about, aſking every body, "What did you think of me?"——"Upon my "Life, Sir, it was prodigious."——"But, how did "I expreſs myſelf upon that Subject?"—"Which?" —— "Where I gave a Deſcription of *Pan,* and "the *Nymphs* (*b*)?"——"Moſt excellently."—— And do you tell me, after this, that you regulate your Deſires and Averſions conformably to Nature? Get you gone. Perſuade ſomebody elſe. Did not you, the other Day, praiſe a Man, contrary to your own Opinion? Did not you flatter a certain Senator? Would you wiſh your own Children to be like him?——"Heaven forbid!"—"Why "then did you praiſe and cajole him?"——"He is "an ingenious young Man, and attentive to Diſ- "courſes."——"How ſo?"—"He admires *me.*" Now indeed you have produced your Proof. After all, what do you think? Do not theſe very People ſecretly deſpiſe you? When therefore a Man, conſcious of no good Action, or Intention, finds ſome Philoſopher ſaying, "You are a great Genius, and "of a frank and candid Diſpoſition;" what do you think

(*b*) Mr. *Upton* obſerves, that theſe florid Deſcriptions were the principal Study of the Sophiſts.

think he ſays, but, "This Man hath ſome Need of "me." Pray tell me, what Action of a great Genius he hath ſhown. You ſee, he hath long converſed with you, hath heard your Diſcourſes, hath heard your Lectures. Hath he turned his Attention to himſelf? Hath he perceived his own Faults? Hath he thrown off his Conceit? Doth he ſeek an Inſtructor?——Yes, he doth.——An Inſtructor how to *live?* No, Fool; but how to *talk*: for it is upon this Account that he admires *you*. Hear what he ſays. "This Man writes with very great "Art, and much more finely than *Dion* (*c*)." That is quite another Thing. Doth he ſay, This is a modeſt, faithful, calm Perſon? But, if he ſaid this too, I would aſk him, ſince he is *faithful*, What is it to be *faithful* (*d*)? And, if he could not tell, I would add, Firſt learn the Meaning of what you ſay, and then ſpeak. While you are in this bad Diſpoſition then, and gaping after Applauders, and counting your Hearers, would you be of Benefit to others? "To-day I had many more Hearers." "Yes, many: we think there were five hundred." You ſay nothing: make them a Thouſand.—— "*Dion* never had ſo great an Audience." "How "ſhould he?"——"And they have a fine Taſte "for Diſcourſes."——"What is excellent, Sir, "will move even a Stone." Here is the Language of a Philoſopher! Here is the Diſpoſition of one, who is to be beneficial to Mankind! Here is the Man, attentive to Diſcourſes! Who hath read the Works of the *Socratic* Philoſophers, as ſuch; not as if they were the Writings of Orators, like *Lyſias* and *Iſocrates*. "*I have often wondered by what Ar-* "*guments,*

(*c*) *Dion* was a *Greek* Writer of thoſe Times; called, for his Eloquence, *Chryſoſtom*, or Golden-mouthed; as one of the Fathers of the Church was afterwards.

(*d*) The Senſe ſeems abſolutely to require, that the latter ουτος ſhould be either expunged or changed into τουτο.

"*guments* (*e*), &c. No: *By what Argument*: that "is the more perfectly accurate Expression." Is this to have read them any otherwise, than as you read little Pieces of Poetry? If you read them as you ought, you would not dwell on such Trifles; but would rather consider such a Passage as this: Anytus *and* Melitus *may kill*; *but they cannot hurt me*. And, *I am always so disposed, as to regard none of my Friends, but that Reason, which, after Examination, appears to me to be the best*. Hence, who ever heard *Socrates* say, "I know, or "teach, any thing?" But he sent different People to different Instructors: so they came to him, desiring to be recommended to the Philosophers; and he took and recommended them. No: but I warrant you, as he accompanied them, he used to give them such Advice as this: "Hear *me* discourse "To-day at the House of *Quadratus* (*f*)."—— Why should I hear you? Have you a Mind to show me how finely you put Words together, Sir? And what Good doth that do you? "But praise "me."——What do you mean by praising you? ——Say, incomparable! prodigious!——Well: I do say it. But, if Praise be that which the Philosophers call by the Appellation of *Good*, what have I to praise you for? If it be a Good to speak well, teach me, and I will praise you.——"What then, "ought these Things to be heard without Plea-"sure?"——By no means. I do not hear even a Harper, without Pleasure; but am I therefore to stand playing upon the Harp? Hear what *Socrates* says to his Judges. "It would not be decent "for me to appear before you, at this Age, com-"posing

(*e*) These Words are the Beginning of *Xenophon*'s Memoirs of *Socrates*; and it was a Debate among the minute Critics, whether *Argument* or *Arguments* was the proper Reading. UPTON.

(*f*) It might be usual for Persons of Fashion to lend their Houses, for Sophists and Orators to declaim in. UPTON.

"posing Speeches, like a Boy." Like a Boy, says he. For it is, without doubt, a pretty Knack, to chuse out Words, and place them together: and then to read or speak them gracefully in public; and, in the midst of the Discourse, to observe, that "he vows by all that is good, there are but "Few capable of these Things." But doth a Philosopher apply to People to hear him? Doth not he attract those who are fitted to receive Benefit from him, in the same manner as the Sun, or their necessary Food doth? What Physician applies to any body to be cured by him? (Though now indeed I hear, that the Physicians at *Rome* apply for Patients; but in my Time they were applied to) "I apply to you, to come and hear that you are "in a bad Way; and that you take care of every "thing, but what you ought: that you know not "what is good or evil; and are unfortunate, and "unhappy." A fine Application! And yet, unless the Discourse of a Philosopher hath this Effect, both that, and the Speaker, are void of Life *(g)*. *Rufus* used to say, If you are at leisure to praise me, I speak to no Purpose. And indeed he used to speak in such a manner, that each of us, who heard him, supposed, that some Person had accused us to him; he so hit upon what was done by us, and placed the Faults of every one, before his Eyes.

§. 2. The School of a Philosopher is a Surgery. You are not to go out of it with Pleasure, but with Pain; for you come there, not in Health: but one of you hath a dislocated Shoulder; another, an Abscess; a third, a Fistula; a fourth, the Headach. And am I then, to sit uttering pretty trifling Thoughts, and little Exclamations, that, when you have praised me, you may each of you go away with the same dislocated Shoulder, the same aching Head,

(g) St. *James* uses the same Word, when he saith, *Faith without Works is dead.*

Head, the ſame Fiſtula, and the ſame Abſceſs, that you brought? And is it for this that young Men are to travel? And do they leave their Parents, their Friends, their Relations, and their Eſtates, that they may praiſe you, while you are uttering little Exclamations? Was this the Practice of *Socrates*? Of *Zeno*? Of *Cleanthes*? "What "then! is there not in ſpeaking, a Style and Man- "ner of Exhortation?"——Who denies it? Juſt as there is a Manner of Confutation, and of Inſtruction. But who ever therefore, added that of *Oſtentation*, for a fourth? For in what doth the exhortatory Manner conſiſt? In being able to ſhow to one and all, the Contradictions in which they are involved; and that they care for every thing rather than what they mean to care for: for they mean the Things conducive to Happineſs; but they ſeek them where they are not to be found. To effect this, muſt a thouſand Seats be placed, and an Audience invited; and you, in a fine Robe, or Cloke, aſcend the Roſtrum, and deſcribe the Death of *Achilles*? Forbear, for Heaven's ſake, to bring, as far as you are able, good Words and Practices into Diſgrace. Nothing, to be ſure, gives more Force to Exhortation, than when the Speaker ſhows, that he hath need of the Hearers! But tell me, who, when he hears you reading, or ſpeaking is ſolicitous about *himſelf*? Or turns his Attention upon *himſelf*? Or ſays, when he is gone away, "The Philoſo- "pher hit me well." Inſtead of this, even though you are in high Vogue, is not all that one Man ſays; "He ſpoke finely about *Xerxes*."——"No, "ſays another; but on the Battle of *Thermopylæ*." Is this the Audience of a Philoſopher?

CHAPTER XXIV.

That we ought not to be affected, by Things not in our own Power.

§. 1. LET not what is contrary to Nature in another, be an Evil to you: for you were not born to be depressed, and unhappy, along with others; but to be happy, along with them. And, if any one is unhappy, remember, that he is so for himself: for God made all Men to enjoy Felicity, and a settled good Condition. He hath furnished all with Means for this Purpose; having given them some Things for their own; others, not for their own. Whatever is subject to Restraint, Compulsion, or Deprivation, not their own: whatever is not subject to Restraint, their own. And the Essence of Good and Evil, he hath placed in Things which are our own; as it became Him, who provides for, and protects us, with paternal Care.

But I have parted with such a one, and he is in Grief.

And why did he esteem what belonged to another, his own? Why did he not consider, while he was pleased with seeing you, that you are mortal, that you are subject to change your Abode? Therefore he bears the Punishment of his own Folly. But to what Purpose, or for what Cause do you too break (*a*) your Spirits? Have not *you* neither studied these Things? But, like trifling, silly Women, considered the Things you delighted in; the Places, the Persons, the Conversations, as if they were to last for ever; and now sit crying, because you

(*a*) There is no need of *Salmasius*'s Change of αντι τινος, &c. to αντιτεινεις, &c. if, for επι τι κλας, one reads επικλᾶς. The τι might arise from a Mistake in writing πι twice over. Επικλασιν is used in the same Sense, in L. 3. c. 26. p. 527. of Mr. *Upton*'s Edition. If κλαω hath it, the present Reading may stand.

you do not see the same People, nor live in the same Place? Indeed you deserve to be so affected, and thus to become more wretched than Ravens or Crows; which, without groaning, or longing for their former State, can fly where they will, build their Nests in another Place, and cross the Seas.

Ay: but this happens from their Want of Reason.

Was Reason then given to us by the Gods, for the Purpose of Unhappiness and Misery, to make us live wretched and lamenting? O, by all means, let every one be immortal! Let nobody go from home! Let us never go from home ourselves, but remain rooted to a Spot, like Plants! And, if any of our Acquaintance should quit his Abode, let us sit and cry; and when he comes back, let us dance, and clap our Hands, like Children. Shall we never wean ourselves, and remember what we have heard from the Philosophers, (unless we have heard them only as juggling Enchanters;) That the World is one great City, and the Substance one, out of which it is formed: that there must necessarily be a certain Rotation of Things: that some must give way to others; some be dissolved, and others rise in their stead: some remain in the same Situation, and others be moved: but that all is full of Friendship: first of the Gods, and then of Men, by Nature endeared to each other: that some must be separated; others live together, rejoicing in the Present, and not grieving for the Absent: and that Man, besides a natural Greatness of Mind, and Contempt of Things independent on Choice, is likewise formed not to be rooted to the Earth: but to go at different Times to different Places; sometimes on urgent Occasions, and sometimes merely for the sake of Observation. Such was the Case of *Ulysses*; who,

Wand'ring from Clime to Clime observant stray'd,
Their Manners noted, and their States survey'd.
Pope's Odyss. I.

And yet, before him, of *Hercules*, to travel over the World,

Just and unjust recording in his Mind,
And, with sure Eyes, inspecting all Mankind.
Pope's Odyss. XVII. v. 580.

To expel and clear away the one, and, in its stead, to introduce the other. Yet how many Friends do you think he must have at *Thebes?* How many at *Argos?* How many at *Athens?* And how many did he acquire in his Travels? He married too, when he thought it a proper Time, and became a Father, and then quitted his Children; not lamenting and longing for them, nor as if he had left them Orphans: for he knew, that no human Creature is an Orphan; but that there is a Father, who always and without Intermission, takes care of all. For he had not merely heard it, as Matter of Talk, that *Jupiter* was the Father of Mankind; but he esteemed and called him his own Father, and performed all that he did, with a View to Him. Hence, he was, in every Place, able to live happy. But it is never possible to make Happiness consistent with a Desire of what is not present. For *(b)* what is happy must have all it wishes for; must resemble a Person satisfied with Food: there must be no Thirst, no Hunger.

But *Ulysses* longed for his Wife, and sat crying on a Rock.

Why: do you mind *Homer*, and his Fables, in every thing? Or, if *Ulysses* really did cry, what was he, but a wretched Man? But what wise and good

(b) Το γαρ ευδαιμονουν απεχειν δει παντα ἃ θελει, πεπληρωμενω τινι εοικεναι. This bears a strong Resemblance to απεχω δε παντα και περισσευω, πεπληρωμαι, &c. *Phil.* iv. 18.

good Man is wretched? The Universe is surely but ill governed, unless *Jupiter* takes care, that his Subjects may be happy like himself. But these are unlawful and profane Thoughts; and *Ulysses*, if he did indeed cry and bewail himself, was not a good Man. For who can be a good Man, who doth not know what he is? And who knows this, and forgets, that all Things made are perishable; and that it is not possible for Man and Man always to live together? What then? To desire Impossibilities is base and foolish: it is the Behaviour of a *(c)* Stranger [to the World]; of one who fights against God, the only way he can, by his Principles.

But my Mother grieves, when she doth not see me.

And why hath not she learnt these Doctrines? I do not say, that Care ought not to be taken that she may not lament; but that we are not to wish absolutely, what is not in our own Power. Now, the Grief of another is not in our Power; but my own Grief is. I will therefore absolutely suppress my own, for that is in my Power; and I will endeavour to suppress another's Grief, as far as I am able: but I will not endeavour it absolutely, otherwise I shall fight against God; I shall resist *Jupiter*, and oppose him, in the Administration of the Universe. And not only my *(d)* Children's Children will bear the Punishment of this Disobedience, and Fighting against God, but I myself too; starting, and full of Perturbation, both in the Day-time, and in my Dreams by Night; trembling at every Message, and having my (*e*) Enjoyment dependent on the

(c) The *Greek* should be pointed, ξενου, θεομαχουντος.

(d) An Allusion to *Homer*.

(*e*) The Translation here follows a Conjecture of *Wolfius*; who reads, for ευπειθειαν, ευπαθειαν. The same Word occurs in B. IV. c. 3. p. 582. of Mr. *Upton*'s Edition; and is there translated in the same manner.

the Intelligence of others. "Somebody is come "from *Rome.*" "No Harm, I hope." Why, what Harm can happen to you, where you are not? ——"From *Greece.*" "No Harm, I hope." Why, at this Rate, every Place may be the Cause of Misfortune to you. Is it not enough for you to be unfortunate where you are, but it must be beyond Sea too, and by Letters? Such is the Security of your Condition!

But what if my Friends there should be dead?

What indeed, but that those are dead, who were born to die. Do you at once wish to live to be old, and yet not to see the Death of any one you love? Do not you know, that, in a long Course of Time, many and various Events must necessarily happen? That a Fever must get the better of one; a Highwayman, of another; a Tyrant, of a third? For such is the World we live in; such they who live in it with us. Heats and Colds, improper Diet, Journies, Voyages, Winds, and various Accidents destroy some, banish others; destine one to an Embassy, another to a Camp. And now, pray, sit in a Flutter about all these Thingt; lamenting, disappointed, wretched, dependent on another; and that not one or two, but ten thousand times ten thousand.

§. 2. Is this what you have heard from the Philosophers? This what you have learnt? Do not you know (*f*) what sort of a Thing a Warfare is? One must keep Guard; another go out for a Spy; another, to Battle too. It is neither possible, that all should be in the same Place, nor indeed better: but you, neglecting to perform the Orders of your General, complain, whenever any thing a little hard is commanded; and do not consider what you make the Army become, as far as lies in your Power.

For,

(*f*) The Translation here follows Mr. *Upton*'s Conjecture, in his *Addenda*.

For, if all ſhould imitate you, nobody will dig a Trench, or throw up a Rampart, or watch, or expoſe himſelf to Danger; but every one will appear uſeleſs to the Expedition. Again: if you were a Sailor in a Voyage, fix upon one Place, and there remain. If it ſhould be neceſſary to climb the Maſt, refuſe to do it; if to run to the Head of the Ship, refuſe to do it. And what Captain will bear you? Would not he throw you over board, as a uſeleſs Piece of Goods, and mere Luggage, and a bad Example to the other Sailors? Thus alſo, in the preſent Caſe: every one's Life is a *(g)* Warfare, and that long and various. You muſt obſerve the Duty of a Soldier, and perform every thing, at the Nod of your General; and even, if poſſible, divine what he would have done. For there is no Compariſon between the above-mentioned General and This, either in Power, or Excellence of Character. You are placed in an extenſive Command, and not in a mean Poſt; but you are a Senator *(h)*: Do not you know, that ſuch a one muſt ſpend but little Time on his Affairs at home; but be much abroad, either commanding or obeying; attending on the Duties either of a Magiſtrate, a Soldier, or a Judge. And now pray, would you be fixed and rooted to the ſame Spot, like a Plant?

Why: it is pleaſant.

Who denies it? And ſo is a Ragout pleaſant; and a fine Woman is pleaſant. Is not this juſt what They ſay who make Pleaſure their End? Do not you perceive whoſe Language you have ſpoken?

(g) This Figure is frequently uſed both by ſacred and profane Authors. See *Job* vii. 1. *Eph.* vi. 12. 1 *Pet.* ii. 11, &c. *Vivere militare eſt. Life is a State of War.* SEN. Epiſt. 96, &c.

(h) Inſtead of Αλλ, αει Βȣλευτης, the true Reading, perhaps, is, Αλλα ει Βȣλευτης; and it is tranſlated accordingly.

That of *Epicureans* and *Catamites*. And while you follow their Practices, and hold their Principles, do you talk to us of the Doctrines of *Zeno* and *Socrates*? Why do not you throw away, to as great a Distance as possible, those Ornaments which belong to others, and which you have nothing to do with? What else do the *Epicureans* desire, than to sleep without Hindrance, and rise (*i*) without Compulsion; and, when they are got up, to yawn at their leisure, and wash their Face; then write and read what they please; then prate about some Trifle or other, and be applauded by their Friends, whatever they say: then go out for a Walk; and, after they have taken a Turn, bathe, and then eat; and then to Bed: in what manner they spent their Time there, why should one say? For it is easily guessed. Come: now do *you* also tell me, what Course of Life *you* desire to lead, who are a Zealot for Truth, and *Diogenes*, and *Socrates*? What would you do at *Athens*? These very same Things? Why then do you call yourself a Stoic? They who falsely pretend to the *Roman* Citizenship, are punished severely: and must those be dismissed with Impunity, who falsely claim so great a Thing, and so venerable a Title, as you do? Or is this impossible; and is there not a divine, and powerful, and inevitable Law, which exacts the greatest Punishments from those, who are guilty of the greatest Offences? For what says this Law? *Let him who claims what doth not belong to him, be arrogant, be vain-glorious, be base, be a Slave: let him grieve, let him envy, let him pity; and, in a word, let him be unhappy, let him lament.*

§. 3. (*k*) What then! would you have me pay my Court to such a one? Would you have me frequent his Door?

If

(*i*) The Conjecture of *Wolfius* (ἀναστῆναι) is a good one; and the Translation hath followed it.

(*k*) What follows hath no Connexion with what immediately preceded; but belongs to the general Subject of the Chapter.

If Reaſon requires it, for your Country, for your Relations, for Mankind, why ſhould you not go? You are not aſhamed to go to the Door of a Shoemaker, when you want Shoes; nor of a Gardener, when you want Lettuce. Why then of the Rich, when you have ſome ſimilar Want?

Ay: but I am not ſtruck with Awe of a Shoemaker.

Nor of a rich Man neither.

I need not flatter a Gardener.

Nor a rich Man neither.

How then ſhall I get what I want?

Why, do I bid you go, in Expectation of *getting* it? No: only that you may do what becomes yourſelf.

Why then, after all, ſhould I go?

That you may have gone; that you may have diſcharged the Duties of a Citizen, of a Brother, of a Friend. And, after all, remember, that you are going to a Shoemaker, to a Gardener, who hath not the Power of any thing great or reſpectable, though he ſhould ſell it ever ſo dear. You are going to buy Lettuces. They are ſold for a Penny, not for a Talent. So here too, the Matter is worth going to his Door about. Well: I will go. It is worth talking with him about *(l)*. Well: I will talk with him.

Ay: but one muſt kiſs his Hand too, and cajole him with Praiſe.

Away with you. That is worth a Talent. It is not expedient for myſelf, nor my Country, nor my fellow Citizens, nor my Friends, to deſtroy the good

(*l*) The Change of the Perſons in theſe Diſcourſes is often ſo ſudden, that it is difficult to diſcover the Speaker; and one can judge only from the general Senſe. The Tranſlator hath endeavoured to give this Paſſage the Turn which ſeems moſt agreeable to the Context, without adhering very literally to the ſeveral Words in the *Greek*. *Epictetus*, in this Paragraph, perſonates the Scholar, whom he is exhorting to viſit a great Man.

good Citizen, and the Friend [in my own Character.]

But one ſhall appear not to have ſet heartily about the Buſineſs, if one fails.

What; have you forgot again, why you went? Do not you know, that a wiſe and good Man doth nothing for Appearance; but for the ſake of having acted well?

What Advantage then is it to him, to have acted well?

What Advantage is it to one, who writes the Name of *Dion* as he ought? The having writ it.

Is there no Reward then?

Why: do you ſeek any greater Reward, for a good Man, than the doing what is fair and juſt? And yet, at *Olympia*, you deſire nothing elſe; but think it enough, to be crowned Victor. Doth it appear to you ſo ſmall and worthleſs a Thing, to be fair, good and happy? Beſides: being introduced by God into this great City, [the World,] and bound to diſcharge, at this time, the Duties of a Man, do you ſtill want Nurſes and a Mamma; and are you (*m*) moved and effeminated by the Tears of poor fooliſh Women? Are you thus determined never to ceaſe being an Infant? Do not you know, that he who acts like a Child, the older he is, ſo much is he the more ridiculous?

§. 4. (*n*) Did you never viſit any one at *Athens*, at his own Houſe?

Yes: whomſoever I pleaſed.

Why: now you are here, be willing to viſit this Perſon, and you will ſtill ſee whom you pleaſe; only let it be without Meanneſs, without Deſire, or Averſion, and your Affairs will go well: but their going well, or not, doth not conſiſt in going to the Houſe,

(*m*) This refers to a former Part of the Chapter.

(*n*) Here, what was ſaid before, about going to a great Man, is again reſumed.

House; and standing at the Door, or not; but lies within, in your own Principles; when you have acquired a Contempt of Things independent on Choice, and esteem none of them your own; but that what belongs to you is only to judge, to think, to exert your Pursuits, your Desires, and Aversions, right. What further Room is there, after this, for Flattery, for Meanness? Why do you still long for the Quiet you enjoyed there (o); for Places familiar to you? Stay a little, and these will become familiar to you, in their Turn; and then, if you are so mean-spirited, weep and lament again at leaving these.

How then am I to preserve an affectionate Temper?

As becomes a noble-spirited and happy Person. For Reason will never tell you to be dejected, and broken-hearted; or to depend on another; or to reproach either God, or Man. Be affectionate in such a manner as to observe all this. But if, from *Affection*, as you call it, you are to be a Slave, and a Wretch, it is not worth your while to be affectionate. And what restrains you from loving any one as a Mortal, as a Person who may be obliged to quit you? Pray did not *Socrates* love his own Children? But it was as became one, who was free, and mindful that his first Duty was, to gain the Love of the Gods. Hence he violated no Part of the Character of a good Man, either in his Defence, or in fixing a Penalty on himself (p). Nor yet

(o) At *Athens*.

(p) It was the Custom at *Athens*, in Cases where no fixed Punishment was appointed by the Law, before the Judges gave Sentence, to ask the Criminal himself, what Penalty he thought he deserved. *Socrates* refused either to comply with this Form himself, or suffer any of his Friends to do it for him; alleging, that the naming a Penalty, was a Confession of Guilt. When the Judges therefore asked him, what Penalty he thought he deserved, he answered, "The highest Honours, and Re-"wards;

yet before, when he was a Senator, or a Soldier. But *we* make use of every Pretence to be mean-spirited; some, on Account of a Child; some, of a Mother; and some, of a Brother. But it is not fit to be unhappy, on the Account of any one; but happy, on the Account of All; and chiefly of God, who hath constituted us for this Purpose. What! did *Diogenes* love nobody; who was so gentle, and benevolent, as chearfully to undergo so many Pains and Miseries of Body, for the common Good of Mankind? Yes: he did love them: but how? As became a Minister of *Jove*; at once taking care of Men, and obedient to God. Hence the whole Earth, not any particular Place, was his Country. And, when he was taken Captive, he did not long for *Athens*, and his Friends and Acquaintance there; but made himself acquainted with the Pirates, and endeavoured to reform them: and, when he was at last sold, he lived at *Corinth*, just as before at *Athens*: and, if he had gone to the *Perrhæbeans* (q), he would have been exactly the same. Thus is Freedom acquired. Hence he used to say, "Ever "since *Antisthenes* made me free (r), I have ceased "to be a Slave." How did *he* make him free? Hear what he says. "He taught me what was "my own, and what not. An Estate is not my "own. Kindred, Domestics, Friends, Reputati-"on, familiar Places, Manner of Life, all belong "to another." "What is your own then?" "The Use of the Appearances of Things. He "showed me, that I have *this*, not subject to Re-"straint,

"wards; and to be maintained in the *Prytaneum*, at the pub-"lic Expence." An Answer which so extremely irritated his Judges, that they immediately condemned him to Death. PLATO. CICERO.

(q) A People towards the Extremity of *Greece*.

(r) *Diogenes* was the Disciple of *Antisthenes*. Compare what *Diogenes* says of *Antisthenes* making him free, with *John* viii. 32—36.

" straint, or Compulsion: no one can hinder or " force me to use them, any otherwise than I please. " Who then, after this, hath any Power over me? " *Philip*, or *Alexander*, or *Perdiccas*, or the *Persian* " King? Whence should they have it? For he " that is to be subdued by Man, must, long before, " be subdued by Things. He therefore, of whom " neither Pleasure, nor Pain, nor Fame, nor " Riches, can get the better; and who is able, " whenever he thinks fit, to throw away his whole " Body, with Contempt, and depart, whose Slave " can he ever be? To whom is he subject?" But if *Diogenes* had taken Pleasure in living at *Athens*, and had been subdued by that Manner of Life, his Affairs would have been at every one's Disposal; and whoever was stronger, would have had the Power of grieving him. How would he have flattered the Pirates, think you, to make them sell him to some *Athenian*, that he might see again the fine *Piræum*, the long Walls, and the Citadel? How would you see them, you Wretch? As a dispirited Slave. And what Good would that do you?—" No: but free."——Show in what manner, free. See, somebody lays hold on you; whoever takes you away from your usual Manner of Life, and says, " You are my Slave: for it is in my " Power to restrain you from living as you like. It " is in my Power to (*s*) afflict and humble you. " Whenever I please, you may be chearful again; " and set out, elated, for *Athens*." What do you say to him who thus enslaves you? What Method will you find of getting free? Or dare you not so much as look up at him; but, without making many Words, supplicate to be dismissed? You ought to go to Prison, Man, with Alacrity, with Speed, and to precede your Conductors. Instead of

(*s*) Instead of ἀνεῖναι, the Sense seems to require ἀνιᾶν; and it is so translated.

of this, do you regret living at *Rome*, and long for *Greece?* And, when you must die, will you then too come crying to us, that you shall no more see *Athens*, nor walk in the *Lycæum?* Have you travelled for *this?* Is it for *this*, that you have been seeking for somebody to do you Good? What Good? That you may the more easily solve Syllogisms, and manage hypothetical Arguments? And is it for this Reason, you left your Brother, your Country, your Friends, your Family, that you might carry back such Improvements as these? So that you did not travel for Constancy, nor for Tranquillity; nor that, secured from Harm, you might complain of no one, accuse no one: that no one might injure you; and that thus you might preserve your relative Duties, without Impediment. You have made a fine Traffic of it, to carry home hypothetical Arguments, and convertible Propositions! If you please too, sit in the Market, and cry them for Sale, as Mountebanks do their Medicines. Why will you not rather deny, that you know even what you have learned; for fear of bringing a Scandal upon Theorems as useless? What Harm hath Philosophy done you? In what hath *Chrysippus* injured you, that you should give a Proof, by your Actions, that Philosophy is of no Value? Had you not Evils enough at home? How many Causes for Grief and Lamentation had you there, even if you had not travelled? But you have added more; and, if you ever get any new Acquaintance and Friends, you will find fresh Causes for groaning; and, in like manner, if you attach yourself to any other Country. To what Purpose therefore do you live? To heap Sorrow upon Sorrow, to make you wretched? And then you tell me this is *Affection.* What Affection, Man? If it be good, it is not the Cause of any Ill: if ill, I will have nothing to do with it. I was born for my own Good; not Ill.

§. 5.

§. 5. What then is the proper Exercise in this Case?

First, the highest, and principal, and obvious, as it were at your Door, is, that when you attach yourself to any thing, it may not be as to what cannot be taken away.

But as to what?

As to something of the same kind with an earthen Pot, or a glass Cup; that, when it happens to be broken, you may remember not to be troubled (*t*). So here too: when you kiss your Child, or your Brother, or your Friend, never intirely give way to the Appearance, nor suffer the Pleasure to diffuse itself as far as it will; but curb it, restrain it, like those who stand behind triumphant Victors, and remind them, that they are men. Do you likewise remind yourself, that you love what is mortal; that you love what is not your own. It is allowed you for the present, not irrevocably, nor for ever; but as a Fig, or a Bunch of Grapes, in the appointed Season. If you long for these in Winter, you are a Fool. So, if you long for your Son, or your Friend, when he is not allowed you, know, you wish for Figs in Winter. For as Winter is to a Fig, so is every Acccident in the Universe, to those Things which are taken away by it. In the next place, represent to yourself Appearances contrary to (*u*) whatever Objects give you Pleasure. What Harm is there, while you are kissing your Child, to say softly, "To-"morrow you will die:" and so to your Friend, "To-morrow either you or I shall go away, and we "shall see each other no more."

But these Sayings are ominous.

And so are some Incantations: but, because they are useful, I do not mind it; only let them be useful. But do you call any thing *ominous*, except what is the Signification of some Ill? Cowardice is *ominous*; Mean-spiritedness is *ominous*; Lamentation, Grief,

(*t*) See *Enchiridion*, c. iii.

(*u*) The Translation here follows Mr. *Upton*'s Conjecture. Ει αυτοις οιςισι, &c.

Grief, Want of Shame. These are Words of bad Omen; and yet we ought not to be scrupulous of using them, as a Guard against the Things they mean. But do you tell me, that a Word is *ominous* which is significant of any thing natural? Say too, that it is *ominous*, for Ears of Corn to be reaped; for this signifies the Destruction of the Corn; but not of the World. Say too, that the Fall of the Leaf is *ominous*; and that a candied Mass should be produced from Figs; and Raisins, from Grapes. For all these are changes from a former, into another State; not a Destruction, but a certain appointed Oeconomy and Administration. Such is Absence, a small Change: such is Death, a greater Change: not from what now is nothing, but to what now is not.

(*w*) What then, shall I be no more?

You will be: but [you will be] some thing else, of which, at present, the World hath no Need: for even *you* were not produced when you pleased, but when the World had Need [of you.] Hence a wise and good Man, mindful who he is, and whence he came, and by whom he was produced, is attentive only how he may fill his Post regularly, and dutifully to God. "Is it thy Pleasure I should "any longer continue in being? I will continue, "free, spirited, agreeably to thy Pleasure: for "Thou hast made me incapable of Restraint, in "what is my own. But hast Thou no farther Use "for me? Fare thou well! I have staid thus long "for thy Sake alone, and no other; and now I "depart in Obedience to Thee."——"How do "you depart?"——"Again: agreeably to thy "Pleasure; as free, as thy Servant, as one sensible "of thy Commands, and thy Prohibitions. But, "while

(*w*) The Translation follows Mr. *Upton*'s Transposition of οὐκ. The Meaning of the Passage is, that, though the personal Existence is dissolved, and destroyed by Death, the Substance, out of which it was produced, remains, under some other Form; which was the Stoic Doctrine.

"while I am employed in thy Service, *what* wouldst "Thou have me be? A Prince, or a private "Man; a Senator, or a Plebeian; a Soldier, or a "General; a Preceptor, or the Master of a Fami-"ly? Whatever Post or Rank Thou shalt assign "me, like *Socrates*, I will die a thousand times ra-"ther than desert it. *Where* wouldst thou have "me be? At *Rome*, or at *Athens*; at *Thebes*, or "at *Gyaros*? Only remember me there. If Thou "shalt send me, where Men cannot live conform-"ably to Nature, I do not depart from thence (*x*), "in Disobedience to thy Will; but as receiving "my Signal of Retreat from Thee. I do not de-"sert Thee: Heaven forbid! but I perceive Thou "hast no Use for me. If a Life conformable to "Nature be granted, I will seek no other Place, "but that in which I am; nor any other Compa-"ny, but those with whom I am."

§. 6. Let these Things be ready at hand, Night and Day. These Things write; these Things read; of these Things talk both to yourself and others. [Ask them,] "Have you any Assistance to give "me for this Purpose?" And again, go and ask another, and another. Then, if any of those Things should happen that are said to be against our Will, immediately this will be a Relief to you; in the first place, that it was not unexpected. For it is a great Matter, upon all Occasions, to [be able to] say (*y*), "I knew that I begot one born to die." Thus do you say too; "I knew that I was liable to die, to "remove, to be exiled, to be imprisoned." If afterwards you turn to yourself, and seek from what Quarter the Event proceeds, you will presently recollect: "It is from Things independent on Choice; "not from what is my own. What then is it to "me?" Then, farther (which is the chief);

(*x*) Ἀπειθῶν. WOLFIUS.

(*y*) This was said by *Xenophon*, when News was brought him, that his Son *Gryllus* was killed in a Battle.

U Who

Who ſent it? The Commander, the General, the City, the Law of the City? Give it me then; for I muſt always obey the Law in all Things. Farther yet: when any Appearance moleſts you (for [to prevent] *that*, is not in your Power,) ſtrive againſt it; and, by Reaſon, conquer it. Do not ſuffer it to gain Strength, nor to lead you on to Conſequences; and repreſent what, and how, it pleaſes. If you are at *Gyaros*, do not repreſent to yourſelf the Manner of Living at *Rome*; how many Pleaſures you uſed to find there, and how many would attend your Return; but be intent on this Point; How he, who lives at *Gyaros*, may live with Spirit and Comfort, at *Gyaros*. And, if you are at *Rome*, do not repreſent to yourſelf the Manner of Living at *Athens*: but conſider only, how you ought to live where you are. Laſtly: to all other Pleaſures oppoſe that of being conſcious, that you are obeying God; and performing, not in Word, but in Deed, the Duty of a wiſe and good Man. How great a Thing is it to be able to ſay to yourſelf, "What others are now ſolemnly arguing in the Schools, and ſeem to carry beyond "Probability, this I am [actually] performing. "They are ſitting and expatiating upon *my* Virtues, and diſputing about *me*, and celebrating "*me*. *Jupiter* hath been pleaſed to let me receive "a Demonſtration of this from myſelf; and indeed that *He* may know, whether he hath a Soldier, a Citizen, ſuch as he ſhould be, and to produce me as a Witneſs to other Men, concerning Things independent on Choice. See that "your Fears were vain, your Appetites vain. Seek "not Good from without: ſeek it in yourſelves, "or you will never find it. For this Reaſon, he "now brings me hither, now ſends me thither; "ſhows me to Mankind, poor, without Authority, "ſick; ſends me to *Gyaros*; leads me to Priſon: "not that he hates me: Heaven forbid! For who "hates the beſt of his Servants? Nor that he "neglects me: for he doth not neglect any one of "the ſmalleſt (z) Things: but to exerciſe me, and "make uſe of me as a Witneſs to others. Ap-"pointed to ſuch a Service, do I ſtill care where I "am, or with whom, or what is ſaid of me, in-"ſtead of being wholly attentive to God, and to "his Orders and Commands?"

§. 7. Having theſe Things always at hand, and practiſing them by yourſelf, and making them ready for Uſe, you will never want any one to comfort and ſtrengthen you. For Shame doth not conſiſt in not having any thing to eat, but in not having Reaſon enough to exempt you from Fear and Sorrow. But, if you once acquire that Exemption, will a Tyrant, or his Guards, or Courtiers, be any thing to you? Will any Deſtination of Offices, or they who offer Sacrifices in the Capitol, on being admitted into the Emperor's Train, give *you* Uneaſineſs, who have received ſo great a Command from *Jupiter*? Only, do not make a Parade of it, nor grow inſolent upon it. But ſhow it by your Actions: and, though no one ſhould perceive it, be content, that you are well, and happy.

CHAPTER XXV.

Concerning Thoſe who deſiſt from their Purpoſe.

§. 1. CONSIDER which of the Things, which you at firſt propoſed to yourſelf, you have retained, which not, and how; which give you Pleaſure, which Pain, in the Reflection; and, if poſſible, recover yourſelf, where you have failed. For the Champions, in this greateſt of Combats, muſt not grow weary; but are even content-

(z) Compare this with the Deſcription of the univerſal Care of Providence, *Matth.* x. 29, 30. and the Occaſion on which it was introduced.

edly to bear Whipping. For this is no Combat of Wrestling or Boxing; where both he who succeeds, and he who doth not succeed, may possibly be of very great Worth, or of little; indeed may be very fortunate, or very miserable: but the Combat is for good Fortune and Happiness itself. What is the Case then? *Here*, even if we have renounced the Contest, no one restrains us from renewing it; nor need we wait for another Four Years, for the Return of another *Olympiad*; but recollecting, and recovering yourself, and returning with the same Zeal, you may renew it immediately: and even if you should again yield, you may again begin: and, if you once get the Victory, you become like one who hath never yielded. Only do not begin, from a Habit of this, to do it with Pleasure, and then, like Quails that have fled the Pit (*a*), go about as if you were a brave Champion, though you have been conquered, all the Games round (*b*).——"The "Appearance of a pretty Girl conquers me." What then? "Have not I been conquered be-"fore? I have a mind to rail at somebody. Well: "have not I railed before?"——You talk to us just as if you had come off unhurt. Like one that should say to his Physician, who had forbidden him to bathe, "Why, did not I bathe before?" Suppose the Physician should answer him, "Well: "and what was the Consequence of your Bathing? "Were not you feverish? Had not you the "Head-ach?" So, when you before railed at somebody, did not you act like an ill-natured Person; like

(*a*) It was a Sport among the *Greeks*, to put Quails in a circular Space, like our Cockpits, and use various Ways of trying their Courage. If the Quail ran away out of the Pit, its Master lost.

(*b*) An Allusion to the *Pythian*, *Isthmian*, *Nemean*, and *Olympic* Games. The Persons who were victorious in all these, were distinguished by a particular Name; signifying, that they had been Conquerors through the whole Circle of the Games. UPTON.

like an impertinent one? Have not you fed this Habit of yours, by Actions familiar to it? When you were conquered by a pretty Girl, did you come off with Impunity? Why then do you talk of what you have done *before*? You ought to remember it, I think, as Slaves do Whipping, so as to refrain from the same Faults.——"But the "Case is unlike; for there it is Pain that causes "the Remembrance: but what is the Pain, what "the Punishment, of my committing Faults? For "when was I ever habituated [by any Suffering] "to avoiding acting ill?"——Therefore the Pains of Experience, whether we will, or not, have their Use.

CHAPTER XXVI.

Concerning those who are in Dread of Want.

§. 1. (a) ARE not you ashamed to be more fearful and mean-spirited than fugitive Slaves? To what Estates, to what Servants, do *they* trust, when they run away, and leave their Masters? Do not they, after carrying off a little with them for the First Days, travel over Land and Sea, contriving first one, then another Method of getting Food? And what Fugitive ever died with Hunger? But *you* tremble, and lie awake by Night, for fear you should want Necessaries. Wretch! are you so blind? Do not you see the Way where the Want of Necessaries leads?

Why, where doth it lead?

Where a Fever, where even a Stone falling on you, leads——to Death. Have not you yourself then, often said this to your Companions? Have

(a) Compare this Chapter with the beautiful and affecting Discourses of our Saviour on the same Subject, *Matth.* vi. 25——34. *Luke* xii. 22——30.

Have not you read, have not you written, many Things of this kind? And how often have you arrogantly boasted, that you are easy with regard to Death?

Ay: but my Family too will starve with Hunger.

What then? Doth their Hunger lead any other Way than yours? Is there not the same Descent? The same State below? Will you not then, in every Want and Necessity, look with Confidence there, where even the most Rich and Powerful, and Kings and Tyrants themselves must descend? You indeed, hungry perhaps; and they, burst with Indigestion and Drunkenness? What Beggar have you almost ever seen, who did not live to Old-age, nay, to extreme Old-age? Chilled with Cold Day and Night, lying on the Ground, and eating only what is barely necessary, they come nearly to an Impossibility of Dying.—Cannot you write? Cannot you keep a School? Cannot you be a Watchman at somebody's Door?

But it is shameful to come to this Necessity.

First therefore, learn what Things are shameful? and then tell us, you are a Philosopher: but at present, do not bear, that even any one else should call you so. Is that shameful to *you*, which is not your own Act? Of which you are not the Cause? Which hath happened to you by Accident, like a Fever, or the Head-ach? If your Parents were poor, or left others their Heirs, or, though they are living, do not assist you, are these Things shameful for *you?* Is this what you have learned from the Philosophers? Have you never heard, that what is shameful is blameable; and what is blameable deserves to be blamed? Whom do you blame for an Action not his own, which he hath not done himself? Did *you* then make your Father such a one [as he is]? Or is it in *your* Power to mend him? Is that permitted you? What then,

must

must you desire what is not permitted; and, when you fail of it, be *ashamed?* Are you thus habituated, even when you are studying Philosophy, to depend upon others, and to hope nothing from yourself? Sigh then, and groan, and eat in Fear that you shall have no Victuals To-morrow. Tremble, lest your Servants should rob you, or run away from you, or die. Thus live on, without ceasing, whoever you are, who have applied to Philosophy in Name only; and, as much as in you lies, have disgraced its Theorems, by showing, that they are unprofitable and useless to those who take up the Profession of them. You have never made Constancy, Tranquillity, and Apathy, the Object of your Desires; have attended on no one upon this Account; but on many, for the Sake of Syllogisms; nor have ever, by yourself, examined any one of these Appearances. "Can I bear this, or can I "not bear it? What remains for me to do?" But, as if all your Affairs went safe and well, you have dwelt upon the Third Class (*b*), that of Security from Failure; that you may never fail——Of what?——Fear, Mean-spiritedness, Admiration of Riches, an unaccomplished Desire, and unsuccessful Aversion. These are the Things which you have been labouring to secure. Ought you not first to have acquired something by the Use of Reason, and then to have provided Security for *that?* Whom did you ever see building a Round of Battlements, without placing them upon a Wall? And what Porter is ever set where there is no Door? But you *study*. Can you show me what you study?

Not to be shaken by Sophistry.

Shaken from what? Show me first, what you have in your Custody; what you measure, or what you weigh; and then accordingly show me the Balance, or the Bushel. What signifies it to go on, ever so long, measuring Dust? Ought you

(*b*) See Introduction, §. 6.

not to ſhow, what makes Men happy, what makes their Affairs proceed as they wiſh? How we may blame no one, accuſe no one; how acquieſce in the Adminiſtration of the Univerſe? Show me theſe Things. "See, I do ſhow them," ſay you; "I will ſolve Syllogiſms to you."——This is the Meaſure, Wretch, and not the Thing meaſured. Hence you now pay the Penalty due for neglecting Philoſophy. You tremble, you lie awake, you adviſe with every body, and if what you are adviſed to doth not pleaſe every body, you think that you have been ill-adviſed. Then you dread Hunger, as you fancy: but it is not Hunger that you dread; but you are afraid, that you ſhall not have a Cook; that you ſhall not have another Perſon for a Butler; another, to pull off your Shoes; a fourth, to dreſs you; others, to rub you; others, to follow you: that, when you have undreſſed yourſelf in the Bathing-room, and ſtretched yourſelf out like thoſe who are crucified, you may be rubbed here and there; and the Perſon who preſides over theſe Operations may ſtand by, and ſay, "Come this "Way; give your Side; take hold on his Head; "turn your Shoulder:" and that, when you are returned home from the Bath, you may bawl out, "Doth nobody bring any thing to eat?" And then, "Take away; wipe the Table." This is your Dread, that you ſhall not be able to lead the Life of a ſick Man. But learn the Life of thoſe in Health: how Slaves live; how, Labourers; how, thoſe who are genuine Philoſophers; how *Socrates* lived, even with a wife and Children; how, *Diogenes*; how, *Cleanthes* (*c*), at once ſtudying and drawing Water. If theſe are the Things you would have,

(*c*) *Cleanthes* was a Stoic Philoſopher, the Diſciple and Succeſſor of *Zeno.* He uſed to draw Water for his Livelihood all Night, and ſtudy all Day. He was ſo poor, that for Want of proper Materials, he uſed write down what he had heard from his Maſter *Zeno,* on Tiles, and Pieces of Bone. The Phyſicians ordered

have, you will have them every-where, and with a fearleſs Confidence.

In what?

In the only Thing that can be confided in; what is ſure, incapable of being reſtrained, or taken away; your own Choice.

§. 2. But why have you contrived to make yourſelf ſo uſeleſs, and good for nothing, that nobody will receive you into their Houſe; nobody take Care of you: but though, if any ſound uſeful Veſſel was thrown out of Doors, whoever finds it, will take it up, and eſteem it as a Gain; yet nobody will take up *you*; but every body eſteem you a Loſs. What, cannot you ſo much as perform the Office of a Dog, or a Cock? Why then do you wiſh to live any longer, if you are ſo worthleſs? Doth any good Man fear, that Food ſhould fail him? It doth not fail the Blind; it doth not fail the Lame. Shall it fail a good Man? A Paymaſter is not wanting to a Soldier, or to a Labourer, or to a Shoemaker; and ſhall one be wanting to a good Man? Is God ſo negligent of his own Inſtitutions; of his Servants; of his Witneſſes, whom alone he makes uſe of as Examples to the Uninſtructed, both that He *is*, and that he adminiſters the Univerſe rightly; and doth not neglect human Affairs; and that no Evil happens to a good Man, either living or dead? What then is the Caſe, when he doth not beſtow Food? What elſe, than that, like a good General, he hath made me a Signal of Retreat? I obey, I follow; ſpeaking well of my Leader, praiſing his Works. For I came when it ſeemed good to him; and again, when it ſeems good to him, I depart: and in Life it was my Buſineſs to praiſe God, both by

ordered him, for a Swelling in his Gums, to abſtain two Days from Food; with which he complied. When he was recovered, they gave him Leave to return to his uſual Diet; which he refuſed; and, ſaying he was now far advanced on his Journey, ſtarved himſelf to Death. DIOG. LAERT.

by myself, to each particular Person, and to the World. Doth he not grant me many Things? Doth he not grant me Affluence? It is not his Pleasure, that I should live luxuriously: for he did not grant that even to *Hercules*, his own Son; but another *(d)* reigned over *Argos* and *Mycenæ*; while *he* lived subject to Command, laboured, and was exercised. And *Eurystheus* was just what he was; neither King of *Argos*, nor *Mycenæ*; not being indeed King of himself. But *Hercules* was Ruler and Governor of the whole Earth and Seas; the Expeller of Lawlessness and Injustice; the Introducer of Justice and Sanctity. And this he effected naked and alone. Again: when *Ulysses* was shipwrecked, and cast away, did his helpless Condition at all deject him? Did it break his Spirit? No: But how did he go to *Nausicaa*, and her Attendants, to ask those Necessaries which it seems most shameful to beg from another?

As the fierce Lion, on the Mountain bred,
Confiding in his Strength———

Confiding in what? Not in Glory, nor in Riches, nor in Dominion; but in his own Strength: that is, in his Principles, concerning what Things are in our own Power; what, not. For these alone are what render us free, render us incapable of Restraint; raise the Head of the Dejected, and make them look, with unaverted Eyes, full in the Face of the Rich, and of the Tyrants: and this was the Gift of the Philosopher *(e)*. But *you* will not set out with Confidence; but trembling, about such Trifles as Clothes and Plate. Wretch! have you thus wasted your Time till now?

But what, if I should be sick?

You will be sick as you ought.

Who

(d) *Eurystheus.*

(e) The Sense would be better, if we read τῆς φιλοσοφίας, of Philosophy.

Who will take care of me?

God: your Friends.

I ſhall lie in a hard Bed.

But like a Man.

I ſhall not have a convenient Room.

You will be ſick in an inconvenient one then.

Who will provide Victuals for me?

They who provide for others too: you will be ſick like *Manes* (*f*).

But, beſides, what will be the Concluſion of my Sickneſs? Any other than Death?

Why, do not you know then, that the Origin of all human Evils, and of Mean-ſpiritedneſs, and Cowardice, is not *Death*; but rather the *Fear* of Death? Fortify yourſelf therefore againſt this. Hither let all your Diſcourſes, Readings, Exerciſes, tend. And then you will know, that thus alone are Men made free.

(*f*) The Name of a Slave, particularly of a Slave who once belonged to *Diogenes*: and perhaps this Expreſſion alludes to ſome Story about him, which is now unknown.

END *of the* THIRD BOOK.

THE DISCOURSES OF *EPICTETUS.*

BOOK IV.

CHAPTER I.

Of Freedom.

§. 1. HE is free, who lives as he likes; who is not subject either to Compulsion, to Restraint, or to Violence: whose Pursuits are unhindered, his Desires successful, his Aversions unincurred. Who then would wish to lead a wrong Course of Life?——" No one."——Who would live deceived, prone to mistake, unjust, dissolute, discontented, dejected?——" No one."——No wicked Man then lives as he likes; therefore neither is he free. And who would live in Sorrow,

Fear,

Fear, Envy, Pity; with disappointed Desires, and incurred Aversions?——"No one."——Do we then find any of the Wicked exempt from Sorrow, Fear, disappointed Desires, incurred Aversions?——"Not one."——Consequently then, not free (*a*).

§. 2. If a Person who hath been twice Consul should hear this, provided you add, "but *you* are "a wise Man; this is nothing to *you*;" he will forgive you. But if you tell him the Truth; that, in point of Slavery, he doth not differ from those who have been thrice sold; what must you expect, but to be beaten? "For how, says he, am I a "Slave? My Father was free, my Mother free (*b*). "Besides, I am a Senator too, and the Friend of "*Cæsar*; and have been twice Consul; and have "myself many Slaves."——In the first place, most worthy Sir, perhaps your Father too was a Slave of the same kind; and your Mother, and your Grandfather, and all your Ancestors successively. But even if they were ever so free, what is that to *you*? For what, if they were of a generous, you of a mean Spirit: they, brave; and you, a Coward: they, sober; and you, dissolute?

§. 3. And, "What, says he, is this towards be"ing a Slave?" (*c*)——Do you think it nothing towards being a Slave, to act against your Will? Compelled, and lamenting?——"Be it so. But "who can compel me, but the Master of All, "*Cæsar*?"——By your own Confession then, you have *one* Master: and let not his being, as you say, Master of All, give you any Comfort; but know, that

(*a*) *Whosoever committeth Sin, is the Servant of Sin.* John viii. 34.

(*b*) *They answered him, We be* Abraham's *Seed, and were never in Bondage to any Man: how sayest thou, Ye shall be made free?* John viii. 33.

(*c*) Mr. *Upton*'s Copy transposes many Pages of this Chapter to their right Place; which, in others, were joined to the last Chapter of the Third Book.

that you are a Slave in a great Family. Thus the *Nicopolitans* too, frequently cry out, "By the Life "of *Cæsar*, we are *free!*"

§. 4. For the present, however, if you please, we will let *Cæsar* alone. But tell me this. Have you never been in Love with any one, either of a servile or liberal Condition?—"Why, what is *that* "to the being either a Slave, or free?"——Was you never commanded any thing by your Mistress, that you did not chuse? Have you never flattered your Slave? Have you never kissed her Feet? And yet, if you were commanded to kiss *Cæsar*'s Feet, you would think it an Outrage, and an Excess of Tyranny. Have you never gone out by Night, where you did not chuse? Have you never spent more than you chose? Have not you sometimes uttered your Words with Sighs and Groans? Born to be reviled, and shut out of Doors? But, if you are ashamed to confess your own Follies, see what *Thrasonides* (d) says, and doth; who, after having fought more Battles perhaps than you, went out by Night, when *Geta* (e) would not dare to go: Nay, had he been compelled to it by him, would have gone roaring, and lamenting his bitter Servitude. And what doth [this Master of his] say afterwards, "A sorry "Girl hath enslaved *me*, whom no Enemy ever en-"slaved."——(Wretch! to be the Slave of a Girl, and a sorry Girl too! Why then do you still call yourself *free?* Why do you boast your military Expeditions?)——Then he calls for a Sword, and is angry with the Person who, out of Kindness, denies it; and sends Presents to her who hates him; and begs, and weeps, and then again is elated on every little Success. But how is he elated even then? Is it so, as neither passionately to desire or fear.

§. 5.

(d) A Character in one of the Comedies of *Menander*, called *The Hated Lover*.

(e) The Name of a Slave.

§. 5. Consider, in Animals, what is our Idea of Freedom. Some keep tame Lions, and feed, and even carry them about with them: and who will say, that any such Lion is free? Nay, doth he not live the more slavishly, the more he lives at ease? And who, that had Sense and Reason, would wish to be one of those Lions? Again: How much do Birds, which are taken and kept in a Cage, suffer, by trying to fly away? Nay, some of them starve with Hunger, rather than undergo such a Life: then, as many of them as are saved, it is scarcely, and with Difficulty, and in a pining Condition; and the Moment they find any Hole, out they hop. Such a Desire have they of natural Freedom, and to be at their own Disposal, and unrestrained.——"And what Harm *(f)* doth this Confinement do "you?"——"What say you? I was born to fly "where I please, to live in the open Air, to sing "when I please. You deprive me of all this, and "say, What *Harm* doth it do you?"

§. 6. Hence we will allow those only to be free, who do not endure Captivity; but, as soon as they are taken, die, and escape. Thus *Diogenes* somewhere says, That the only way to Freedom is to die with Ease. And he writes to the *Persian* King; "You can no more enslave the *Athenians*, than you "can Fish."——"How? What, shall not I take "them?"—"If you do take them, says he, they "will leave you, and be gone, like Fish. For "take a Fish, and it dies. And, if the *Athenians* "too die, as soon as you have taken them, of what "Use are your warlike Preparations?"—This is the Voice of a free Man, who had examined the Matter in earnest; and, as it might be expected, found it out. But, if you seek it where it is not, what Wonder, if you never find it?

§. 7. A Slave wishes to be immediately set free. Think you it is because he is desirous to pay his Fine

(f) Wolfius, very rightly, for καλὸν reads κακὸν.

Fine to the Officer (*g*)? No: but becauſe he fancies, that, for want of acquiring his Freedom, he hath hitherto lived under Reſtraint, and unproſperouſly. "If I am once ſet free, ſays he, it is all "Proſperity: I care for no one; I ſpeak to All, as "their Equal, and on a Level with them. I go "where I will, I come when (*h*), and how I will." He is at laſt made free; and preſently, having nowhere to eat, he ſeeks whom he may flatter, with whom he may ſup. He then either ſubmits to the baſeſt and moſt infamous Proſtitution; and, if he can obtain Admiſſion to ſome great Man's Table, falls into a Slavery much worſe than the former: or, if the Creature, void of Senſe and right Taſte, happens to acquire an affluent Fortune, he doats upon ſome Girl, laments, and is unhappy, and wiſhes for Slavery again. "For what Harm did it do "me? Another clothed me, another ſhod me, "another fed me, another took care of me when "I was ſick. It was but in a few Things, by way "of Return, I uſed to ſerve him. But now, mi-"ſerable Wretch! what do I ſuffer, in being a "Slave to many, inſtead of one! Yet, if I can ob-"tain the Equeſtrian Rings (*i*), I ſhall live with the "utmoſt Proſperity and Happineſs." In order to obtain them, he firſt ſuffers what he deſerves; and, as ſoon as he hath obtained them, it is all the ſame again. "But then, ſays he, if I do but get a mi-"litary Command, I ſhall be delivered from all my "Troubles." He gets a military Command. He ſuffers as much as the vileſt Rogue of a Slave: and, nevertheleſs, he aſks for a ſecond Command, and a third: and when he hath put the finiſhing Hand, and is made a Senator, then he is a Slave indeed.

X When

(*g*) See p. 99. Note (*d*).

(*h*) It ſeems neceſſary, that οθεν and οπυ ſhould be οταν and οπως; and they are ſo tranſlated.

(*i*) A Gold Ring was the peculiar Ornament of the *Roman* Knights, by which they were diſtinguiſhed from the Plebeians. UPTON.

When he comes into the Aſſembly, it is then that he undergoes his fineſt and moſt ſplendid Slavery.

§. 8.———(*k*). Not to be a Fool; but to learn what *Socrates* taught; the Nature of Things: and not to adapt Pre-conceptions raſhly to particular Subjects. For the Cauſe of all human Evils is, the not being able to adapt general Pre-conceptions to particular Caſes. But different People have different Opinions. One thinks the Cauſe of his Evils to be, that he is ſick. By no means: but that he doth not adapt his Pre-conceptions right. Another, that he is poor: another, that he hath a harſh Father and Mother: another, that he is not in the good Graces of *Cæſar*. This is nothing elſe, but not underſtanding how to adapt our Pre-conceptions. For, who hath not a Pre-conception of Evil, that it is hurtful? That it is to be avoided? That it is by all means to be prudently guarded againſt? One Pre-conception doth not contradict another, except when it comes to be adapted. What then is this Evil, thus hurtful, and to be avoided? "Not to "be the Friend of *Cæſar*," ſaith one. He is gone; he fails in the adapting; he is embarraſſed; he ſeeks what is nothing to the purpoſe. For, if he gets to be *Cæſar*'s Friend, he is never the leſs diſtant from what he ſought. For what is it that every Man ſeeks? To be ſecure, to be happy, to do what he pleaſes without Reſtraint, and without Compulſion. When he becomes the Friend of *Cæſar* then, doth he ceaſe to be reſtrained? To be compelled? Is he ſecure? Is he happy? Whom ſhall he aſk? Whom can we better credit than this very Man, who hath been his Friend? Come forth and tell us, whether you ſleep more quietly now, or before you were the Friend of *Cæſar*? You preſently hear him cry, "Leave off, for Heaven's "ſake, and do not inſult me. You know not the "Miſeries I ſuffer: there is no Sleep for me; but "one

(*k*) Something is here wanting in the Original.

" one comes, and ſaith, that *Cæſar* is already awake; " another, that he is juſt going out. Then follow " Perturbations, then Cares." Well: and when did you uſe to ſup more pleaſantly; formerly, or now? Hear what he ſays about this too. When he is not invited, he is diſtracted: and if he is, he ſups like a Slave with his Maſter, ſolicitous all the while, not to ſay or do any thing fooliſh. And what think you? Is he afraid of being whipped, like a Slave? How can he hope to eſcape ſo well? No: but as becomes ſo great a Man, *Cæſar*'s Friend, of loſing his Head.—And when did you bathe more quietly; when did you perform your Exerciſes more at your leiſure; in ſhort, which Life would you rather wiſh to live, your preſent, or the former? I could ſwear, there is no one ſo ſtupid and inſenſible (*l*), as not to deplore his Miſeries, in proportion as he is more the Friend of *Cæſar*.

§. 9. Since then, neither they who are called Kings (*m*), nor the Friends of Kings, live as they like; who, after all, are free? Seek, and you will find: for you are furniſhed by Nature with Means for diſcovering the Truth. But, if you are not able by theſe alone to find the Conſequence, hear them who have ſought it. What do they ſay? Do you think Freedom a Good?—" The greateſt."—Can any one then, who attains the greateſt Good be unhappy, or unſucceſsful in his Affairs?—" No."—As many, therefore, as you ſee unhappy, lamenting, unproſperous, confidently pronounce them not free.—" I do."—Henceforth then we have done with buying and ſelling, and ſuch like ſtated Conditions of becoming Slaves. For, if you have made theſe Conceſſions properly, whether a great or a little King, a Conſular, or one twice a Conſul, be unhappy, he is not free.—" Agreed."

X 2 §. 10.

(*l*) Αναλγητος for αναλγης. Upton.

(*m*) The Stoics held the wiſe Man to be the only real King. Upton.

§. 10. Further then, anſwer me this: Do you think Freedom to be ſomething great, and noble, and valuable?——"How ſhould I not?"——Is it poſſible then, that he who acquires any thing ſo great, and valuable, and noble, ſhould be of an abject Spirit?——"It is not."——Whenever then you ſee any one ſubject to another, and flattering him, contrary to his own Opinion, confidently ſay, that He too is not free: and not only if he doth it for a Supper, but even if it be for a Government; nay, a Conſulſhip: but call thoſe indeed little Slaves, who act thus for the ſake of little Things; and the others, as they deſerve, great Slaves——"Be "this too agreed."——Well: do you think Freedom to be ſomething independent and ſelf-determined?——"How can it be otherwiſe?"——Him then, whom it is in the Power of another to reſtrain or to compell, affirm confidently, to be not free. And do not mind his Grandfathers, or Great Grandfathers; or inquire, whether he hath been bought or ſold: but, if you hear him ſay, from his Heart, and with Emotion, *my Maſter*, though twelve Lictors ſhould march before him, call him a Slave. And, if you ſhould hear him ſay, *Wretch, that I am! what do I ſuffer!* call him a Slave. In ſhort, if you ſee him wailing, complaining, unproſperous, call him a Slave in Purple.——"Suppoſe then "he doth nothing of all this?"——Do not yet ſay, he is free; but learn whether his Principles are liable to Compulſion, to Reſtraint, or Diſappointment; and, if you find this to be the Caſe, call him a Slave, keeping Holiday during the *Saturnalia* (*n*). Say, that his Maſter is abroad: he will come preſently; and you will know what he ſuffers. ——"Who will come?"——Whoever hath the Power either of beſtowing, or taking away, any of

(*n*) The Feaſt of *Saturn*, in which the Slaves had a Liberty of ſitting at Table with their Maſters; in Memory of the Equality of Conditions under his Reign.

of the Things, he wishes for.——" Have we so "many Masters then?"——We have. For, prior to all such, we have the Things themselves for our Masters; now they are many: and it is through these, that it becomes necessary that such as have the Disposal of them, should be our Masters too. For no one fears *Cæsar* himself; but Death, Banishment, Loss of Goods, Prison, Disgrace. Nor doth any one love *Cæsar*, unless he be a Person of great Worth: but we love Riches, the Tribunate, the Prætorship, the Consulship. When we love, and hate, and fear these Things, they who have the Disposal of them must necessarily be our Masters. Hence we even worship them as Gods. For we consider, that whoever hath the Disposal of the greatest Advantages, is a Deity: and then we subjoin falsely, *but such a one hath the Power of the greatest Advantages*; *therefore he is a Deity*. For, if we subjoin falsely, the Inference arising from thence must be false likewise.

§. 11. " What is it then that makes a Man free " and independent? For neither Riches, nor Con- " sulship, nor Command of Provinces, or King- " doms, make him so; but something else must " be found"—What is it that preserves any one from being hindered and restrained in Writing?— " The Science of Writing."—In Music?—" The " Science of Music."—Therefore, in Life too, the Science of Living. As you have heard it in general then, consider it likewise in Particulars. Is it possible for Him to be unrestrained, who desires any of those Things, that are in the Power of others? —" No."—Can he avoid being hindered?—" No." —Therefore neither can he be free. Consider then, whether we have nothing, or all, in our own Power alone, or whether some Things are in our own Power and some in that of others.—" What do you " mean?"——When you would have your Body perfect, is it in your own Power, or is it not?—

" It is not."——When you would be healthy?—
" Nor this."——When you would be handſome?
—" Nor this."——Live or die?——" Nor this."
——Body then is not our own; but ſubject to every thing ſtronger than itſelf.—" Agreed."—Well: is it in your own Power to have an Eſtate when you pleaſe, and as long as you pleaſe, and ſuch a one as you pleaſe?—" No."—Slaves?—" No."—Clothes?—" No."—A Houſe?—" No."—Horſes?
" Indeed none of theſe."——Well: if you would ever ſo fain have your Children live, or your Wife, or your Brother, or your Friends, is it in your own Power?—" No, nor this."——Will you ſay then, that there is *nothing* independent, which is in your own Power alone, and unalienable? See then, if you have any thing of this ſort.—" I do not know."
——But, conſider it thus: Can any one make you aſſent to a Falſhood?——" No one."——In the Topic of Aſſent then, you are unreſtrained and unhindered.——" Agreed:"——Well: and can any one compell you to exert your Purſuits, towards what you do not like?——" He can. For when
" he threatens me with Death, or Fetters, he com-
" pells me to exert them."——If then you were to deſpiſe dying, or being fettered, would you any longer regard him?—" No."—Is deſpiſing Death then an Action in our Power, or is it not?—" It
" is."—Is it therefore in your Power alſo, to exert your Purſuits towards any thing, or is it not?——
" Agreed, that it is. But in whoſe Power is my
" avoiding any thing?"—This too is in your own.
—" What then, if, when I am exerting myſelf to
" walk, any one ſhould reſtrain me?"—What Part of you can he reſtrain? Can he reſtrain your Aſſent?—" No: but my Body."—Ay, as he may a Stone.—" Be it ſo. But ſtill I walk no more."
—And who told you, that Walking was an Action of your own, that cannot be reſtrained? For I only ſaid, that your exerting yourſelf towards it could

could not be restrained. But where there is need of Body, and its Assistance, you have already heard, that nothing is in your Power.——"Be this too "agreed."——And can any one compell you to desire against your Will?——"No one."——Or to propose, or intend, or, in short, not to make use of the Appearances which present themselves to you?——"Nor this. But when I desire any thing, "he will restrain me from obtaining what I de-"sire."—If you desire any thing that is your own, and that cannot be restrained, how can He restrain you?—"By no means."—And pray who tells you, that he who desires what depends on another, cannot be restrained?——"May not I desire Health "then?"——By no means: nor any thing else that depends on another: for what is not in your own Power, either to procure, or to preserve, when you will, *that* belongs to another. Keep off not only your Hands from it, but, far prior to these, your Desires. Otherwise you have given yourself up a Slave: you have put your Neck under the Yoke, if you admire any of the Things not your own, but subject and mortal, to which soever of them you are attached.——"Is not my Hand my "own?"——It is a Part of you; but it is, by Nature, Clay; liable to Restraint, to Compulsion; a Slave to every thing stronger than itself. And why do I say your *Hand?* You ought to possess your whole *Body* as a paultry Ass, with a Pack-saddle on, as long as may be, as long as it is allowed you. But, if there should come a Press (*o*), and a Soldier should lay hold on it, let it go. Do not resist, or murmur: otherwise you will be first beat, and lose the Ass after all. And, since you are to consider the Body [itself] in this manner, think what remains to do, concerning those Things which are provided for the Sake of the Body. If *that* be an

 Ass,

(*o*) Beasts of Burthen and Carriages are pressed, for the Use of Armies, when Need requires.

Aſs, the reſt are Bridles, Pack-ſaddles, Shoes, Oats, Hay, for the Aſs. Let theſe go too. Quit them more eaſily and expeditiouſly, than the Aſs. And when you are thus prepared, and thus exerciſed, to diſtinguiſh what belongs to others from your own; what is liable to Reſtraint, from what is not; to eſteem the one your own Property, the other not; to keep your Deſire, to keep your Averſion, carefully turned to this Point; whom have you any longer to fear?—“ No one.”—For about what ſhould you be afraid? About what is your own, in which conſiſts the Eſſence of Good and Evil? And who hath any Power over *this*? Who can take it away? Who can hinder you? No more than God [can be hindered]. But are you afraid for Body, for Poſſeſſions, for what belongs to others, for what is nothing to you? And what have you been ſtudying all this while, but to diſtinguiſh between your own, and not your own; what is in your Power, and what is not in your Power; what is liable to Reſtraint, and what is not? And for what Purpoſe have you applied to the Philoſophers? That you might be never the leſs diſappointed and unfortunate? No doubt you will be exempt from Fear and Perturbation! And what is *Grief* to *you*? For [nothing but] what we fear, when expected, affects us with Grief, when preſent. And what will you any longer paſſionately wiſh for? For you have a temperate and ſteady Deſire of Things dependent on Choice, as they are good, and preſent: and you have no Deſire of Things independent on Choice, ſo as to leave room for that irrational and impetuous, and immoderately haſty Paſſion.

§. 12. Since then you are thus affected with regard to *Things*, what *Man* can any longer be formidable to you? What hath *Man* formidable to Man, either in Appearance, or Speech, or mutual Intercourſe? No more than Horſe to Horſe, or Dog to Dog, or Bee to Bee. But *Things* are formidable

to

to every one, and when-ever any Person can either confer or take away these from another, *He* becomes formidable too.—" How (*p*) then is the Citadel" [the Seat of Tyranny] " to be destroyed?"—Not by Sword or Fire, but by Principle. For if we should demolish that which is in the Town, shall we have demolished also that of a Fever, of pretty Girls, in short, the Citadel within ourselves; and turned out the Tyrants, to whom we are subject upon all Occasions, every Day; sometimes the same, sometimes others? From hence we must begin; from hence demolish the Citadel; turn out the Tyrants: give up Body, its Parts, Riches, Power, Fame, Magistracies, Honours, Children, Brothers, Friends: esteem all these as belonging to others. And, if the Tyrants be turned out from hence, why should I besides demolish the [external] Citadel; at least, on my own account? For what doth it do to *me* by standing? Why should I turn out the Guards? For in what Point do they affect *me*? It is against others they direct their Fasces, their Staves, and their Swords. Have I ever been restrained from what I willed; or compelled against my Will? Indeed how is this possible? I have ranged my Pursuits under the Direction of God. Is it His Will, that I should have a Fever? It is my Will too. Is it His Will, that I should pursue any Thing? It is my Will too. Is it His Will that I should desire? It is my Will too. Is it His Will, that I should obtain any Thing? It is mine too. Is it not His Will? It is not mine. Is it his Will, that I should be tortured (*q*)? Then it is my Will to be tortured. Is it his Will, that I should die? Then it is my

(*p*) *Epictetus* here personates one desirous of recovering the Liberty of the City, in which he lives. There were Citadels, erected from time to time in *Greek* Cities, to support Tyrants: and they and the Citadels were destroyed together, whenever it could be done.

(*q*) The Translation here is agreeable to Mr. *Upton*'s Copy.

my Will to die. Who can any longer restrain or compell me, contrary to my own Opinion? No more than *Jupiter* [can be restrained]. It is thus that cautious Travellers act. Doth any one hear, that the Road is beset by Robbers? He doth not set out alone; but waits for the Retinue of an Embassador, or Quæstor, or a Proconsul: and, when he hath joined himself to their Company, goes along in Safety. Thus doth the prudent Man act in the World. There are many Robberies, Tyrants, Storms, Distresses, Losses of Things the most dear. Where is there any Refuge? How can he go along unattacked? What Retinue can he wait for, to go safely through his Journey? To what Company join himself? To some rich Man? To some Consular Senator? And what Good will that do me? He is [often] stript himself; groans and laments, And what if my Fellow-Traveller himself should turn against me, and rob me? What shall I do? I will be the Friend of *Cæsar*. While I am his Companion, no one will injure me. Yet, before I can become illustrious enough for this, what must I bear and suffer! How often, and by how many, must I be robbed! And then, if I do become the Friend of *Cæsar*, he too is mortal: and if, by any Accident, he should become my Enemy, where can I best retreat? To a Desart? Well: and doth not a Fever come there? What can be done then? Is it not possible to find a Fellow-Traveller, safe, faithful, brave, incapable of being surprised? A Person, who reasons thus, understands and considers, that, if he joins himself to God, he shall go safely through his Journey.——"How do you "mean, join himself?"——That whatever is the Will of God, may be *his* Will too: whatever is not the Will of God, may not be *his*.——"How "then can this be done?"——Why, how otherwise than by considering the Exertions of God's Power, and his Administration? What hath he given me, me, my own, and independent? What hath he reserved to himself? He hath given me whatever depends upon Choice. The Things in my Power he hath made incapable of Hindrance or Restraint. But how could he make a Body of Clay (r) incapable of Hindrance? Therefore he hath subjected [that, and] Possessions, Furniture, House, Children, Wife, to the Revolution of the Universe. Why then do I fight against God? Why do I will to retain what depends not on Will? What is not granted absolutely; but how? In such a Manner, and for such a Time, as was thought proper. But he who gave, takes away (s). Why then do I resist? Not to say, that I shall be a Fool in contending with a stronger than myself; what is a prior Consideration, I shall be unjust. For whence had I these Things, when I came into the World? My Father gave them to me. And who gave them to *him*? And who made the Sun? Who, the Fruits? Who, the Seasons? Who, their Connexion and Relation to each other? And, after you have received all, and even your very Self from another, are you angry with the Giver; and complain, if He takes any thing away from you? Who are you; and for what Purpose did you come? Was it not He who brought you here? Was it not He who showed you the Light? Hath not He given you Assistants? Hath not He given you Senses? Hath not He given you Reason? And as whom did He bring you here? Was it not as a Mortal? Was it not as one to live, with a little Portion of Flesh upon Earth, and to see his Administration; to behold the Spectacle with him, and partake of the Festival for a short Time? After having beheld the Spectacle, and the Solemnity, then, as long as it is permitted you, will you not depart, when He leads you

(r) See B. I. c. 1. §. 3.

(s) *The Lord gave, and the Lord hath taken away.* Job i. 21.

you out, adoring and thankful for what you have heard and seen?——"No: but I would enjoy "the Feast still longer."——So would the Initiated too be longer in their Initiation; so, perhaps, would the Spectators at *Olympia* see more Combatants. But the Solemnity is over. Go away. Depart, like a grateful and modest Person: make room for others. Others too must be born, as you were; and, when they are born, must have a Place, and Habitations, and Necessaries. But, if the first do not give way, what [Room] is there left? Why are you insatiable? Why are you unconscionable? Why do you crowd the World?——"Ay: but I "would have my Wife and Children with me too."——Why, are they *your's*? Are they not the Giver's? Are they not His who made *you* also? Will you not quit what belongs to another then? Will you not yield to your Superior?——"Why "then did he bring me into the World upon these "Conditions?"——Well: if it is not worth your while, depart (*t*). He hath no Need of a discontented Spectator. He wants such as may share the Festival; make Part of the Chorus: who may rather extoll, applaud, celebrate the Solemnity: He will not be displeased to see the Wretched and Fearful dismissed from it. For, when they were present, they did not behave as at a Festival, nor fill a proper Place; but lamented, found fault with the Deity, Fortune, their Companions: insensible both of their Advantages, and their Powers, which they received

(*t*) And is this all the Comfort, every serious Reader will be apt to say, which one of the best Philosophers, in one of his noblest Discourses, can give to the good Man under severe Distress? "Either tell yourself, that present Suffering, void of "future Hope, is no Evil; or give up your Existence, and "mingle with the Elements of the Universe!" Unspeakably more rational, and more worthy of infinite Goodness, is our blessed Master's Exhortation to the persecuted Christian: "Re-"joice, and be exceeding glad, for great is your Reward in "Heaven."

received for contrary Purposes; the Powers of Magnanimity, Nobleness of Spirit, Fortitude, and the Subject of present Enquiry, Freedom.—"For "what Purpose then have I received these Things?" ——To use them.——"How long?"——As long as He, who lent them, pleases. If then they are not necessary, do not attach yourself to them, and they will not be so: do not tell yourself, that they are necessary, and they are not.

§. 13. This should be our Study from Morning till Night, beginning from the least and frailest Things, from an earthen Vessel, from a Glass. Afterwards, proceed to a Suit of Clothes, a Dog a Horse, an Estate: from thence to your Self, Body, Parts of the Body, Children, Wife, Brothers. Look every-where around you, and throw them from yourself. Correct your Principles. See that nothing cleave to you, which is not your own; nothing grow (u) to you, that may give you Pain, when it is torn away. And say, when you are daily exercising yourself as you do here, not that you act the Philosopher (admit this to be an insolent Title), but that you are asserting your Freedom. For this is true Freedom. This is the Freedom, that *Diogenes* gained from *Antisthenes*; and declared, it was impossible, that he should ever after be a Slave, to any one. Hence, when he was taken Prisoner, how did he treat the Pirates? Did he call any of them Master? (I do not mean the Name, for I am not afraid of a Word, but the Disposition from whence the Word proceeds.) How did he reprove them for feeding their Prisoners ill? How was he sold? Did he seek a Master? (w) No: but a Slave. And when he was sold, how did he converse with his Lord? He immediately disputed with him, that he ought not to be dressed nor shaved in the manner he was; how he ought to bring up his Children.

(u) Mr. *Upton*'s Conjecture.
(w) See p. 137. Note (c).

Children. And where is the Wonder? For if the same Master had bought an Instructor for his Children; in the Exercises of the *Palæstra*, would he in those Exercises have treated him as a Servant, or as a Master? And so if he had bought a Physician or an Architect? In every Subject, the Skilful must necessarily be superior to the Unskilful. What else then can he be but Master, who possesses the universal Knowledge of Life? For who is Master in a Ship? The Pilot. Why? Because whoever disobeys him is a Loser.——"But a Master can "put me in Chains."——Can he do it then without being a Loser?——"So I, among others, used "to think."——But, because he must be a Loser, for that very Reason it is not in his Power: for no one acts unjustly, without being a Loser.—"And "what Loss doth he suffer, who puts his own Slave "in Chains?"—What think you? The very putting him in Chains. This you yourself must grant, if you would preserve the Doctrine, that Man is not a wild, but a gentle Animal. For when is it, that a Vine is in a bad Condition?——"When it "is in a Condition contrary to its Nature."——When a Cock?——"The same."——Therefore a Man too. What then is his Nature? To bite, and kick, and throw into Prison, and cut off Heads? No: but to do good, to assist, to indulge the Wishes of others. Whether you will, or not then, he is in a bad Condition, when-ever he acts unreasonably.——"And so, was not *Socrates* in a "bad Condition?"——No: but his Judges and Accusers.——"Nor *Helvidius*, at *Rome*?"——No: but his Murderer.——"How do you talk?"——(*x*) Why, just as you do. You do not call that Cock in a bad Condition, which is victorious, and wounded; but that which is conquered, and comes

(*x*) The Translation here follows a different Pointing from Mr. *Upton*, Πως λεγεις; ως και συ. Αλεκτρυονα, &c.

comes off unhurt. Nor do you call a Dog happy, which neither hunts nor toils; but when you ſee him ſweating, and in pain, and panting, with the Chace. In what do we talk Paradoxes? If we ſay, that the Evil of every thing conſiſts in what is contrary to its Nature, is this a Paradox? Do not you ſay it with regard to all other Things? Why therefore, in the Caſe of Man alone, do you take a different Turn? But farther: it is no Paradox to ſay, that by Nature Man is gentle, and ſocial, and faithful.——"This is (y) none neither."——How then [is it a Paradox to ſay,] that, when he is whipped, or impriſoned, or beheaded, he is not hurt? If he ſuffers nobly, doth not he come off even the better, and a Gainer? But he is the Perſon hurt, who ſuffers the moſt miſerable and ſhameful Evils: who, inſtead of a Man, becomes a Wolf, or Viper, or a Hornet.

§. 14. Come then: let us recapitulate what hath been granted. The Man who is unreſtrained, who hath all Things in his Power as he wills, is free: but he who may be reſtrained, or compelled, or hindered, or thrown into any Condition againſt his Will, is a Slave.——"And who is unreſtrained?"——He that deſires none of thoſe Thing, that belong to others.——"And what are thoſe Things, which belong to others?"——Thoſe which are not in our own Power, either to have, or not to have; or to have them of ſuch a Sort, or in ſuch a State. Body, therefore, belongs to another; its Parts, to another; Poſſeſſions, to another. If then you attach yourſelf to any of theſe as your own, you will be puniſhed, as he deſerves, who deſires what belongs to others. This is the Way, that leads to Freedom;

(y) This Anſwer implies a ſilent Conceſſion, that it is no Paradox to affirm, the Evil of every thing to conſiſt, in what is contrary to its Nature.

dom; this the only Deliverance from Slavery; to be able at length to ſay, from the Bottom of one's Soul,

Conduct me, Jove, *and thou*, O Deſtiny,
Where-ever Your Decrees have fix'd my Lot.

§. 15. But what ſay you, Philoſopher? A Tyrant ſummons you to ſpeak ſomething unbecoming you. Will you ſay it, or will you not?——"Stay, "let me conſider."——Would you conſider *now?* And what did you uſe to conſider, when you were in the Schools? Did not you Study what Things are good, and evil, and what indifferent?——"I did."——Well: and what were the Opinions which pleaſed us?——"That juſt and (z) fair "Actions were good; unjuſt and baſe ones, evil." ——Is living a Good?——"No."——Dying, an Evil?——"No."——A Priſon?——"No."—— And what did a mean and diſhoneſt Speech, the betraying a Friend, or the flattering a Tyrant, appear to us?——"Evils."——Why then are you ſtill conſidering, and have not already conſidered, and come to a Reſolution? For what Sort of a Conſideration is this? *Whether I ought, when it is in my Power, to procure myſelf the greateſt Good, inſtead of procuring myſelf the greateſt Evil.* A fine and neceſſary Conſideration, truly, and deſerving mighty Deliberation! Why do you trifle with us, Man? There never was any ſuch Point conſidered: nor, if you really imagined what was fair and honeſt to be good, what baſe and diſhoneſt, evil, and all other Things indifferent, would you ever be at ſuch a Stand as this, or near it: but you would preſently be able to diſtinguiſh, by your Underſtanding, as you do by your Sight. For do you ever conſider, whether black is white: or light, heavy? Do not you follow the plain Evidence of your

(z) The Tranſlation here follows Mr. *Upton's* Conjecture.

your Senſes? Why then do you ſay, that you are now conſidering, whether Things indifferent are to be avoided, rather than Evils? The Truth is, you have no Principles: for neither doth the one Sort of Things appear to you indifferent, but the greateſt Evils; nor the other Evils, but Matters of no Concern to you. For thus you have accuſtomed yourſelf from the firſt. "Where am I? "In the School? And is there an Audience? I "talk as the Philoſophers do. But am I got out "from the School? Away with this Stuff, that "belongs only to Scholars and Fools. This Man "is accuſed by the Teſtimony of a Philoſopher, "his Friend: this Philoſopher turns Paraſite; that "hires himſelf out for Money; a third doth it "in the very Senate. Who doth not wiſh what "appears [to himſelf to be right]? His (*a*) Prin-"ciples exclaim from within."———You are a poor cold Lump of Opinion, conſiſting of mere Words; on which you hang, as by a Hair. But preſerve yourſelf firm, and make a due Uſe of the Appearances; remembering, that you are to be exerciſed in Things. In what manner do you hear, I do not ſay, that your Child is dead, (for how ſhould you bear that?) but that your Oil is ſpilled, your Wine drank out? That any one, while you are bawling, might only ſay this; "Philoſopher, "you talk otherwiſe in the Schools. Why do you "deceive us? Why, when you are a Worm, do "you call yourſelf a Man?" I ſhould be glad to be near one of theſe Philoſophers, while he is revelling in Debauchery, that I might ſee how he exerts himſelf, and what Sayings he utters; whether he remembers his Title, and the Diſcourſes which he hears, or ſpeaks, or reads.

(*a*) There is much Obſcurity, and ſome Variety of Reading, in ſeveral Lines of the Original, in this Place; and I am not certain, whether the Tranſlation hath given the true Senſe; but it is the beſt I could make of it.

§. 16. "And what is all this to Freedom?"—— Truly nothing else is, but this, whether you rich People will or not.——"And who is your Evi-"dence of this?"——Who, but yourselves? Who have a powerful Master, and live by his Motion and Nod, and faint away, if he doth but look sternly upon you: who pay your Court to old Men, and old Women, and say, "I cannot do this, it is "not in my Power." Why is it not in your Power? Did not you just now contradict me, and say, you were free?——"But *Aprylla* (*b*) hath "forbid me."——Speak the Truth then, Slave, and do not run away from your Masters; nor deny them, nor dare to assert your Freedom, when you have so many Proofs of your Slavery. One might indeed find some Excuse for a Person, compelled by Love to do something contrary to his Opinion, even when at the same time he sees what is best, and yet hath not Resolution enough to follow it; since he is with-held by something violent, and in some measure, divine. But who can bear you, who are in Love with old Men and old Women; and wipe their Noses, and wash them, and bribe them with Presents, and wait upon them when they are sick, like a Slave; at the same time wishing they may die, and enquiring of the Physician, whether their Distemper be yet mortal? And again, when for these great and venerable Magistracies and Honours, you kiss the Hands of the Slaves of others; so that you are the Slave of those who are not free themselves! And then you walk about in State, a Prætor, or a Consul. Do not I know how you came to be Prætor; whence you received the Consulship; who gave it you? For my own Part, I would not even live, if I must live by *Felicio*'s Means, and bear his Pride, and slavish Insolence. For I know what a Slave is, blinded by what he thinks good Fortune. §. 17.

(*b*) Probably some rich old Woman, from whom the Speaker had Expectations.

§. 17. Are you free yourſelf then? (It will be ſaid.) By Heaven I wiſh and pray for it. But I cannot yet face my Maſters. I ſtill pay a Regard to my Body, and ſet a great Value on keeping it whole; though at the ſame time it is not whole *(c)*. But I can ſhow you one who was free, that you may no longer ſeek an Example. *Diogenes* was free.——"How ſo?"——Not becauſe he was of free Parents, for he was not: but becauſe he was ſo himſelf; becauſe he had caſt away all the Handles of Slavery; nor was there any Way of getting at him, nor any-where to lay hold on him, to enſlave him. Every thing ſat looſe upon him, every thing only juſt hung on. If you took hold on his Poſſeſſions, he would rather let them go, than follow you for them: if on his Leg, he let go his Leg: if his Body, he let go his Body: Acquaintance, Friends, Country, juſt the ſame. For he knew whence he had them, and from whom, and upon what Conditions he received them. But he would never have forſaken his true Parents the Gods, and his real Country; nor have ſuffered any one to be more dutiful and obedient to them than he: nor would any one have died more readily for his Country than he. For he never ſought when it would be proper for him to act for the ſake of *(d)* any thing elſe, [except his real Country the Univerſe;] but he remembered, that every thing that exiſts is from thence, and carried on by it, and commanded by its Ruler. Accordingly, ſee what he himſelf ſays and writes. "Upon this Account, ſays he, O *Diogenes*, it is in your Power to converſe as you will with the *Perſian* Monarch, and with *Archidamus*, King of the *Lacedemonians*."——Was it becauſe *he* was born of

Y 2

(*c*) *Epictetus* here alludes to his own Lameneſs. See p. 28 and 50.

(*d*) This Paſſage hath great Difficulties in the Original. I have given it what appeared to me the beſt Senſe. But I am ſtill doubtful.

of free Parents? Or was it because *they* were descended from Slaves, that all the *Athenians*, and all the *Lacedemonians*, and *Corinthians*, could not converse with them as they pleased; but feared and paid Court to them? Why then is it in *your* Power, *Diogenes?* "Because I do not esteem this "sorry Body as my own. Because I want nothing. "Because these [Principles,] and nothing else, are "a Law to me." These were the Things that suffered him to be free.

§. 18. And that you may not think, that I show you the Example of a Man clear of Incumbrances; without a Wife or Children, or Country or Friends, or Relations, to bend and draw him aside: take *Socrates*, and consider him, who had a Wife and Children, but not as his own; a Country, Friends, Relations; but only as long as it was proper, and in the manner that was proper; and all these he submitted to the Law, and to the Obedience due to it. Hence, when it was proper to fight, he was the first to go out, and exposed himself to Danger, without the least Reserve. But when he was sent by the Thirty Tyrants to apprehend *Leo* (e); because he esteemed it a base Action, he did not deliberate about it; though he knew, that, perhaps, he might die for it. But what did that signify to *him?* For it was something else that *he* wanted to preserve, not his paultry Flesh: but his Fidelity, his Honour, free from Attack, or Subjection. And afterwards, when he was to make a Defence for his Life, doth he behave like one who had Children? Or a Wife? No:

(e) *Socrates*, with Four other Persons, was commanded by the Thirty Tyrants of *Athens* to fetch *Leo* from the Isle of *Salamis*, in order to be put to Death. His Companions executed their Commission; but *Socrates* remained at home, and chose rather to expose his Life to the Fury of the Tyrants, than be accessary to the Death of an innocent Person. He would most probably have fallen a Sacrifice to their Vengeance, if the Oligarchy had not shortly after been dissolved. See PLATO's *Apology*.

No: (*f*) but like a ſingle Man. And how doth he behave, when he was to drink the Poiſon? When he might have eſcaped, and *Crito* perſuaded him to get out of Priſon, for the Sake of his Children, what doth he ſay? Doth he eſteem it a fortunate Opportunity? How ſhould he? But he conſiders what is becoming, and neither ſees nor regards any thing elſe. "For I am not deſirous, ſays he, to "preſerve this pitiful Body; but that [Part of me] "which is improved and preſerved by Juſtice, and "impaired and deſtroyed by Injuſtice." *Socrates* is not to be baſely preſerved. He, who refuſed to vote for what the *Athenians* commanded: he, who contemned the Thirty Tyrants: he, who held ſuch Diſcourſes on Virtue, and moral Beauty: ſuch a Man is not to be preſerved by a baſe Action; but is preſerved by dying, not by running away. For even a good Actor is preſerved by leaving off when he ought; not by going on to act beyond his Time. "What then will become of your Children?" "If "I had gone away into *Theſſaly*, you would have "taken care of them; and will there be no one to "take care of them, when I am departed to *Hades*?" You ſee how he ridicules, and plays with Death. But, if it had been you or I, we ſhould preſently have proved, by philoſophical Arguments, that thoſe, who act unjuſtly, are to be repaid in their own Way; and ſhould have added, "If I eſcape, I "ſhall be of Uſe to many; if I die, to none." Nay, if it had been neceſſary, we ſhould have crept through a Mouſe-hole to get away. But how ſhould *we* have been of Uſe to any? For where muſt they have dwelt? If we were uſeful alive, ſhould we not be of ſtill more Uſe to Mankind, by dying when we ought, and as we ought? And now the Remembrance of the Death of *Socrates* is not leſs, but even more uſeful to the World, than that of the Things which he did and ſaid when alive.

(*f*) Mr. *Upton*'s Copy.

§. 19. Study these Points, these Principles, these Discourses; contemplate these Examples, if you would be free, if you desire the Thing in Proportion to its Value. And where is the Wonder, that you should purchase so great a Thing at the Price of others, so many, and so great? Some hang themselves, others break their Necks, and sometimes even whole Cities have been destroyed, for that which is reputed Freedom: and will not you, for the Sake of the true, and secure, and inviolable Freedom, repay God what he hath given, when he demands it? Will you not study, not only as *Plato* says, to die, but to be tortured, and banished, and scourged; and, in short, to give up all that belongs to others. If not, you will be a Slave among Slaves, though you were ten thousand Times a Consul: and, even though you should rise to the Palace, you will be never the less so. And you will feel, that though Philosophers (as *Cleanthes* says) do, perhaps, talk contrary to common Opinion, yet not contrary to Reason. For you will find it true in fact, that the Things that are eagerly followed and admired, are of no Use to those, who have gained them: while they who have not yet gained them, imagine, that, if they are acquired, every Good will come along with them: and then, when they are acquired, there is the same Feverishness, the same Agitation, the same Nauseating, and the same Desire of what is absent. For Freedom is not procured by a full Enjoyment of what is desired, but by proving the Desire to be a wrong one. And, in order to know that this is true, take the same Pains about these, which you have taken about other Things. Lie awake to acquire a Set of Principles, that will make you free. Instead of a rich old Man, pay your Court to a Philosopher. Be seen about his Doors. You will not get any Disgrace by being seen there. You will not return empty, or unprofited, if you go as you ought. However, try at least. The Trial is not dishonourable.

CHAP-

CHAPTER II.

Of Complaisance (a).

§. 1. TO this Point you muſt attend before all others: Not to be ſo attached to any one of your former Acquaintance or Friends, as to condeſcend to the ſame Behaviour with his; otherwiſe you will undo yourſelf. But, if it comes into your Head, *I ſhall appear odd to him, and he will not treat me as before*, remember, that there is nothing to be had for nothing: nor is it poſſible, that he who acts in the ſame manner, ſhould not be the ſame Perſon. Chuſe then, whether you will be loved by thoſe you were formerly, and be like your former ſelf; or be better, and not meet with the ſame Treatment. For, if this is preferable, immediately incline altogether that way, and let no other Kinds of Reaſoning draw you aſide: for no one can improve while he is wavering (b). If then you prefer this to every thing, if you would be fixed only on this, and employ all your Pains about it, give up every thing elſe. Otherwiſe this Wavering will affect you both Ways; you will neither make a due Improvement, nor preſerve the Advantages you had before. For before, by ſetting your Heart intirely on Things of no Value, you were agreeable to your Companions. But you cannot excell in both Kinds: but muſt neceſſarily loſe as much of the one, as you partake of the other. If you do not drink with thoſe, with whom you uſed to drink, you cannot appear equally agreeable to them. Chuſe then, whether you would be a Drunkard, and agreeable to them, or ſober, and diſ-

(a) Compare this Chapter with *Matt.* vi. 24. *No Man can ſerve two Maſters.*

(b) See *James* i. 8.

disagreeable to them. If you do not sing with those, with whom you used to sing, you cannot be equally dear to them. Here too then, chuse which you will. For if it is better to be modest and decent, than to have it said of you, *What an agreeable Fellow!* give up the rest; renounce it; withdraw yourself; have nothing to do with it. But, if this doth not please you, incline, with your whole Force, the contrary Way. Be one of the Catamites; one of the Adulterers. Act all that is consequent to such a Character, and you will obtain what you would have. Jump up in the Theatre too, and roar out in praise of the Dancer. But Characters so different are not to be confounded. You cannot act both *Thersites* and *Agamemnon*. If you would be *Thersites*, you must be hump-backed and bald: If *Agamemnon*, tall and handsome, and a Lover of those who are under your Care.

CHAPTER III.

What Things are to be exchanged for others.

§. 1. WHEN you have lost any thing external, have this always at hand, what you have got instead of it: and, if that be of more Value, do not by any means say, "I am a Loser:" whether it be a Horse for an Ass; an Ox for a Sheep; a good Action for a Piece of Money; a due composedness of Mind for a dull Jest; or Modesty for indecent Discourse. By continually remembring this, you will preserve your Character such as it ought to be. Otherwise consider, that you are spending your Time in vain; and all that you are now applying your Mind to, you are going to spill and overset. And there needs but little, and a small Deviation from Reason, to destroy and overset all. A Pilot doth not need the same Apparatus to overset a Ship, as to save it; but, if he he turns it a little to the Wind, it is loſt: even if he ſhould not do it by Deſign, but only for a Moment be thinking of ſomething elſe, it is loſt. Such is the Caſe here too. If you do but nod a little, all that you have hitherto collected is gone. Take heed then to the Appearances of Things. Keep yourſelf awake over them. It is no inconſiderable Matter you have to guard; but Modeſty, Fidelity, Conſtancy, Enjoyment (*a*), Exemption from Grief, Fear, Perturbation; in ſhort, Freedom. For what will you ſell theſe? Conſider what the Purchaſe is worth.—"But ſhall I not get ſuch "a Thing inſtead of it?"—Conſider, if you do get it (*b*), what it is that you obtain for the other. I have Decency; another the Office of a Tribune: I have Modeſty; he hath the Prætorſhip. But I do not make Acclamations where it is unbecoming: I ſhall not riſe (*c*) up [to do Honour to another] in a Caſe where I ought not: for I am free, and the Friend of God, ſo as to obey him willingly: but I muſt not value any thing elſe; neither Body, nor Poſſeſſions, nor Fame; in ſhort, nothing. For it is not His Will, that I ſhould value them. For, if this had been his Pleaſure, he would have made them my Good, which now he hath not done: therefore I cannot tranſgreſs his Commands.—"In every thing pre-"ſerve your own proper Good."—"But what of "the reſt?"—"Preſerve *them* too according as it "is permitted, and ſo far as to behave agreeably "to Reaſon in relation to them; contented with "this alone. Otherwiſe you will be unfortunate, "diſappointed, reſtrained, hindered." Theſe are the Laws, theſe the Statutes, tranſmitted from thence.

(*a*) See p. 277. Note (*e*).

(*b*) I ſuſpect, that τυγχάνων ſhould be ου τυγχανων, and then the Tranſlation will be,—Conſider, on the other hand, if you do not get that, what you obtain inſtead of it.

(*c*) Probably *Epictetus* here alludes to the jumping up in the Theatre, in favour of ſome Actor, mentioned in the preceding Chapter, and in the fourth Chapter of the third Book.

thence. Of these one ought to be an Expositor, and to these obedient, not to those of *Masurius* (*d*) and *Cassius*.

CHAPTER IV.

Concerning Those who earnestly desire a Life of Repose.

§. 1. REMEMBER, that it is not only the Desire of Riches and Power, that renders us mean, and subject to others, but even of Quiet, and Leisure, and Learning, and Travelling. For, in general, valuing any external Thing whatever, subjects us to another. Where is the Difference then, whether you desire to be a Senator, or not to be a Senator? Where is the Difference whether you desire Power, or to be out of Power? Where is the Difference, whether you say, "I am "in a wretched Way, I have nothing to do; but "am tied down to Books, as inactive as if I were "dead;"——or, "I am in a wretched Way, I "have no Leisure to read?" For as Levees and Power are among Things external, and independent on Choice, so likewise is a Book. For what purpose would you read? Tell me. For if you rest merely in being amused, and learning something, you are insignificant and miserable. But if you refer it to what you ought, what is that but a prosperous Life? And if Reading doth not procure you a prosperous Life, of what Use is it? "But "it doth procure a prosperous Life (say you); "and therefore I am uneasy at being deprived of "it."——And what sort of Prosperity is that, which

(*d*) Two famous Lawyers. This Passage is an Instance of the manner of Speaking, less usual among the *Greek* and *Roman*, than the Eastern Writers; where enjoining one Thing, and forbidding another, means only that the first should be preferred in case of Competition.

which every thing, I do not say *Cæsar*, or the Friend of *Cæsar*, but a Crow, a Piper, a Fever, ten thousand other Things, can hinder? But nothing is so essential to Prosperity, as the being perpetual, and unhindered. I am now called to do something. I now go therefore, and will be attentive to the Bounds and Measures, which ought to be observed; that I may act modestly, steadily, and without Desire or Aversion with regard to Externals (*a*). In the next place, I am attentive to other Men; what they say, and how they are moved: and that, not from Ill-nature, nor that I may have an Opportunity for Censure or Ridicule: but I turn to myself, [and ask,] "Am I also guilty of the same "Faults; and how then shall I leave them off?" (*b*) Once I too was faulty; but, God be thanked, not now. Well: when you have done thus, and been employed in this manner, have not you done as good a Work, as if you had read a thousand Lines, or written as many? For are you uneasy at not reading while you are eating, or bathing, or exercising? Are not you satisfied with performing these Actions conformably to what you have read? Why then do you not think uniformly about every thing?

(*a*) The Readers, perhaps, may grow tired, with being so often told, what they will find it very difficult to believe, That, because Externals are not in our own Power, they are nothing to us. But, in Excuse for this frequent Repetition, it must be considered, that the Stoics had reduced themselves to a Necessity of dwelling on this Consequence, extravagant as it is, by rejecting stronger Aids. One cannot indeed avoid highly admiring the very Few, who attempted to amend and exalt themselves, on this Foundation. No one, perhaps, ever carried the Attempt so far in Practice; and no one ever spoke so well in support of the Argument, as *Epictetus*. Yet, notwithstanding his great Abilities, and the Force of his Example, one finds him strongly complaining of the want of Success: and one sees from this Circumstance, as well as from many others in the Stoic Writings, That Virtue cannot be maintained in the World, without the Hope of a future Reward.

(*b*) Τοτε, perhaps should be ποτε; and is so translated.

thing? When you approach *Cæsar*, or any other Perſon, if you preſerve yourſelf unpaſſionate, unalarmed, ſedate; if you are rather an Obſerver of what is done, than [yourſelf] obſerved; if you do not envy thoſe who are preferred to you; if the Materials of Action do not ſtrike you; what do you want? Books? How, or to what End? For is not this a kind of Preparation for Living, but Living itſelf, made up of Things different? Juſt as if a Champion, when he enters the Liſts, ſhould fall a crying, becauſe he is not exerciſing without. It was for this, that you uſed to be exerciſed. For this, were the Poiſers, the Duſt (*c*), the young Fellows, your Antagoniſts. And do you now ſeek for theſe, when it is the time for Buſineſs? This is juſt as if, in the Topic of Aſſent, when we are preſented with Appearances, of which ſome are evidently true, others not, inſtead of diſtinguiſhing them, we ſhould want to read Diſſertations on Evidence.

§. 2. What then is the Cauſe of this? That we have neither read nor written, in order to treat the Appearances that occur to us, conformably to Nature, in our Behaviour. But we ſtop at learning what is ſaid, and being able to explain it to others; at ſolving Syllogiſms, and ranging hypothetical Arguments. Hence, where the Study is, there too is the Hindrance. Do you deſire abſolutely what is out of your Power? Be reſtrained then, be hindered, be diſappointed. But if we read Diſſertations about the exertion of the Efforts, not merely to ſee what is ſaid about the Efforts, but to exert them well: on Deſire and Averſion, that we may not be diſappointed of our Deſires, nor incur our Averſions:

(*c*) The Olympic Champions uſed to rub themſelves with Duſt and Sand: which, as they were anointed, was neceſſary to give them the better Hold on each other. See Mr. *Upton*'s Note on L. III. c. 15. p. 419. l. 10.

Averſions: on the Duties of Life, that, mindful of our Relations, we may do nothing irrationally, nor contrary to them: we ſhould not be provoked at being hindered in our Reading; but ſhould be contented with the Performance of Actions ſuitable to us, and ſhould not compute as we have hitherto been accuſtomed to compute. "To-day I have "read ſo many Lines; I have written ſo many;" but, "To-day I have uſed my Efforts as the Phi-"loſophers direct. I have reſtrained my Deſires "abſolutely; I have applied my Averſion only to "Things dependent on Choice. I have not been "terrified by ſuch a one, nor put out of Counte-"nance by ſuch another. I have exerciſed my "Patience, my Abſtinence, my Beneficence." And thus we ſhould thank God for what we ought to thank him. But now we reſemble the Vulgar in another way alſo, and do not know it. One is afraid, that he ſhall not be in Power; *you* (*d*), that you ſhall. By no means be afraid of it, Man; but as you laugh at *him*, laugh at *yourſelf*. For there is no Difference, whether you thirſt, like one in a Fever, or dread Water, like him who is bit by a mad Dog. Elſe, how can you ſay, like *Socrates*, "If it ſo pleaſes God, ſo let it be?" Do you think that *Socrates*, if he had fixed his Deſires on the Leiſure of the *Lycèum*, or the Academy, or the Converſation of the Youth there, Day after Day, would have made ſo many Campaigns as he did ſo readily? Would not he have lamented and groaned; "How wretched am I! now muſt I be miſe-"rable here, when I might be ſunning myſelf in "the *Lycèum*?" Was that your Buſineſs in Life then, to ſun yourſelf? Was it not to be proſperous? To be unreſtrained? Unhindered? And how could he have been *Socrates*, if he had lamented thus?

(*d*) The Tranſlation follows the Conjecture of *Wolfius*.

thus? How could he, after that, have written Pæans in a Prison?

§. 3. In short then, remember this, that whatever external to your own Choice you esteem, you destroy that Choice. And not only Power is external to it, but the being out of Power too: not only Business, but Leisure too.——"Then, must I live "in this Tumult now?"——What do you call a Tumult?——"A Multitude of People."——And where is the Hardship? Suppose it is the *Olympic* Games. Think it a public Assembly. There too some bawl out one Thing, some do another; some push the rest. The Baths are crowded. Yet who of us is not pleased with these Assemblies, and doth not grieve to leave them? Do not be hard to please, and squeamish at what happens. "Vinegar is dis-"agreeable, [says one]; for it is sour. Honey is "disagreeable, says a second; for it disorders my "Constitution. I do not like Vegetables, says a "third. Thus too [say others] I do not like Re-"tirement; it is a Desart: I do not like a Crowd; "it is a Tumult."—Why, if Things are so disposed, that you are to live alone, or with few, call this Condition a Repose; and make use of it as you ought. Talk with yourself: exercise the Appearances presented to your Mind: work up your Preconceptions to Accuracy. But if you light on a Crowd, call it one of the public Games, a grand Assembly, a Festival. Endeavour to share in the Festival with the rest of the World. For what Sight is more pleasant to a lover of Mankind, than a great Number of Men? We see Companies of Oxen, or Horses, with Pleasure. We are highly delighted to see a great many Ships. Who is sorry to see a great many Men?—"But they stun me "with their Noise."—Then your Hearing is hindered; and what is that to *you?* Is your Faculty of making a right Use of the Appearances of Things hindered too? Or who can restrain you from using your

your Desire and Aversion, your Powers of Pursuit and Avoidance, conformable to Nature? What Tumult is sufficient for this? Do but remember the general Rules. *What is mine? What not mine? What is allotted me? What is the Will of God, that I should do now? What is not his Will?* A little while ago it was His Will, that you should be at leisure, should talk with yourself, write about these Things, read, hear, prepare yourself. You have had sufficient Time for this. At present He says to you, "Come now to the Combat. Show us what you "have learned; how you have wrestled." How long would you exercise by yourself? It is now the Time to show, whether you are of the Number of those Champions who merit Victory, or of those who go about the World, conquered in all the Games round. Why then are you out of Humour? There is no Combat without a Tumult. There must be many preparatory Exercises, many Acclamations, many Masters, many Spectators.—"But "I would live in quiet."—Why then, lament and groan, as you deserve. For what greater Punishment is there to the Uninstructed, and Disobedient to the Orders of God, than to grieve, to mourn, to envy; in short, to be disappointed, and unhappy? Are not you willing to deliver yourself from all this?—And how shall I deliver myself?—Have not you heard, that you must absolutely with-hold Desire, and apply Aversion to such Things only, as are dependent on Choice? That you must give up all, Body, Possessions, Fame, Books, Tumults, Power, Exemption from Power? For to which soever your Propension is, you are a Slave; you are under Subjection; you are made liable to Restraint, to Compulsion; you are altogether the Property of others. But have that of *Cleanthes* always ready,

Conduct me, Jove; *and Thou,* O Destiny.

Is

Is it Your Will, that I ſhould go to *Rome?* Conduct me to *Rome.* To *Gyaros?*—To *Gyaros.* To *Athens?*—To *Athens.* To Priſon?—To Priſon. If you once ſay, "When is one to go to *Athens?*" you are undone. This Deſire, if it be unaccompliſhed, muſt neceſſarily render you diſappointed; and, if fulfilled, vain on what ought to elate you: on the contrary, if you are hindered, wretched, by incurring what you do not like. Therefore give up all theſe Things.—"*Athens* is a fine Place." —But it is a much finer Thing to be happy, impaſſive, tranquil, not to have what concerns you dependent on others.—"*Rome* is full of Tumults "and Viſits."—But Proſperity is worth all Difficulties. If then it be a proper Time for theſe, why do not you withdraw your Averſion from them? (What Neceſſity is there for you to be made to carry your Burden, by being cudgelled like an Aſs?) Otherwiſe conſider, that you muſt always be a Slave to him, who hath the Power to procure your Diſcharge, to every one who hath the Power of hindering you; and muſt worſhip him, like your evil Genius.

§. 4. The only way to real Proſperity (let this Rule be at hand Morning, Noon, and Night,) is, a Reſignation of Things independent on Choice; to eſteem nothing as a Property; to deliver up all Things to our tutelar Genius, and to Fortune; to make thoſe the Governors of them, whom *Jupiter* hath made ſo; to be ourſelves devoted to that only, which is our Property; to that which is incapable of Reſtraint; and whatever we read, or write, or hear, to refer all to this.

§. 5. Therefore I cannot call any one induſtrious, if I hear only that he reads, or writes; nor even if he adds the whole Night to the Day, do I call him ſo, unleſs I know to what he refers it. For not even *you* would call Him induſtrious, who ſits up for the Sake of a Girl; nor therefore in the other

other Caſe do *I*. But, if he doth it for Fame, I call him ambitious; if for Money, avaritious; if from the Deſire of Learning, bookiſh; but not induſtrious. But, if he refers his Labour to his ruling Faculty, in order to treat and regulate it conformably to Nature, then only I call him induſtrious. For never either praiſe or blame any Perſon, on account of outward Actions that are common to all; but on the account of Principles. Theſe are the peculiar Property of each Individual, and the Things which make Actions good or bad.

§. 6. Mindful of this, be pleaſed with the preſent, and contented with whatever it is the Seaſon for. If you perceive any of thoſe Things, which you have learned and ſtudied, occurring to you in Action, rejoice in them. If you have laid aſide Ill-nature and Reviling; if you have leſſened your Harſhneſs, indecent Language, Inconſiderateneſs, Effeminacy; if you are not moved by the ſame Things as formerly; if not in the ſame manner as formerly; you may keep a perpetual Feſtival: To-day, becauſe you have behaved well in one Affair: To-morrow, becauſe in another. How much better a Reaſon for Sacrifice is this, than obtaining a Conſulſhip, or a Government? Theſe Things you have from yourſelf, and from the Gods. Remember this, Who it is that gave them, and to whom, and for what Purpoſe. Habituated once to theſe Reaſonings, can you ſtill think there is any Difference, in what Place you are to pleaſe God? Are not the Gods every-where at the ſame Diſtance? Do not they every-where equally ſee what is doing?

CHAPTER V.

Concerning the Quarrelsome, and Ferocious.

§. 1. A WISE and good Person neither quarrels with any one himself, nor, as far as possible, suffers another. The Life of *Socrates* affords us an Example of this too, as well as of the other [Virtues]; who not only every-where avoided quarrelling himself, but did not even suffer others to quarrel. See in *Xenophon's Symposium*, how many Quarrels he ended; how, again, he bore with *Thrasymachus*, with *Polus*, with *Callicles*; how, with his Wife, how, with his Son, who attempted to confute him, and cavilled with him. For he well remembered, that no one is Master of the ruling Faculty of another; and therefore he desired nothing but what was his own.——"And what is "that?"——Not that this [or that] Person (*a*) should be moved conformably to Nature; for that belongs to others; but that while they act in their own Way, as they please, he should nevertheless be affected, and live conformably to Nature, only doing what belongs to himself, in order to make them too live conformably to Nature. For this is the Point, that a wise and good Person hath in view. To have the Command of an Army? No: but if it be allotted him, to preserve on this Subject of Action, the right Conduct of his own ruling Faculty. To marry? No: but if a Marriage be allotted him, to preserve himself, on this Subject of Action, conformable to Nature. But, if he would have his Wife, or his Child, exempt from Fault, he would have that his own, which belongs to others. And being instructed, consists in this very Point,

(*a*) Perhaps for κινῃ αὐτος τι, should be read, κινηται αὐτος; and the Translation follows this Conjecture.

Point, To learn what Things are our own, and what belong to others.

§. 2. What room is there then for quarrelling, to a Person thus disposed? For doth he wonder at any thing that happens? Doth it appear new to him? Doth not he expect worse and more grievous Injuries from bad People, than happen to him? Doth he not reckon it so much gained, as they come short of the last Extremities? Such a one hath reviled you.—You are much obliged to him, that he hath not struck you.—But he hath struck you too.—You are much obliged to him, that he hath not wounded you too.—But he hath wounded you too.—You are much obliged to him, that he hath not killed you. For when did he ever learn, or from whom, that he is a gentle, that he is a social Animal: that the very Injury itself is a great Mischief to the Injurious? As then he hath not learned these Things, nor believes them, why should he not follow what appears for his Interest? Your Neighbour hath thrown Stones. What then? Is it any Fault of *yours*? But your Goods are broken. What then? Are you a Piece of Furniture? No; but your Essence consists in the Faculty of Choice. What Behaviour then is assigned you, in Return? If you consider yourself as a Wolf—to bite again, to throw more Stones. But if you ask the Question, as a Man, examine your Treasure: see what Faculties you have brought into the World with you. Are they Dispositions to Ferocity? To Revenge? When is a Horse miserable? When he is deprived of his natural Faculties. Not when he cannot crow, but when he cannot run. And a a Dog? not when he cannot fly, but when he cannot hunt. Is not a Man then also unhappy in the same manner? Not he, who cannot strangle Lions, or grasp Statues (*b*), (for he hath received no Fa-

(*b*) Like *Hercules* and *Diogenes*. See p. 228. Note (*b*).

culties for this purpose from Nature ;) but who hath lost his Rectitude of Mind, his Fidelity. Such a one is the Person, who ought to be publicly lamented, for the Misfortunes into which he is fallen: not, by Heaven, either he who is born *(c)* or dies ; but he, whom it hath befallen while he lives to lose what is properly his own : not his paternal Possessions, his paultry Estate, or his House, his Lodging, or his Slaves, (for none of these are a Man's own ; but all belonging to others, servile, dependent, and given at different Times, to different Persons, by the Disposers of them ;) but his personal Qualifications as a Man, the Impressions which he brought into the World stampt upon his Mind : such as we seek in Money ; and, if we find them, allow it to be good ; if not, throw it away. "What "Impression hath this Piece of Money ?"—"*Tra*"*jan's*." "Give it me."—*Nero's (d)*." Throw it away. It is false : it is good for nothing. So in the other Case. "What Impression have his Prin"ciples ?" "Gentleness, social Affection, Patience, "Good-nature." Bring them hither. I receive them. I make such a Man a Citizen ; I receive him for a Neighbour, a fellow Traveller. Only see that he hath not the *Neronian* Impression. Is he passionate ? Is he resentful ? Is he querulous ? Would he, if he took the Fancy, break the Head of those who fall in his way ? Why then do you call

(c) An Allusion to a Passage in *Euripides*. The general Sense of which is, That we ought to lament the Person who is born, from a Consideration of the Evils into which he is coming, and to rejoice over the Dead, who is at rest from his Labours. UPTON.

There is an Account in *Herodotus*, of a People of *Thrace*, who used to assemble, and condole with a Family where any one was born ; and, on the contrary, exprefs great Joy and Congratulation where-ever there happened a Death. L. 5. c. 4.

(d) Nero being declared an Enemy by the Senate, his Coin was, in consequence of this, prohibited and destroyed.

call him a Man? For is every thing diſtinguiſhed by a mere outward Form? Then ſay, juſt as well, that a Piece of Wax is an Apple, or that it hath the Smell and Taſte too. But the external Figure is not enough: nor, conſequently, is it ſufficient to make a Man, that he hath a Noſe and Eyes, if he hath not the proper Principles of a Man. Such a one doth not underſtand Reaſon, or apprehend when he is confuted. He is an Aſs. Another is dead to the Senſe of Shame. He is a worthleſs Creature (*e*); any thing, rather than a Man. Another ſeeks whom he may kick or bite: ſo that he is neither Sheep nor Aſs. But what then? He is a wild Beaſt.

§. 3. "Well: but would you have me deſpiſed "then?"—By whom? By thoſe who know you? And how can They deſpiſe you, who know you to be gentle and modeſt? But, perhaps, by thoſe who do not know you? And what is that to You? For no other Artiſt troubles himſelf about the Ignorant. ——"But People will be much the readier to at-"tack me."——Why do you ſay *me*? Can any one hurt your Choice, or reſtrain you from treating conformably to Nature, the Appearances that are preſented to you? Why then are you diſturbed, and deſirous to make yourſelf appear formidable? Why do not you make public Proclamation, that you are at Peace with all Mankind, however they may act; and that you chiefly laugh at thoſe, who ſuppoſe they can hurt you. "Theſe Wretches nei-"ther know who I am, or in what conſiſt my "Good and Evil: or that there is no Acceſs for "*them* to what is really *mine*." Thus the Inhabitants of a fortified City laugh at the Beſiegers. "What Trouble now are theſe People giving "themſelves for nothing? Our Wall is ſecure; we

(*e*) The Name of ſome Animal would ſuit better here, than the Epithet ἀχρηστος. But χοῖρος, a Hog, is a Word too unlike; and I can think of no better.

"have Provisions for a very long Time, and every other Preparation." These are what render a City fortified, and impregnable: but nothing but its Principles render the human Soul so. For what Wall is so strong, what Body so impenetrable, or what Possession so unalienable, or what Dignity so secured against Stratagems? All Things else, every-where else, are mortal, easily reduced; and whoever, in any degree, fixes his Mind upon them, must necessarily be subject to Perturbation, Despair, Terrors, Lamentations, disappointed Desires, and incurred Aversions.

§. 4. And will we not fortify then the only Place of Security that is granted us; and, withdrawing ourselves from what is mortal and servile, diligently improve what is immortal, and by Nature free? Do we not remember, that no one either hurts or benefits another: but the Principle, which we hold concerning every thing, doth it? It is this that hurts us; this that overturns us. Here is the Fight, the Sedition, the War. It was nothing else, that made *Eteocles* and *Polynices* Enemies, but their Principle concerning Empire, and their Principle concerning Exile: that the one seemed the extremest Evil; the other, the greatest Good. Now the very Nature of every one is to pursue Good, to avoid Evil; to esteem him as an Enemy and Betrayer, who deprives us of the one, and involves us in the other, though he be a Brother, or a Son, or Father. For nothing is more nearly related to us than Good. So that if Good and Evil consist in Externals, there is no Affection between Father and Son, Brother and Brother; but all is every-where full of Enemies, Betrayers, Sycophants. But if a right Choice be the only Good, and a wrong one the only Evil, what further room is there for quarrelling, for reviling? About what? About what is nothing to us? Against whom? Against the Ignorant, against the

the Unhappy, againſt thoſe who are deceived in Things of the greateſt Importance?

§. 5. Mindful of this, *Socrates* lived in his own Houſe, patiently bearing a furious Wife, a ſenſeleſs Son. For what were the Effects of her Fury? The throwing as much Water as ſhe pleaſed on his Head, the trampling (f) a Cake under her Feet. "And what is this to me, if I think ſuch Things "nothing to me? This very Point is my Buſineſs: "and neither a Tyrant, nor a Maſter, ſhall reſtrain "my Will; nor Multitudes, though I am a ſingle "Perſon; nor one ever ſo ſtrong, though I am "ever ſo weak. For this is given by God to every "one, free from Reſtraint."

§. 6. Theſe Principles make Friendſhip in Families, Concord in Cities, Peace in Nations. They make a Perſon grateful to God, every-where in good Spirits, [about Externals,] as belonging to others, as of no Value. But we, alas! are able indeed to write and read theſe Things, and to praiſe them when they are read; but very far from being convinced by them. Therefore what is ſaid of the *Lacedemonians*,

Lions at Home, Foxes at Epheſus,

may be applied to us too: Lions in the School, but Foxes out of it.

(f) *Alcibiades* ſent a fine great Cake, as a Preſent to *Socrates*: which ſo provoked the Jealouſy of the meek *Xantippe*, that ſhe threw it down, and ſtampt upon it. *Socrates* only laughed, and ſaid, "Now you will have no Share in it yourſelf." UPTON *from* ÆLIAN.

CHAPTER VI.

Concerning Those who grieve at being pitied.

§. 1. IT vexes me, ſay you, to be pitied. Is this *your* Affair then, or *theirs*, who pity you? And further: How is it in your Power to prevent it?——"It is, if I ſhow them, that I do not need "Pity."——But are you now in ſuch a Condition, as not to need Pity, or are you not?——"I think "I am. But theſe People do not pity me for what, "if any thing, would deſerve Pity, my Faults; "but for Poverty, and want of Power, and Sick- "neſſes, and Deaths, and other Things of that "Kind."——Are you then prepared to convince the World, that none of theſe Things is in reality an Evil: but that it is poſſible for a Perſon to be happy, even when he is poor, and without Honours, and Power? Or are you prepared to appear to them, rich and powerful? The laſt of theſe is the Part of an arrogant, ſilly, worthleſs Fellow. Obſerve too, by what Means this Fiction muſt be carried on. You muſt hire ſome paultry Slaves, and get poſſeſſed of a few little Pieces of Plate, and often ſhow them in public; and, though they are the ſame, endeavour to conceal that they are the ſame: you muſt have gay Clothes, and other Finery; and make a Show of being honoured by your great People; and endeavour to ſup with them, or be *thought* to ſup with them; and uſe ſome vile Arts with your Perſon, to make it appear handſomer and genteeller than it really is. All this you muſt contrive, if you would take the ſecond Way not to be pitied. And the firſt is impracticable, as well as tedious, to undertake the very Thing, that *Jupiter* himſelf could not do: to convince all Mankind what Things are really good and evil. Is this granted you? The only Thing granted you is, to convince

convince *yourself*: and you have not yet done that: and do you, notwithſtanding, undertake to convince *others*? Why, who hath lived ſo long with you, as you have with yourſelf? Who is ſo likely to have Faith in you, in order to be convinced by you, as you in yourſelf? Who is a better Wiſher, or a nearer Friend to you, than you to yourſelf? How is it then, that you have not yet convinced yourſelf. Should not you (*a*) now turn theſe Things every way in your Thoughts? What you were ſtudying was this: to learn to be exempt from Grief, Perturbation, and Meanneſs, and to be free. Have not you heard then, that the only way that leads to this is, to give up what doth not depend on Choice: to withdraw from it; and confeſs, that it belongs to others? What kind of Thing then is another's Opinion about you?——"Independent "on Choice."——Is it nothing then to *you*?——"Nothing."——While you are ſtill piqued and diſturbed about it then, do you think, that you are convinced concerning Good and Evil.

§. 2. Letting others alone then, why will you not be your own Scholar and Teacher? Let others look to it, whether it be for their Advantage to think and act contrary to Nature: but no one is nearer to me than myſelf. What then is the Meaning of this? I have heard the Reaſonings of Philoſophers, and aſſented to them: yet, in fact, I am never the more relieved. Am I ſo ſtupid, and yet in other Things, that I had an Inclination to, I was

(*a*) The Text here is either corrupt, or very elliptical and obſcure; and the Tranſlation conjectural. *Ανω κατα* hath the ſame Senſe in the next Page but one, which is aſſigned to it here. The *και* before *μανθανειν* is omitted, as being probably a Corruption of the laſt Syllable of the preceding Word, written twice over. Mr. *Upton*'s MS. cuts the Difficulty ſhort, by leaving out ſeveral Words; in conſequence of which, the Tranſlation would be; *How is it then, that you have not yet brought yourſelf to learn to be exempt*, &c.

was not found very stupid: but I quickly learned Grammar, and the Exercises of the *Palæstra*, and Geometry, and the Solution of Syllogisms. Hath not Reason then convinced me? And yet there is no one of the other Things, that I so much approved or liked from the very first. And now I read concerning these Subjects, I hear Discourses upon them, I write about them, and I have not yet found any Reasoning of greater Strength than this. What then do I want? Is it not, that the contrary Principles are not removed out of my Mind? Is it not, that I have not strengthened these Opinions by Exercise, nor accustomed them to occur in Action; but, like Arms thrown aside, they are grown rusty, and do not fit me? Yet neither in the *Palæstra*, nor writing, nor reading, nor solving Syllogisms, am I contented with mere Learning: but I turn the Arguments every way, which are presented to me, and I compose others; and the same of convertible Propositions. But the necessary Theorems, by which I might become exempted from Fear, Grief, Passion, unrestrained and free, I neither exercise, nor study, with a proper Application. And then I trouble myself, what others will say of me; whether I shall appear to them worthy of Regard; whether I shall appear happy.—Will you not see, Wretch, what you can say of *yourself*? What sort of Person you appear to *yourself*, in your Opinions, in your Desires, in your Aversions, in your Pursuits, in your Preparation, in your Intention, in the other proper Works of a Man? But, instead of that, do you trouble yourself, whether *others* pity you?—"Very true. But I am pitied improperly."—Then are not you *pained* by this? And is not he who is in Pain to be pitied.—"Yes."—How then are you pitied improperly? For you render yourself worthy of Pity by what you suffer upon being pitied.

§. 3.

§. 3. What ſays *Antiſthenes* then? Have you never heard? "It is kingly, O *Cyrus*, to do well, "and to be ill ſpoken of." My Head is well, and all around me think it akes. What is that to *me?* I am free from a Fever; and they compaſſionate me, as if I had one. "Poor Soul, what a long "while have you had this Fever!" I ſay too, with a diſmal Countenance, Ay, indeed, it is now a long time that I have been ill.—"What can be "the Conſequence then?"——What pleaſes God. And at the ſame time I ſecretly laugh at them, who pity me. What forbids then, but that the ſame may be done in the other Caſe? I am poor: but I have right Principles concerning Poverty. What is it to me then, if People pity me for my Poverty? I am not in Power, and others are: but I have ſuch Opinions as I ought to have concerning Power, and the want of Power. Let them ſee to it, who pity me. But I am neither hungry, nor thirſty, nor cold. But, becauſe they are hungry and thirſty, they ſuppoſe me to be ſo too. What can I do for them then? Am I to go about, making Proclamation, and ſaying, Do not deceive yourſelves, good People, I am very well: I regard neither Poverty, nor want of Power, nor any thing elſe, but right Principles. Theſe I poſſeſs unreſtrained. I care for nothing farther.—But what trifling is this? How have I right Principles, when I am not contented to be what I am; but am out of my Wits, how I ſhall appear?—But others will get more, and be preferred to me.—Why, what is more reaſonable, than that they who take pains for any thing, ſhould get moſt in that Particular, in which they take pains? They have taken pains for Power; you, for right Principles: they, for Riches; you, for a proper Uſe of the Appearances of things. See whether they have the Advantage of you in that, for which you have taken pains, and which they neglect: if they aſſent better, concerning the

natural

natural Bounds and Limits of Things; if their Desires are less disappointed than yours, their Aversions less incurred; if they take a better Aim in their Intention, in their Purposes, in their Pursuits: whether they preserve a becoming Behaviour, as Men, as Sons, as Parents, and so on in respect of the other Relations of Life. But, if they are in Power, and you not (*b*): why will you not speak the Truth to yourself; that *you* do nothing for the sake of Power; but that *they* do every thing? And it is very unreasonable, that he who carefully seeks any thing, should be less successful than he who neglects it.—" No: but since I take Care to have " right Principles, it is more reasonable that I should " have Power."—Yes, in respect to what you take Care about, your Principles. But give up to others the Things, in which they have taken more Care than you. Else it is just as if, because you have right Principles, you should think it fit, that when you shoot an Arrow, you should hit the Mark better than an Archer, or that you should forge better than a Smith. Therefore let alone taking pains about Principles, and apply yourself to the Things which you wish to possess, and then fall a crying, if you do not suceeed; for you deserve to cry. But now you say, that you are engaged in other Things; intent upon other Things: and it is a true Saying, that one Business doth not suit with another. One Man, as soon as he rises and goes out, seeks to whom he may pay his Compliments; whom he may flatter; to whom he may send a Present; how he may please the Dancer [in vogue]; how, by doing ill-natured Offices to one, he may oblige another. Whenever he prays, he prays for nothing like these: whenever he sacrifice, he sacrifices for Things like these. To these he transfers the *Pythagorean* Precept;

Let

(*b*) I have translated thus, on the Supposition, that ου in the Original ought to be repeated.

Let not the stealing God of Sleep surprise, &c.

(*c*) *Where have I failed* in Point of Flattery? *What have I done?* Any thing like a free, brave-spirited Man? If he should find any thing of this Sort, he rebukes and accuses himself. "What "Business had you to say that? For could not "you have lied? Even the Philosophers say, there "is no Objection against telling a Lye."

§. 4. But on the other hand, if you have in reality been careful about nothing else, but to make a right Use of the Appearance of Things; as soon as you are up in a Morning, consider, what do I want in order to be free from Passion? What, to enjoy Tranquillity? What am I? Am I mere worthless Body? Am I Estate? Am I Reputation? None of these. What then? I am a reasonable Creature. What then is required of me? Recollect your Actions. *Where have I failed*, in any Requisite for Prosperity? *What have I done*, either unfriendly, or unsociable? *What have I omitted*, that was necessary in these Points?

§. 5. Since there is so much Difference then in your Desires, your Actions, your Wishes, would you yet have an equal Share with others in those Things, about which you have not taken Pains, and they have? And do you wonder, after all, and are you out of Humour, if they pity you? But they are not out of Humour, if you pity them. Why? Because they are convinced, that they are in Possession of their proper Good; but you are not convinced that you are. Hence you are not contented with your own Condition; but desire theirs: whereas they are contented with theirs, and do not desire yours. For, if you were really convinced, that it is *you* who are in Possession of what is good, and that *they* are mistaken, you would not so much as think what they say about you.

CHAP-

(*c*) See the *Pythagorean* Verses (quoted in B. III. c. 10.) of which these Questions are a Parody.

CHAPTER VII.

Of Fearlessness.

§. 1. WHAT makes a Tyrant formidable? His Guards, say you, and their Swords; they who belong to the Bed-chamber; and they who shut out those, who would go in. What is the Reason then, that, if you bring a Child to him when he is surrounded by his Guards, it is not afraid? Is it because the Child doth not know what they mean? Suppose then, that any one doth know what is meant by Guards, and that they are armed with Swords; and, for that very Reason, comes in the Tyrant's Way, beings desirous, on account of some Misfortune, to die, and seeking to die easily by the Hand of another: Doth such a Man fear the Guards? No: for he wants the very Thing, that renders them formidable. Well then: if any one, without an absolute Desire to live or die, but, as it may happen, comes in the Way of a Tyrant, what restrains his approaching him without Fear? Nothing. If then another should think concerning his Estate, or Wife, or Children, as this Man doth concerning his Body; and, in short, from some Madness or Folly, should be of such a Disposition, as not to care whether he hath them, or hath them not; but, as Children, playing with Shells, make a Difference indeed in the Play, but do not trouble themselves about the Shells; so he should pay no Regard to the Materials [of Action]; but apply himself to the playing with, and Management of, them; what Tyrant, what Guards, or their Swords, are any longer formidable to such a Man?

§. 2.

§. 2. And is it possible, that any one should be thus disposed towards these Things from Madness (*a*); and the *Galileans*, from mere Habit; yet that no one should be able to learn, from Reason and Demonstration, that God made all Things in the World, and the whole World itself, unrestrained and perfect; and all its Parts for the Use of the Whole? All other Creatures are indeed excluded from a Power of comprehending the Administration of the World; but a reasonable Being hath Abilities for the Consideration of all these Things: both that it [self] is a Part, and what Part; and that it is fit the Parts should submit to the Whole. Besides, being by Nature constituted noble, magnanimous, and free, it sees, that, of the Things which relate to it, some are unrestrained and in its own Power, some restrained, and in the Power of others: the unrestrained, such as depend on Choice; the restrained, such as do not depend on it. And, for this Reason, if it esteems its Good and its Interest to consist in Things unrestrained, and in its own Power, it will be

(*a*) *Epictetus*, probably, means, not any remaining Disciples of *Judas* of *Galilee*, but the Christians, whom *Julian* afterwards affected to call *Galileans*. It helps to confirm this Opinion, that *M. Antoninus* (L. 2. §. 3.) mentions them, by their proper Name of Christians, as suffering Death out of mere Obstinacy. It would have been more reasonable, and more worthy the Character of these great Men, to have enquired into the Principles, on which the Christians refused to worship Heathen Deities, and by which they were enabled to support their Sufferings with such amazing Constancy, than rashly to pronounce their Behaviour the Effect of Obstinacy and Habit. *Epictetus* and *Antoninus* were too exact Judges of human Nature, not to know, that Ignominy, Tortures, and Death, are not, merely on their own Account, Objects of Choice: nor could the Records of any Time or Nation, furnish them with an Example of Multitudes of Persons of both Sexes, of all Ages, Ranks, and natural Dispositions, in distant Countries, and successive Periods, resigning whatever is most valuable and dear to the Heart of Man, from a Principle of *Obstinacy*, or the mere Force of *Habit*: not to say, that Habit could have no Influence on the first Sufferers.

be free, prosperous, happy, unhurt, magnanimous, pious; thankful (*b*) to God for every thing; never finding fault with any thing, never censuring any thing that is brought to pass by him. But, if it esteems its Good, and its Interest, to consist in Externals, and Things independent on Choice, it must necessarily be restrained, be hindered, be enslaved to those who have the Power over those Things which it admires, and fears; it must necessarily be impious, as supposing itself injured by God, and unequitable, as claiming more than its Share; it must necessarily too be abject, and mean-spirited.

§. 3. What forbids, but that he, who distinguishes these Things, may live with an easy and light Heart, quietly expecting whatever may happen, and bearing contentedly what hath happened? Would you have Poverty [be my Lot]? Bring it; and you shall see what Poverty is, when it hath got one to act it well. Would you have Power? Bring Toils too along with it. Banishment? Where-ever I go, it will be well with me there: for it was well with me *here*, not on account of the Place, but of the Principles, which I shall carry away with me; for no one can deprive me of these: on the contrary, they alone are my Property, and cannot be taken away; and retaining them, suffices me where-ever I am, or what-ever I do.——" But it is now time to die."—— What is it that you call dying (*c*)? Do not talk of the Thing in a Tragedy Strain; but say, as the Truth is, that it is Time for a compound Piece of Matter to be resolved back into its Original. And where is the Terror of this? What Part of the World is going to be lost? What is going to happen new, or prodigious? Is it for this, that a Tyrant is formidable? Is it on this Account, that

(*b*) This agrees with *Eph.* v. 20. *Giving Thanks always for all Things unto God*——.

(*c*) The Translation here follows Mr. *Upton*'s Manuscript, and Emendation.

that the Swords of his Guards seem so large and sharp? Try these Things upon others. For my Part, I have examined the Whole. No one hath an Authority over me. God hath made me free: I know his Commands: after this, no one can enslave me. I have a proper Assertor of my Freedom; proper Judges. Is it not of my Body, that you are the Master? What is that to *me* then? Of that Trifle my Estate? What is that to *me* then? Is it not of Banishment and Chains, that you are the Master? Why, all these again, and my whole Body I give up to you: when-ever you please, make a Trial of your Power, and you will find how far it extends.

§. 4. Whom then can I any longer fear? Those who belong to the Bed-chamber? Lest they should do——What? Shut me out? If they find me desirous to come in, let them.——"Why do you "come to the Door then?"——Because it is fitting for me, that while the Play lasts, I should play too.——"How then are you incapable of being "shut out?"——Because, if I am not admitted, I would not wish to go in; but would much rather, that Things should be as they are: for I esteem what God wills, to be better than what I will (*d*). I give myself up a Servant and a Follower to him. I pursue, I desire, in short, I *will* along with Him. Being shut out doth not relate to *me*; but to those who push to get in. Why then do not I push too? Because I know, that there is not any Good distributed there to those who get in. But when I hear any one congratulated on the Favour of *Cæsar*, I say, What hath he got?——"A Province (*e*)." ——Hath he then got such Principles too, as he ought to have?——"A public Charge."——Hath

(*d*) *Nevertheless not as I will, but as Thou wilt.* Matth. xxvi. 39.

(*e*) The Translation of this Passage follows the Conjecture of *Wolfius*.

he then got with it the Knowledge how to uſe it too? If not, why ſhould I be thruſt about any longer to get in? Some one ſcatters Nuts and Figs. Children ſcramble and quarrel for them; but not Men: for they think them Trifles. But, if any one ſhould ſcatter Shells, not even Children would ſcramble for theſe. Provinces are diſtributing. Let Children look to it. Money. Let Children look to it. Military Command, a Conſulſhip. Let Children ſcramble for them. Let theſe be ſhut out, be beat, kiſs the Hands of the Giver, of his Slaves. But, to me, they are but mere Figs and Nuts.——"What then is to be done?"——If you miſs them, while he is throwing them, do not trouble yourſelf about it: but, if a Fig ſhould fall into your Lap, take it, and eat it; for one may pay ſo much Regard even to a Fig. But, if I am to ſtoop and throw down one, or be thrown down by another, and flatter thoſe who are got in, a Fig is not worth this, nor any other of the Things which are not really good, and which the Philoſophers have perſuaded me not to eſteem as good.

§. 5. Show me the Swords of the Guards.——"See how big, and how ſharp they are."——What then do theſe great and ſharp Swords do?——"They kill."——And what doth a Fever do?——"Nothing elſe."——And a Tile?——"Nothing elſe."——Would you have me then be ſtruck with an awful Admiration of all theſe, and worſhip them, and go about a Slave to them all? Heaven forbid! But, having once learnt, that every thing that is born muſt likewiſe die, (that the World may not be at a Stand, or the Courſe of it hindered), I no longer make any Difference, whether this be effected by a Fever, or a Tile, or a Soldier: but, if any Compariſon is to be made, I know, that the Soldier will effect it with leſs Pain, and more ſpeedily. Since then I neither fear any of thoſe Things, which he can inflict upon me, nor covet

covet any thing which he can beſtow, why do I ſtand any longer in Awe of a Tyrant? Why am I ſtruck with Aſtoniſhment? Why do I fear his Guards? Why do I rejoice, if he ſpeaks kindly to me, and receives me graciouſly; and relate to others, in what Manner he ſpoke to me? For is He *Socrates*, or *Diogenes*, that his Praiſe ſhould ſhow what I am? Or have I ſet my Heart on imitating his Manners? But, to keep up the Play, I go to him, and ſerve him, as long as he commands nothing unreaſonable or improper. But, if he ſhould ſay to me, "Go to *Salamis*, and bring *Leo* (*f*)," I anſwer him, Seek another, for I play no longer. ——"Lead him away."——I follow, in Sport. ——"But your Head will be taken off."——And will his own always remain on; or yours, who obey him?——"But you will be thrown out, unburied."——If *I* am the Corpſe, *I* ſhall be thrown out; but if *I* am ſomething elſe than the Corpſe (*g*); ſpeak more handſomely, as the Thing is, and do not think to fright me. Theſe Things are frightful to Children and Fools. But if any one, who hath once entered into the School of a Philoſopher, doth not know what he himſelf is, he deſerves to be frighted, and to flatter what he lately flattered; if he hath not yet learnt, that he is neither Fleſh, nor Bones, nor Nerves; but that which makes uſe of theſe, and regulates and comprehends the Appearances of Things.

§. 6. "Well: but theſe Reaſonings make Men "deſpiſe the Laws."——And what Reaſonings then render thoſe, who uſe them, more obedient to the Laws? But the Law of Fools is no Law. And yet, ſee how theſe Reaſonings render us properly diſpoſed, even towards ſuch Perſons, ſince they

(*f*) An Alluſion to the Story, mentioned in the firſt Chapter of this Book, p. 324. Note (*e*).

(*g*) See p. 288. Note (*w*).

they teach us, not to claim, in Opposition to them, any thing wherein they have it in their Power to be superior to us. They teach us to give up Body, to give up Estate, Children, Parents, Brothers, to yield every thing, to let go every thing, excepting only Principles; which even *Jupiter* hath excepted, and decreed to be every one's own Property. What Unreasonableness, what Breach of the Laws, is there in this? Where you are superior and stronger, there I give way to *you*: Where, on the contrary, I am superior, do you submit to *me*; for this hath been my Study, and not yours. Your Study hath been to walk upon a *Mosaic* Floor, to be attended by your Servants and Clients, to wear fine Clothes, to have a great Number of Hunters, Fiddlers, and Players. Do I lay any Claim [to these?] but [on the other hand,] have you then studied Principles, or even your own rational Faculty? Do you know, of what Parts it consists? How they are connected; what are its Articulations; what Powers it hath, and of what Kind? Why then do you take it amiss, if another, who hath studied them, hath the Advantage of you in these Things?——"But they are of all Things "the greatest."——Well: and who restrains you from being conversant with them, and attending to them ever so carefully? Or who is better provided with Books, with Leisure, with Assistants? Only turn your Thoughts now-and-then to these Matters; bestow but a little Time upon your own ruling Faculty. Consider what it is you have, and whence it came, that uses all other Things, that examines them all, that chuses, that rejects. But while you employ yourself about Externals, you will have those indeed, such as no one else hath; but your ruling Faculty, such as you like to have it, sordid and neglected.

CHAP.

CHAPTER VIII.

Concerning such as hastily run into the philosophic Dress.

§. 1. NEVER commend or censure any one for common Actions, nor ascribe them either to Skilfulness or Unskilfulness; and thus you will at once be free both from Rashness and Ill-nature. Such a one bathes in a mighty little Time. Doth he therefore do it ill? Not at all. But what? In a mighty little Time.——"Is every "thing well done then?"——By no means. But what is done from good Principles is well done; what from bad ones, ill. But till you know from what Principle any one acts, neither commend nor censure the Action. But the Principle is not easily judged of from the external Appearances. Such a one is a Carpenter. Why? He uses an Axe. What signifies that? Such a one is a Musician: for he sings. What signifies that? Such a one is a Philosopher. Why? Because he wears a Cloke and long Hair. What then do Mountebanks wear? And so, when People see any of these acting indecently, they presently say, "See (*a*) what the Phi-"losopher doth." But they ought rather, from his acting indecently, to say, he is no Philosopher. For, if indeed the Idea, which we have of a Philosopher, and his Profession, was, to wear a Cloke and long Hair, they would say right: but, if it be rather to keep himself free from Faults, since he doth not fulfil his Profession, why do not they deprive him of his Title? For this is the Way with regard to other Arts. When we see any one handle an Axe aukwardly, we do not say, "Where is "the Use of this Art? See how ill Carpenters per-"form."

(*a*) Perhaps the true Reading is ὅ ὁ φιλοσοφος.

"form." But we say the very contrary: "This "Man is no Carpenter; for he handles an Axe "aukwardly." So, if we hear any one sing badly, we do not say, "Observe how Musicians sing." but rather, "This Fellow is no Musician." It is with regard to Philosophy alone, that People are thus affected. When they see any one acting contrary to the Profession of a Philosopher, they do not take away his Title; but, laying it down, that he is a Philosopher, and then assuming from the very Fact that he behaves indecently, they infer, that Philosophy is of no Use.

§. 2. "What then is the Reason of this?" Because we pay some Regard to the Pre-conception which we have of a Carpenter, and a Musician, and so of other Artists; but not of a Philosopher; which being thus vague and confused, we judge of it only from external Appearances. And of what other Art do we take up our Judgment from the Dress and the Hair? Hath it not Theorems too, and Materials, and an End, [to distinguish it?] What then is the Subject-matter of a Philosopher? Is it a Cloke?——No: but Reason. What his End? To wear a Cloke?——No: but to have his Reason correct. What are his Theorems? Are they how to get a great Beard, or long Hair?——No: but rather, as *Zeno* expresses it, To know the Elements of Reason, what each of them is in particular, and how they are adapted to each other, and what are their Consequences.

§. 3. Why then will you not first see, whether, by acting in an unbecoming Manner, he answers his Profession, and so proceed to blame the Study? Whereas now, when you act soberly yourself, you say, from what he appears to do amiss, "Observe "the *Philosopher!*" As if it was decent to call a Person, who doth such Things, a *Philosopher*. And, again, "This is *philosophical!*" But you do not say, "Observe the Carpenter, or observe the Mu-"sician,"

"sician," when you know one of them to be an Adulterer, or see him to be a Glutton. So, in some small Degree, even You perceive, that the profession of a Philosopher is; but are misled, and confounded by your own Carelessness. But indeed even they, who are called Philosophers, enter upon their Profession by Things which are common to them with others. As soon as they have put on a Cloke, and let their Beard grow, they cry, "I am "a Philosopher." Yet no one says, "I am a Mu-"sician;" because he hath bought a Fiddle and Fiddlestick; nor, "I am a Smith;" because he is drest in the *Vulcanian* Cap and Apron. But they take their Name from their Art, not from their Habit.

§. 4. For this Reason, *Euphrates* was in the Right to say, "I long endeavoured to conceal my "embracing the Philosophic Life; and it was of "Use to me. For, in the first place, I knew that, "what I did right, I did it not for Spectators; but "for myself. I eat in a proper Manner, for my-"self. I had a composed Look, and Walk, all for "God and myself. Then, as I fought alone, I was "alone in Danger. Philosophy was in no Danger, "on my doing any thing shameful, or unbecom-"ing: nor did I hurt the rest of the World; "which, by offending as a Philosopher, I might "have done. For this Reason, they who were ig-"norant of my Intention, used to wonder, that "while I conversed, and lived intirely with Philo-"sophers, I never took up the Character. And "where was the Harm, that I should be discovered "to be a Philosopher, by my Actions, and not by "the usual Badges. See how I eat, how I drink, "how I sleep, how I bear, how I forbear; how I "assist others; how I make use of my Desires, "how of my Aversions; how I preserve the natu-"ral and acquired Relations, without Confusion, "and without Impediment. Judge of me from "hence, if you can. But, if you are so deaf and "blind, that you would not suppose *Vulcan* himself "to be a good Smith, unless you saw the Cap upon "his Head, where is the Harm of not being found "out by so foolish a Judge?"

§. 5. It was thus too that *Socrates* concealed himself from the Generality; and some even came and desired him to recommend them to Philosophers. Did he use to be displeased then, like us; and say, What! do not you take *me* for a Philosopher? No; he took and recommended them; contented with only being a Philosopher, and rejoicing in not being vexed, that he was not thought one. For he remembered his Business: and what is the Business of a wise and good Man? To have many Scholars? By no means. Let those see to it, who have made this their Study. Well then: is it to be a perfect Master of difficult Theorems? Let others see to that too. In what then was he, and did he desire to be, somebody? In what constituted his Hurt or Advantage? "If, says he, any one can "hurt me, I am doing nothing. If I depend for "my Advantage upon another, I am nothing. Do "I wish for any thing, and it doth not come to "pass? I am unhappy." To such a Combat he invited every one, and, in my Opinion, yielded to no one. But do you think it was by making Proclamation, and saying, "I am such a one?" Far from it: but by *being* such a one For this, again, is Folly and Insolence to say, "I am impassive and "undisturbed. Be it known to you, Mortals, that "while *you* are fluctuating and bustling about for "Things of no Value, *I* alone am free from all "Perturbation."——Are you then so far from being contented with having no Pain yourself, that you must needs make Proclamation: "Come hi- "ther, all you who have the Gout, or the Head- "ake, or a Fever, or are lame, or blind; and see

"me

" *me* free from every Distemper." This is vain and shocking, unless you could show, like *Æscula-pius*, by what Method of Cure they may presently become as free from Distempers as yourself, and bring your own Health as a Proof of it.

§. 6. Such is the Cynic, honoured with the Sceptre and Diadem from *Jove*: who says, " That you " may see, O Mankind, that you do not seek " Happiness and Tranquillity where it is, but " where it is not; behold, I am sent an Example " to you, from God; who have neither (*b*) Estate, " nor House, nor Wife, nor Children, nor even a " Bed, or Coat, or Furniture. And see how heal- " thy I am. Try me: and, if you see me free " from Perturbation, hear the Remedies, and by " what Means I was cured." This now is benevolent and noble. But consider whose Business it is.——*Jupiter*'s, or his whom he judges worthy of this Office; that he may never discover any thing to the World, by which he may invalidate his own Testimony, which he gives for Virtue, and against Externals.

No sickly Pale his beauteous Features wear,
Nor from his Cheek he wipes the languid Tear.

HOMER.

And not only this, but he doth not desire or seek for Company or Place, or Amusement, as Boys do the Vintage Time, or Holy-Days: always fortified by virtuous Shame, as others are by Walls, and Gates, and Centinels.

§. 7. But now they, who have only such an Inclination to Philosophy, as bad Stomachs have to some Kinds of Food, of which they will presently grow sick, immediately run to the Sceptre, to the Kingdom,

(*b*) See p. 257. Note (*m*).

Kingdom. They let grow their Hair, assume (*d*) the Cloke, bare the Shoulder, wrangle with all they meet; and even, if they see any one in a thick warm Coat, wrangle with him. First harden yourself against all Weather, Man. Consider your Inclination; whether it be not that of a bad Stomach, or of a longing Woman. First study to conceal what you are; philosophise a little while by yourself. Fruit is produced thus. The Seed must first be buried in the Ground, lie hid there some time, and grow up by degrees, that it may come to Perfection. But, if it produces the Ear before the Stalk hath its proper Joints, it is imperfect, and of the Garden of *Adonis* (*e*). Now *you* are a poor Plant of this Kind. You have blossomed too soon: the Winter will kill you. See what Countrymen say about Seeds of any Sort, when the warm Weather comes too early. They are in great Anxiety, for fear the Seeds should shoot out too luxuriantly; and then, one Frost taking them (*f*), shows how prejudicial their Forwardness was. Beware you too, Man. You have shot out luxuriantly; you have sprung forth towards a trifling Fame, before the proper Season. You seem to be somebody, as a Fool may among Fools. You will be taken by the Frost: or rather, you are already frozen downwards, at the Root: you still blossom indeed a little at the Top, and therefore you think you are still alive and flourishing. Let *us*, at least, ripen

(*d*) Which were the Characteristics of the Cynics.

(*e*) At the Feast of *Adonis*, there were carried about little Earthen Pots, filled with Mould, in which grew several Sorts of Herbs. These were called Gardens: and from thence the Gardens of *Adonis* came to be proverbially applied to Things unfruitful or fading; because those Herbs were only sowed so long before the Festival, as to sprout forth and be green at that Time, and then were presently cast into the Water. See POTTER's *Grecian* Antiquities, Chap. 20. p. 363.

(*f*) Here is a strong Similitude to the Seed in the Gospels, that sprung up quickly, and withered.

ripen naturally. Why do you lay us open? Why do you force us? We cannot yet bear the Air. Suffer the Root to grow; then the first, then the second, then the third Joint of the Stalk to spring from it; and thus (*g*) Nature will force out the Fruit, whether I will or not. For who that is big with, and full of such Principles, doth not perceive too his own Qualifications, and exert his Efforts to correspondent Operations? Not even a Bull is ignorant of his own Qualifications, when any wild Beast approaches the Herd, nor waits for any one to encourage him; nor a Dog, when he spies any Game. And, if I have the Qualifications of a good Man, shall I wait for you to qualify me for my own proper Operations? but believe me, I have them not yet. Why then would you wish *me* to be withered before my Time, as *you* are?

CHAPTER IX.

Concerning a Person who was grown immodest.

(*a*) §. 1. WHEN you see another in Power, set against it, that you have the Advantage of not wanting Power. When you see another rich, see what you have instead of Riches: for, if you have nothing in their Stead, you are miserable. But if you have the Advantage of not needing Riches, know, that you have something more than he hath, and of far greater Value. Another possesses a handsome Woman; you, the Happiness of not desiring a handsome Woman. Do

(*g*) This Passage hath some Difficulty in the Original; and, probably, may have been corrupted. The Translation hath given what seems to be the Sense.

(*a*) They, who are desirous of taking Refuge in Heathenism from the Strictness of the Christian Morality, will find no great Consolation in reading this Chapter of *Epictetus*.

Do you think these are little Matters? And what would those very Persons, who are rich, and powerful, and possess handsome Women, give, that they were able to despise Riches and Power, and those very Women whom they love, and whom they acquire! Do not you know of what Nature the Thirst of one in a Fever is? It hath no Resemblance to that of a Person in Health. He drinks, and is satisfied. But the other, after being delighted a very little while, grows sick, turns the Water into Choler, throws it up, hath Pain in his Bowels, and becomes more violently thirsty. Of the same Nature is it to have Riches, or Dominion, or enjoy a fine Woman, with Fondness of any one of these Things. Jealousy takes place; Fear of losing the beloved Object; indecent Discourses, indecent Designs; unbecoming Actions.

§. 2. "And what, say you, do I lose all the "while?"——You were modest, Man, and are so no longer. Have you lost nothing? Instead of *Chrysippus* and *Zeno*, you read *Aristides* (*b*) and *Euenus* (*c*). Have you lost nothing then? Instead of *Socrates* and *Diogenes*, you admire him who can corrupt and entice the most Women. You set out your Person, and would be handsome, when you are not. You love to appear in fine Clothes, to attract the Eyes of the Women; and, if you anywhere meet with (*d*) a good Perfumer, you esteem yourself a happy Man. But formerly you did not so much as think of any of these Things; but only where you might find a decent Discourse, a worthy Person, a noble Design. For this Reason, you used to sleep like a Man; to appear in public like a Man; to wear a manly Dress; to hold Discourses worthy of a Man. And after this, do you tell me, you

(*b*) An indecent Poet of *Miletus*.

(*c*) A Writer of amorous Verses.

(*d*) The Translation follows Mr. *Upton*'s Conjecture of Μυροποιῷ.

you have loſt nothing? What then do Men loſe nothing but Money? Is not Modeſty to be loſt? Is not Decency to be loſt? Or may he, who loſes theſe, ſuffer no Damage? You indeed perhaps no longer think any thing of this Sort to be a Damage. But there was once a Time, when you accounted this to be the only Damage and Hurt; when you were anxiouſly afraid, leſt any one ſhould ſhake your Regard from theſe Diſcourſes and Actions. See, it is not ſhaken by another; but by yourſelf. Fight againſt yourſelf, recover yourſelf to Decency, to Modeſty, to Freedom. If you had formerly been told any of theſe Things of me, that any one prevailed on me to commit Adultery, to wear ſuch a Dreſs as yours, to be perfumed, would not you have gone and laid violent Hands on the Man, who thus abuſed me? And will you not now then help yourſelf? For how much eaſier is that Aſſiſtance? You need not kill, or fetter, or affront, or go to Law with any one; but merely to talk with yourſelf, who will moſt readily be perſuaded by you, and with whom no one hath greater Credit than you. And, in the firſt place, condemn your Actions: but when you have condemned them, do not deſpair of yourſelf, nor be like thoſe poor-ſpirited People, who when they have once given Way, abandon themſelves intirely, and are carried along, as by a Torrent. Take Example from the wreſtling Maſters. Hath the Boy fallen down? Get up again, they ſay; wreſtle again, till you have acquired Strength. Be you affected in the ſame Manner. For, be aſſured, that there is nothing more tractable than the human Mind. You need but will, and it is done, it is ſet right: as, on the contrary, you need but nod over the Work, and it is ruined. For both Ruin and Recovery are from within.

§. 3.

§. 3. "And, after all, what Good will this do "me?"——(e) What greater Good do you seek? From impudent, you will become modest; from indecent, decent; from dissolute, sober. If you seek any greater Things than these, go on as you do. It is no longer in the Power of any God to save you.

CHAPTER X.

What Things we are to despise, and on what to place a distinguished Value.

§. 1. THE Doubts and Perplexities of all Men are concerning Externals. What they shall do? How it may be? What will be the Event? Whether this Thing may happen, or that? All this is the Talk of Persons engaged in Things independent on Choice. For who says, How shall I do, not to assent to what is false? How, not to dissent from what is true? If any one is of such a good Disposition, as to be anxious about these Things, I will remind him: Why are you anxious? It is in your own Power. Be assured. Do not rush upon Assent before you have applied the natural Rule. Again, if (a) he be anxious, for fear

(e) *Epictetus* here asserts, that the only Benefit of Reformation is, being reformed; and that they, who look for any other, are incapable of being reformed, even by God himself; and so may go on, and be as bad as they please. Suppose a Prince should publish a Proclamation, that the only Advantage of Loyalty was being loyal; and, if any of his Subjects looked for any other, he might be a Rebel with impunity: what Effect must this have, compared with the Declaration, *Rev.* xxii. 11, 12. *He that is unjust, let him be unjust still: and he that is filthy, let him be filthy still: and he that is righteous, let him be righteous still: And behold, I come quickly, and my* Reward *is with Me, to give to every Man, according as his Works shall be.*

(a) I read the Text, in this Place, as *Wolfius* appears by his Translation to have done.

fear his Desire should be ineffectual and disappointed, or his Aversion incurred, I will first kiss him, because, slighting what others are in a Flutter and terrified about, he takes care of what is his own; where his very Being is: then I will say to him; If you would not be disappointed of your Desires, or incur your Aversions, desire nothing that belongs to others; be averse to nothing not in your own Power; otherwise your Desire must necessarily be disappointed, and your Aversion incurred. Where is the Doubt here? Where the room for, *How will it be? What will be the Event?* And, *Will this happen, or that?* Now is not the Event independent on Choice?——"Yes."——And doth not the Essence of Good and Evil consist in what depends on Choice?——"Yes."——It is in your Power then, to treat every Event conformably to Nature? Can any one restrain you?——"No "one."——Then do not say to me any more, *How will it be?* For, however it be, you will set it right, and the Event to you will be lucky.

§. 2. Pray what would *Hercules* have been, if he had said, "What can be done to prevent a great "Lion, or a great Boar, or savage Men, from "coming in my Way?" Why, what is that to you? If a great Boar should come in your Way, you will fight the greater Combat: if wicked Men, you will deliver the World from wicked Men.—"But "then if I should die by this Means?"——You will die a good Man, in the Performance of a gallant Action. For since, at all Events, one must die, one must necessarily be found doing something, either tilling, or digging, or trading, or serving a Consulship, or sick of an Indigestion, or a Flux. At what Employment then would you have Death find you? For my Part I would have it be some humane, beneficent, public-spirited, gallant Action. But if I cannot be found doing any such great Things, yet, at least, I would be doing what I am

incapable

incapable of being restrained from, what is given me to do, correcting myself, improving that Faculty which makes use of the Appearances of Things, to procure Tranquillity, and render to the several Relations of Life their Due; and, if I am so fortunate, advancing to the third Topic, a Security of judging right. If Death overtakes me in such a Situation, it is enough for me, if I can stretch out my Hands to God, and say, "The Opportu-"nities which Thou hast given me, of compre-"hending and following [the Rules] of thy Admi-"nistration, I have not neglected. As far as in me "lay, I have not dishonoured Thee. See how I "have used my Perceptions; how, my Pre-con-"ceptions. Have I at any time found fault with "Thee? Have I been discontented at Thy Dispen-"sations; or wished them otherwise? Have I "transgressed the Relations of Life? I thank "Thee, that Thou hast brought me into Being. I "am satisfied with the Time that I have enjoyed "the Things, which Thou hast given me. Receive "them back again, and assign them to whatever "Place Thou wilt; for they were (*b*) all Thine, and "Thou gavest them to me (*c*)."

§. 3. Is it not enough to make one's Exit in this State of Mind? And what Life is better, and more becoming than that of such a one? Or what Conclusion

(*b*) *Thine they were, and Thou gavest them me.* John xvii. 6.

(*c*) I wish it were possible to palliate the Ostentation of this Passage, by applying it to the ideal perfect Character: but it is in a general Way, that *Epictetus* hath proposed such a dying Speech, as cannot, without shocking Arrogance, be uttered by any one born to die. Unmixt as it is with any Acknowledgement of Faults or Imperfections at present, or with any Sense of Guilt on Account of the past, it must give every sober Reader a very disadvantageous Opinion of some Principles of the Philosophy, on which it is founded, as contradictory to the Voice of Conscience, and formed on absolute Ignorance, or Neglect, of the Condition and Circumstances of such a Creature as Man.

clusion happier? But, in order to attain these Advantages, there are no inconsiderable Things, both to be taken and lost. You cannot wish both for a Consulship and these too, nor take Pains to get an Estate and these too, or be solicitous both about your Servants and yourself. But, (*d*) if you wish any thing absolutely, of what belongs to others, what is your own is lost. This is the Nature of the Affair. Nothing is to be had for nothing. And where is the Wonder? If you would be Consul, you must watch, run about, kiss Hands, be wearied down with waiting at the Doors of others, must say and do many slavish Things, send Gifts to many, daily Presents to some. And what is the Consequence [of Success]? Twelve Bundles of Rods (*e*); to sit three or four times on the Tribunal; to give the *Circensian* Games, and Suppers (*f*) in Baskets to all the World: or let any one show me what there is in it more than this. Will you then be at no Expence, no Pains to acquire Apathy, Tranquillity, to sleep sound while you do sleep, to be thoroughly awake while you are awake, to fear nothing, to be anxious for nothing? But, if any thing belonging to you be lost, or idly wasted, while you are thus engaged, or another gets what you ought to have had, will you immediately begin fretting at what hath happened? Will you not compare the Exchange you have made? How much for how much? But you would have such great Things for nothing, I suppose. And how can you? One Business doth not suit with another: you cannot bestow your Care both upon Externals and your own ruling Faculty (*g*). But, If you would have the former, let the latter alone; or you will succeed in neither, while you are drawn

(*d*) See *Enchiridion*, c. xiii.

(*e*) The Ensigns of the Consular Office.

(*f*) These were distributed by the great Men in *Rome* to their Clients, as a Reward for their Attendance.

(*g*) *Ye cannot serve God and* Mammon. *Matth.* vi. 24.

different Ways, towards both. On the other hand, if you would have the latter, let the former alone. ——"The Oil will be spilled, the Furniture will "be spoiled:"——but still I shall be free from Passion.——"There will be a Fire when I am not "in the Way, and the Books will be destroyed:" ——but still I shall treat the Appearances of Things conformably to Nature.——"But I shall "have nothing to eat."——If I am so unlucky, dying is a safe Harbour. That is the Harbour for all, Death: that is the Refuge; and, for that Reason, there is nothing difficult in Life. You may go out of Doors when you please, and be troubled with Smoke no longer.

§. 4. Why then are you anxious? Why do you keep yourself waking? Why do not you calculate where your Good and Evil lies: and say, they are both in my own Power; neither can any deprive me of the one, or involve me, against my Will, in the other. Why then do not I lay myself down and snore? What is my own, is safe. Let what belongs to others look to itself, who carries it off, how it is given away by Him, that hath the Disposal of it. Who am I, to will, that it should be so and so? For is the Option given to me? Hath any one made Me the Dispenser of it? What I have in my own Disposal is enough for me. I must make the best I can of this. Other Things must be as the Master of them pleases.

§. 5. Doth any one, who hath these Things before his Eyes, lie awake [like *Achilles*,] and shift from Side to Side? What would he have, or what doth he want? *Patroclus*, or *Antilochus* (g), or *Menelaus*? Why, did he ever think any one of his Friends immortal? Why, when had not he it before his Eyes, that the Morrow, or the next Day,

(g) *Antilochus* and *Menelaus* are not mentioned, or referred to, in the Passage of *Homer*, to which *Epictetus* alludes.

Day, himſelf, or that Friend, might die?——"Ay, very true, ſays he: but (*h*) I reckoned, that "he would ſurvive me, and bring up my Son."——Becauſe you were a Fool, and reckoned upon (*i*) Uncertainties. Why then do you blame yourſelf; but ſit crying, like a Girl?——"But he uſed "to (*k*) ſet my Dinner before me."——Becauſe he was alive, Fool; but now he cannot. But *Automedon* will ſet it before you; and, if he ſhould die, you will find ſomebody elſe. What if the Pipkin, in which your Meat uſed to be cooked, ſhould happen to be broken; muſt you die with Hunger, becauſe you have not your old Pipkin (*l*)? Do not you ſend and buy a new one?

What greater Evil (ſays he) *could afflict my Breaſt?*

Is *this* your Evil then? And, inſtead of removing it, do you accuſe your Mother, that ſhe did not foretell it to you, that you might have ſpent your whole Life in grieving from that Time forward?

§. 6. Do not you think now, that *Homer* compoſed all this on Purpoſe to ſhow us, that the nobleſt, the ſtrongeſt, the richeſt, the handſomeſt of Men, may, nevertheleſs, be the moſt unfortunate and wretched, if they have not the Principles they ought to have?

(*h*) Αδηλα ωυ, perhaps, ſhould be *αδηλα δηλα ωυ.*

(*i*) *I hop'd* Patroclus *might ſurvive, to rear*
My tender Orphan, with a Parent's Care. POPE.

(*k*) *Thou too,* Patroclus, *(thus his Heart he vents)*
Haſt ſpread th' inviting Banquet in our Tents. POPE.

(*l*) This is a wretched Idea of Friendſhip; but a neceſſary Conſequence of the Stoic Syſtem. What a fine Contraſt to this gloomy Conſolation are the noble Sentiments of an Apoſtle! Value your deceaſed Friend, ſays *Epictetus*, as a broken Pipkin; forget him, as a Thing worthleſs, loſt, and deſtroyed. St. *Paul*, on the contrary, comforts the mourning Survivors; bidding them, *not ſorrow, as thoſe who have no Hope:* but remember, that the Death of good Perſons is only a Sleep; from which they ſhall ſoon ariſe to a happy Immortality.

CHAPTER XI.

Of Purity and Cleanlineſs.

§. 1. SOME doubt whether Sociableneſs be comprehended in the Nature of Man: and yet theſe very Perſons do not ſeem to me to doubt, but that Purity is by all means comprehended in it; and that by this, if by any thing, it is diſtinguiſhed from brute Animals. When therefore we ſee any Animal cleaning itſelf, we are apt to cry, with Wonder, It is like a human Creature. On the contrary, if an Animal is accuſed [of Dirtineſs], we are preſently apt to ſay, by way of Excuſe, that it is not a human Creature. Such Excellence do we ſuppoſe to be in Man, which we firſt received from the Gods. For, as they are by Nature pure and uncorrupt, in proportion as Men approach to them by Reaſon, they are tenacious of Purity and Incorruption. But, ſince it is impracticable that their Eſſence, compoſed of ſuch Materials, ſhould be abſolutely pure, it is the Office of Reaſon to endeavour to render it as pure as poſſible.

§. 2. The firſt and higheſt Purity, or Impurity, then, is that which is formed in the Soul But you will not find the Impurity of the Soul and Body to be alike. For what elſe [of Impurity] can you find in the Soul, than that which renders it filthy with regard to its Operations? Now the Operations of the Soul are its Purſuits and Avoidances, its Deſires, Averſions, Preparations, Intentions, Aſſents. What then is that which renders it defiled and impure in theſe Operations? Nothing elſe than its perverſe Judgments. So that the Impurity of the Soul conſiſts in wicked Principles; and its Purification in the forming right Prin-

Principles; and that is pure which hath right Principles; for that alone is unmixed and undefiled in its Operations.

§. 3. Now we ſhould, as far as poſſible, endeavour after ſomething like this in the Body too. It is impoſſible but, in ſuch a Compoſition as Man, there muſt be a Defluxion of Rheum. For this Reaſon, Nature hath made Hands, and the Noſtrils themſelves as Channels to let out the Moiſture. If any one therefore ſnuffs it up again, I ſay, that he performs not the Operation of a Man. It was impoſſible, but that the Feet muſt be bemired and ſoiled from what they paſs through. Therefore Nature hath prepared Water and Hands. It was impoſſible, but that ſome Filth muſt cleave to the Teeth from Eating. Therefore, ſhe ſays, waſh your Teeth. Why? That you may be a Man, and not a wild Beaſt, or a Swine. It was impoſſible, but, from Perſpiration, and the Preſſure of the Clothes, ſomething dirty, and neceſſary to be cleaned, ſhould remain upon the Body. For this, there is Water, Oil, Hands, Towels, Bruſhes, Sope, and other neceſſary Apparatus, for its Purification.——No: a Smith indeed will get the Ruſt off his Iron, and have proper Inſtruments for that Purpoſe: and you yourſelf will have your Plates waſhed before you eat; unleſs you are quite dirty and ſlovenly: but you will not waſh nor purify your Body.——"Why ſhould I?" (ſay you.)——I tell you again, in the firſt place, that you may be like a Man; and, in the next, that you may not offend thoſe with whom you converſe. * * * (*a*) Without being ſenſible of it, you do ſomething like this. Do you think you deſerve to ſtink? Be it ſo. But do thoſe deſerve [to ſuffer by] it who

(*a*) Something here ſeems to be loſt. Or, perhaps, the Words, *without being ſenſible of it, you do ſomething like this,* ought to be inſerted after, *neglected him.*

sit near you? who are placed at a Table with you? Who salute you? Either go into a Desert, as you deserve, or live solitary at Home, and smell yourself: for it is fit you should enjoy your Nastiness alone. But, to what Sort of Character doth it belong, to live in a City, and behave so carelessly and inconsiderately? If Nature had trusted even a Horse to your Care, would you have overlooked and neglected him? Now consider your Body as committed to you, instead of a Horse. Wash (*b*) it, rub it, take care that it may not be any one's Aversion, nor disgust any one. Who is not more disgusted at a stinking, unwholesome-looking Sloven, than at a Person who hath been rolled in Filth? The Stench of the one is adventitious from without; but that which arises from Want of Care, is a Kind of inward Putrefaction.——"But "*Socrates* bathed but seldom."——But his Person looked clean, and was so agreeable and pleasing, that the most beautiful and noble Youths were fond of him, and desired rather to sit by him, than by those who had the finest Persons. He might have omitted both Bathing and Washing, if he had pleased; and yet Bathing, though seldom, had its Effect.——"But *Aristophanes* calls him, one of the "*squalid slip-shod Philosophers.*"——Why, so he says too, that he walked in the Air, and stole Clothes from the *Palæstra.* Besides, all who have written of *Socrates*, affirm quite the contrary; that he was not only agreeable in his Conversation, but in his Person too. And, again, they write the same of *Diogenes.* For we ought not to fright the World from Philosophy, by the Appearance of our Person;

(*b*) Here, probably, should be added——if you do not chuse warm Water, with cold. These Words in the *Greek* are transferred to a Place, where they are absolutely unintelligible. They were, probably, at first, omitted by chance; then supplied at the Bottom of the Page; and then transcribed, as if that had been their proper Place.

Perſon; but to ſhow ourſelves chearful and eaſy, by the Care of our Perſons (*c*), as well as by other Marks. "See, all of you, that I have nothing; "that I want nothing. Without Houſe, without "City, and an Exile, (if that happens to be the "Caſe (*d*),) and without a Home, I live more ea-"ſily and proſperouſly than the Noble and Rich. "Look upon my Perſon too, that it is not injured "by coarſe Fare."——But, if any one ſhould tell me this, with the Habit and the Viſage of a condemned Criminal, what God ſhould perſuade me to come near Philoſophy, while (*e*) it renders Men ſuch Figures? Heaven forbid! I would not do it, even if I was ſure to become a wiſe Man for my Pains. I declare, for my own Part, I would rather that a young Man, on his firſt Inclination to Philoſophy, ſhould come to me finically dreſſed, than with his Hair ſpoiled and dirty. For there appears in him ſome Idea of Beauty, and Deſire of Decency: and where he imagines it to be, there he applies his Endeavours. One hath nothing more to do, but to point it out to him, and ſay, "You "ſeek Beauty, young Man; and you do well. Be "aſſured then, that it ſprings from the rational "Part of you. Seek it there, where the Purſuits "and Avoidances, the Deſires and Averſions, are "concerned. Herein conſiſts your Excellence: "but the paultry Body is by Nature Clay. Why "do you trouble yourſelf, to no Purpoſe, about "it? You will be convinced by Time, if not o-"therwiſe, that it is nothing." But, if he ſhould come to me bemired, dirty, with Whiſkers down to his Knees, what can I ſay to him? By what Si-

 militude

(*c*) In Times of Mourning or Danger, the Antients expreſſed their Senſe of their Situation by neglecting their Perſons.

(*d*) As it was the Caſe of *Diogenes*.

(*e*) For ὥστε, perhaps, ἔστε may be the true Reading; and it is ſo tranſlated.

militude allure him? For what hath he studied, which hath any Resemblance to Beauty, that I may transfer his Attention, and say, that Beauty is not there, but here? Would you have me tell him, that Beauty doth not consist in Filth, but in Reason? For hath he any Desire of Beauty? Hath he any Appearance of it? Go, and argue with a Hog, not to roll in the Mire.

§. 4. It was in the Quality of a young Man that loved Beauty, that *Polemo* (*f*) was touched by the Discourses of *Xenocrates*. For he entered with some Incentives to the Study of Beauty, though he sought in the wrong Place. And indeed Nature hath not made the very Brutes dirty, which live with Man. Doth a Horse wallow in the Mire? Or a good Dog? But Swine, and filthy Geese, and Worms, and Spiders, which are banished to the greatest Distance from human Society. Will you then, who are a Man, chuse not to be even one of the Animals, that are conversant with Man; but rather a Worm, or a Spider? Will you not bathe sometimes, be it in whatever Manner you please? Will you never use Water to wash yourself? Will you not come clean, that they who converse with you may have some Pleasure in you? But will you accompany us, a mere Lump of Nastiness, even to the Temples; where it is not lawful for any one so much as to spit, or blow his Nose?

§. 5. What then, would any body have you dress yourself out to the utmost? By no means; except in those Things where our Nature requires it; in Reason, Principles, Actions: but, in our Persons, only as far as Neatness, as far as not to give Offence. But if you hear, that it is not right to wear Purple, you must go, I suppose, and roll your Cloke in the Mud, or tear it.—— " But where " should

(*f*) See p. 198. Note (*e*).

"ſhould I have a fine Cloke?"——You have Water, Man; waſh it.———"What an amiable (g) "Youth is here? How worthy this old Man, to "love, and be loved!"——A fit Perſon to be truſted with the Inſtruction of our Sons and Daughters, and attended by young People, as Occaſion may require,——to read them Lectures on a Dung-hill! Every Deviation proceeds from ſomething human: but this approaches very nearly towards being not human.

CHAPTER XII.

Of Attention.

§. 1. WHEN you let go your Attention for a little while, do not fancy you may recover it when-ever you pleaſe: but remember this, That, by means of the Fault of To-day, your Affairs muſt neceſſarily be in a worſe Condition for the future. Firſt, what is the ſaddeſt Thing of all, a Habit ariſes of not attending; and then a Habit of deferring the Attention, and always driving (a) off from time to time, and procraſtinating a proſperous Life, a Propriety of Behaviour, and the Thinking and Acting conformably to Nature. Now, if the Procraſtination of any thing is advantageous, the abſolute Omiſſion of it is ſtill more advantageous: but, if it be not advantageous, why do not you preſerve a conſtant Attention?——"I would "play To-day."——What then? Ought you not to do it, with proper Attention to yourſelf?—— "I would ſing."———Well: and what forbids but that you may ſing, with Attention to yourſelf? For

(g) The Youth, probably, means the Scholar, who neglects Neatneſs; and the old Man, the Tutor, that gives him no Precept or Example of it.

(a) Ειωθει, perhaps, ſhould be ωθειται.

For there is no Part of Life exempted, to which Attention doth not extend. For will you do it the worſe by attending, and the better by not attending? What elſe in Life is beſt performed by inattentive People? Doth a Smith forge the better by not attending? Doth a Pilot ſteer the ſafer by not attending? Or is any other, even of the minuteſt Operations, performed the better by Inattention? Do not you perceive, that, when you have let your Mind looſe, it is no longer in your Power to call it back, either to Propriety, or Modeſty, or Moderation? But you do every thing as it happens: you follow your Inclinations.

§. 2. To what then am I to attend?

Why, in the firſt Place, to thoſe univerſal Maxims, which you muſt always have at hand; and not ſleep, or get up, or drink, or eat, or converſe without them: that no one is the Maſter of another's Choice; and it is in Choice alone that Good and Evil conſiſt. No one therefore is the Maſter either to procure me any Good, or to involve me in any Evil: but I alone have the Diſpoſal of myſelf, with regard to theſe Things. Since theſe then are ſecured to me, what need have I to be troubled about Externals? What Tyrant is formidable? What Diſtemper? What Poverty? What Offence?——"I have not pleaſed ſuch a one."——Is he my Concern then? Is he my Conſcience?—"No."——Why do I trouble myſelf any further about him then?——"But he is thought to be of "ſome Conſequence."——Let him look to that, and they who think him ſo. But I have One, whom I muſt pleaſe, to whom I muſt ſubmit, whom I muſt obey; God, and thoſe (*b*) who are next Him. He hath entruſted me with myſelf, and made

(*b*) The tutelar Genius, and Fortune. Of the former, ſee B. I. ch. 14. §. 2. Of both, ſee B. IV. ch. 4. §. 4. By changing και τοις into και τοι, the Tranſlation will be; *But, next to Him, He hath intruſted me with myſelf.*

made my Choice subject to myself alone, having given me Rules for the right Use of it. If I follow the proper Rules in Syllogisms, in convertible Propositions, I do not regard, nor care for any one, who says any thing contrary to them. Why then am I vext at being censured in Matters of greater Consequence? What is the Reason of this Perturbation? Nothing else, but that in this Instance I want Exercise. For every Science despises Ignorance, and the Ignorant; and not only the Sciences, but even the Arts. Take any Shoemaker, take any Smith you will, and he laughs at the rest of the World, with regard to his own Business.

§. 3. In the first place then, these are the Maxims we must have ready, and do nothing without them; but direct the Soul to this Mark, to pursue nothing external, nothing that belongs to others, but as He, who hath the Power, hath appointed: Things dependent on Choice are to be pursued always; and the rest, as it is permitted. Besides this, we must remember, who we are, and what Name we bear, and endeavour to direct the several Offices of Life to the rightful Demands of its several Relations: what is the proper Time for Singing, what for Play, in what Company: what will be the Consequence of our Performance: whether our Companions will despise us, or we ourselves: when to employ Raillery, and whom to ridicule: upon what Occasions to comply, and with whom; and then, in complying, how to preserve our own Character.

§. 4. Where-ever you deviate from any of these Rules, the Damage is immediate; not from any thing external, but from the very Action itself.— "What then, is it possible, by these Means, to be "faultless!" Impracticable: but this is possible, to use a constant Endeavour to be faultless. For we shall have Cause to be satisfied, if, by never remitting this Attention, we shall be exempt at least

from

from a few Faults. But now, when you ſay, I will begin to attend To-morrow; be aſſured, it is the ſame Thing as if you ſay, "I will be ſhameleſs, "impertinent, baſe, To-day: it ſhall be in the "Power of others to grieve me: I will be paſſionate, "I will be envious To-day." See to how many Evils you give yourſelf up.——"But all will be "well To-morrow."——How much better To-day? If it be for your Intereſt To-morrow, much more To-day, that it may be in your Power To-morrow too, and that you may not defer it again to the third Day.

CHAPTER XIII.

Concerning Such as readily diſcover their own Affairs.

§. 1. WHEN any one appears to us to diſcourſe frankly of his own Affairs, we too are ſome Way induced to diſcover our Secrets to him; and we ſuppoſe this to be acting with Frankneſs. Firſt, becauſe it ſeems unfair, that, when we have heard the Affairs of our Neighbour, we ſhould not, in return, communicate ours to him; and, beſides, we think, that we ſhall not appear of a frank Character in concealing what belongs to ourſelves. Indeed it is often ſaid, "I have "told you all my Affairs; and will you tell me "none of yours? Where do People act thus?" Laſtly, it is ſuppoſed, that we may ſafely truſt him who hath already truſted us: for we imagine, that he will never diſcover our Affairs, for fear we, in our Turn, ſhould diſcover his. It is thus that the Inconſiderate are caught by the Soldiers at *Rome.* A Soldier ſits by you, in a common Dreſs, and begins to ſpeak ill of *Cæſar.* Then you, as if you had received a Pledge of his Fidelity, by his firſt beginning the Abuſe, ſay likewiſe what you think; and ſo you are led away in Chains to Execution.

§. 2.

§. 2. Something like this is the Caſe with us in general. But when one hath ſafely intruſted his Secrets to me, ſhall I, in Imitation of him, truſt mine to any one who comes in my Way? The Caſe is different. I indeed hold my Tongue, (ſuppoſing me to be of ſuch a Diſpoſition) but he goes, and diſcovers them to every body: and then, when I come to find it out, if I happen to be like him, from a Deſire of Revenge, I diſcover his; and aſperſe, and am aſperſed. But, if I remember, that one Man doth not hurt another, but that every one is hurt and profited by his own Actions, I indeed keep to this, not to do any thing like him: yet, by my own talkative Folly, I ſuffer what I do ſuffer.

§. 3. "Ay: but it is unfair, when you have "heard the Secrets of your Neighbour, not to com-"municate any thing to him, in return."——Why, did I aſk you to do it, Sir? Did you tell me your Affairs, upon Condition that I ſhould tell you mine, in return? If you are a Blab, and believe all you meet to be Friends, would you have *me* too become like you? But, what if the Caſe be this: that you did right in truſting your Affairs to *me*, but it is not right that I ſhould truſt *you?* Would you have me run headlong, and fall? This is juſt as if I had a ſound Barrel, and you a leaky one: and you ſhould come and depoſite your Wine with me to put it into my Barrel; and then ſhould take it ill, that, in my Turn, I did not truſt you with my Wine. No. You have a leaky Barrel. How then are we any longer upon equal Terms? You have depoſited your Affairs with an honeſt Man, and a Man of Honour; one who eſteems his own Actions alone, and nothing external, to be either hurtful or profitable. Would you have me depoſite mine with you; a Man who have diſhonoured your own Faculty of Choice, and who would get a paultry Sum, or a Poſt of Power or Preferment at

Court,

Court, even if, for the Sake of it, you were to kill your own Children, like *Medea?* Where is the Equality of this? But show me, that you are faithful; a Man of Honour, steady; show me, that you have friendly Principles; show me, that your Vessel is not leaky; and you shall see, that I will not stay till you have trusted your Affairs to me; but I will come and intreat you to hear an Account of mine. For who would not make use of a good Vessel? Who despises a benevolent and friendly Adviser? Who will not gladly receive one to share the Burden, as it were, of his Difficulties; and, by sharing, to make it lighter?—"Well: "but I trust *you*, and you do not trust *me*."—In the first place, you do not really trust me; but you are a Blab, and therefore can keep nothing in. For, if the former be the Case, trust *only* me. But now, whomever you see at leisure, you sit down by him, and say, "My dear Friend, there is not a "Man in the World that wishes me better, or hath "more Kindness for me, than you; I intreat you "to hear my Affairs." And this you do to those, with whom you have not the least Acquaintance. But, if you do [really] trust me, it is plainly as [thinking me] a Man of Fidelity and Honour; and not because I have told you my Affairs. Let me alone then, till I too am of this Opinion [with regard to You]. Show me, that, if a Person hath told his Affairs to any one, it is a Proof of his being a Man of Fidelity and Honour. For, if this was the Case, I would go about and tell my Affairs to the whole World; if, upon that Account, I should become a Man of Fidelity and Honour. But that is no such Matter; but requires a Person to have no ordinary Principles.

§. 4. If then you see any one taking Pains for Things that belong to others, and subjecting his Choice to them, be assured, that this Man hath a thousand Things to compell and restrain him. He hath

hath no Need of burning Pitch, or the torturing Wheel, to make him tell what he knows; but the Nod of a Girl, for Inſtance, will ſhake his Purpoſe; the Good-will of a Courtier, the Deſire of a public Poſt, of an Inheritance; ten thouſand other Things of that Sort. It muſt therefore be remembered in general, that ſecret Diſcourſes require Fidelity, and a certain Sort of Principles. And where at this Time, are theſe eaſily to be found? Pray let any one ſhow me a Perſon of ſuch a Diſpoſition as to ſay, I trouble myſelf only with thoſe Things which are my own, incapable of Reſtraint, by Nature free. This I eſteem the Eſſence of Good. Let the reſt be as it may happen. It makes no Difference to me.

END *of the* DISCOURSES.

THE ENCHIRIDION, OR MANUAL, OF *EPICTETUS.*

THE

ENCHIRIDION.

I.

OF Things, ſome are in our Power, and others not. In our Power are Opinion, Purſuit, Deſire, Averſion, and in one Word, whatever are our own Actions. Not in our Power, are Body, Property, Reputation, Command, and, in one Word, whatever are not our own Actions.

Now, the Things in our Power are, by Nature, free, unreſtrained, unhindered: But thoſe not in our Power, weak, ſlaviſh, reſtrained, belonging to others. Remember then, that, if you ſuppoſe Things by Nature ſlaviſh, to be free; and what belongs to others, your own; you will be hindered; you will lament; you will be diſturbed; you will find fault both with Gods and Men. But, if you ſuppoſe, that only to be your own, which is your own; and what belongs to others, ſuch as it really is; no one will ever compell you; no one will reſtrain you: you will find fault with no one; you will accuſe no one, you will do no one Thing againſt your Will: no one will hurt you: you will not have an Enemy; for you will suffer no Harm.

Aiming therefore at such great Things, remember, that you must not allow yourself to be carried, even with a slight Tendency, towards the Attainment of the others (*a*): but that you must entirely quit some of them, and for the present postpone the rest. But, if you would both have these, and Command, and Riches, at once, perhaps you will not gain so much as the latter; because you aim at the former too: but you will absolutely fail of the former; by which alone Happiness and Freedom are procured.

Study, therefore, to be able to say to every harsh Appearance, "You are but an Appearance, and "not absolutely the Thing you appear to be." And then examine it by those Rules which you have: and first, and chiefly, by this: Whether it concerns the Things which are in our own Power, or those which are not; and, if it concerns any thing not in our Power, be prepared to say, that it is nothing to *you*.

II.

REMEMBER that *Desire* promises the Attainment of that of which you are desirous; and *Aversion* promises the Avoiding of that to which you are averse: that he who fails of the Object of his Desire, is disappointed: and he who incurs the Object of his Aversion, wretched. If then, you confine your Aversion to those Objects only, which are contrary to that natural Use of your Faculties, which you have in your own Power, you will never incur any thing to which you are averse. But if you are averse to Sickness, or Death, or Poverty, you will be wretched. Remove Aversion, then, from

(*a*) The Translation follows Mr. *Upton's* Conjecture, of ἀλλων for αὐτων.

from all Things that are not in our Power, and transfer it to Things contrary to the Nature of what is in our Power. But, for the present, totally suppress Desire: for, if you desire any of the Things not in our own Power, you must necessarily be disappointed; and of those which are, and which it would be laudable to desire, nothing is yet in your Possession. (*b*) Use only [the requisite Acts] of Pursuit and Avoidance; and even these lightly, and with Gentleness, and Reservation.

III.

WITH regard to whatever Objects either delight the Mind, or contribute to Use, or are loved with fond Affection, remember to tell yourself, of what Nature they are, beginning from the most trifling Things. If you are fond of an Earthen Cup, that it is an Earthen Cup of which you are fond: for thus, if it is broken, you will not be disturbed. If you kiss your Child, or your Wife, that you kiss a Being subject to the Accidents of Humanity; and thus you will not be disturbed, if either of them dies.

IV.

WHEN you are going about any Action, remind yourself of what Nature the Action is. If you are going to bathe, represent to yourself the Things, which usually happen in the Bath: some Persons dashing the Water; some pushing and crowding; others giving abusive Language; and others stealing [the Clothes]. And thus you will more safely go about this Action, if you say to yourself, "I "will now go bathe, and preserve my own Mind in

(*b*) The Sense is, that he, who is only beginning to philosophise, hath yet nothing right within him to desire, or set his Heart upon; therefore, till he hath, he must not set his Heart upon any thing. But in the mean time, he must make use of the *Pursuits* and *Avoidances*; *i. e.* perform the common Actions of Life: but these outward Movements must be cautious and gentle; and the inward Movements of Desire be quite restrained.

"a State conformable to Nature." And in the ſame manner with regard to every other Action. For thus, if any Impediment ariſes in Bathing, you will have it ready to ſay, "It was not only to "bathe that I deſired, but to preſerve my Mind in a "State conformable to Nature; and I ſhall not "preſerve it ſo, if I am out of Humour at Things "that happen."

V.

Men are diſturbed, not by Things, but by the Principles and Notions, which they form concerning Things. Death, for Inſtance, is not terrible, elſe it would have appeared ſo to *Socrates*. But the Terror conſiſts in our Notion of Death, that it is terrible. When therefore we are hindered, or diſturbed, or grieved, let us never impute it to others, but to ourſelves; that is, to our own Principles. It is the Action of an uninſtructed Perſon to lay the Fault of his own bad Condition upon others; of one entering upon Inſtruction, to lay the Fault on himſelf; and of one perfectly inſtructed, neither on others, nor on himſelf.

VI.

Be not elated on any Excellence not your own. If a Horſe ſhould be elated, and ſay, "I am hand-"ſome," it would be ſupportable. But when you are elated, and ſay, "I have a handſome Horſe," know, that you are elated on what is, in fact, only the Good of the Horſe. (*c*) What then is your own? The Uſe of the Appearances of Things. So that when you behave conformably to Nature, in the Uſe of theſe Appearances, you will be elated with Reaſon; for you will be elated on ſome Good of your own.

VII.

(*c*) The Tranſlation follows Mr. *Upton*'s Correction of the Text in this Chapter.

VII.

As in a Voyage, when the Ship is at Anchor, if you go on Shore, to get Water, you may amuſe yourſelf with picking up a Shell-fiſh, or an Onion, in your Way; but your Thoughts ought to be bent towards the Ship, and perpetually attentive, leſt the Captain ſhould call; and then you muſt leave all theſe Things, that you may not be thrown into the Veſſel, bound Neck and Heels, like a Sheep. Thus likewiſe in Life, if, inſtead of an Onion, or a Shell-fiſh, ſuch a Thing as a Wife or a Child be granted you, there is no Objection: but if the Captain calls, run to the Ship, leave all theſe Things, regard none of them. But, if you are old, never go far from the Ship: leſt, when you are called, you ſhould be unable to come in time.

VIII.

Require not Things to happen as you wiſh; but wiſh them to happen as they do happen; and you will go on well.

IX.

Sickness is an Impediment to the Body, but not to the Faculty of Choice, unleſs itſelf pleaſes. Lameneſs is an Impediment to the Leg, but not to the Faculty of Choice: and ſay this to yourſelf with regard to every thing that happens. For you will find it to be an Impediment to ſomething elſe; but not to yourſelf.

X.

Upon every Accident, remember to turn towards yourſelf, and enquire, what Powers you have for making a proper Uſe of it. If you ſee a handſome Perſon, you will find Continence a Power againſt this: if Pain be preſented to you, you will find Fortitude: if Ill-Language, you will find Patience. And thus habituated, the Appearances of Things will not hurry you away along with them.

XI.

Never say of any thing, "I have lost it;" but, "I have restored it." Is your Child dead? It is restored. Is your Wife dead? She is restored. Is your Estate taken away? Well: and is not that likewise restored? "But he who took it away is a "bad Man." What is it to you, by whose Hands He, who gave it, hath demanded it back again? While He gives you to possess it, take care of it; but as of something not your own, as Passengers do of an Inn.

XII.

If you would improve, lay aside such Reasonings as these. "If I neglect my Affairs, I shall not "have a Maintainance: if I do not correct my Ser-"vant, he will be good for nothing." For it is better to die with Hunger, exempt from Grief and Fear, than to live in Affluence with Perturbation: and it is better your Servant should be bad, than you unhappy.

Begin therefore from little Things. Is a little Oil spilt? A little Wine stolen? Say to yourself, "This is the Purchase paid for Apathy, for Tran-"quillity; and nothing is to be had for nothing." And when you call your Servant, consider, it is possible he may not come at your Call; or, if he doth, that he may not do what you would have him do. But he is by no means of such Importance (*d*), that it should be in his Power to give you any Disturbance.

XIII.

(*e*) If you would improve, be content to be thought foolish and stupid with regard to Externals.

Do

(*d*) Thus some MSS. Changing in others καλως into κακως, the Translation will be——It is not so well with Him, and ill with You.

(*e*) There is a great Likeness to Christian Phrases and Doctrines in this Chapter.

Do not wish to be thought to know any thing; and though you should appear to be somebody to others, distrust yourself. For, be assured, it is not easy at once to preserve your Faculty of Choice in a State conformable to Nature, and [to secure] Externals: but while you are careful about the one, you must of Necessity neglect the other.

XIV.

If you wish your Children, and your Wife, and your Friends, to live for ever, you are stupid: for you wish Things to be in your Power, which are not so; and, what belongs to others, to be your own. So likewise, if you wish your Servant to be without Fault, you are a Fool; for you wish Vice not to be Vice (*f*), but something else. But, if you wish to have your Desires undisappointed, this is in your own Power. Exercise, therefore, what is in your Power. He is the Master of every other Person, who is able to confer, or remove, whatever that Person wishes either to have or to avoid. Whoever then would be free, let him wish nothing, let him decline nothing, which depends on others; else he must necessarily be a Slave.

XV.

Remember that you must behave [in Life] as at an Entertainment (*g*). Is any thing brought round to you? Put out your Hand, and take your Share, with Moderation. Doth it pass by you? Do not stop it. Is it not yet come? Do not stretch forth your Desire towards it, but wait till it reaches you. Thus [do] with regard to Children, to a Wife, to public Posts, to Riches; and you will be some time or other a worthy Partner of the Feasts of the Gods. And if you do not so much as take the Things which are set before you, but are able even to despise

(*f*) *i. e.* dependent on Persons own Choice.

(*g*) An Allusion to the Custom in the antient Entertainments, of carrying round the Dishes to each of the Guests. Upton.

pise them, then you will not only be a Partner of the Feasts of the Gods, but of their Empire also. For, by thus doing, *Diogenes* and *Heraclitus* (*b*), and others like them, deservedly became, and were called, divine.

XVI.

When you see any one weeping for Grief, either that his Son is gone abroad, or dead, or that he hath suffered in his Affairs; take heed, that the Appearance may not hurry you away with it. But immediately make the Distinction within your own Mind; and have it ready to say, "It is not "the Accident [itself] that distresses this Person, "for it doth not distress another Man; but the "Judgment, which he forms concerning it." As far as Words go, however, do not disdain to condescend to him; and even, if it should so happen, to groan with him. Take heed, however, not to groan inwardly too.

XVII.

Remember that you are an Actor in a Drama, of such a Kind as the Author pleases to make it. If short, of a short one; if long, of a long one. If it be his Pleasure you should act a poor Man, a Cripple, a Governor, or a private Person, see that you act it naturally. For this is your Business, to act well the Character assigned you: to chuse it, is another's.

XVIII.

When a Raven happens to croak unluckily, let not the Appearance hurry you away with it: but immediately make the Distinction to yourself; and say, "None of these Things is portended to *me*; "but either to my paultry Body, or Property, or "Reputation, or Children, or Wife. But to *me* "all Portents are lucky, if I will. For which-ever "of

(*b*) For *Heraclitus*, I suspect, should be read *Hercules*.

"of these Things happens, it is in my Power to "derive Advantage from it."

XIX.

You may be unconquerable, if you enter into no Combat, in which it is not in your own Power to conquer. When, therefore, you see any one eminent in Honours, or Power, or in high Esteem on any other Account, take heed not to be hurried away with the Appearance, and to pronounce him happy: for, if the Essence of Good consists in Things in our own Power, there will be no room for Envy, or Emulation. But, for your Part, do not wish to be a General, or a Senator, or a Consul, but [to be] free: and the only way to this, is, a Contempt of Things not in our own Power.

XX.

REMEMBER, that not he who gives Ill Language, or a Blow, affronts; but the Principle, which represents these Things as affronting. When therefore, any one provokes you, be assured, that it is your own Opinion which provokes you. Try, therefore, in the first place, not to be hurried away with the Appearance. For, if you once gain Time and Respite, you will more easily command yourself.

XXI.

LET Death and Exile, and all other Things which appear terrible, be daily before your Eyes; but chiefly Death: and you will never entertain any abject Thought, nor too eagerly covet any thing.

XXII.

IF you have an earnest Desire of attaining to Philosophy, prepare yourself from the very first, to be laughed at, to be sneered by the Multitude, to hear them say, "He is returned to us a Philoso-"pher all at once;" and, "Whence this super-"cilious Look?" Now, for your Part, do not have a supercilious Look indeed; but keep steadily to those Things which appear best to you, as one

one appointed by God to this Station. For remember, that, if you adhere to the same Point, those very Persons who at first ridiculed, will afterwards admire you. But, if you are conquered by them, you will incur a double Ridicule.

XXIII.

If you ever happen to turn your Attention to Externals, so as to wish to please any one, be assured, that you have ruined your Scheme of Life (*i*). Be contented then, in every thing, with being a Philosopher: and, if you wish to be thought so likewise by any one, appear so to yourself, and it will suffice you.

XXIV.

Let not such Considerations as these distress you. "I shall live in Dishonour; and be no-body any-"where." For, if Dishonour is an Evil, you can no more be involved in any Evil by the Means of another, than be engaged in any thing base. Is it any Business of yours then, to get Power, or to be admitted to an Entertainment? By no means. How then, after all, is this a Dishonour? And how is it true, that you will be *no-body any-where*; when you ought to be some-body in those Things only, which are in your own Power, in which you may be of the greatest Consequence? "But my "Friends will be unassisted."——What do you mean by unassisted? They will not have Money from you; nor will you make them *Roman* Citizens. Who told you then, that these are among the Things in our own Power; and not the Affair of others? And who can give to another the Things which he hath not himself? "Well: but get them "then, that we too may have a Share." If I can get them with the Preservation of my own Honour, and

(*i*) *If I yet pleased Men, I should not be the Servant of Christ.* Gal. i. 10.

and Fidelity, and greatneſs of Mind, ſhow me the Way, and I will get them: but, if you require me to loſe my own proper Good, that you may gain what is no Good, conſider how unequitable and fooliſh you are. Beſides: which would you rather have a Sum of Money; or a Friend of Fidelity and Honour? Rather aſſiſt me then to gain this Character, than require me to do thoſe Things by which I may loſe it. Well: but my Country, ſay you, as far as depends upon me, will be unaſſiſted. Here again, what Aſſiſtance is this you mean? "It will not have Porticos, nor Baths, of "your providing." And what ſignifies that? Why, neither doth a Smith provide it with Shoes, or a Shoemaker with Arms. It is enough, if every one fully performs his own proper Buſineſs. And were you to ſupply it with another Citizen of Honour and Fidelity, would not (*k*) he be of Uſe to it? Yes. Therefore neither are you yourſelf uſeleſs to it. "What Place then, ſay you, ſhall I "hold in the State?" Whatever you can hold with the Preſervation of your Fidelity and Honour. But if, by deſiring to be uſeful to that, you loſe theſe, of what Uſe can you be to your Country, when you are become faithleſs, and void of Shame?

XXV.

Is any one preferred before you at an Entertainment, or in a Compliment, or in being admitted to a Conſultation? If theſe Things are good you ought to rejoice, that *he* hath got them: and, if they are evil, do not be grieved, that *you* have not got them. And remember, that you cannot, without uſing the ſame Means [which others do] to acquire Things not in our own Power, expect to be thought worthy of an equal Share of them. For how

(*k*) I have followed the Conjecture of a Friend, who thinks ωφελεις ſhould be ωφελει, to preſerve an Oppoſition between the Perſon ſignified by it, and the συ αυτος in the next Sentence.

how can he, who doth not frequent the Door of any [great] Man, doth not attend him, doth not praiſe him, have an equal Share with him who doth? You are unjuſt then, and unſatiable, if you are unwilling to pay the Price for which theſe Things are ſold, and would have them for nothing. For how much are Lettuces ſold? A Half-penny, for Inſtance. If another then, paying a Half-penny, takes the Lettuces, and you, not paying it, go without them, do not imagine, that he hath gained any Advantage over you. For as he hath the Lettuces, ſo you have the Half-penny, which you did not give. So, in the preſent Caſe, you have not been invited to ſuch a Perſon's Entertainment; becauſe you have not paid him the Price for which a Supper is ſold. It is ſold for Praiſe: it is ſold for Attendance. Give him then the Value, if it be for your Advantage. But, if you would, at the ſame time, not pay the one, and yet receive the other, you are inſatiable, and a Blockhead. Have you nothing then, inſtead of the Supper? Yes indeed you have; the not praiſing him, whom you do not like to praiſe; the not bearing with his Behaviour at coming in *(l)*.

XXVI.

THE Will of Nature may be learned from thoſe Things, in which we do not differ from each other. As, when our Neighbour's Boy hath broken a Cup, or the like, we are preſently ready to ſay, "Theſe "are Things that will happen." Be aſſured then, that, when your own Cup likewiſe is broken, you ought to be affected juſt as when another's Cup was broken. Transfer this, in like manner, to greater Things. Is the Child or Wife of another dead? There is no one who would not ſay, "This "is

(l) Or, according to the Reading in *Simplicius*—the Attendants in his Antechamber.

"is a human Accident." But if any one's (*m*) own Child happens to die, it is presently, "Alas! "how wretched am I!" But it should be remembered, how we are affected in hearing the same Thing concerning others.

XXVII.

As a Mark (*n*) is not set up for the Sake of missing the Aim, so neither doth the Nature of Evil exist in the World.

XXVIII.

If a Person had delivered up your Body to any-one, whom he met in his Way, you would certainly be angry. And do you feel no Shame in delivering up your own Mind to be disconcerted, and confounded by any one, who happens to give you ill Language?

XXIX (*o*).

XXX.

Duties are universally measured by Relations. Is any one a Father? In this are implied, as due, Taking Care of him; submitting to him in all Things; patiently receiving his Reproaches, his Correction. But he is a bad Father. Is your natural Tie then to a *good* Father? No: but to a Father. Is a Brother unjust? Well: preserve your own

(*m*) Natural Affection prompts us to grieve for a Wife or a Child, and to sympathize with the Griefs of others: whence Christianity teaches us *to weep with them who weep:* yet forbidding us, in any Case, to *sorrow as without Hope*. Stoicism carries Truth into Absurdity; while Christian Philosophy makes all Truths coincide, uniting Fortitude with Tenderness and Compassion.

(*n*) Happiness, the Effect of Virtue, is the Mark which God hath set up for us to aim at. Our missing it, is no Work of His; nor so properly any Thing real, as a mere Negative and Failure of our own.

(*o*) This Chapter, except some very trifling Differences, is the same with the Fifteenth of the Third Book of the Discourses; therefore unnecessary to be repeated here.

own Situation towards him. Consider not what *he* doth; but what *you* are to do, to keep your own Faculty of Choice in a State conformable to Nature. For another will not hurt you, unless you please. You will then be hurt, when you *think* you are hurt. In this manner, therefore, you will find, from [the Idea of] a Neighbour, a Citizen, a General, the [corresponding] Duties, if you accustom yourself to contemplate the [several] Relations.

XXXI.

BE assured, that the essential Property of Piety towards the Gods, is, to form right Opinions concerning them, as existing (*p*), and as governing the Universe with Goodness and Justice. And fix yourself in this Resolution, to obey them, and yield to them, and willingly follow them in all Events, as produced by the most perfect Understanding. For, thus you will never find Fault with the Gods, nor accuse them as neglecting you. And it is not possible for this to be effected any other way (*q*), than by withdrawing yourself from Things not in our own Power, and placing Good or Evil in those only which are. For if you suppose any of the Things, not in our own Power, to be either good or evil; when you are disappointed of what you wish, or incur what you would avoid, you must necessarily find fault with, and blame the Authors. For every Animal is naturally formed to fly and abhor Things that appear hurtful, and the Causes of them; and to pursue and admire those which appear beneficial, and the Causes of them. It is impracticable then, that one who supposes himself to be hurt, should rejoice in the Person who, he thinks, hurts him; just as it is impossible to rejoice in the Hurt itself. Hence, also, a Father is reviled by a Son, when he doth not impart to him the Things

(*p*) *He that cometh to God, must believe that He is; and that He is a Rewarder of them that diligently seek Him.* Heb. xi. 6.

(*q*) Αλλως τι, should be αλλως δε.

Things which he takes to be good: and the ſuppoſing Empire to be a Good, made *Polynices* and *Eteocles* mutually Enemies. On this account the Huſbandman, the Sailor, the Merchant; on this account thoſe who loſe Wives and Children, revile the Gods. For where Intereſt is, there too is Piety placed. So that, whoever is careful to regulate his Deſires and Averſions as he ought, is, by the very ſame Means, careful of Piety likewiſe. But it is alſo incumbent on every one to offer Libations, and Sacrifices, and Firſt Fruits, conformably to the Cuſtoms of his Country, with Purity; and not in a ſlovenly manner, nor negligently, nor ſparingly, nor beyond his Ability.

XXXII.

WHEN you have Recourſe to Divination, remember, that you know not what the Event will be, and you come to learn it of the Diviner: but of what Nature it is, you know before you come; at leaſt, if you are a Philoſopher. For if it is among the Things not in our own Power, it can by no means be either good or evil. Do not, therefore, bring either Deſire or Averſion with you to the Diviner, (elſe you will approach him trembling;) but firſt acquire a diſtinct Knowledge, that every Event is indifferent, and nothing to *you*, of whatever Sort it may be; for it will be in your Power to make a right Uſe of it; and this no one can hinder: then come with Confidence to the Gods, as your Counſellors: and afterwards, when any Counſel is given you, remember what Counſellors you have aſſumed; and whoſe Advice you will neglect, if you diſobey. Come to Divination, as *Socrates* preſcribed, in Caſes, of which the whole Conſideration relates to the Event, and in which no Opportunities are afforded by Reaſon, or any other Art, to diſcover the Thing propoſed to be learned. When, therefore, it is our Duty to ſhare the Danger of a Friend, or of our Country, we ought not to conſult

ſult the Oracle, whether we ſhall ſhare it with them, or not. For though the Diviner ſhould forewarn you, that the Victims are unfavourable, this means no more, than that either Death, or Mutilation, or Exile, is portended. But we have Reaſon within us: and it directs, even with theſe Hazards, to ſtand by our Friend and our Country. Attend therefore to the greater Diviner, the *Pythian* God; who caſt out of the Temple, the Perſon who gave no Aſſiſtance to his Friend, while another was murdering him.

XXXIII.

IMMEDIATELY preſcribe ſome Character and Form [of Behaviour] to yourſelf, which you may preſerve, both alone, and in Company.

Be for the moſt part ſilent: or ſpeak merely what is neceſſary, and in few Words. We may, however enter, though ſparingly, into Diſcourſe ſometimes, when Occaſion calls for it: but not on any of the common Subjects, of Gladiators, or Horſe Races, or athletic Champions, or Feaſts; the vulgar Topics of Converſation: but principally not of Men, ſo as either to blame, or praiſe, or make Compariſons. If you are able then, by your own Converſation, bring over that of your Company to proper Subjects: but, if you happen to be taken among Strangers, be ſilent.

Let not your (*r*) Laughter be much, nor on many Occaſions, nor profuſe.

Avoid Swearing, if poſſible, altogether; if not, as far as you are able.

Avoid public and vulgar Entertainments: but, if ever an Occaſion calls you to them, keep your Attention upon the Stretch, that you may not imperceptibly ſlide into vulgar Manners. For be aſſured, that if a Perſon be ever ſo ſound himſelf, yet, if his Companion be infected, he who converſes with him will be infected likewiſe.

Provide

(*r*) See *Eccleſ.* ii. 2. vii. 3—6. *Ecclus.* xix. 30. xxi. 20.

Provide Things relating to the Body no farther than mere Uſe; as Meat, Drink, Cloathing, Houſe, Family. But ſtrike off, and reject, every thing relating to Show and Delicacy.

As far as poſſible, before Marriage, preſerve yourſelf pure from Familiarities with Women: and, if you indulge them, let it be lawfully (*s*). But do not therefore be troubleſome, and full of Reproofs, to thoſe who uſe theſe Liberties; nor frequently boaſt, that you yourſelf do not.

If any one tells you, that ſuch a Perſon ſpeaks ill of you, do not make Excuſes about what is ſaid of you, but anſwer; "He doth not know my other "Faults, elſe he would not have mentioned only "theſe."

It is not neceſſary for you to appear often at public Spectacles: but if ever there is a proper Occaſion for you to be there, do not appear more ſolicitous for any one, than for yourſelf; that is, wiſh Things to be only juſt as they are, and him only to conquer who is the Conqueror: for thus you will meet with no Hindrance. But abſtain entirely from Acclamations, and Deriſion, and violent Emotions. And when you come away, do not diſcourſe a great deal on what hath paſſed, and what doth not contribute to your own Amendment. For it would appear by ſuch Diſcourſe, that you were immoderately ſtruck with the Show.

Go not [of your own Accord] to the Rehearſals of any [Authors], nor appear [at them] readily. But if you do appear, preſerve your Gravity and Sedateneſs, and at the ſame time avoid being moroſe.

 When

(*s*) Public Proſtitutes were allowed by the Laws at *Rome* and in *Greece*. The Miſchiefs, occaſioned by Perſons of this Character, ſcarcely ſo much as hinted by the Stoic Philoſopher, are the Subject of many beautiful Reflexions in the Book of *Proverbs*.

When you are going to confer with any one, and particularly of those in a superior Station, represent to yourself how *Socrates* (*t*), or *Zeno*, would behave in such a Case, and you will not be at a Loss to make a proper Use of whatever may occur.

When you are going to any of the People in Power, represent to yourself, that you will not find him at home: that you will not be admitted [into the House]: that the Doors [of his Apartment] will not be opened to you: that he will take no Notice of you. If, with all this, it be your Duty to go, bear what happens, and never say [to yourself], "It "was not worth so much." For this is vulgar, and like a Man disconcerted by Externals (*u*).

In Parties of Conversation, avoid a frequent and excessive mention of your own Actions, and Dangers. For, however agreeable it may be to yourself to mention the Risques you have run, it is not equally agreeable to others to hear your Adventures. Avoid, likewise, an Endeavour to excite Laughter. For this is a slippery Point, which may throw you into vulgar Manners: and, besides, may be apt to lessen you in the Esteem of your Acquaintance. Approaches to indecent Discourse are likewise dangerous. Whenever, therefore, any thing of this Sort happens, if there be a proper Opportunity, rebuke him who makes Advances that way: or, at least, by Silence, and Blushing, and a forbidding Look, show yourself to be displeased by such Talk.

XXXIV.

(*t*) It should be observed here, that, the Mind being thus naturally affected by the Thought of imitating a superior Character, Christians enjoy a singular Advantage, in not being left to study and copy the imperfect and faulty Patterns of Persons no way particularly related to them; but having an authentic Delineation of divine Excellence, familiarized to their Apprehensions in Him, who, both in acting and suffering for us, *hath left us an Example, that we should follow his Steps.*

(*u*) A late Editor of the *Enchiridion* hath proposed to read διαπεπληγμενα instead of διαβεβλημενα.

XXXIV.

If you are ſtruck by the Appearance of any promiſed Pleaſure, guard yourſelf againſt being hurried away by it: but let the Affair wait your Leiſure, and procure yourſelf ſome Delay. Then bring to your Mind both Points of Time; that in which you ſhall enjoy the Pleaſure, and that in which you will repent and reproach yourſelf, after you have enjoyed it: and ſet before you, in Oppoſition to theſe, how you will rejoice and applaud yourſelf, if you abſtain. And even, though it ſhould appear to you a ſeaſonable Gratification, take heed, that its enticing, and agreeable, and attractive Force may may not ſubdue you: but ſet in Oppoſition to this, how much better it is, to be conſcious of having gained ſo great a Victory.

XXXV.

When you do any thing from a clear Judgment that it ought to be done, never ſhun the being ſeen to do it, even though the World ſhould make a wrong Suppoſition about it: for, if you do not act right, ſhun the Action itſelf; but, if you do, why are you afraid of thoſe who cenſure you wrongly?

XXXVI.

As the Propoſition, *Either it is Day, or it is Night,* is extremely proper for a disjunctive Argument, but quite improper in a conjunctive one *(w)*: ſo, at a Feaſt, to chuſe the largeſt Share, is very ſuitable to the bodily Appetite, but utterly inconſiſtent with the ſocial Spirit of an Entertainment. When you eat with another, then remember, not only the Value of thoſe Things which are ſet before you, to the Body; but the Value of that Behaviour, which ought to be obſerved towards the Perſon who gives the Entertainment.

(w) The Stoics were ſo fond of Logic, that we muſt not wonder if *Epictetus* took a Simile from thence, which to others muſt appear a ſtrange one.

XXXVII.

If you have assumed any Character above your Strength, you have both made an ill Figure in that, and quitted one which you might have supported.

XXXVIII.

As, in walking, you take care not to tread upon a Nail, or turn your Foot; so likewise take care not to hurt the ruling Faculty of your Mind. And, if we were to guard against this in every Action, we should undertake the Action with the greater Safety.

XXXIX.

The Body is to every one the measure of the Possessions proper for it; as the Foot is of the Shoe. If, therefore, you stop at this, you will keep the Measure: but, if you move beyond it, you must necessarily be carried forward, as down a Precipice: as in the Case of a Shoe, if you go beyond its Fitness to the Foot, it comes first to be gilded, then purple (*x*), and then studded with Jewels. For to that which once exceeds a due Measure, there is no Bound.

XL.

Women from fourteen Years old are flattered with the Title of Mistresses, by the Men. Therefore, perceiving that they are regarded only as qualified to give the Men Pleasure, they begin to adorn themselves; and in that, to place all their Hopes. It is worth while, therefore, to fix our Attention on making them sensible, that they are esteemed for nothing else, but the Appearance of a decent, and modest, and discreet Behaviour (*y*).

XLI.

(*x*) Purple was of high Honour and Price among the Antients.

(*y*) The original Words here, κοσμιαι και αιδημονες εν σωφροσυνη, are almost the same with, εν καταστολη κοσμιω μετα αιδους και σωφροσυνης, 1 Tim. ii. 9.

XLI.

It is a Mark of want of Genius, to ſpend much Time in Things relating to the Body; as, to be long in our Exerciſes, in Eating, and Drinking, and in the Diſcharge of other animal Functions. Theſe ſhould be done incidentally, and ſlightly; and our whole Attention be engaged in the Care of the Underſtanding.

XLII.

When any Perſon doth ill by you, or ſpeaks ill of you, remember that he acts, or ſpeaks, from a Suppoſition of its being his (z) Duty. Now, it is not poſſible, that he ſhould follow what appears right to you, but what appears ſo to himſelf. Therefore, if he judges from a wrong Appearance, He is the Perſon hurt; ſince He too is the Perſon deceived. For, if any one ſhould ſuppoſe a true Propoſition to be falſe, the Propoſition is not hurt; but he who is deceived [about it]. Setting out then from theſe Principles, you will meekly bear a Perſon who reviles you: for you will ſay, upon every Occaſion, "It ſeemed ſo to him."

XLIII.

Every Thing hath two Handles; the one, by which it may be borne; the other, by which it cannot. If your Brother acts unjuſtly, do not lay hold on the Action by the Handle of his Injuſtice; for by that it cannot be borne: but by the Oppoſite, that he is your Brother, that he was brought up

(z) *Epictetus* ſeems, in part, to be miſtaken here. For, perhaps, it is oftener from having no Thought at all about Duty, or preferring Inclination to it, than from having a wrong Notion of it; that Perſons are ſlanderous and injurious: beſides, that wrong Notions often ariſe from Neglect, or Partiality. Suppoſing all bad Actions to proceed intirely from Ignorance, or Miſtake, puts them on a Level, in point of Freedom from Guilt, with good ones. But, ſince many proceed from thence, more or leſs, the Doctrine of this Chapter is, in a conſiderable Degree, right: and, ſo far as it is, very ſtrongly calls to one's Mind that divine Interceſſion—*Forgive them! For they know not what they do!*

up with you: and thus you will lay hold on it, as it is to be borne.

XLIV.

THESE Reasonings are unconnected: "I am "richer than you; therefore I am better:" "I am "more eloquent than you; therefore I am better." The Connexion is rather this: "I am richer than "you; therefore my Property is greater than "yours:" "I am more eloquent than you; there-"fore my Style is better than yours." But *you*, after all, are neither Property, nor Style.

XLV.

DOTH any one bathe (*a*) in a mighty little time? Do not say, that he doth it ill; but, in a mighty little time. Doth any one drink a great Quantity of Wine? Do not say, that he doth ill; but, that he drinks a great Quantity. For, unless you perfectly understand the Principle, [from which any one acts], how should you know, if he acts ill? Thus you will not run the Hazard of assenting to any Appearances, but such as you fully comprehend.

XLVI.

NEVER call yourself a Philosopher; nor talk a great deal among the Unlearned about Theorems; but act conformably to them. Thus, at an Entertainment, do not talk how Persons ought to eat; but eat as you ought. For remember, that in this manner *Socrates* also universally avoided all Ostentation. And when Persons came to him, and desired to be recommended by him to Philosophers, he took and recommended them: so well did he bear being overlooked. So that if ever any Talk should happen among the Unlearned, concerning [philosophic] Theorems, be you, for the most part silent. For there is great Danger in immediately throwing out what you have not digested. And, if any one tells you, that you know nothing, and you are not nettled at it, then you may be sure, that you have begun your

(*a*) See B. IV. c. 8. of the Discourses.

your Business. For Sheep do not throw up the Grass, to show Shepherds how much they have eaten: but, inwardly digesting their Food, they outwardly produce Wool, and Milk. Thus, therefore, do you likewise, not show Theorems to the Unlearned; but the Actions produced by them, after they have been digested.

XLVII.

WHEN you have brought yourself to supply the Necessities of your Body, at a small Price, do not pique yourself upon it: nor, if you drink Water, be saying upon every Occasion, "I drink Water." But first consider, how much more sparing and patient of Hardship the Poor are, than we. But if at any time you would enure yourself by Exercise to Labour, and bearing hard Trials, [do it] for your own Sake, and not for the World: do not grasp (*b*) Statues; but, when you are violently thirsty, take a little cold Water in your Mouth, and spurt it out, and tell no body.

XLVIII.

THE Condition and Characteristic of a Vulgar Person is, that he never expects either Benefit or Hurt from himself; but from Externals. The Condition and Characteristic of a Philosopher is, that he expects all Hurt and Benefit from himself. The Marks of a Proficient are, that he censures no one, praises no one, blames no one, accuses no one; says nothing concerning himself as being any body, or knowing any thing: when he is, in any Instance, hindered, or restrained, he accuses himself; and, if he is praised, he secretly laughs at the Person who praises him; and, if he is censured, he makes no Defence. But he goes about with the Caution of infirm People [after Sickness, or an Accident], dreading to move any thing that is set right, before it is perfectly fixed. He suppresses (*c*) all Desire in himself:

(*b*) See B. III. c. 12. of the Discourses.

(*c*) See c. 2. Note (*b*).

himſelf: he transfers his Averſion to thoſe Things only, which thwart the proper Uſe of our own Faculty of Choice: the Exertion of his active Powers towards any thing is very gentle: if he appears ſtupid, or ignorant, he doth not care; and, in a word, he watches himſelf as an Enemy, and one in Ambuſh.

XLIX.

WHEN any one ſhows himſelf vain, on being able to underſtand and interpret the Works of *Chryſippus*, ſay to yourſelf, "Unleſs *Chryſippus* had written obſcurely, this Perſon would have had no Subject for his Vanity. But what do *I* deſire? To underſtand Nature, and follow her. I aſk then, who interprets her; and, finding *Chryſippus* doth, I have Recourſe to him. I do not underſtand his Writings. I ſeek therefore one to interpret *them*." So far there is nothing to value myſelf upon. And when I find an Interpreter, what remains is, to make uſe of his Inſtructions. This alone is the valuable Thing. But, if I admire nothing but merely the Interpretation, what do I become more than a Grammarian, inſtead of a Philoſopher? Except, indeed, that, inſtead of *Homer*, I interpret *Chryſippus*. When any one therefore deſires me to read *Chryſippus* to him, I rather bluſh, when I cannot ſhow my Actions agreeable, and conſonant to his Diſcourſe.

L.

WHATEVER Rules you have deliberately propoſed to yourſelf [for the Conduct of Life,] abide by them, as ſo many Laws, and as if you would be guilty of Impiety in tranſgreſſing any of them: and do not regard what any one ſays of you; for this, after all, is no Concern of yours. How long then will you defer to think yourſelf worthy of the nobleſt Improvements, and, in no Inſtance, to tranſgreſs the Diſtinctions of Reaſon? You have received the Philoſophic Theorems, with which you ought

ought to be converſant: and you have been converſant with them. What other Matter then do you wait for, to throw upon that the Delay of reforming yourſelf? You are no longer a Boy; but a grown Man *(d)*. If therefore you will be negligent and ſlothful, and always add Procraſtination to Procraſtination, Purpoſe to Purpoſe, and fix Day after Day, in which you will attend to yourſelf; you will inſenſibly continue without Proficiency, and, living and dying, perſevere in being one of the Vulgar. This Inſtant then think yourſelf worthy of living as a Man grown up, and a Proficient. Let whatever appears to be the beſt, be to you an inviolable Law. And if any Inſtance of Pain, or Pleaſure, or Glory, or Diſgrace be ſet before you, remember, that now is the Combat, now the *Olympiad* comes on, nor can it be put off; and that, by once being worſted, and giving way, Proficiency is loſt, or [by the contrary] preſerved. Thus *Socrates* became perfect, improving himſelf by every thing; (*e*) attending to nothing but Reaſon. And though you are not yet a *Socrates*, you ought however to live as one deſirous of becoming a *Socrates*.

LI.

THE firſt and moſt neceſſary Topic in Philoſophy, is, that of the Uſe of [practical] Theorems; as that, *We ought not to lie:* the ſecond is, that of Demonſtrations; as, *Whence it is, that we ought not to lie:* the third, that which gives Strength and Articulation to the other two; as, *Whence this is a Demonſtration.* For what is Demonſtration? What is

(*d*) The ſame Words, Ανηρ τελειος, in the ſame Senſe, are uſed *Eph.* iv. 13. (where they are oppoſed to νηπιοι, v. 14.) *James* iii. 2. and Ανθρωπος τελειος, *Col.* i. 28. and τελειος, ſingly, 1 *Cor.* ii. 6. *Phil.* iii. 15. *Heb.* v. 14. where it is oppoſed to νηπιος, v. 13. Which Word is uſed alſo, 1 *Cor.* iii. 1. as μειρακιον is here.

(*e*) *Plato*, in his *Crito*, introduces *Socrates* ſaying this of himſelf. UPTON.

is Consequence? What Contradiction? What Truth? What Falshood? The third Topic then is necessary, on the Account of the second: and the second, on the Account of the first. But the most necessary, and that whereon we ought to rest, is the first. But we act just on the contrary. For we spend all our Time on the third Topic, and employ all our Diligence about that, and entirely neglect the first. Therefore, at the same time that we lie, we are mighty ready to show how it is demonstrated, that Lying is not right.

LII.

UPON all Occasions, we ought to have these Maxims ready at hand.

Conduct me, Jove, *and Thou,* O Destiny,
Where-ever Your Decrees have fix'd my Station.
I follow chearfully: and, did I not,
Wicked and wretched, I must follow still (*f*).

Who-e'er yields properly to Fate, is deem'd
Wise among Men, and knows the Laws of Heaven (*g*).

And this Third:

(*h*) "O *Crito*, if it thus pleases the Gods, thus "let it be. *Anytus* and *Melitus* may kill me indeed: but hurt me they cannot."

(*f*) From a Poem of *Cleanthes.*
(*g*) From *Euripides.*
(*h*) From *Plato's Crito,* and *Apology.*

The END *of the* ENCHIRIDION.

FRAGMENTS

OF

EPICTETUS.

FRAGMENTS

OF

EPICTETUS,

FROM

STOBÆUS, ANTONIUS, *and* MAXIMUS (*a*).

I.

A LIFE entangled with Fortune, resembles a wintry Torrent: for it is turbulent, and muddy, and difficult to pass, and violent and noisy, and of short Continuance.

A Soul

(*a*) According to *Fabricius*, in his *Bibliotheca Græca*, L. V. c. 30. *Stobæus* was a Heathen: at least, he cites only Heathen Authors. He lived about the Beginning of the Fifth Century. *Maximus* was a Christian, of the Seventh; and *Antonius*, surnamed *Melissa*, or the Bee, of the Eighth Century, or later; some say, of the Twelfth. Their Collections are printed together. The Editions of *Stobæus* are extremely incorrect: and in him and *Maximus*, the Names of the Authors quoted, either were frequently wrong originally, or have been altered since. This may have happened to *Antonius* also: and, consequently, some of the Sayings ascribed to *Epictetus* may not have been his. Indeed, many of these Fragments have very little the Turn of his other Discourses. The two first, particularly, have a much stronger Resemblance of the Style and Manner of *M. Antoninus*.

A Soul converſant with Virtue, reſembles a perpetual Fountain: for it is clear, and gentle, and potable, and ſweet, and communicative, and rich, and harmleſs, and innocent.

II.

If you would be good, firſt believe that you are bad.

III.

It is better to offend ſeldom (owning it when we do), and act often wiſely, than to ſay, we ſeldom err, and offend frequently.

IV.

Chastise your Paſſions, that they may not puniſh you.

V.

Be not ſo much aſhamed of what is void of Glory, as ſtudious to ſhun what is void of Truth.

VI.

If you would be well ſpoken of, learn to ſpeak well of others. And, when you have learned to ſpeak well of them, endeavour likewiſe to do well to them; and thus you will reap the Fruit of being well ſpoken of by them.

VII.

Freedom is the Name of Virtue; and Slavery, of Vice: and both theſe are Actions of Choice. But neither of them belongs to Things, in which Choice hath no Share. But Fortune (b) is accuſtomed to diſpoſe at her Pleaſure of the Body, and thoſe Things relating to the Body in which Choice hath no Share. For no one is a Slave, whoſe Choice is free. Fortune is an evil Chain to the Body; and Vice, to the Soul. For he whoſe Body is unbound, and whoſe Soul is chained, is a Slave. On the contrary, he whoſe Body is chained, and his Soul unbound, is free. The Chain of the Body, Nature unbinds by Death; and Vice, by (c) Money: the Chain

(b) The Senſe abſolutely requires, that ψυχη ſhould be τυχη; and it is ſo tranſlated.

(c) Perhaps, by bringing a Judge, or a Jailer. However, the Senſe is not clear.

Chain of the Soul, Virtue unbinds, by Learning, and Experience, and philoſophic Exerciſe.

VIII.

If you would live with Tranquillity and Content, endeavour to have all who live with you, good. And you will have them good, by inſtructing the Willing, and diſmiſſing the Unwilling (*d*). For together with the Fugitives, will Wickedneſs and Slavery fly: and with thoſe who remain with you, will Goodneſs and Liberty be left.

IX.

(*e*) It is ſcandalous, that he who ſweetens his Drink by the Gifts of the Bees, ſhould, by Vice, embitter Reaſon, the Gift of the Gods.

X.

No one, who is a Lover of Money, a Lover of Pleaſure, or a Lover of Glory, is likewiſe a Lover of Mankind: but only he who is a Lover of Virtue.

XI.

As you would not wiſh to ſail in a large, and finely decorated, and gilded Ship, and ſink: ſo neither is it eligible to inhabit a grand and ſumptuous Houſe, and be in a Storm [of Paſſions and Cares].

XII.

When we are invited to an Entertainment, we take what we find: and, if any one ſhould bid the Maſter of the Houſe ſet Fiſh, or Tarts, before him, he would be thought abſurd. Yet, in the World, we aſk the Gods for what they do not give us; and that, though they have given us ſo many Things.

(*d*) The Tranſlation omits επειτα κεχειρωμενους, which is in *Antonius* and *Maximus*, but not in *Stobæus*.

(*e*) This Sentence is aſcribed to *Pythagoras*, by *Antonius* and *Maximus de rationali. Serm.* 27. p. 75.

XIII.

THEY are pretty Fellows indeed, ſaid he, who value themſelves on Things not in our own Power. I am a better Man than you, ſays one; for I have many Eſtates, and you are pining with Hunger. I have been Conſul, ſays another: I am a Governor, a third; and I have a fine Head of Hair, ſays a fourth. Yet one Horſe doth not ſay to another, "I am better than you; for I have a great "deal of Hay, and a great deal of Oats; and I "have a Gold Bridle, and embroidered Trap"pings:" but, "I am ſwifter than you." And every Creature is better or worſe, from its own good or bad Qualities. Is Man, then, the only Creature, which hath no natural good Quality? And muſt we conſider Hair, and Clothes, and Anceſtors, [to judge of him]?

XIV.

PATIENTS are diſpleaſed with a Phyſician, who doth not preſcribe to them; and think he gives them over. And why are none ſo affected towards a Philoſopher, as to conclude, he deſpairs of their Recovery to a right Way of Thinking, if he tells them nothing, which may be for their Good?

XV.

THEY who have a good Conſtitution of Body, ſupport Heats and Colds: and ſo they, who have a right Conſtitution of Soul, bear [the Attacks of] Anger, and Grief, and immoderate Joy, and the other Paſſions.

XVI.

EXAMINE yourſelf, whether you had rather be rich, or happy: and, if rich, be aſſured, that this is neither a Good, nor altogether in your own Power: but, if happy, that this is both a Good, and in your own Power: ſince the one is a temporary Loan of Fortune (*f*), and the other depends on Choice.

XVII.

(*f*) Τῆς εὐδαιμονίας ſeems to be merely an Interpolation, and is omitted in the Tranſlation.

XVII.

As when you ſee a Viper, or an Aſp, or a Scorpion, in an Ivory or Gold Box, you do not love, or think it happy, on Account of the Magnificence of the Materials, in which it is incloſed; but ſhun and deteſt it, becauſe it is of a pernicious Nature: ſo likewiſe, when you ſee Vice lodged in the midſt of Wealth, and the ſwelling Pride of Fortune, be not ſtruck by the Splendour of the Materials, with which it is ſurrounded; but deſpiſe the baſe Alloy of its Manners.

XVIII.

RICHES are not among the Number of Things, which are good: Prodigality is of the Number of thoſe, which are evil: Rightneſs of Mind, of thoſe which are good. Now Rightneſs of Mind invites to Frugality, and the Acquiſition of Things that are good: but Riches invite to Prodigality, and ſeduce from Rightneſs of Mind. It is difficult therefore for a rich Perſon to be right-minded; or a right-minded Perſon, rich (g).

XIX.

(h)——JUST as if you had been bred and born in a Ship, you would not *be* eager to become the Pilot. For neither would the Ship have any natural and perpetual Connexion (i) with you there; nor have Riches here; but Reaſon every where. That therefore, which is natural and congenial to you, Reaſon, think likewiſe to be in a peculiar Manner your own, and take care of it.

(g) *How hardly ſhall they that have Riches, enter into the Kingdom of God!* Mark x. 23.

(h) The former Part of the Sentence ſeems to be wanting; in which, probably, the Author had ſaid, That they who have hereditary Wealth, ſhould not think the Management of it their chief Concern: juſt as, *&c.*

(i) Συνεϛα ſhould, perhaps, be συνηπται.

XX.

If you were born in *Persia*, you would not endeavour to live in *Greece*; but to be happy in the Place where you are. Why then, if you are born in Poverty, do you endeavour to be rich, and not to be happy in the Condition where you are?

XXI.

As it is better to lie straitened for Room upon a little Couch in Health, than to toss upon a wide Bed in Sickness; so it is better to contract yourself within the Compass of a small Fortune, and be happy, than to have a great one, and be wretched.

XXII.

It is not Poverty that causes Sorrow; but covetous (*k*) Desires: nor do Riches deliver from Fear; but Reasoning. If, therefore, you acquire a Habit of Reasoning, you will neither desire Riches, nor complain of Poverty.

XXIII.

A Horse is not elated, and doth not value himself on his fine Manger or Trappings, or Saddle-cloths; nor a Bird, on the warm Materials of its Nest: but the former, on the Swiftness of his Feet; and the latter, of its Wings. Do not you, therefore, glory in your Eating, or Dress; or, briefly, in any external Advantage; but in Good nature and Beneficence.

XXIV.

There is a Difference between living well, and living profusely. The one arises from Contentment, and Order, and Decency, and Frugality: the other from Dissoluteness, and Luxury, and Disorder, and Indecency. In short, to the one belongs true Praise; to the other, Censure. If, therefore, you would live well, do not seek to be praised for Profuseness:

XXV.

(*k*) The *Latin* Translator supposes, that ευθυμια should be επιθυμια, which the Sense requires.

XXV.

LET the first satisfying of Appetite be always the Measure to you of eating and drinking; and Appetite itself the Sawce and the Pleasure. Thus you will never take more [Food] than is necessary, nor will you want Cooks: and you will be contented with whatever Drink falls in your Way (*l*).

XXVI.

BE careful not to (*m*) thrive by the Meats in your Stomach; but by Chearfulness in the Soul. For the former, as you see, are evacuated, and carried off together; but the latter, though the Soul be (*n*) separated, remains uncorrupted, and sincere.

XXVII.

IN every Feast remember, that there are two Guests to be entertained, the Body, and the Soul: and that what you give the Body, you presently lose; but what you give the Soul, remains for ever.

XXVIII.

DO not mix Anger with Profusion, and set them before your Guests. Profusion makes its Way through the Body, and is quickly gone: but Anger, when it hath penetrated the Soul, abides for a long Time. Take care, not to be transported with Anger, and affront your Guests, at a great Expence; but rather delight them at a cheap Rate, by gentle Behaviour.

 XXIX.

(*l*) I have not translated the Fragment which follows this in Mr. *Upton*; because I do not understand it.

(*m*) There are various Readings of this Fragment; but none which makes the Sense very clear.

(*n*) It is doubtful whether the Meaning be, that the Effect of a chearful Behaviour will remain after the Person is dead, or after he is separated from the Company.

XXIX.

Take care at your Meals, that the Attendants be not more in Number than those whom they are to attend. For it is absurd, that many Persons should wait on a few Chairs.

XXX.

It would be best, if both while you are personally making your Preparations, and while you are feasting at Table, you could give among the Servants Part of what is before you *(o)*. But, if such a Thing be difficult at that Time, remember, that you, who are not weary, are attended by those who are; you, who are eating and drinking, by those who are not; you who are talking, by those who are silent; you who are at Ease, by those who are under Constraint (*p*): and thus you will never be heated into any unreasonable Passion yourself; nor do any Mischief, by provoking another.

XXXI.

Strife and Contention are always absurd; but particularly unbecoming at Table Conversations. For a Person warmed with Wine will never either teach, or be convinced by, one who is sober. And where-ever Sobriety is wanting, the End will show, that you have exerted yourself to no Purpose.

XXXII.

Grashoppers are musical; but Snails are dumb. The one rejoice in being wet; and the others, in being warm. Then the Dew calls out the one; and for this they come forth: but, on the contrary, the Noon-day Sun awakens the other; and in this they sing. If, therefore, you would be

(*o*) *Gesner*, for κυβερνας, reads κοινωνεις, which seems the best Sense, and is followed in the Translation.

(*p*) There is something strikingly beautiful and humane in this Consideration about Servants.

be a muſical and harmonious Perſon, whenever, in Parties of Drinking, the Soul is bedewed with Wine, ſuffer her not to go forth, and defile herſelf. But when, in Parties of Converſation, ſhe glows by the Beams of Reaſon, then command her to ſpeak from Inſpiration, and utter the Oracles of Juſtice.

XXXIII.

CONSIDER him, with whom you converſe, in one of theſe three Ways; either as ſuperior to you [in Abilities], or inferior, or equal. If ſuperior, you ought to hear him, and be convinced: if inferior, to convince (*q*) him: if equal, to agree with him: and thus you will never be found guilty of Litigiouſneſs.

XXXIV.

IT is better, by yielding to Truth, to conquer Opinion; than by yielding to Opinion, to be defeated by Truth.

XXXV.

IF you ſeek Truth, you will not ſeek to conquer by all poſſible Means: and, when you have found Truth, you will have a Security againſt being conquered.

XXXVI.

TRUTH conquers by itſelf; Opinion, by foreign Aids.

XXXVII.

IT is better, by living with one free Perſon, to be fearleſs, and free, than to be a Slave in Company with many.

XXXVIII.

WHAT you avoid ſuffering yourſelf, attempt not to impoſe on others. You avoid Slavery, for inſtance: take care not to enſlave. For, if you can bear to exact Slavery from others, you appear to have been firſt yourſelf a Slave. For Vice hath no

(*q*) Ἀπειθεῖν, probably, ſhould be πείθειν; and is ſo tranſlated. The α ſeems to have been added from the preceding Word.

no Communication with Virtue; nor Freedom with Slavery. As a Person in Health would not wish to be attended by the Sick, nor to have those who live with him be in a State of Sickness; so neither would a Person who is free, bear to be served by Slaves, or to have those who live with him in a State of Slavery.

XXXIX.

WHOEVER you are, that would live at a Distance from Slaves, deliver yourself from Slavery. And you will be free, if you deliver yourself from [the Power of] Appetite. For neither was *Aristides* called Just, nor *Epaminondas*, Divine, nor *Lycurgus*, a Preserver, because they were rich, and were served by Slaves; but because, being poor, they delivered *Greece* from Slavery.

XL.

IF you would have your House securely inhabited, imitate the *Spartan Lycurgus*. And as he did not inclose his City with Walls, but fortified the Inhabitants with Virtue, and preserved the City always free; so do you likewise: not surround yourself with a great Court-yard, nor raise high Towers; but strengthen those that live with you by Benevolence, and Fidelity, and Friendship. And thus nothing hurtful will enter, even if the whole Band of Wickedness was set in Array against it.

XLI.

DO not hang your House round with Tablets, and Pictures; but adorn it with Sobriety. For those are merely foreign, and a *(a)* fading Deception of the Eyes: but this, a congenial, and indelible, and perpetual Ornament to the House.

XLII.

(r.) In *Stobæus*, the Word is επικουρος. *Gesner*, whom Mr. *Upton* follows, guessed it should be επιηρος. Επικηρος, which the Translation supposes, is a less Alteration, and makes a proper Opposition to what follows.

XLII.

INSTEAD of Herds of Oxen, endeavour to assemble Flocks of Friends about your House.

XLIII.

As a Wolf resembles a Dog, so doth a Flatterer, and an Adulterer, and a Parasite, resemble a Friend. Take heed, therefore, that, instead of Guardian Dogs, you do not inadvertently admit ravening Wolves.

XLIV.

HE is void of true Taste, who strives to have his House admired, by decorating it with a showish Outside: but to adorn our Characters by the Gentleness of a communicative Temper, is at once a Proof of good Taste, and good Nature.

XLV.

IF you admire little Things, in the first Place, you will never (s) be thought to deserve great ones: but, if you despise little Things, you will be greatly admired.

XLVI.

NOTHING is meaner than the Love of Pleasure, the Love of Gain, and Insolence. Nothing is nobler than Magnanimity, Meekness, and Good-nature.

XLVII.

——— PRODUCING the Sentiments of those intractable Philosophers, who do not think [the Enjoyment of] Pleasure to be [in itself] the natural State of Man; but merely an adventitious Circumstance of those Things, in which his natural State consists, Justice, Sobriety, and Freedom. For what manner of Reason then should the Soul rejoice, and feel a Serenity from the lesser Good of the Body, as *Epicurus* says [it doth]; and not be pleased with its own Good, which is the very greatest? And yet Nature hath given me likewise a Sense of Shame: and

(s) Πρωτον μεγαλων αξιωθηση is the Text of *Stobæus*. Mr. *Upton* puts in ουκ, which the Translation follows. Απαξιωθηση is a smaller Change, and the same Sense.

and I am covered with Blushes, when I think I have uttered any indecent Expression. This Emotion will not suffer me to lay down Pleasure as [in itself] a Good, and the End of Life.

XLVIII.

THE Ladies at *Rome* have *Plato's Republic* in their Hands, because he allows a Community of Wives: for they attend merely to the Words of the Author, and not to his Sense. For he doth not first order one Man and one Woman to marry and live together, and then allow a Community of Wives: but he abolishes that kind of Marriage, and introduces one of another kind (*t*). And, in general, Men are pleased in finding out Excuses for their own Faults. Yet Philosophy says, it is not fit even to move a Finger without some Reason.

XLIX.

THE more rarely the Objects of Pleasure occur, the more delightful they are.

L.

WHENEVER any one exceeds Moderation, the most delightful Things may become the most undelightful.

LI.

AGRIPPINUS was justly entitled to Praise on this Account, that, though he was a Man of the highest Worth, he never praised himself; but blushed, even if another praised him. And he was a Man of such a Character, as to write in Praise of every harsh Event that befell him: if he was feverish, of a Fever; if disgraced, of Disgrace; if banished, of Banishment. And, when once, as he was going to dine, a Messenger brought him word, that *Nero* ordered him to Banishment; Well then, says *Agrippinus*, we will dine at *Aricia* (*u*).

LII.

(*t*) This, and other shocking Things in *Plato's Republic*, shew how apt even wise Men are to err, without a Guide.

(*u*) See Discourses, B. I. c. 1.

LII.

DIOGENES affirmed no Labour to be good, unless the End was a due State and Tone of the Soul, and not of the Body.

LIII.

As a true Balance is neither set right by a true one, nor judged by a false one: (*w*) so likewise a just Person is neither set right by just Persons, nor judged by unjust ones.

LIV.

As what is straight hath no need of what is straight, so neither what is just, of what is just, [to assist or amend it].

LV.

Do not give Judgment from another Tribunal, before you have been judged yourself at the Tribunal of Justice (*x*).

LVI.

If you would give a just Sentence, mind neither Parties, nor Pleaders; but the Cause itself.

LVII.

You will commit the fewest Faults in judging, if you are faultless in your own Life.

LVIII.

It is better, by giving a just Judgment, to be (*y*) blamed by him who is deservedly condemned, than by giving an unjust Judgment, to be justly censured by Nature.

LIX.

As the Touch-stone which tries Gold, is not itself tried by the Gold; such is he, who hath the Rule of judging.

LX.

It is scandalous for a Judge to be judged by others.

LXI.

(*w*) Compare this and the next Fragment with 1 *Cor.* ii. 15.
(*x*) See *Rom.* xiv. 10.
(*y*) The Antithesis seems to require, that ἀξίως should be ἀδίκως, and the Translation——unjustly blamed by him, who is condemned.

LXI.

As nothing is ſtraighter than what is ſtraight, ſo nothing is juſter than what is juſt (*z*).

LXII.

WHO among you do not admire the Action of *Lycurgus* the *Lacedemonian*? For when he had been deprived of one of his Eyes, by one of the Citizens, and the People had delivered the young Man to him, to be puniſhed in whatever Manner he ſhould think proper; *Lycurgus* forbore to give him any Puniſhment. But, having inſtructed, and rendered him a good Man, he brought him into the Theatre: and, while the *Lacedemonians* were ſtruck with Admiration; "I received," ſays he, "this "Perſon from you, injurious and violent; and I re-"ſtore him to you gentle, and a good Citizen."

LXIII.

WHEN *Pittacus* had been unjuſtly treated by ſome Perſon, and had the Power of chaſtiſing him, he let him go; ſaying, "Forgiveneſs is better than Pu-"niſhment: for the one is the Proof of a gentle, "the other of a ſavage Nature."

LXIV.

—— But, above all, this is the Buſineſs of Nature, to connect and mutually adapt the Exertion of the active Powers (*a*) to the Appearance of what is fit and beneficial.

LXV.

IT is the Character of the moſt mean-ſpirited and fooliſh Men, to ſuppoſe they ſhall be deſpiſed by others; unleſs, by every Method, they hurt thoſe who are firſt their Enemies (*b*).

LXVI.

(*z*) The Stoics held all Virtues, and all Faults to be equal: and this Fragment is one of their Illuſtrations of that Paradox.

(*a*) The Text has της—φανlασιας; but the true Reading ſeems evidently to be τη φανlασια; and this the Tranſlation follows.

(*b*) Το δε οιεσθαι ευκαταφρονητους τοις αλλοις εσεσθαι, εαν μη τους πρωτους εχθρους παντι τροπω βλαψωμεν, σφοδρα αγεννων και ανοητων ανθρωπων.

LXVI.

WHEN you are going to attack any one with Vehemence and Threatning, remember to say first to yourself, that you are [by Nature] a gentle Animal, and that by doing nothing violent, you shall live without Repentance, and without need of being set right.

LXVII.

WE ought to know, that it is not easy for a Man to form a Principle of Action, unless he daily speaks and hears the same Things, and, at the same time, accommodates them to the Use of Life.

LXVIII.

NICIAS was so intent on Business, that he often asked his Domestics, whether he had bathed, and whether he had dined.

LXIX.

WHILE *Archimedes* was intent on his *Diagrams*, his Servants drew him away by Violence, and anointed (*c*) him, and, after his Body was anointed, he traced his Figures upon *that*.

LXX.

WHEN *Lampis*, the Sea Commander, was asked how he acquired Riches: "A great deal," said he, "without Difficulty, but a little with Labour."

LXXI.

SOLON, when he was silent at an Entertainment, being asked by *Periander*, whether he was silent for want of Words, or from Folly; "No Fool," answered he, "can be silent at a Feast."

LXXII.

ανθρωπων. Φαμεν γαρ τον ευκαταφρονητον, νοεισθαι μεν και κατα το δυνατον ειναι βλαψαι. Αλλα πολυ μαλλον νοειται κατα το δυνατον ειναι ωφελειν.

This is the Whole of the Fragment: of which only the first Part, which is too good to be omitted, is translated. The rest I do not understand.

(*c*) The Ancients anointed the Body every Day.

LXXII.

CONSULT nothing so much, upon every Occasion, as Safety. Now it is safer to be silent, than to speak: and omit speaking whatever is not accompanied with Sense and Reason.

LXXIII.

As Light-houses in Havens, by kindling a great Flame from a few Faggots, afford a considerable Assistance to Ships wandering on the Sea: so an illustrious Person, in a State harrassed by Storms, while he is contented with little himself, confers great Benefits on his Fellow-Citizens.

LXXIV.

——As you would certainly, if you undertook to steer a Ship, learn the Steersman's Art. For it will be in your Power, as in that Case, to steer the whole Ship: so, in this, the whole State.

LXXV.

IF you have a mind to adorn your City by consecrated Monuments, first consecrate in yourself the most beautiful Monument of Gentleness, and Justice, and Benevolence.

LXXVI.

You will confer the greatest Benefits on your City, not by raising the Roofs, but by exalting the Souls [of your Fellow-Citizens]. For it is better, that great Souls should live in small Habitations, than that abject Slaves should burrow in great Houses.

LXXVII.

Do not variegate the Structure of your Walls with *Eubæan* and *Spartan* Stone: but adorn both the Minds of the Citizens, and of those who govern them, by the *Grecian* Education. For Cities are made good Habitations by the Sentiments of those who live in them; not by Wood and Stone.

LXXVIII.

As, if you were to breed Lions, you would not be solicitous about the Magnificence of their Dens, but the Qualities of the Animals [themselves]: so, if if you undertake to preſide over your Fellow-Citizens, be not ſo ſolicitous about the Magnificence of the Buildings, as careful of the Fortitude of thoſe who inhabit them.

LXXIX.

As a ſkilful Manager of Horſes doth not feed the good Colts, and ſuffer the unruly ones to ſtarve; but feeds them both alike; only whips one more, to make him draw equally with his Fellow: ſo a Man of Care, and Skill in the Art of Civil Government, endeavours to do *(d)* Good to the well-diſpoſed Citizens, but not at once to deſtroy thoſe that are otherwiſe. He by no means denies Subſiſtence to either of them: only he diſciplines and urges on, with the greater Vehemence, him who reſiſts Reaſon and the Laws.

LXXX.

As neither a Gooſe is alarmed by Gaggling, nor a Sheep by Bleating, ſo neither be you terrified by the Voice of a ſenſeleſs Multitude.

LXXXI.

As you do not comply with a Multitude, when it injudiciouſly aſks of you any Part of your own Property: ſo neither be diſconcerted by a Mob, when it endeavours to force you to any unjuſt Compliance.

LXXXII.

PAY in, before you are called upon, what is due to the Public, and you will never be aſked for what is not due.

LXXXIII.

As the Sun doth not wait for Prayers and Incantations, to be prevailed on to riſe, but immediately ſhines forth, and is received with univerſal Salutation; ſo neither do you wait for Applauſes, and Shouts, and Praiſes, in order to do Good; but be a vo-

(d) The *Latin* Verſion ſuppoſes that ποιεῖ ſhould be εὐποιεῖ. This the Senſe ſeems to require; and it is ſo tranſlated.

a voluntary Benefactor; and you will be beloved like the Sun (*e*).

LXXXIV.

A SHIP ought not to be fixed by one Anchor; nor Life on a single Hope (*f*).

LXXXV.

WE ought not to stretch either our Legs or our Hopes to a Point they cannot reach.

LXXXVI.

THALES, being asked, what was the most universally enjoyed of all Things, answered, "Hope: "for they have it, who have nothing else."

LXXXVII.

IT is more necessary for the Soul to be cured, than the Body: for it is better to die, than to live ill.

LXXXVIII.

PYRRHO used to say, "There is no Difference "between living and dying." A Person asked him, Why then do not you die? "Because," answered *Pyrrho*, "there is no Difference (*g*)."

LXXXIX.

NATURE is admirable, and, as *Xenophon* says, fond of Life. Hence we love, and take Care of the Body, which is of all Things the most unpleasant and squalid. For if we were obliged, only for five Days, to take care of our Neighbour's Body, we could not support it. For only consider what it would be, when we get up in a Morning, to wash the Teeth of others, and do all requisite Offices besides. In reality, it is wonderful we should love a Thing, which every Day demands so much Attendance. I stuff this Sack, and then I empty it again. What is more troublesome? But I must obey

(*e*) This Simile is peculiarly beautiful; and hath the Force of an Argument in the Discourse of a Stoic, who held the Sun to be animated, and intelligent.

(*f*) This Fragment, in *Stobæus*, is ascribed to *Socrates*.

(*g*) See Discourses, B. I. c. 27. Note (*a*).

obey God. Therefore I ſtay, and bear to waſh, and feed, and clothe this paultry, miſerable Body. When I was younger, he commanded me ſomething ſtill more, and I bore it. And will you not, when Nature, which gave the Body, takes it away, bear that? "I love it;" ſay you. Well: this is what I have juſt been obſerving: and this very Love hath Nature given you: but ſhe alſo ſays, "Now let it go, and have no farther Trouble."

XC.

WHEN a young Man dies, [an old one] accuſes the Gods, that, at the Time when He ought to be at reſt, he is encumbered with the Troubles of Life. Yet, (*h*) nevertheleſs, when Death approaches, he wiſhes to live; and ſends for the Phyſician, and intreats him to omit no Care or Pains. It is marvellous, that Men ſhould not be willing either to live, or die.

XCI.

To a longer and worſe Life, a ſhorter and better is by all Means to be preferred by every one.

XCII.

WHEN we are Children, our Parents deliver us to the Care of a Tutor; who is continually to watch over us, that we get no Hurt. When we are become Men, God delivers us to the Guardianſhip of an implanted Conſcience. We ought by no means then to deſpiſe this Guardian: for it will both diſpleaſe (*i*) God, and we ſhall be Enemies to our own conſcious Principle.

XCIII.

RICHES ought to be uſed as the Materials of ſome Action; and not upon every Occaſion alike.

XCIV.

ALL Men ſhould rather wiſh for Virtue than Wealth; which is dangerous to the Fooliſh: for Vice

F f

(*h*) Ἧττον is dropt out of the Text, probably, by Reaſon of the Similitude of the next Word ὅταν.

(*i*) Απαρεϛον, perhaps, ſhould be απαρεϛοι.

Vice is increaſed by Riches. And in proportion as any one is deſtitute of Underſtanding, into the more injurious Exceſs he flies out, by having the Means of gratifying the Rage of his Pleaſures.

XCV.

WHAT ought not to be done, be not even ſuſpected [or, entertain not even a Thought] of doing (*k*).

XCVI.

DELIBERATE much before you ſay and do any thing: for it will not be in your Power to recall what is ſaid or done.

XCVII.

EVERY Place is ſafe to him who lives with Juſtice.

XCVIII.

CROWS pick out the Eyes of the Dead, when they are no longer of any Uſe. But Flatterers deſtroy the Soul of the Living, and blind its Eyes.

XCIX.

THE Anger of a Monkey, and the Threats of a Flatterer, deſerve equal Regard.

C.

KINDLY receive thoſe, who are willing to give good Advice: but not thoſe, who upon every Occaſion are eager to flatter. For the former truly ſee what is advantageous: but the latter conſider only the Opinions of their Superiors; and imitate the Shadows of Bodies, by nodding Aſſent to what they ſay.

CI.

A MONITOR ought, in the firſt place, to have a Regard to the Delicacy and Senſe (*l*) of Shame of the Perſon admoniſhed. For they, who are hardened againſt a Bluſh, are incorrigible.

CII.

(*k*) This Fragment is aſcribed to *Pythagoras*, STOB. *Serm.* I.

(*l*) Φημης in *Antonius* and *Maximus* is αισχυνης. And it is ſo tranſlated here.

CII.

It is better to admonish than reproach: for the one is mild and friendly; the other, harsh and affronting: and the one corrects the Faulty; the other only convicts them.

CIII.

(*m*) Communicate to Strangers, and Persons in Need, according to your Ability (*n*). For he who gives nothing to the Needy, shall receive nothing in his own Need.

CIV.

A Person once brought Clothes to a Pirate, who had been cast ashore, and almost killed by the Severity of the Weather; then carried him to his House, and furnished him with other Conveniences. Being reproached by some Person, for doing Good to bad People; "I have paid this Regard," answered he, "not to the Man, but to human Nature."

CV.

We ought not to chuse every Pleasure: but that, which tends to something good.

CVI.

It is the Character of a wise Man, to resist Pleasure; and of a Fool, to be enslaved by it.

CVII.

In all Vice, Pleasure being presented like a Bait, draws sensual Minds to the Hook of Perdition.

CVIII.

Chuse rather to punish your Appetites, than to be punished by them.

CIX.

No one is free, who doth not command himself.

(*m*) This and the following Fragment are from *Antonius* and *Maximus*, and in the Margin stand there, *Democriti*, *Isocratis*, & *Epicteti*: so, probably, they ought to be put in the second Class.

(*n*) The Expression in the Original is the same with *Luke* xi. 41.

CX.

THE Vine bears three Clusters. The first, of Pleasure; the second, of Intoxication; the third, of Outrage (*o*).

CXI.

Do not talk much over Wine, to show your Learning: for your Discourse will be loathsome.

CXII.

HE is a Drunkard, who takes more than three Glasses: and though he be not drunk, he hath exceeded Moderation.

CXIII.

(*p*) LET Discourse of God be renewed every Day, preferably to our Food.

CXIV.

THINK oftener of God, than you breathe.

CXV.

IF you always remember, that God stands by, an Inspector of whatever you do, either in Soul or Body: you will never err, either in your Prayers or Actions; and you will have God abiding with you.

CXVI.

As it is pleasant to view the Sea from the Shore: so it is pleasant to one who hath escaped, to remember his past Labours.

CXVII.

THE Intention of the Law is, to benefit human Life: but it cannot, when Men themselves chuse to suffer: for it discovers its proper Virtue in the Obedient.

CXVIII.

As Physicians are the Preservers of the Sick; so are the Laws, of the Injured.

CXIX.

THE justest Laws are the truest.

CXX.

(*o*) This Saying is likewise ascribed to *Pythagoras*.
(*p*) See *Deut.* vi. 7. *Psal.* lxxi. 15, 24. cv. 2.

CXX.

It is decent to yield to a Law, to a Governor, and to a wiſer Man.

CXXI.

Things, done contrary to Law, are the ſame as if they were undone.

CXXII.

In Proſperity, it is very eaſy to find a Friend; in Adverſity, nothing is ſo difficult.

CXXIII.

Time delivers Fools from Grief: and Reaſon, wiſe Men.

CXXIV.

He is a Man of Senſe, who doth not grieve for what he hath not; but rejoices in what he hath.

CXXV.

Epictetus being aſked, how a Perſon might grieve his Enemy, anſwered, "By doing as well as "poſſible himſelf."

CXXVI.

Let no wiſe Man eſtrange himſelf from the Government of the State: for it is both impious to withdraw from being uſeful to thoſe that need it, and cowardly to give way to the Worthleſs. For it is fooliſh to chuſe rather to be governed ill, than to govern well.

CXXVII.

Nothing is more (q) becoming a Governor, than to deſpiſe no one, nor be inſolent; but to preſide over all impartially.

CXXVIII.

Any Perſon may live happy in Poverty; but few, in Wealth and Power. So great is the Advantage of Poverty, that no (r) Man, obſervant of the Laws of Life, would change it for diſreputable

 Wealth:

(q) Αλλο ſeems a falſe Reading for *μαλλον*.

(r) If any one thinks this Senſe of νομιμος harſh, or unſuitable, he may read, φρονιμος, *prudent.*

Wealth: unleſs, indeed, *Themiſtocles*, the Son of *Neocles*, the moſt wealthy of the *Athenians*, in a Poverty of Virtue, was better than *Ariſtides* and *Socrates*. But both himſelf and his Wealth are periſhed, and without a Name. For a bad Man loſes all in Death; but Virtue is eternal.

CXXIX.

[REMEMBER] that ſuch is, and was, and will be, the Nature of the World; nor is it poſſible that Things ſhould be otherwiſe, than they now are: and that not only Men, and other Animals upon Earth, partake of this Change and Transformation, but the Divinities alſo. For indeed even the four Elements are transformed and changed up and down: and Earth becomes Water, and Water Air, and this again is transformed into other Things. And the ſame Manner of Transformation happens from Things above to thoſe below. Whoever endeavours to turn his Mind towards theſe Points, and perſuade himſelf to receive with Willingneſs what cannot be avoided, he will paſs his Life with Moderation and Harmony.

CXXX.

HE who is diſcontented with Things preſent, and allotted by Fortune, is unſkilful in Life. But he who bears them, and the Conſequences ariſing from them, nobly and rationally, is worthy to be eſteemed a good Man.

CXXXI.

ALL Things obey, and are ſubſervient to, the World (*u*); the Earth, the Sea, the Sun, and other Stars, and the Plants and Animals of the Earth. Our Body likewiſe obeys it, in being ſick, and well, and young, and old, and paſſing thro' the other Changes, whenever That decrees. It is therefore reaſonable, that

(*u*) The Stoics often confound the Idea of God with that of the World.

that what depends on ourſelves, that is, our Judgment, ſhould not be the only Rebel to it. For the World is powerful, and ſuperior, and conſults the beſt for us, by governing us in Conjunction with the Whole. Farther: Oppoſition, beſides that it is unreaſonable, and produces nothing except a vain Struggle, throws us likewiſe into Pain and Sorrows.

(a) *The following* FRAGMENTS *are ascribed jointly to* EPICTETUS *and other Authors.*

I.

CONTENTMENT, as it is a short and delightful Way, hath much Gracefulness and little Trouble.

II.

FORTIFY yourself with Contentment; for this is an impregnable Fortress.

III.

PREFER nothing to Truth, not even the Choice of Friendship, lying within the Reach of the Passions: for by them Justice is both confounded and darkened.

IV.

TRUTH is an immortal and an eternal Thing. It bestows, not a Beauty which Time will wither, nor a Boldness of which the Sentence of a Judge can *(b)* deprive us; but [the Knowledge of] what is just and lawful, distinguishing from them, and confuting, what is unjust.

V.

WE should have neither a blunt Sword, nor an *(c)* ineffectual Boldness of Speech.

VI.

NATURE has given Man one Tongue, but two Ears, that we may hear twice as much as we speak.

VII.

(*a*) I have followed Mr. *Upton*'s Division: but many Fragments in the foregoing Class properly belong to this.

(*b*) Αφαιρει την, probably, should be αφαιρετην, and is so translated.

(*c*) This saying is ascribed by *Stobæus* to *Socrates*. Ατακτον, disorderly, is there απρακτον, ineffectual: which I have preferred.

VII.

NOTHING is in reality either pleaſant or unpleaſant by Nature; but all Things are effected by Cuſtom.

VIII.

CHUSE the beſt Life: for Cuſtom will make it pleaſant.

IX.

CHUSE rather to leave your Children well inſtructed, than rich. For the Hopes of the Learned are better than the Riches of the Ignorant.

X.

A DAUGHTER is a Poſſeſſion to a Father; which is not his own.

XI.

THE ſame Perſon adviſed the Leaving Modeſty to Children, rather than Gold.

XII.

THE Reproach of a Father is an agreeable Medicine: for the Profit is greater than the Pain.

XIII.

HE who ſucceeds in a Son-in-Law, finds a Son: he who fails in one, loſes likewiſe a Daughter.

XIV.

THE Worth of Learning, like that of Gold, is eſteemed in every Place.

XV.

HE who exerciſes Wiſdom, exerciſes the Knowledge of God.

XVI.

THERE is no Animal ſo beautiful, as a Man adorned by Learning.

XVII.

WE ought to fly the Friendſhip of the Wicked, and the Enmity of the Good.

XVIII.

NECESSITOUS Circumſtances prove Friends, and detect Enemies.

XIX.

XIX.

We ought to do well by our Friends, when they are preſent; and ſpeak well of them, when they are abſent.

XX.

Let not him think he is loved by any, who loves none.

XXI.

We ought to chuſe both a Phyſician and a Friend, not the moſt agreeable, but the moſt uſeful.

XXII.

If you would lead a Life without Sorrow, conſider Things which will happen, as if they had already happened.

XXIII.

Be exempt from Grief; not like irrational Creatures, from Inſenſibility; nor from Inconſiderateneſs, like Fools: but like a Man of Virtue, making Reaſon the Remedy for Grief.

XXIV.

They whoſe Minds are the leaſt grieved by Calamities, and whoſe Actions ſtruggle the moſt againſt them, are the greateſt both in public and in private Life.

XXV.

They who are well inſtructed, like thoſe who are exerciſed in the *Palæſtra*, if they happen to fall, quickly and dextrouſly riſe again from Misfortunes.

XXVI.

We ought to call in Reaſon, like a good Phyſician, to our Aſſiſtance in Misfortunes.

XXVII.

A Fool intoxicated by a long Courſe of good Fortune, as by one of Drinking, becomes more ſenſeleſs.

XXVIII.

Envy is the Adverſary of the Fortunate.

XXIX.

XXIX.

HE who remembers what Man is, is diſcontented at nothing which happens.

XXX.

A PILOT and a fair Wind are neceſſary to a happy Voyage: Reaſon and Art, to a happy Life.

XXXI.

GOOD Fortune, like ripe Fruit, ought to be enjoyed while it is preſent.

XXXII.

HE is unreaſonable, who is diſpleaſed at Events, which happen from natural Neceſſity.

The following FRAGMENTS *are omitted by Mr.* UPTON: *but as they ſtand under the Name of* ARRIAN, *and ſeem to be in the Spirit of* EPICTETUS, *they are added here.*

I.

(*a*) WHAT does it ſignify to me, ſays he, whether the Univerſe is compoſed of Atoms or (*b*) uncompounded Subſtances, or of Fire and Earth? Is it not ſufficient to know the Eſſence of Good and Evil, and the proper Bounds of the Deſires and Averſions; and, beſides thoſe, of the active Powers; and by the making uſe of theſe as ſo many certain Rules, to order the Conduct of Life, and bid theſe Things, which are above us, farewell: which, perhaps, are incomprehenſible to human Underſtanding: but, if one ſhould ſuppoſe them ever ſo comprehenſible, ſtill, what is the Benefit of them, when comprehended? And muſt it not be ſaid, that He gives Himſelf Trouble to no Purpoſe, who allots theſe Things as neceſſary to the Character of a Philoſopher.——"What then, is the *Delphic* Admonition, *Know Thyſelf*, ſuperfluous?"——"No, ſurely, "ſays he."——"What then doth it mean?" If any one ſhould admoniſh a Performer in a Chorus to *know himſelf*, would not he attend to it as a Direction about his (*c*) Motions——.

II.

(*a*) *Stob. de Diis & Phyſiol. Serm.* 211. p. 714. Ed. *Francof.* 1581.

(*b*) I have tranſlated αμερων as it ſtands in the Text; but, poſſibly, it might originally be no more than a marginal Interpretation of ατομων, changing the Full Point into a Comma; or, according to *Geſner*'s Tranſlation, a Corruption of ομοιομεριων.

(*c*) The Sentence ſeems imperfect.

II.

(*d*) THE ſame Perſon being aſked, Wherein the Diligent have the Advantage of the Slothful? anſwered, Wherein the Pious have the Advantage of the Impious; in good Hopes.

III.

(*e*) WALLS give to Cities, and Cultivation of the Underſtanding to Minds, Ornament and Security.

IV.

(*f*) WHEN a young Man was giving himſelf Airs in a public Place; and ſaying, that he was grown wiſe, by converſing with many wiſe Men; I have converſed too, anſwered ſomebody, with many rich Men, but I am not grown rich.

V.

(*g*) SOCRATES, being ſent for by (*h*) *Archelaus*, as deſigning to make him a rich Man, returned him this Anſwer: "Four Quarts of Meal are ſold "at *Athens* for five Farthings, and the Fountains "run with Water. If what I have is not ſufficient for me, yet I am ſufficiently able to make a "ſhift with that; and thus it becomes ſufficient "for me. Do not you perceive, that it makes no "Difference in the Goodneſs of *Polus* [the Player's] "Voice, whether he performs the Part of *Oedipus* "in his regal State, or when he is a Wanderer, "and a Beggar at *Colonus*? And ſhall a brave "Man

(*d*) *Maximus*, περι φιλοπονιας, *Serm.* 118. p. 374.
(*e*) *Ant.* & *Max. de diſciplinâ.* *Serm.* 210. p. 704.
(*f*) Ibid.
(*g*) *Stobæus*, *Compar. Paupertatis* & *Divitiarum.* *Serm.* 237. p. 778.
(*h*) *Archelaus*, the Philoſopher, was the Maſter of *Socrates*: but the Perſon here mentioned was King of *Macedon*, who vainly endeavoured to get *Socrates* to his Court. The Envy of *Ariſtophanes* upon this Occaſion is ſaid to have produced that infamous Piece of Scurility and Buffoonery his *Comedy of the Clouds.* See *Bayle*, in the Article *Archelaus.*

"Man appear worse than *Polus*, and not perform "well in whatever Personage is imposed upon him "by the Deity? Shall he not imitate *Ulysses*, who "made no worse Figure in Rags than in a fine purple "Robe (*i*)?"

VI.

THERE are some Persons who are calmly of a high Spirit, and do all the same Things quietly, and as it were without Anger, which those do who are hurried with strong Passion. We are to guard, therefore, against the Faults of such Persons, as being much worse than that of violent Anger. For People of the latter Character are quickly satiated with Vengeance; whereas the others extend it to a longer Time, like Persons in a slow Fever.

(*i*) *Stobæus. Quod Eventus*, &c. p. 324. 329.

INDEX.

INDEX.

APPENDIX.

THE learned Dr. TAYLOR, Editor of *Lysias* and *Demosthenes*, having honoured me with his Opinion, concerning some Passages, about which he was consulted, I am enabled by his Observations to make the following Improvements to this Work.

Page 32. Add to Note (*b*)——It seems probable, that a great deal is wanting; and that οτι ανθρωπικα belongs to one Story, and τι ουν, εφη, to another.

P. 67. But how then came any such Suspicions ...... Perhaps the Sense is, Whence arise our Suspicions, Jealousies, and Fears, concerning our Children, if we have no natural Affection towards them?

P. 87. Add to Note (*d*)——Or, perhaps, εμαθον should be εμαθες.

P. 102. This your Victory, this your Conclusion ..... Perhaps *Victory* and *Conclusion* should change Places.

P. 126. To Note (*b*) add——But, as διατιλλω occurs not elsewhere, and reading it here will make an improper Repetition of nearly the same Sense, and διαθειναι τινα signifies, to do something to another, L. 4. c. 7. p. 628. edit. *Upt.* and in *Lysias, Apol. in Sim.* p. 79. *contra Agorat.* p. 235, it will be best to preserve the present Reading, and to translate it——What doth he lose, who makes him such?

P. 149. To Note (*i*) add——*Prov.* viii. 34. and *Ecclus* xiv. 23. speak of *waiting and hearkening at the Doors of Wisdom.* Yet the Passage, to which Mr. *Upton* refers, p. 577, of his Edition, and p. 327 of this Translation, favours the received Reading.

P. 150. To Note (*l*) add——Probably here is an Allusion to the Proverb, cited by *Wolfius*, επι θυρσης καθιζεσθαι, of which see *Suidas*.

P. 161. To Note (*c*) add——Yet possibly the Sense of αυδην may be couched under αδε.

P. 211. To Note (*b*) add——But a much better, and almost certain Conjecture is, to read απαλλαττομενους instead of πλαττομενους. And then the Translation will be——Concerning those, who return, or, were returning home, on account of Sickness.

P. 223.

APPENDIX.

P. 223. To Note (*b*) add——But, on farther Consideration, the Sense of returning or departing, which αναλυω hath, *Luke* xii. 36. *Phil.* i. 23. and αναλυσις, 2 *Tim.* iv. 6. seems proper here: and the Translation may be——You go to the Theatre, or thence to some other Place. For Persons often move from one Place to another, merely because they are amused in none.

P. 227. To Note (*f*) add——But probably it should be changed into ποθου, and the Translation be——What Occasion for Anger, for Desire . . . . These two *Greek* Words are confounded elsewhere. And the same Alteration seems needful in *Porphyr. de Abst.* L. I. § 2.

P. 229. To Note (*i*) add——He is sensible however, that ανατοιχειν is not exactly to throw one's self on *one* Side; and stands condemned by *Phrynicus*, as a low Expression.

P. 244. To Note (*a*) add——Or we may suppose απαντη to be a Gloss, or a casual Repetition of the same Word occurring in the Line before: and so translate, *there exists the Knowledge*, &c.

P. 270. To Note (*d*) add——Or, perhaps, rather the former ουτος should be left out.

P. 279. To Note (*b*) add——Yet, possibly, the present Reading may stand, and be translated, *But your Life is a perpetual Magistracy.*

P. 298. To Note (*e*) add——Or του φιλοσοφου may mean, *Of the philosophic Principle.*

P. 305. To Note (*b*) add——Or the latter οπου θελω may be a Repetition of the Transcriber.

P. 323. To Note (*d*) add——For ολων I have taken the Reading of Mr. *Upton*'s Copy, αλλων.

P. 329. To Note (*b*) add——Yet I would not insert a Negative unnecessarily.

P. 332. Note (*c*). For, *rub themselves with*, put, *throw on their Antagonists.*

P. 341. To Note (*e*) add——Perhaps also what follows, and particularly ωδι προβατον, is corrupt.

P. 345. To Note (*a*) add——But this Omission was probably owing to the Transcribers skipping from μαθειν to the like Word μανθανειν. Possibly, instead of leaving out και, we should rather suppose, that something before it is left out. And in all Likelihood the true Translation of ιν εχη ανω κατω, instead of *should not you*, &c. is the following: *is not this, i. e.* undertaking to convince others instead of yourself, *inverting the Order of Things?*

P. 371. The Notes (*h*) and (*i*) should change Places.

APPENDIX.

P. 373. Add to Note (*a*)——Or rather, after the next Word: and the Translation should be, *Yet now, without being sensible of it, you do something like this, even in the present Case. Consider your Body*, &c. But still the Separation of οιει from και νυν is somewhat unnatural, and takes off from the Spirit and Quickness of the Repartee.

P. 374. Squalid ..... The original Word signifies, in general, pale. And, probably, *Aristophanes* meant the Paleness, which proceeds from a sedentary studious Life. But *Epictetus* plainly understood him, of that unwholesome Look, which Want of Cleanliness gives.

P. 377. To Note (*a*) add———Or, as *Casaubon* conjectures, απωθειν. Or, perhaps, as Mr. *Upton* proposes, υπερτιθεμενον should be υπερτιθεμενος.

P. 378. Is he my Conscience ..... Κριμα signifies, p. 652. l. 6. and p. 660. l. 5. of Mr. *Upton*'s Edition, the Judgment, which any one passes in his own Mind.

P. 394. To Note (*b*) add———For nothing appears, to support so great an Encomium of that Philosopher: whereas *Hercules* and *Diogenes* were Favourites of the Stoics, and particularly of our Author; and the latter professed himself an Imitator of the former. But then he was never deified. And therefore may we not put in his stead, Διονυσος, *Bacchus*? They are joined by the Ancients. See *Qu. Curt.* L. VIII. c. 5. and *Hor. Epist.* II. 1. 5. 10. And they will stand here in their proper Order. But this may be thought too licentious a Change. And, to say nothing of *Hercules*, *Bacchus* was by no means remarkable for Abstemiousness.

P. 404. To Note (*u*) add———This Reading he hath taken from an Edition in 1554, said to be made from a better Manuscript than the common Editions. He understands it to mean, *struck and affected over-strongly by Externals.* Διαβεβλημενος means, averse from, L. II. c. 26. in the beginning, and *Philostrat. vit. Apollon.* VIII. 7. 3. But from the vulgar Sense, *calumniated*, it may mean here, one to whom Externals have been misrepresented, who hath a Misconception of the World.

P. 416. And Vice, by Money ..... Perhaps for η κακια should be read ευτυχια, a Turn of good Fortune.

F I N I S.

Milton Keynes UK
Ingram Content Group UK Ltd.
UKHW020628250424
441651UK00004B/106

9 781013 344770